LESSONS FOR
EXTENDING DIVISION

GRADES 4-5

THE TEACHING ARITHMETIC SERIES

Teaching
ARITHMETIC

LESSONS FOR
EXTENDING
DIVISION

▲▲▲▲▲

GRADES 4-5

MARYANN WICKETT
MARILYN BURNS

MATH SOLUTIONS PUBLICATIONS
SAUSALITO, CA

Math Solutions Publications
A division of
Marilyn Burns Education Associates
150 Gate 5 Road, Suite 101
Sausalito, CA 94965
www.mathsolutions.com

Library of Congress Cataloging-in-Publication Data

Wickett, Maryann.
   Lessons for extending division : grades 4/5 / Maryann Wickett, Marilyn
Burns.
     p. cm.
Includes index.
   ISBN 0-941355-46-2 (alk. paper)
   1. Division—Study and teaching (Elementary) I. Burns, Marilyn, 1941–
II. Title.
   QA115.W63 2003
    372.7'2—dc21

                       2003013247

Editor: Toby Gordon
Production: Melissa L. Inglis
Cover & interior design: Leslie Bauman
Composition: TechBooks

Printed in the United States of America on acid-free paper
07 06 05 04 03   ML   1 2 3 4 5

A Message from Marilyn Burns

We at Marilyn Burns Education Associates believe that teaching mathematics well calls for increasing our understanding of the math we teach, seeking greater insight into how children learn mathematics, and refining lessons to best promote children's learning. All of our Math Solutions Professional Development publications and inservice courses have been designed to help teachers achieve these goals.

Our publications include a wide range of choices, from books in our new Teaching Arithmetic and Lessons for Algebraic Thinking series to resources that link math and literacy; from books to help teachers understand mathematics more deeply to children's books that help students develop an appreciation for math while learning basic concepts.

Our inservice offers five-day courses, one-day workshops, and series of school-year sessions throughout the country, working in partnership with school districts to help implement and sustain long-term improvement in mathematics instruction in all classrooms.

To find a complete listing of our publications and workshops, please visit our Web site at *www.mathsolutions.com*. Or contact us by calling (800) 868-9092 or sending an e-mail to *info@mathsolutions.com*.

We're eager for your feedback and interested in learning about your particular needs. We look forward to hearing from you.

A DIVISION OF MARILYN BURNS EDUCATION ASSOCIATES

CONTENTS

COMPUTATION PRACTICE

ADDITIONAL ACTIVITIES   225

ASSESSMENTS   239

BLACKLINE MASTERS   257

INDEX   267

ACKNOWLEDGMENTS

We wish to thank the following teachers and their students for allowing us to teach these lessons and for sharing their invaluable support, enthusiasm, encouragement, ideas, feedback, and hard work.

Karen Krantz—Paloma Elementary School, San Marcos, CA

Richard Kharas—Seymour School, Syracuse, New York

Larry Dovenbarger—Carrillo School, San Marcos, CA

Carol Scurlock—Discovery School, San Marcos, CA

Nicole McClymonds—Carrillo School, San Marcos, CA

Bill Wickett—Reynolds School, Oceanside, CA

Patti Reynolds—Carrillo School, San Marcos, CA

Eunice Hendrix-Martin—Carrillo School, San Marcos, CA

Kristin Whelan—Carrillo School, San Marcos, CA

Danielle Ross—Park School, Mill Valley, CA

The students of room 19—Carrillo School, San Marcos, CA

INTRODUCTION

Division computation, often referred to as long division, is a cornerstone of many fourth- and fifth-grade mathematics curricula and typically consumes vast amounts of instructional time. It is often a source of agony and frustration for both students and their teachers. However, there is another way, and that's what this book offers.

Michael's first words to me were, "I'm stupid and I don't do division." His teacher explained that Michael, a new student in his fourth-grade class, appeared to have given up on life and himself. When I began the lesson *An Introduction to Division Computation: If You Hopped Like a Frog,* Michael sat down, pulled the hood of his Big Dog sweatshirt over his head, and hid his eyes in the crook of his elbow. I carefully watched Michael and noticed him peeking when I read about a chameleon's tongue being half as long as its body length. I noticed him peeking again when I posed the question, "If I were a chameleon, how long would my tongue be?"

While the students worked to figure the lengths of their tongues if they were chameleons, I sat and talked with Michael. I discovered that he could multiply by ten and also subtract reasonably accurately and efficiently, tools he could use to solve long division problems. Making use of Michael's skills, together we figured the length his tongue would be if he were a chameleon, a notion he found absurd and amusing. He was interested in the problem and successfully completed it. Michael was hooked! Together, we figured the length his friend's tongue would be if he were a chameleon. Michael then said that he didn't need my help anymore, but he asked that I still sit next to him. "Just in case," he explained. I watched Michael as he figured out the lengths his tablemates' tongues would be if they were chameleons. He verified his results with each person at the table and, to everyone's delight, the results checked.

I continued to work on other days with Michael and his class. Some days he asked me to sit beside him and give occasional reminders, but Michael learned to do long division accurately and efficiently.

In a different class, after students had experienced the same lesson and also the lessons in the Long Division in Contexts section of this book, I asked students to complete the assessment *Easy, Medium, and Hard.* Wendi, a student who had initially struggled but had gained confidence and skill during her study of division, wrote the following problem as an example of a problem of medium difficulty:

100)300,436,287

She explained, "The numbers are big, so it looks hard. But dividing and multiplying by one hundred is easy. Keeping track of what I'm doing is tricky, so I think the problem is medium." As Wendi worked on solving the problem, she exclaimed, "Oh my gosh, the remainder is the same as the last two digits in the dividend! I bet that's because I divided by one hundred." Her pleasure with her discovery was evident by her excitement. I was impressed with her confidence, persistence, and willingness to explore division in such a playful, curious way. Michael and Wendi are examples of what can be.

Goals for Division Instruction

Division is an important focus of mathematics instruction beginning in the third grade and continuing in the fourth and fifth grades. Students with a firm foundation in division should be able to

- ▲ explain that division involves equal groups;
- ▲ recognize the two types of division problems—sharing (or partitioning) and grouping—and be able to think flexibly about both;
- ▲ represent remainders in different ways, choosing a representation that is appropriate within the context of the problem being solved;
- ▲ represent division problems symbolically in three ways—$100 \div 25 = 4$, $25\overline{)100}$ with 4 above, and $\frac{100}{25} = 4$;

- ▲ use division facts up to $144 \div 12$ accurately and efficiently;
- ▲ divide by ten and multiples of ten accurately and efficiently;
- ▲ calculate problems with up to two-digit divisors and three- and four-digit dividends accurately and efficiently;
- ▲ interpret division in real-world situations;
- ▲ solve problems that involve division;
- ▲ explain how division relates to multiplication and subtraction.

Traditionally, instruction in division has focused on two objectives: learning the division facts and developing computational fluency in division. These are important goals, and reaching them calls for developing in children a firm understanding of the concept of division and how division relates to the other operations. Time spent by students on searching for, learning from, and applying patterns and building a strong conceptual understanding is critical for students' proficiency with division computation. Students should be able to compute mentally as well as with paper and pencil. They should be able to explain their thinking and why it makes sense. They should know when an answer is reasonable. They should be able to interpret remainders. The lessons in this book address these goals and support students' growth toward accuracy and efficiency in division computation based on understanding.

A Closer Look at the Mathematics

The lessons in the book are organized into five sections. The first section contains four introductory lessons that provide a foundation for the lessons in the next four sections, each of which then focuses on a particular aspect of the mathematics of division. Two of the introductory lessons—*Silent Division* and *The Divisor Stays the*

Same—engage students in looking for and learning from patterns that help them see relationships among dividends, divisors, quotients, and remainders. *Investigating Factors* strengthens students' understanding of the connection between division and multiplication. *An Introduction to Division Computation: If You Hopped Like a Frog* uses the information in a children's book to present an algorithm for division computation. Following are descriptions of the content of the lessons in the next four sections, which build on these introductory experiences.

MORE PATTERNS WITH DIVISORS, DIVIDENDS, AND QUOTIENTS

Mathematics is built on patterns, and instruction should, as much as possible, provide students repeated experiences with exploring, defining, applying, and learning from patterns. Our approach in this section continues the learning begun in Chapters 1 and 2 in the introductory section. Here we present two lessons—*The Dividend Stays the Same* and *The Quotient Stays the Same*—to provide students additional opportunities to consider the relationships among dividends, divisors, quotients, and remainders by examining patterns in sequences of problems.

The patterns students explore and apply include

▲ the effects on the quotient when the divisor remains the same but the dividend is either doubled or multiplied by ten. For example:

$8 \div 4 = 2$

$16 \div 4 = 4$ The dividend doubled, the divisor remained the same, and the quotient also doubled.

$8 \div 4 = 2$

$80 \div 4 = 20$ The dividend was multiplied by ten, the divisor remained the same, and the quotient was also multiplied by ten. (See Chapter 2, "The Divisor Stays the Same," for a more detailed explanation.)

▲ the effects on the quotient when the divisor is multiplied or divided by another number and the dividend remains the same. For example:

$16 \div 4 = 4$

$16 \div 8 = 2$ The dividend remained the same, the divisor was multiplied by two, and the quotient was divided by two. (See Chapter 1, "Silent Division," for a more detailed explanation.)

▲ the effect on the quotient when the divisor is larger than the dividend.

$1 \div 2 = 0 \text{ R1 or } \frac{1}{2}$ $2 \div 3 = 0 \text{ R2 or } \frac{2}{3}$

$1 \div 3 = 0 \text{ R1 or } \frac{1}{3}$ $2 \div 4 = 0 \text{ R2 or } \frac{2}{4}$

$1 \div 4 = 0 \text{ R1 or } \frac{1}{4}$ $2 \div 5 = 0 \text{ R2 or } \frac{2}{5}$

(See Chapter 5, "The Dividend Stays the Same," for additional information.)

▲ the relationship between the dividend and the divisor that must occur to generate different problems with the same quotient.

$4 \div 2 = 2$ $4 \div 3 = 1 \text{ R1}$

$6 \div 3 = 2$ $5 \div 4 = 1 \text{ R1}$

$10 \div 5 = 2$ $10 \div 9 = 1 \text{ R1}$

The dividend is twice the divisor or the divisor is half the dividend.   The dividend is one more than the divisor.

(See Chapter 6, "The Quotient Stays the Same," for a more detailed explanation.)

More detailed information about these patterns is included in the "Teaching Notes" section of Chapters 1, 2, 5, and 6.

DIVISIBILITY RULES

It's generally obvious to most adults that in order for a number to be divisible by 2 (which means there is a whole number answer with no remainder), the number has to be even. And it's also generally obvious that numbers divisible by 5 must end in 0 or 5, and numbers divisible by 10 must end in 0. However, rules for thinking about when numbers are divisible by 3 or 6, for example, aren't as obvious, even to many adults. In this section, we introduce students to rules for divisibility by 2, 5, and 10, and then by 3 and 6, by engaging them in looking for and describing patterns from which such rules emerge. When a rule is not obvious from investigating patterns, such as the rule for divisibility by 3, we suggest how to present the rule to help students understand it as well as learn to apply it.

This section includes three lessons that specifically and directly address the rules—*Exploring Divisibility Rules for Two, Five, and Ten; Exploring Divisibility Rules for Three;* and *Exploring Divisibility Rules for Six.* These three lessons together span four days of instruction. We also include in this section another lesson based on a children's book—*A Remainder of One.* This lesson gives children the opportunity to think about divisibility rules and remainders while also connecting their mathematics learning to the creativity of children's literature.

Following are the divisibility rules we present in these chapters:

Divisibility by two: A number is divisible by 2 if it is even. Or another way to express the rule is: A number is divisible by 2 if it has a 0, 2, 4, 6, or 8 in the ones place. Examples: 34, 56, and 342.

Divisibility by three: A number is divisible by 3 if the sum of its digits is divisible by 3. Examples: 63, 105, 3,015. (**Note:** If the digits of a number are added and it's unclear if the sum is a multiple of 3, then add the digits of the sum. If the sum of the digits of the sum is divisible by 3, so is the original number. For example: The sum of the digits of 9,576 is 27. Add 2 and 7 and the sum is 9. Nine is a multiple of 3 and is divisible by 3, making 9,576 a multiple of 3 and divisible by 3.)

Divisibility by four: The rule used in the context of the lesson *A Remainder of One* is that every other number in the list of numbers divisible by 2 is also divisible by 4. This test makes sense to the students. For your own information, another way to present a divisibility test for 4 is this: A number is divisible by 4 if the last two digits of the number are 00 or the last two digits of the number form a number divisible by 4. Examples: 100, 116, 264.

Divisibility by five: A number is divisible by 5 if it has a 0 or a 5 in the ones place. Examples: 15, 60, 120, 255.

Divisibility by six: A number is divisible by 6 if it divisible by both 2 and 3. Another way to express the rule is: A number is divisible by 6 if it is even and the sum of its digits is divisible by 3. Examples: 36, 42, 168, 174, 96.

Divisibility by ten: A number is divisible by 10 if it has a 0 in the ones place. Examples: 10, 210, 3,050.

There are divisibility rules for seven, eight, and nine as well. The divisibility rule for seven is neither simple nor efficient for children to use. Information about the divisibility rules for eight and nine can be found in the "Teaching Notes" section of Chapter 9, "Exploring Divisibility Rules for Six."

LONG DIVISION IN CONTEXTS

There are two important goals for the lessons in this section. One is to reinforce for students the purpose for and usefulness of learning to compute. The other is to help students develop the computational skills they need to divide efficiently and accurately. We link these two goals in this section because we believe that too often, computational methods are taught in isolation and as ends in themselves, rather than as tools for children to have available as they engage in doing mathematics.

Contexts not only relate computation to real-world situations but also have the added benefit of providing students with ways to verify their answers. The lessons in this section—*Grape Licorice, The Yarn Lesson*, and *Beans and Scoops*—have this feature and extend the learning from *An Introduction to Division Computation: If You Hopped Like a Frog* in the introductory section. After solving the problems presented, students check their answers with the physical materials suggested by the contexts.

In each lesson, we follow a similar routine:

1. Present the context of the problem situation.
2. Ask students to solve the problem individually or in pairs.
3. Lead a discussion for students to share their results and methods.
4. When possible, have students verify the answer with concrete materials.
5. Introduce and/or reinforce an algorithm.

The problems included in this section model both interpretations of division. For example, *Grape Licorice* involves the students in the sharing, or partitioning, interpretation of division; the *Yarn Lesson* and *Beans and Scoops* involve them in the grouping interpretation of division. The computational methods students use for both interpretations are the same, but the structures of the problems in the two contexts differ.

Another issue that we think is important to address in this section is the choice we've made to teach a division algorithm that is different from the standard "divide, multiply, subtract, bring down" method and is also different from the traditional "short division" method teachers sometimes teach. The alternative algorithm we introduce is shown in some textbook series, and we prefer it because it asks students to think about the number being divided in its entirety, not digit by digit, thus providing the opportunity for students to rely on their number sense and bring meaning to what they are doing. For example, when solving a problem such as 676 divided by 18, as presented in Chapter 13, "Beans and Scoops," students who use the "divide, multiply, subtract, bring down" method begin by looking at the first digit in the dividend and then ask: "How many eighteens go into six?" Some actually record a 0 above the 6 in the hundreds place while others don't, but they all move on, sometimes actually moving their fingers to uncover the next digit in the dividend, and ask the question: "How many eighteens go into sixty-seven?" Both times, students are incorrectly referring to the meaning of the digits, first referring to 600 as 6, and then to 670 as 67. Also, it's typical for students to learn this algorithm by rote, rarely if ever thinking about why dividing, then multiplying, then subtracting, and finally, bringing down the next digit makes sense. While we do not teach or recommend teaching this algorithm, you will see evidence of it in some of the samples of student work.

The alternative algorithm that we introduce builds on the idea that dividing can be accomplished by doing repeated subtractions, just as we think of multiplying as doing repeated additions. In this alternative algorithm, students focus on the entire dividend, 676, and ask: "About how many eighteens can I subtract from six hundred seventy-six?" Then they rely on thinking about what they've learned about multiplying numbers by 10 or multiples of 10. For example, since ten 18s are 180, a student might begin by recording the partial quotient of 10, subtracting 180 from 676, and then continue by subtracting additional groups of 18. Or a student might reason that since $10 \times 18 = 180$, then $20 \times 18 = 360$, so he will begin with a partial quotient of 20, subtracting 360 to see what's left.

Both the traditional algorithm and the suggested alternative will produce the same answer and are equally efficient. However, while all students' work relating to the traditional algorithm is identical (except that some students put zeroes in front of quotients, as mentioned earlier, and others do not), the alternative algorithm allows for variations. Following are several ways that a student can use this alternative algorithm when solving a problem. You'll see examples like these in the student work shown in various chapters.

```
   2 ⌐               2 ⌐                1 ⌐
   5 │               5 │                2 │
  10 │ 37 R10       10 │ 37 R10         2 │
  10 │              20 ┘               2 │
  10 ┘            18)676              10 │
18)676            −360               20 ┘ 37 R10
 −180              316             18)676
  496             −180              −360
 −180              136              316
  316              −90             −180
 −180               46              136
  136              −36              −36
  −90               10              100
   46                                −36
  −36                                 64
   10                                −36
                                      28
                                     −18
                                      10
```

One more thought about the alternative algorithm: You'll see in the student work we've included in the book that students have used two different formats for recording this alternative algorithm. This is because in some of the classes where we tried these ideas, teachers had their own preferences for the specifics of recording. Following is an alternative way to record each of the three samples shown above.

```
      37 R10              37 R10              37 R10
18)676              18)676              18)676
 -180 | 10           -360 | 20           -360 | 20
  496                 316                 316
 -180 | 10           -180 | 10           -180 | 10
  316                 136                 136
 -180 | 10            -90 | 5            -36 | 2
  136                  46                 100
  -90 | 5            -36 | 2             -36 | 2
   46                  10                  64
  -36 | 2                               -36 | 2
   10                                     28
                                        -18 | 1
                                          10
```

Our instructional recommendation is to give students the broadest range of options possible when doing mathematics. What's important to us is that students have at least one, and ideally more than one, way to compute accurately and efficiently. Also, a focus on fostering students' understanding guides all of our instructional decisions, and it's important to us that students learn to make sense of whatever procedures they use. If the alternative algorithm is new for you, we suggest that you become comfortable with it and augment your instruction by presenting it to your students. We have found that it helps all students focus on the meaning of division, the relationship between division and multiplication, and the relationship between division and subtraction. Also, we've found the alternative algorithm to be especially useful for students who have difficulty mastering the traditional algorithm.

We hope we've made a convincing enough case for you to try introducing to your students the alternative algorithm we've included in these lessons and to enjoy the success that we've experienced, even with struggling students.

COMPUTATION PRACTICE

While contexts are extremely beneficial for helping students see the usefulness of division and for learning methods for computing, we don't want to imply that all practice must involve contexts. Asking students to think about division problems isolated from any situation serves the purpose not only of providing practice but also of using the numbers themselves as contexts for furthering students' understanding and skills. The issue is one of providing balance so students have sufficient experience relating division to problem situations and sufficient experience honing their computational skills.

We have not included practice pages in this book. We trust that you have sufficient resources for all the practice you want to provide for your students. However, in the lessons in this section, we suggest some alternative ways to engage students in computation practice. We include three games—the *Division Game,* the *Factor Game,* and *Leftovers with 100*—and one other activity—*Division Riddles.* Our goal is to give you some additional alternatives for providing students much needed practice with division while also continuing to engage them in thinking and reasoning.

The Structure of the Lessons

In order to help you with planning and teaching the lessons in this book, each is organized into the following sections:

Overview To help you decide if the lesson is appropriate for your students, this is a nutshell description of the mathematical goals of the lesson and what the students will be doing.

Materials This section lists the special materials needed along with quantities. Not included in the list are regular classroom supplies such as pencils and paper. Worksheets that need to be duplicated are included in the Blackline Masters section at the back of the book.

Time The number of class periods is provided, sometimes with a range allowing for different-length periods. It's also indicated for some activities that they are meant to be repeated from time to time.

Teaching Directions The directions are presented in a step-by-step format.

Teaching Notes This section addresses the mathematics underlying the lesson and at times provides information about the prior experiences or knowledge that students need.

The Lesson This is a vignette that describes what actually occurred when the lesson was taught to one or more classes. While the vignette mirrors the plan described in the teaching directions, it elaborates with details that are valuable for preparing and teaching the lesson. Samples of student work are included.

Extensions This section is included for some of the lessons and offers follow-up suggestions.

Questions and Discussion Presented in a question-and-answer format, this section addresses issues that came up during the lesson and/or have been posed by other teachers.

Although they are organized similarly, the lessons presented here vary in several ways. Some span one class period, others take longer, and some are suitable to repeat throughout the year, giving students a chance to revisit ideas and extend their learning. Some use manipulative materials, others ask students to draw pictures, and some ask students to reason and calculate mentally. While some lessons seem more suited for beginning experiences, at times it's beneficial for more experienced students to engage in them as well. An activity that seems simple can reinforce students' understanding, thus building confidence, or give them a fresh way to look at a familiar concept. Also, a lesson that initially seems too difficult or advanced can be ideal for introducing students to thinking in a new way.

How to Use This Book

Teaching the lessons described in the seventeen chapters requires at least twenty-eight days of instruction, not including time for repeat experiences, as recommended for some lessons, or for the ideas for extensions suggested at the end of many lessons or the additional activities or assessments suggested at the end of the book.

While it's possible to spend more than five consecutive weeks on these lessons, we don't think that's the best decision. In our experience, children require time to consider and absorb ideas and concepts, and we would rather spend a three-week period and then wait two months or so before returning for another three-week period, or arrange for three chunks of time, each about two weeks or so, spaced throughout the year. When students return to an idea after a break, they bring not only the learning they've done in other areas but also a fresh look that some distance can provide.

The four introductory lessons build a foundation for others in the book and we suggest that you not skip these lessons. The other lessons are categorized into different aspects of division, as explained earlier in "A Closer Look at the Mathematics." The sections and the chapters within the sections are listed in an order that reflects our experiences but may be changed to fit the needs of your particular students. Two more sections appear at the end of the book. Additional Activities provides other related division experiences presented in shortened format. Assessments suggests ways to keep track of your students' learning.

Throughout the lessons, we ask children to work in pairs. There are many ways to assign partners. Some teachers have children change partners every day, while others have their students keep the same partners throughout a unit of study. In some classrooms, children choose their own partners; in some classrooms, the teacher assigns partners randomly, by drawing names, for example; in other classrooms, the teacher chooses which children will work together or simply asks each student to turn and talk to the person sitting beside or across from him or her. There are a variety of ways to organize students to work in pairs, and what works best with one group of children may not be the best way for another group.

Because student participation is key to learning, we expect students to share their thinking throughout the lessons in this book. Students present their ideas in whole-class discussions, complete individual writing assignments, and talk in small groups, often preceded by a form of pair sharing called dyads, based on the work of Dr. Julian Weissglass, a mathematics education professor at the University of California at Santa Barbara. A dyad is an opportunity for all children to be listened to by another and for all children to listen. The following are the basic guidelines for using dyads:

▲ Each person is given equal time to share and listen.
▲ The listener doesn't interrupt the person who is talking. The listener also doesn't give advice, analyze, or break in with comments.
▲ The listener doesn't share what the talker has said with anyone else.

This confidentiality allows children to more fully explore their ideas without fear of being ridiculed or having mistakes shared publicly. It has been our experience that using these rules have given shy, less verbal children more opportunity to voice their ideas. In many cases, as these students gain confidence by sharing in a safe environment, they share more in whole-class discussions, which often results in deeper thinking and understanding of the mathematics along with increased confidence. Using dyads frequently also helps keep more students engaged in the learning process.

Some children are more willing to share ideas than others. It's important, however, that all students learn to participate fully in our math classes. To facilitate this, we do the following:

▲ We make it part of the classroom culture and our expectations that all students are capable and can think. Even more, they are expected to think and always do their best. Anything less is not acceptable.

▲ We support students by using our behavior as a model, and we constantly think about and explore ideas with them. We don't expect students to believe that we know everything—we don't!

▲ To support students' thinking and development of strategies to use, we pose a question and then give students a few moments of quiet "think time," when all students are expected to focus their attention.

▲ After students have a few moments to form their own thoughts, we often use a form of pair sharing called dyads, as described previously.

▲ Whole-class discussions play a big role in our teaching. Before beginning a discussion, we provide students the opportunity to think about the topic at hand, through think time, a writing assignment, or a dyad. When students come to a whole-class discussion prepared, the discussion is more lively and interesting and provides more opportunity for both the students and us to learn.

▲ In whole-class discussions, students usually share strategies that they have used. We record these strategies on the chalkboard or some other highly visible place in the classroom, giving students a reference list of ideas.

As effective as the last strategy is, occasionally a student will still get stuck. In this instance, it often helps to ask a question such as the following:

How might you begin?
What do you think the problem is asking you to do?
What would happen if . . . ?
Can you draw a picture that represents the problem or find a pattern?
Can you think of a smaller, similar problem?

Our role as teachers is to be supportive and encouraging of all students. Listening carefully with a curious attitude about what children have to say is one way. Writing their responses on the board or a chart during class discussions is another way. Responding to their thinking with probing questions is another way still. When teachers demonstrate these behaviors, students know that they and their thinking are being valued. Sometimes this means putting aside any preconceived ideas and expectations of hoped-for responses. Being listened to and respected is highly motivating and longer lasting than quick words of praise. Quick words of praise can limit children and actually cause them not to try new ideas for fear of loss of praise or of disappointing the teacher. The focus should be on children expressing their thinking and reasoning processes, not just giving correct answers.

It's likely you'll choose to use these lessons along with other instructional materials or learning activities. It's important, however, to be consistent so that in all lessons you encourage students to make sense of ideas, communicate about their reasoning both orally and in writing, and apply their learning to problem-solving situations.

CHAPTER ONE
SILENT DIVISION

Overview

In this lesson, students explore the effects of changes to the dividend on the quotient when the divisor remains constant and the effects of changes to the divisor on the quotient when the dividend remains constant. Students use this knowledge to develop strategies for solving increasingly complex problems by using what they already know about simpler, related problems. Students use the vocabulary of division—*dividend, divisor, quotient*—to describe patterns they notice, reinforcing their understanding of each term and what it represents in the context of division problems. The lesson provides computational practice, develops students' number sense, builds their estimation skills, and enhances their ability to judge the reasonableness of answers.

Materials

▲ none

Time

▲ one class period followed by shorter explorations several times a week

Teaching Directions

1. Write on the board a problem all students can solve, for example, $4 \div 2 =$.

2. Explain to the students they will be exploring division problems that are related and they'll be able to use what they know about easier problems such as $4 \div 2$ to solve more complex problems.

3. Ask students to raise a hand when they've solved $4 \div 2$.

4. When all hands are up, give the chalk to a student and ask him or her to write the answer on the board. Explain that if a student doesn't want to go to the board to write an answer, that student should shake his or her head "no" and someone else will get the chance.

5. When a student has recorded the answer to 4 ÷ 2, ask the rest of the students to indicate their agreement with the answer by putting their thumbs up, their disagreement with the answer by putting their thumbs down, or uncertainty or confusion by putting their thumbs sideways.

6. Write a second related problem beneath the first. For example, 40 ÷ 2 =. Repeat Steps 3, 4, and 5.

7. Review the vocabulary: *dividend, divisor, quotient.* Use these words often to encourage students to use them as they discuss patterns they notice in the two problems solved thus far. For example, the second dividend is ten times larger than the first. Record this information as shown below:

$4 \div 2 = 2$

$40 \div 2 = 20$ *(dividend × 10) ÷ same divisor = quotient × 10*

8. Explain to students the rules for a silent lesson:
  ▲ A star drawn on the board indicates the beginning of the activity and silence by everyone, including the teacher.
  ▲ When a problem is written on the board, students should indicate when they know the answer by raising their hands.
  ▲ When a student writes the answer on the board, the other students indicate agreement with the answer with thumbs up, disagreement with thumbs down, or uncertainty or confusion with sideways thumbs.

9. Draw a star on the board and write the first problem. (See pages 6, 7, 9, and 11 for possible sequences of problems.) Wait until each student has a hand up, indicating they've all solved the problem, then hand the chalk to one student to write the answer on the board. When the student has written the answer, wait for the other students to use their thumbs to indicate their agreement, disagreement, uncertainty, or confusion. When the correct answer has been written and agreed upon, write a new, related problem and repeat the process.

10. Continue until four or more related problems have been written and solved.

11. Erase the star to indicate that students may again talk. Lead a class discussion, focusing on the changes in the dividend, divisor, and quotient in each problem. Record for each problem after the first one as shown in Step 7.

12. Repeat the activity on other days using a different series of problems each time. Always include a discussion of the patterns students notice about how changing the dividend or the divisor affects the quotient.

Teaching Notes

There are two important things to keep in mind for children to gain the greatest benefit from this lesson. First, it's critical that a discussion follows each series of problems the students solve. The discussion encourages and supports students' understanding of the patterns and increases the chances that they will be able to apply the patterns to solve increasingly complex division problems. Second, in order to explore different patterns, students need repeated experiences with this activity spread out over several weeks. The structure of this activity allows for exploration of many division relationships. See the "Extensions" section on page 10 for additional ideas.

Among the patterns the students explore are the effects of changes to the dividend on the quotient when the divisor remains the same. When a dividend is multiplied or divided by a number, and the divisor remains the same, then the quotient changes just as the dividend did, by being multiplied or divided by the same number. For example, if the dividend doubles and the divisor remains the same, then the quotient will double. This is because the total amount doubles, but the number of groups or the number in each group remains the same. Therefore, the quotient must also double. To clarify this idea, consider this situation: If you divide four cookies into two groups, there are two in each group ($4 \div 2 = 2$). If you double the number of cookies from four to eight cookies, and again divide them into two groups, the number in each group is now four, which is doubled from the first quotient of two ($8 \div 2 = 4$).

Students also explore the effects on the quotient when the dividend remains the same and the divisor changes by being multiplied or divided by another number. If the dividend remains the same, changes to the divisor will have the inverse effect on the quotient. Using the cookie example again, four cookies divided into two groups results in two cookies per group ($4 \div 2 = 2$). Double the divisor, or number of groups, while the number of cookies, the dividend, remains the same, and the problem becomes four cookies divided into four groups. That's one cookie per group ($4 \div 4 = 1$). The number of cookies remained the same, but the number of groups doubled. The same four cookies had to be divided among four groups rather than two. As a result, the quotient was halved from two to one.

In the beginning, writing the division problems using $\div$ to show the operation makes it easier for students to find patterns, since the quotients appear in a list. Later, when students are comfortable with the activity, it's appropriate to write division problems using fractional notation and the $\overline{)}$ sign. Vary how you represent problems so students become familiar and comfortable with all three forms of division.

The word *silent* in *Silent Division* refers to the instructional strategy used during the activity. A star on the board indicates that everyone, including the teacher, must be silent until the star is erased. Students indicate when they know an answer by raising their hands. Then each indicates his or her agreement with answers written on the board with a thumb, putting it up if he or she agrees, down if he or she disagrees, or sideways if he or she is uncertain. When students get stuck, you can provide help in written form. Benefits of the silent strategy include focused attention by students and the elimination of blurting. Also, students have commented that the silence gives them time to think.

The Lesson

▲▲▲

Note: The following conversation models how to introduce the students to the structure and process of *Silent Division,* although it's not done silently in this initial learning experience.

To begin, I wrote the following problem on the board:

$4 \div 2 =$

I said, "Today we're going to explore some related division problems. Some problems will be easy, like the one I wrote on the board, and you can use what you know about the easier problems to help you solve more difficult problems." I paused a moment, then continued. "Raise a hand when you know the answer to four divided by two."

When all hands were up, I asked, "Who would like to come to the board and write the answer to the first problem?" All hands flew into the air, as students were eager for the opportunity to write on the board. I handed the chalk to Becky, who came to the board and wrote *2.* I asked the students to indicate their agreement with Becky's answer by putting their thumbs up if they agreed, down if they disagreed, or sideways if they were uncertain. All thumbs were up. I wrote a second problem beneath the first, changing the 4 to 40:

$4 \div 2 = 2$

$40 \div 2 =$

"Raise a hand when you know the answer," I reminded the students. I handed the chalk to Serge, who came to the board and wrote *20.*

"What's the first number of a division problem called?" I asked as I pointed to the 4 in the first problem. Several hands went up.

Lorenzo said, "Product?" I shook my head.

Vanessa said, "Divisor?" Again I shook my head. Only one hand remained up. I called on Dustin.

"Is it . . . ?" Dustin began, then paused and shrugged his shoulders. It was clear the students in this class didn't know the terms *dividend, divisor*, and *quotient.* I decided to introduce the terminology and then reinforce it by using it repeatedly in this and other lessons.

I explained, "In this problem, the four is called the dividend and represents the entire amount." I wrote *dividend* above the 4 in the first problem to reinforce the vocabulary for the students. I continued, "The two is called the divisor and it tells us one of two things. It either tells us how many groups we have to make or tells us how many are in each group." I wrote *divisor* above the first 2. Some students nodded, indicating their understanding, while many looked blank. I didn't worry about this, as I knew that during the lesson these words would be used often and the students would become more comfortable with them. "The answer to a division problem is called the quotient. It answers the question, How many are in each group? or How many groups are there? It depends on the situation." I wrote *quotient* above the last 2 as follows:

$$\overset{\text{dividend} \quad \text{divisor} \quad \text{quotient}}{4 \div 2 = 2}$$
$$40 \div 2 = 20$$

To change the direction of the conversation, I said, "Let's look at the dividend in the two problems we've solved. What do you notice?"

Joelle said, "You added a zero to get the second dividend."

I replied, "I agree that there is one more zero in the second dividend. Adding a zero is the result of multiplying by what number?" Joelle looked uncertain. I paused to give all students the chance to consider my question.

"Can I call on someone else?" Joelle asked. I nodded. She called on Krystal.

"If you multiply by ten, that's like adding a zero in the ones place," Krystal said.

I wrote the following on the board:

$$4 \div 2 = 2$$
$$40 \div 2 = 20 \quad (dividend \times 10)$$

"What do you notice about the divisors?" I asked next.

"They stayed the same," Cole said. I wrote on the board:

$$4 \div 2 = 2$$
$$40 \div 2 = 20 \quad (dividend \times 10) \div$$
$$\qquad\qquad\qquad\quad same\ divisor$$

"What do you notice about the quotients?" I then asked.

Lisa said, "The second one multiplied by ten." I wrote on the board:

$$4 \div 2 = 2$$
$$40 \div 2 = 20 \quad (dividend \times 10) \div same$$
$$\qquad\qquad\qquad divisor = quotient \times 10$$

"The dividend multiplied by ten and so did the quotient," Shane commented. "I wonder if that always happens."

"That's one of the things we'll find out as we explore *Silent Division*," I replied. "You might be wondering why it's called *Silent Division*. We haven't been very silent; in fact, we've talked a lot. But in just a moment, I'm going to draw a star on the board. The star means we all must remain quiet, including me, until I erase the star. As long as the star is on the board, no one should talk. After I draw the star, I'll write a problem on the board. When you've figured out the answer, raise a hand, just as we've done so far. I'll hand the chalk to someone to come to the board and write the answer. If I try to hand you the chalk and you don't want to write the answer on the board, shake your head 'no' and I'll offer the chalk to someone else. When someone records an answer, the rest of you need to put your thumbs up to show agreement, down to show disagreement, or sideways if you're not sure. If you write an answer and you see thumbs down, you may change your answer or hand the chalk to someone else. Then I'll write a new problem, and so on. Are there questions?"

Jamie asked, "If we aren't sure, we just put our thumb sideways?" I nodded.

John asked, "What if we get stuck?"

"If you can't figure out the answer yourself, you may hand the chalk to someone else," I said. There were no more questions.

BEGINNING SILENT DIVISION

To begin, I drew a star on the board. Everyone was silent. I wrote on the board:

$$2 \div 2 =$$

Hands immediately popped up. I handed Vanessa the chalk. She came to the board and wrote *1*. The other students immediately responded with thumbs up. I took the chalk back and wrote another problem on the board underneath the first one:

$$2 \div 2 = 1$$
$$20 \div 2 =$$

Again, many hands popped up quickly. Kimi came to the board and wrote *10* and received thumbs up from her classmates. Kimi smiled and returned to her seat. I wrote a third problem on the board:

$$2 \div 2 = 1$$
$$20 \div 2 = 10$$
$$200 \div 2 =$$

Students were not quite as confident this time as they had been before, as fewer students raised their hands and those that did, did so more slowly. Andy came to the board and wrote *100*, and the other students indicated their agreement with their thumbs. I wrote the next problem:

$$2 \div 2 = 1$$
$$20 \div 2 = 10$$
$$200 \div 2 = 100$$
$$2,000 \div 2 =$$

Kiera came to the board and wrote *1,000*. The students agreed with Kiera. I then erased the star so we could talk about the patterns in the dividends, divisors, and quotients.

A Class Discussion

Pointing to the first two problems, I asked, "What did you notice about the dividends in the first two problems?" I waited until about half the students had their hands up and then called on Krystal.

"The dividend in the second problem has one more zero than the one in the first problem," Krystal explained. "The dividend is two in problem one and twenty in problem two. A zero was added."

"What number could you use to multiply by two to get twenty?" I asked. I wanted the students to be clear about what causes a zero to be added to the ones place.

"You could multiply by ten," Krystal said with uncertainty. I nodded. I wrote the following on the board next to the second problem:

$$2 \div 2 = 1$$
$$20 \div 2 = 10 \quad (dividend \times 10)$$
$$200 \div 2 = 100$$
$$2,000 \div 2 = 1,000$$

"What do you notice about the divisors in the first two problems?" I continued.

"They stayed the same," Kendra said. Several students nodded their agreement. I wrote on the board:

$$2 \div 2 = 1$$
$$20 \div 2 = 10 \quad (dividend \times 10) \div$$
$$\qquad\qquad\qquad same\ divisor$$
$$200 \div 2 = 100$$
$$2,000 \div 2 = 1,000$$

"What do you notice about the quotients in the first two problems?" I asked.

Clare explained, "The second one is ten times bigger than the first one."

"Put your thumb up if you agree with Clare's explanation," I said. "Put your thumb down if you disagree or sideways if you're not sure." Thumbs were up. I wrote on the board:

$$2 \div 2 = 1$$
$$20 \div 2 = 10 \quad (dividend \times 10) \div same$$
$$\qquad\qquad\qquad divisor = quotient \times 10$$
$$200 \div 2 = 100$$
$$2,000 \div 2 = 1,000$$

Continuing on, I said, "Let's look at the second and third problems to see what changes and what stays the same."

"I know something that changes—the first number," Joelle volunteered. She then paused to refer to the labels I'd written on the board earlier in the lesson, then continued, "The dividend multiplies by ten to go from twenty to two hundred."

"The divisors stay the same," Lisa said.

"And the quotient is multiplied by ten, too," Erin added.

"I agree with what each of you said," I replied as I recorded the following on the board:

$$2 \div 2 = 1$$
$$20 \div 2 = 10 \quad (dividend \times 10) \div same$$
$$\qquad\qquad\qquad divisor = quotient \times 10$$
$$200 \div 2 = 100 \quad (dividend \times 10) \div same$$
$$\qquad\qquad\qquad divisor = quotient \times 10$$
$$2,000 \div 2 = 1,000$$

"Can I tell what happens in the last problem?" Shane asked. I nodded. "The dividend added a zero, or multiplied by ten, the divisor stayed the same, and the quotient added a zero by multiplying by ten."

I said, "Use your thumb to show me if you agree or disagree with Shane's explanation." The students responded with thumbs up. I recorded what Shane shared on the board:

$2 \div 2 = 1$

$20 \div 2 = 10$ *(dividend × 10) ÷ same divisor = quotient × 10*

$200 \div 2 = 100$ *(dividend × 10) ÷ same divisor = quotient × 10*

$2,000 \div 2 = 1,000$ *(dividend × 10) ÷ same divisor = quotient × 10*

"Can we do it again?" Lorenzo and several other students asked. I nodded.

"Before I draw a new star on the board, are there any questions or comments about *Silent Division*?" I asked.

"It was fun," Becky shared. "I was really interested in how the dividend and quotient change in the same way. I didn't expect that."

"I liked getting to write on the board," Kiera said. "I had the answer when I put my hand up, but by the time I got to the board to write the answer, I forgot. Then I had to think of it again."

"Being the person who writes an answer on the board can be scary," I replied. "You kept your wits and you were able to figure out the answer again and write it on the board correctly. Being able to think on your feet like that is a good life skill."

REPEATING SILENT DIVISION

There were no other comments so I again drew a star on the board. The students immediately became silent and focused their attention on the board. I wrote:

$30 \div 30 =$

All hands immediately popped up. I handed the chalk to Clare, who came to the board, correctly wrote the answer, then turned to check that her classmates' thumbs were up. I continued in this way, writing a problem, having a student write the quotient, and waiting for others to respond.

$30 \div 30 = 1$

$300 \div 30 = 10$

$3,000 \div 30 = 100$

$3,000 \div 300 = 10$

$3,000 \div 3,000 = 1$

$30,000 \div 3,000 = 10$

In the first few problems, I changed only the dividend and left the divisor the same. To prevent the students from overgeneralizing this pattern, I changed the divisor in the next two problems and kept the dividend the same.

Andy came to the board to complete $3,000 \div 300$:

$3,000 \div 300 = 100$

He received thumbs down from most of the students. He studied the problem a moment and shrugged. To assist Andy, I wrote on the board next to the problem:

$3,000 \div 300 = 100$ $100 \times 300 =$

The students knew they could check a division answer by multiplying the quotient by the divisor to see if the answer was the dividend, as it should be. Andy mentally multiplied one hundred times three hundred and wrote *30,000* as the product. With a look of confusion, he shrugged and wrote on the board:

Can I choose someone else?

I nodded and he handed the chalk to Dustin, who came to the board, erased Andy's answer to $3,000 \div 300$, and correctly wrote *10*. When I next increased the divisor, the new problem was $3,000 \div 3,000$, and Kendra quickly came to the board and with confidence correctly wrote the quotient as *1*.

A Class Discussion

After erasing the star, I began the discussion by asking what was the same and what was different about the first two problems. John explained, "The dividend of thirty in the first problem was multiplied by ten, so it became three hundred in the second problem. The divisor stayed the same. Because the dividend was multiplied by ten, the quotient has to multiply by ten.

It was one and then it became ten." The students indicated their agreement with John by giving him thumbs up. I recorded on the board:

$$30 \div 30 = 1$$
$$300 \div 30 = 10 \qquad \textit{(dividend} \times 10) \div$$
$$\textit{same divisor} =$$
$$\textit{quotient} \times 10$$

$$3{,}000 \div 30 = 100$$
$$3{,}000 \div 300 = 10$$
$$3{,}000 \div 3{,}000 = 1$$
$$30{,}000 \div 3{,}000 = 10$$

Kiera continued by explaining that the second dividend was multiplied by ten to make the third dividend, which also meant the quotient had to be multiplied by ten, and the divisors stayed the same.

Sylas raised his hand. "I got it until we got to the fourth problem. The dividends stayed the same, and this time the divisors changed. The divisor in the third problem was multiplied by ten, but the quotient wasn't multiplied by ten. I don't get it!"

The students started talking among themselves. I asked for their attention and said, "I hear many of you talking about Sylas's comment. To be sure everyone has a chance to talk and everyone has the chance to listen, I'd like you to talk with your partner. First, one of you will talk for thirty seconds while the other listens without interruption. At the end of thirty seconds, I'll ask you to switch roles so the first talker can listen and the first listener can talk. Then we'll talk together as a class." The room came to life as students shared their ideas about why increasing the divisor caused the quotient to decrease. At the end of thirty seconds, I reminded the students to switch roles. At the end of another thirty seconds, I asked for everyone's attention.

Krystal was first to share. "I think when the divisor went up, the quotient went down because the divisor tells the number of groups or how many in each group. If you increase the number of

groups, then the number in each group will go down if the dividend stays the same, and it did."

"I don't get it," Kendra moaned.

"I think I know what Krystal means," Erin said. "If I have six cookies and I want to put them in three groups, then there are two cookies in a group. But if I have six cookies and I put them in six groups, I have the same cookies but more groups, so the number in the groups will go down."

"Oh yeah!" Dustin said with wonder. "Six divided by three is two, and six divided by six is one . . . more groups, less cookies!!"

I wrote on the board the following summary of Erin's and Dustin's ideas to help the others see what they had explained:

$$6 \div 3 = 2$$
$$6 \div 6 = 1 \qquad \textit{same dividend} \div$$
$$\textit{(divisor} \times 2) = \textit{quotient} \div 2$$

"So what did change from the third problem to the fourth?" I asked to refocus the class.

Becky explained, "The dividends stayed the same, the divisor went up ten times, and the quotient was divided by ten." I recorded Becky's thinking on the board:

$$30 \div 30 = 1$$
$$300 \div 30 = 10 \qquad \textit{(dividend} \times 10) \div$$
$$\textit{same divisor} =$$
$$\textit{quotient} \times 10$$

$$3{,}000 \div 30 = 100 \qquad \textit{(dividend} \times 10) \div$$
$$\textit{same divisor} =$$
$$\textit{quotient} \times 10$$

$$3{,}000 \div 300 = 10 \qquad \textit{same dividend} \div$$
$$\textit{(divisor} \times 10) =$$
$$\textit{quotient} \div 10$$

$$3{,}000 \div 3{,}000 = 1$$
$$30{,}000 \div 3{,}000 = 10$$

"I figured it out a different way," Cole said. "I thought, 'What number times three hundred equals three thousand?' It can only be ten times three hundred, so I knew the quotient had to be ten."

I said, "Cole makes an important point. The quotient times the divisor gives the dividend. In this case the dividend is three thousand. Multiplying the divisor of three hundred by the quotient of ten results in the dividend of three thousand." I recorded on the board Cole's explanation beneath Becky's.

$30 \div 30 = 1$

$300 \div 30 = 10$ *(dividend × 10) ÷ same divisor = quotient × 10*

$3,000 \div 30 = 100$ *(dividend × 10) ÷ same divisor = quotient × 10*

$3,000 \div 300 = 10$ *same dividend ÷ (divisor × 10) = quotient ÷ 10*
10 × 300 = 3,000

$3,000 \div 3,000 = 1$

$30,000 \div 3,000 = 10$

I asked, "Can we verify other problems using Cole's thinking?" Most students nodded.

"It's easy to show Cole's idea works," Erin said. "One times thirty equals thirty. The first problem checks."

"Ten times thirty equals three hundred," Dustin shared.

"And one hundred times thirty equals three thousand," Kimi added.

I recorded on the board Erin's, Dustin's, and Kimi's ideas:

$30 \div 30 = 1$ $1 \times 30 = 30$

$300 \div 30 = 10$ *(dividend × 10) ÷ same divisor = quotient × 10*
10 × 30 = 300

$3,000 \div 30 = 100$ *(dividend × 10) ÷ same divisor = quotient × 10*
100 × 30 = 3,000

$3,000 \div 300 = 10$ *same dividend ÷ (divisor × 10) = quotient ÷ 10*
10 × 300 = 3,000

$3,000 \div 3,000 = 1$

$30,000 \div 3,000 = 10$

There were no more comments, so I continued until we had completed all the problems as follows, including checking the division by using multiplication:

$30 \div 30 = 1$ $1 \times 30 = 30$

$300 \div 30 = 10$ *(dividend × 10) ÷ same divisor = quotient × 10*
10 × 30 = 300

$3,000 \div 30 = 100$ *(dividend × 10) ÷ same divisor = quotient × 10*
100 × 30 = 3,000

$3,000 \div 300 = 10$ *same dividend ÷ (divisor × 10) = quotient ÷ 10*
10 × 300 = 3,000

$3,000 \div 3,000 = 1$ *same dividend ÷ (divisor × 10) = quotient ÷ 10*
1 × 3,000 = 3,000

$30,000 \div 3,000 = 10$ *(dividend × 10) ÷ same divisor = quotient × 10*
10 × 3,000 = 30,000

REPEATING SILENT DIVISION

The students were excited by their discoveries and eager to do another series of problems. Once again I drew a star on the board, and the students solved the following problems using the same procedure as before:

$60 \div 6 = 10$

$66 \div 6 = 11$

$660 \div 6 = 110$

$660 \div 3 = 220$

$660 \div 1\frac{1}{2} = 440$

$660 \div 3 = 220$

$1,320 \div 3 = 440$

In the first two problems of this series, the change in the two dividends is the result of adding one more group. In this case, each group had six, so six was added to the dividend. In the fifth problem, students encountered a fraction in the divisor.

The dividend remained the same, the divisor was the previous divisor divided by two, and as a result the quotient doubled.

To bring the lesson to a close, I asked the students what they thought of *Silent Division*.

Kimi said, "I was surprised at the hard problems I could do in my head."

Dustin added, "It was sort of like a riddle. You knew enough that if you thought about what you knew, you could figure out the next problem."

"I liked writing on the board," Andy said. "When I got stuck it was OK, because I got to have someone else help."

Kiera said, "I wonder what would happen if you changed both the dividend and the divisor at the same time. Like, what if you started with six divided by three and changed it to sixty divided by thirty?" I wrote on the board:

$6 \div 3 =$

$60 \div 30 =$

"Hey, that's weird," Lorenzo said. "I think the answers are the same. Six divided by three is two, and sixty divided by thirty is two. But both the dividend and the divisor were multiplied by ten." I wrote the answers:

$6 \div 3 = 2$

$60 \div 30 = 2$

Becky said, "I think it worked that way because you increased the total things to be divided ten times and you also increased the number of groups to put them in ten times. That's why I think the answer didn't change." Several students nodded. I recorded:

$6 \div 3 = 2$

$60 \div 30 = 2$ *(dividend × 10) ÷ (divisor × 10) = same quotient*

Lisa said pensively, "It was quiet so I could think."

Dustin added a final comment: "I had time to think and solve the problem. Sometimes I even had time to check my answer. I didn't feel rushed." Many students nodded their agreement with Lisa and Dustin. No one had anything else to add, so I ended the lesson for that day.

EXTENSIONS

I continued with *Silent Division* several times per week over the next five or six weeks. As the students became more familiar with the activity, I introduced the other two ways of writing division problems, each time making sure the students understood which number was the dividend, which was the divisor, and which was the quotient and connecting the meaning of each within the context of division. For example, below are three ways to present the same set of problems:

$4 \div 4 = 1$	$4\overline{)4}\,^{1}$	$\frac{4}{4} = 1$
$40 \div 4 = 10$	$4\overline{)40}\,^{10}$	$\frac{40}{4} = 10$
$400 \div 4 = 100$	$4\overline{)400}\,^{100}$	$\frac{400}{4} = 100$
$4,000 \div 4 = 1,000$	$4\overline{)4000}\,^{1000}$	$\frac{4000}{4} = 1,000$

Below are some of the many series of problems you could use.

Multiplying the Dividend by Ten

$4 \div 4 =$ $60 \div 60 =$

$40 \div 4 =$ $600 \div 60 =$

$400 \div 4 =$ $6,000 \div 60 =$

$4,000 \div 4 =$ $60,000 \div 60 =$

Multiplying the Divisor by Ten

$5,000 \div 5 =$

$5,000 \div 50 =$

$5,000 \div 500 =$

$5,000 \div 5,000 =$

Multiplying the Dividend by Two

$20 \div 4 =$

$40 \div 4 =$

$80 \div 4 =$

$160 \div 4 =$

Multiply and Dividing the Dividend by Ten and Doubling the Divisor

$48 \div 8 =$

$480 \div 8 =$

$4,800 \div 8 =$

$4,800 \div 16 =$

$4,800 \div 32 =$

$480 \div 32 =$

$48 \div 32 =$

Introducing Other Notation

$50 \div 50 =$ $60 \div 6 =$

$50 \overline{)50} =$ $\frac{60}{6} =$

$50 \overline{)500} =$ $\frac{600}{6} =$

$500 \overline{)500} =$ $\frac{600}{60} =$

$500 \overline{)5000} =$ $\frac{660}{60} =$

Division with Remainders

$11 \div 5 =$

$16 \div 5 =$

$21 \div 5 =$

$26 \div 5 =$

$31 \div 5 =$

Combining Ideas

$4 \div 4 =$

$8 \div 4 =$

$8 \div 2 =$

$16 \div 4 =$

$160 \div 4 =$

$160 \div 8 =$

$160 \div 80 =$

$160 \div 40 =$

$320 \div 80 =$

$400 \div 80 =$

$480 \div 80 =$

$4,800 \div 80 =$

$4,800 \div 160 =$

Questions and Discussion

▲▲

▲ Why do you do this activity silently?

I do the activity silently for several reasons. First, the silence seems to increase the children's attention and focus. Perhaps this is because it's different to learn silently. Children are using only one sense to take in information. Perhaps it's the change from the usual mode of instruction. What's important is that the children are focused and learning. Another benefit of using a star to indicate silence is that children who tend to blurt out their thinking aren't allowed this behavior. Also, the silence seems to slow things down, giving more students quality time to think and process, as Lisa and Dustin shared at the end of the vignette.

▲ What is the importance of the class discussions?

It's during the class discussions that students explore the connections and relationships among the problems. They consider and discuss how the relationships and patterns they notice can help them solve more complex, related problems. Many students will not make these connections on their own. The class discussions guide, support, and encourage these understandings and their application to solving more difficult problems.

▲ Doesn't the silence make it difficult to help or correct students?

When helping or correcting a student in a silent lesson, I can't rely on verbal explanations, which may or may not make sense to the child. Instead, I must think about other ways to help that child through his or her difficulty. Often I rely more on making connections among ideas or using pictures that can help. When I find general confusion among the students, however, I simply erase the star, indicating that it's OK to talk, and we have a discussion to clear up the confusion. Then I draw the star again and we continue with the activity. However, doing this is the exception rather than the norm.

▲ After the star is erased, what questions are effective for guiding the discussion?

The questions I ask vary according to the situation. As a place to start, I consider the goal I was trying to achieve by selecting particular problems. For example, if my goal was for students to explore the effects on the quotient of dividing the dividend in half while the divisor remained constant, my questioning would focus on this idea. Also, I'm guided by the apparent needs of my students and the patterns and connections they are making among problems and ideas. The key is to keep in mind the mathematics to be taught while listening and responding carefully and thoughtfully to the students.

The following are some general questions that are effective to get a discussion going:

What did you notice?

What patterns did you see?

What's different about the dividends? The divisors?

What would happen if . . . ?

How do you know this information is reasonable?

What did you learn or discover?

What are you still wondering about?

Once the discussion is going, the mathematics to be explored and the students' comments, insights, and questions should guide the conversation and further questions you can raise for the students to consider.

CHAPTER TWO
THE DIVISOR STAYS THE SAME

Overview

This lesson focuses on the relationships among dividends, divisors, quotients, and remainders expressed as whole numbers. Students investigate the patterns that occur in quotients when the divisor stays the same. To model for the whole class how partners will later conduct the investigation, students first divide by two and three the numbers from one to fifteen and then discuss the patterns they notice. Next, working in pairs, students divide the numbers from one to fifteen by four and then the class discusses the patterns. Finally, pairs choose a divisor from five to ten, use it to divide the numbers from one to fifty, and write about the patterns they find. In a whole-group discussion, students examine one another's work, share patterns they notice, and make generalizations based on their observations.

Materials

▲ chart paper

Time

▲ Four class periods followed by shorter discussions spread over several weeks

Teaching Directions

1. Write on the board the following list of division problems, stopping about halfway through the list and asking students to predict the problems you'll write next.

$1 \div 2 =$	$5 \div 2 =$
$2 \div 2 =$	$6 \div 2 =$
$3 \div 2 =$	$7 \div 2 =$
$4 \div 2 =$	$8 \div 2 =$

$9 \div 2 =$ $13 \div 2 =$

$10 \div 2 =$ $14 \div 2 =$

$11 \div 2 =$ $15 \div 2 =$

$12 \div 2 =$

2. When you've completed the list, discuss the vocabulary *dividend, divisor,* and *quotient.* Write on the board: *dividend ÷ divisor = quotient.*

3. Ask for student volunteers to choose a problem and then come to the board to write the quotient for that problem. Have students indicate their agreement with the answer by putting their thumbs up if they agree, down if they disagree, or sideways if they're unsure or don't know. Students may represent answers differently—for example, $3\frac{1}{2}$ or 3 R1—but ask them all to be sure to include the quotient with the remainder as a whole number (3 R1).

4. Talk with the class about how to solve $1 \div 2$, as this is typically confusing for students. Model the solution concretely. For example, talk about dividing one pencil between two students. Since breaking the pencil in half isn't allowed, each of the two students gets zero pencils and the pencil becomes a remainder of one.

5. Discuss and record on the board patterns the students notice about the quotients in the division problems listed.

6. On the board next to the list of division problems from Step 1, write a second list the same as the first, except this time using the divisor of three instead of two. Before students solve the problems, ask them to make predictions about the remainders. Record student's predictions on the board.

$1 \div 3 =$ $9 \div 3 =$

$2 \div 3 =$ $10 \div 3 =$

$3 \div 3 =$ $11 \div 3 =$

$4 \div 3 =$ $12 \div 3 =$

$5 \div 3 =$ $13 \div 3 =$

$6 \div 3 =$ $14 \div 3 =$

$7 \div 3 =$ $15 \div 3 =$

$8 \div 3 =$

7. Have students solve the problems as in Step 3.

8. For the rest of the period, lead a class discussion about the patterns students notice or errors in any of the quotients. Discussion questions could include the following:

What do you notice about the dividends? The divisors?

What patterns do you notice in the quotients?

What do you notice about the remainders?

The Divisor Stays the Same   15

9. Before the next day's class, copy onto chart paper the two lists of problems from Steps 1 and 6. (Represent all remainders as whole numbers.) Add a third set of problems with dividends from one to fifteen and the divisor of four.

$1 \div 2 = 0 \ R1$	$1 \div 3 = 0 \ R1$	$1 \div 4 =$
$2 \div 2 = 1$	$2 \div 3 = 0 \ R2$	$2 \div 4 =$
$3 \div 2 = 1 \ R1$	$3 \div 3 = 1$	$3 \div 4 =$
$4 \div 2 = 2$	$4 \div 3 = 1 \ R1$	$4 \div 4 =$
$5 \div 2 = 2 \ R1$	$5 \div 3 = 1 \ R2$	$5 \div 4 =$
$6 \div 2 = 3$	$6 \div 3 = 2$	$6 \div 4 =$
$7 \div 2 = 3 \ R1$	$7 \div 3 = 2 \ R1$	$7 \div 4 =$
$8 \div 2 = 4$	$8 \div 3 = 2 \ R2$	$8 \div 4 =$
$9 \div 2 = 4 \ R1$	$9 \div 3 = 3$	$9 \div 4 =$
$10 \div 2 = 5$	$10 \div 3 = 3 \ R1$	$10 \div 4 =$
$11 \div 2 = 5 \ R1$	$11 \div 3 = 3 \ R2$	$11 \div 4 =$
$12 \div 2 = 6$	$12 \div 3 = 4$	$12 \div 4 =$
$13 \div 2 = 6 \ R1$	$13 \div 3 = 4 \ R1$	$13 \div 4 =$
$14 \div 2 = 7$	$14 \div 3 = 4 \ R2$	$14 \div 4 =$
$15 \div 2 = 7 \ R1$	$15 \div 3 = 5$	$15 \div 4 =$

10. Ask students to work in pairs to solve the third set of problems and write about the patterns they notice. Then lead a class discussion for students to share patterns they discovered.

11. Ask pairs to choose a divisor from five to ten, solve division problems with dividends from one to fifty, and write about patterns they discover. Write the following on the board to support and guide students' writing:

As you look for patterns, think about the following:

▲ *Which dividends don't have remainders? What is the pattern?*
▲ *Which dividends have R1? R2? R3 and so on? What patterns do you notice?*
▲ *What's the largest remainder you found for your divisor? Why do you think this is so?*

If students finish early, give them another divisor to explore.

12. Lead a class discussion about one divisor. The divisor of nine was used in the vignette, but any divisor from five to ten can be used. Discussion questions could include the following:

▲ What do you notice about the remainders for each divisor?
▲ What do you notice about dividends that have remainders of zero? One? Two? (And so on.)

Also, during the discussion, review both models of division. For example, $15 \div 2$ can represent fifteen divided into two groups of seven with one left over or fifteen divided into groups of two, resulting in seven groups of two with one left over.

Teaching Notes

This lesson provides students the opportunity to investigate, in depth, relationships in division problems among dividends, divisors, quotients, and remainders expressed as whole numbers. The lesson also helps reinforce students' understanding of how we interpret division problems. For example, if we share three pencils between two children, each child will get one pencil and one pencil will be left over; we can represent this problem and answer as $3 \div 2 = 1$ R1. If, however, the problem is to share three cookies between two children, then it's possible to solve the problem either by leaving the leftover cookie whole and reporting it as the remainder ($3 \div 2 = 1$ R1) or by dividing it into two pieces ($3 \div 2 = 1\frac{1}{2}$). Deciding when each of these two possible answers is appropriate depends on the context of the problem. However, when a problem is presented without a context, either answer is correct, as is 1.5.

This lesson focuses on quotients with remainders written as whole numbers and guides students to look for relationships between remainders and the other parts of division problems. While students typically have a good deal of experience representing remainders in answers to division problems as whole numbers, they don't often have the chance to investigate the relationships among dividends, divisors, quotients, and remainders expressed as whole numbers. Following are some of the ideas that emerge from the lesson:

▲ Remainders should always be less than the divisors.
▲ If a remainder is larger than the divisor, this means that there is enough to make another group, and the quotient should be larger.
▲ When the dividend and divisor are the same number, the quotient is 1.
▲ When the dividend is twice the divisor, the quotient is 2.
▲ When the dividend is one more than the divisor, the quotient is 1 R1.
▲ When the remainder is zero, the dividend is a multiple of the divisor . . . or, stating this another way, the divisor is a factor of the dividend.

Your students may notice some or all of these relationships, as well as others not included here or in the vignette.

Also, while students in these grade levels typically are asked to solve division problems with large numbers, many still need practice thinking about problems with small divisors. This investigation provides practice with divisors from two to ten, using them to help students deepen their understanding of the meaning of remainders and their relationships to dividends and divisors.

The Lesson

▲▲

DAY 1

As the students settled, I listed the following problems on the board:

$1 \div 2 =$ $3 \div 2 =$
$2 \div 2 =$ $4 \div 2 =$

$5 \div 2 =$ $11 \div 2 =$
$6 \div 2 =$ $12 \div 2 =$
$7 \div 2 =$ $13 \div 2 =$
$8 \div 2 =$ $14 \div 2 =$
$9 \div 2 =$ $15 \div 2 =$
$10 \div 2 =$

"What do you notice about these problems?" I asked. Most hands went up and I called on Toshi.

"The first numbers are going up," she said.

Pointing to the first number in the first problem, I asked, "In division, what's this number called?"

"The divisor?" Jameson offered with hesitation.

"This is the divisor," I said as I pointed to the second number of the first problem. No one had any other ideas.

"The first number of each problem in this entire column of division problems is called the dividend," I explained as I wrote *dividend* above the 1 in the first problem. "When division problems are written in this form," I continued, pointing to the list, "the second number is the divisor. The divisor is the number you divide by. The answer is called the quotient." I wrote above the first problem: *dividend ÷ divisor = quotient*. Reinforcing vocabulary in this way facilitates communication about ideas.

To return to Toshi's idea, I said, "Toshi, you said the first numbers go up by one. What's another word you could use to mean first numbers?"

Toshi quickly replied, "Dividend. The dividends go up by one."

I recorded Toshi's idea on the board:

Toshi: The dividends go up by 1.

Natalia shared her thoughts next. "I noticed two things. The problems are in numerical order is one thing. I also noticed that the divisors are all two."

I recorded Natalia's ideas on the board:

Natalia: The problems are in numerical order and the divisors are all 2.

No one had any other ideas to share, so I asked, "Who would like to volunteer to write the answer for one of the division problems I wrote on the board?" Hands leaped into the air. "You can choose any problem that you'd like," I added and

called on Eli. He came to the board and wrote *2* for 4 ÷ 2. I said to the rest of the class, "Four divided by two equals two. If you agree, please put your thumb up. If you disagree, put your thumb down. If you don't know or aren't sure, put your thumb sideways." All thumbs were up. I knew that all of the students would agree with the answer, but I asked them to respond anyway to establish this procedure for the rest of the lesson.

I continued, "Eli, please hand the chalk to someone else so he or she can write the answer to another problem. If the chalk is handed to you and you don't want to come to the board to write a quotient, or answer, for one of the problems, just say 'No, thank you.'"

Eli handed the chalk to Vicki. Vicki came to the board and wrote *3* for the problem 6 ÷ 2. Her classmates showed their agreement by putting their thumbs up. Vicki handed the chalk to Kaleb and we continued in this fashion.

The students wrote answers for the problems without remainders first. For 7 ÷ 2, Natalia recorded *3 R1*. Then, for 9 ÷ 2, Daniel recorded $4\frac{1}{2}$. When I've taught this lesson in other classes, students in some have used only the form that Natalia did and in others have used only fractions, as Daniel did, or even decimals, representing Daniel's answer as 4.5. All of these are acceptable answers for this lesson, but I was interested in having the students investigate patterns in the remainders. Therefore, after the students had indicated that they agreed with his answer, I said to Daniel, "Your answer is correct. Can you also write the remainder as a whole number in the form that Natalia used?" Daniel nodded and did so. I use this same response whenever a student represents the remainder as a fraction or a decimal.

I added, "It's important to remember that there are often different ways to represent an answer. For the rest of the problems, you may want to write the answer in more than one way, but please be sure first to write the remainder as a whole number." I pointed to R1 as Natalia and now Daniel had recorded and added, "I'm interested today in having you think about the remainders as whole numbers." Then I reversed Daniel's two answers to model for the students how they should record the rest of the answers.

The students continued, some writing the remainders only as whole numbers and some writing them as fractions or decimals as well. Finally, there were answers for all but the first problem, 1 ÷ 2, and no one volunteered for it. (This is also typical in classes.)

dividend	÷	divisor	=	quotient		
1	÷	2	=			
2	÷	2	=	1		
3	÷	2	=	1 R1		
4	÷	2	=	2		
5	÷	2	=	2 R1		
6	÷	2	=	3		
7	÷	2	=	3 R1		
8	÷	2	=	4		
9	÷	2	=	4 R1,	$4\frac{1}{2}$	
10	÷	2	=	5		
11	÷	2	=	5 R1,	$5\frac{1}{2}$,	5.5
12	÷	2	=	6		
13	÷	2	=	6 R1		
14	÷	2	=	7		
15	÷	2	=	7 R1,	7.5,	$7\frac{1}{2}$

I said, "No one seems to want to solve the last problem, one divided by two. Let's solve it together. Let's look for patterns in the answers you've written so far to help us figure out the answer to one divided by two. What patterns do you notice?"

Cameron said, "The biggest remainder is one."

"Why do you think that is?" I asked. Cameron shrugged. Others put their hands up. I called on Nalani.

"If the remainder were two, you'd have another group," she said.

"What does the remainder mean?" I asked.

Joaquin said, "It tells that there were extras."

Raku added, "It tells that only a part of a group was left. In these problems, the remainder means that one out of a group of two was left." Several students nodded.

I wrote Cameron's idea on the board:

Cameron: The biggest remainder is one.

Tim shared a different idea: "The quotients starting with the second problem go no remainder, remainder, no remainder, remainder. I think if you follow the pattern backward, then one divided by two should have a remainder." I paraphrased Tim's idea as I wrote it on the board:

Tim: Every other quotient has a remainder. The quotient after 1 ÷ 2 has no remainder, so 1 ÷ 2 must have a remainder.

Tim nodded his agreement with what I'd written.

Andrew raised his hand. "I agree with Tim and I think the remainder has to be one. If it's two or three or four and so on, then there are enough left over to make more groups of two."

Andrew: The remainder for 1 ÷ 2 has to be 1.

No one had anything to add, so I asked, "Who would like to write the answer for one divided by two?" Raku volunteered. She wrote: *0 R1*.

"That makes sense," Benito said. "There's another pattern to the quotients, I just noticed. If you ignore the remainders for a minute, the other part of the quotients go one, one, two, two, three, three, and like that. The second and third problem have ones, so the first problem should probably be zero, like Raku said." Some students nodded and some still looked confused.

To help those still confused, I decided to model the problem concretely. I picked up a pencil and said, "Suppose I had one pencil to share between two students and I didn't want to break the pencil. How many pencils would each of the two students get?"

"Zero," many students said.

"If you could break the pencil, each student would get one-half," Kaleb noted.

I responded first to Kaleb's comment and then to the answer most of the class gave. "Yes, but I don't want to break the pencil. While giving each student one-half would work if we were dividing cookies or pizza, it won't work for pencils. In this case, each student would get zero pencils. How many would be left over?" I asked.

"One," the students responded together.

Toshi commented, "Zero remainder one fits the rest of the pattern better than one-half."

No one else had a comment to make. I then wrote another set of problems on the board beside the first set, again with dividends from one to fifteen, but each with the divisor of three.

$1 \div 3 =$ $9 \div 3 =$
$2 \div 3 =$ $10 \div 3 =$
$3 \div 3 =$ $11 \div 3 =$
$4 \div 3 =$ $12 \div 3 =$
$5 \div 3 =$ $13 \div 3 =$
$6 \div 3 =$ $14 \div 3 =$
$7 \div 3 =$ $15 \div 3 =$
$8 \div 3 =$

I said, "Let's write quotients as we did with the first set of problems. This time, let's just show the remainders as whole numbers."

Sara said, "I notice the pattern of the dividends is the same as the last group of problems, but the divisors are all threes instead of twos."

"What do you think the patterns will be for the remainders?" I asked.

Kurt said, "In the first group of problems the pattern was every other problem had a remainder of one. I think the pattern when we divide by three will be different. I think it will be no remainder, no remainder, remainder, no remainder, no remainder, remainder." I recorded Kurt's idea on the board:

Kurt

NR

NR

R

NR

NR

R

•

•

•

When I finished recording, I explained, "I used NR to mean no remainder and R to mean remainder. The three dots at the end of the list mean the pattern continues on."

Vicki shared next. "I think the pattern of the remainders will be remainder two, remainder three, remainder four, remainder five, remainder six, and just keep going." I recorded Vicki's idea on the board next to Kurt's:

Kurt	Vicki
NR	R2
NR	R3
R	R4
NR	R5
NR	R6
R	•
•	•
•	•
•	

Damon was next to share, and I recorded his idea. "I think every other quotient will have no remainder. The remainders will start with two and go up by one each time."

Tim shared another idea. "I think the first problem will have a remainder of one, then a remainder of two, then no remainder, remainder one, remainder two, no remainder, remainder one, remainder two, and on like that. I don't think the remainder can be bigger than two because if it is, there's enough for another group." I added Tim's idea to the board.

Raku shared her idea next. "I think it will go remainder two, remainder one, no remainder, remainder two, remainder one, no remainder."

After I recorded Raku's idea, no other students wanted to share.

Kurt	Vicki	Damon	Tim	Raku
NR	R2	NR	R1	R2
NR	R3	R2	R2	R1
R	R4	NR	NR	NR
NR	R5	R3	R1	R2
NR	R6	NR	R2	R1
R	•	R4	NR	NR
•	•	•	•	•
•	•	•	•	•
•		•	•	•

I commented, "You've shared some interesting ideas about the quotients. Let's see what happens. Who would like to begin by choosing a problem from the list to solve?" Students were eager and hands waved in the air. We proceeded as before. I gave the chalk to Sara and she recorded the answer of 2 to 6 ÷ 3. The others indicated their agreement with thumbs up. Sara then passed the chalk to another volunteer, who came to the board and wrote an answer. We continued in this way, with the rest of the students indicating their agreement, disagreement, or uncertainty with their thumbs. If a student's answer had received a thumbs-down, I would have stopped and led a discussion about the problem; however, this did not occur in this class. Also, if a student made an

error and no one objected, I didn't interrupt but left the error for us to deal with when all problems had an answer. With this class, the completed list had two errors, for 1 ÷ 3 and 7 ÷ 3.

$1 \div 3 = 1\ R2$	$9 \div 3 = 3$
$2 \div 3 = 0\ R2$	$10 \div 3 = 3\ R1$
$3 \div 3 = 1$	$11 \div 3 = 3\ R2$
$4 \div 3 = 1\ R1$	$12 \div 3 = 4$
$5 \div 3 = 1\ R2$	$13 \div 3 = 4\ R1$
$6 \div 3 = 2$	$14 \div 3 = 4\ R2$
$7 \div 3 = 2\ R2$	$15 \div 3 = 5$
$8 \div 3 = 2\ R2$	

"Please study the quotients of these problems carefully and see what you notice," I said. I was hoping the students would notice the errors.

After giving the students a few moments to consider the list, I asked the students to share their ideas with their partners. I said, "First one of you talks for thirty seconds while the other listens. At the end of thirty seconds I'll ask you to change roles so the first talker listens and the first listener talks. Remember, no interruptions." I gave the signal to begin and the room came alive as the students shared their ideas. At the end of thirty seconds, I asked the students to change roles. At the end of the second thirty seconds, I asked for everyone's attention. Several students raised their hands immediately, eager to share.

"What did you notice about the quotients?" I asked.

Susan began, "Seven divided by three and eight divided by three have the same quotient."

"Tell us some more about that," I encouraged.

Susan continued, "They can't both equal two remainder two. It doesn't make sense, but I'm not sure why." Susan paused a few moments, then said, "Can I call on somebody who knows why?" I nodded and she called on Robyn.

The Divisor Stays the Same 21

Robyn explained, "The dividend tells how many you're starting with. In one problem the dividend is seven, and in the other it's eight. The three means you want to make groups of three. The answer just has to be different if you start out with different amounts and you want to make the same size groups."

Cameron said, "I know another way to explain it. Multiplication and division are opposites. If you multiply the whole number part of the quotient with the divisor and add the remainder, you should get the dividend. I did that with eight divided by three equals two remainder two. Multiply two times three and that's six. Then add the remainder of two to six and that makes eight. Then I did the same thing with seven divided by three equals two remainder two. Two times three is six; add the remainder of two and it equals eight, not seven. Seven divided by three equals two remainder two is wrong. It should be two remainder one. Two times three is six and add the remainder of one and it equals seven. It works."

Becki shared next. "If you look at the pattern of remainders, it goes no remainder, remainder one, remainder two. According to the pattern, the answer to seven divided by three should be two remainder one."

No one had anything else to add, so I said, "If you think the quotient to seven divided by three should be two remainder one, please put your thumb up; if you disagree, put your thumb down; and if you're not sure, put your thumb sideways." Most thumbs were up.

Because a few students hadn't put their thumbs up, I said to the class, "Sometimes it helps to explain a problem by relating it to a situation. There are a lot of ways to interpret seven divided by three. One way is seven balloons divided among three people." I stopped and wrote on the board:

7 balloons divided among 3 people = ?

"What would happen if we divided seven balloons among three people?" I asked. "Talk with your neighbor about this."

After giving the students time to talk, I brought them back to attention and called on Vicki.

"They each got two balloons," she said. "Then there's one extra."

"How would we write the answer?" I asked. Most hands went up.

"It's two remainder one," Natalia said.

Kaleb was waving his hand to get my attention. He said, "I don't agree with two divided by three equals zero remainder two. I think it should be zero remainder three." Kaleb stopped and got a very surprised look on his face. "No, wait! I got confused. I thought the remainder should be the same as the divisor, but it should really be the same as the dividend. Oops! It's right the way it is."

Raku shared, "I think one divided by three equals one remainder two is wrong. It makes no sense to me. The first one means how many of something there is. How can each group get the whole amount and still have two extras? If I wanted to share one cookie with three friends, I couldn't give each friend one cookie when there was only one cookie to begin with."

"What do you think the correct answer is?" I asked. Raku shrugged. No one volunteered to explain further. To relate the problem to a situation, I took a marker from a nearby basket of supplies and said, "I have one marker in my hand. I want to divide it among three people, Becki, Amy, and Tanner. How many markers will each person get if I divide them equally?"

Kaleb quickly replied, "Well, one thing is for sure: they'd get ink all over them!" The students giggled.

"I guess that means we can't break the marker apart," I replied. "In that case, how many markers does each student get?"

"Zero," the class chorused.

"How many are left over?" I asked, holding up the one marker.

"One," the class responded in unison.

I said, "The answer to one divided by three is zero remainder one." I corrected the answer that was on the board: $1 \div 3 = 0\ R1$.

To move the conversation forward, I asked, "Do you agree that two divided by three is zero remainder two?" Some students nodded their heads while several others looked uncertain. I took two markers and modeled as I had before. "I have two markers and three students, Becki, Amy, and Tanner. How many markers will each get if I divide them equally?" Hands began to go up. "Tell me in a whisper voice," I said.

"Zero remainder two," the students said, verifying the answer on the board. The list was now correct.

$1 \div 3 = 0\ R1$	$9 \div 3 = 3$
$2 \div 3 = 0\ R2$	$10 \div 3 = 3\ R1$
$3 \div 3 = 1$	$11 \div 3 = 3\ R2$
$4 \div 3 = 1\ R1$	$12 \div 3 = 4$
$5 \div 3 = 1\ R2$	$13 \div 3 = 4\ R1$
$6 \div 3 = 2$	$14 \div 3 = 4\ R2$
$7 \div 3 = 2\ R1$	$15 \div 3 = 5$
$8 \div 3 = 2\ R2$	

The class period was over. I planned to continue the discussion the next day, so I copied both sets of fifteen problems from the board onto chart paper.

DAY 2

Before class I posted the chart with the two sets of problems from the previous day. I added a third set of problems for the students to solve and discuss, again with dividends from one to fifteen and this time with the divisors all four.

To begin the lesson, I said to the students, "Please copy down and solve the fifteen new problems. Use your own recording sheet, but work with your partner to solve the problems. When you've solved all fifteen problems, your next job is to look for patterns as we did before and write about them on your paper." There were no questions and the students began.

Observing the Students

For students who had difficulty with the problem $1 \div 4$, I reminded them of the marker problem, saying, "If I had one marker and I wanted to divide it among four students, how many markers would each student get?" This reference to a previous concrete experience provided enough support so the students were able to move forward.

Tim called me over. He said, "I just figured something out. I noticed that all the multiples of four don't have a remainder. Then I looked up on the chart and noticed the multiples of three don't have a remainder when dividing by three and the same thing with the twos. That's amazing."

"I agree with your observation," I said. "Do you suppose it's true for five and six and other numbers?"

"I think it's true for all numbers, actually," Tim replied. I nodded as Tim began to write about the pattern he had noticed. (See Figure 2–1.)

Alexa asked me about a pattern she noticed in the quotients. "I'm curious. I want to figure out why there were four of the same numbers before going to a new number. Is it connected to the remainder patterns? I think it is, but I'm not sure. The remainder pattern goes no remainder, remainder one, remainder two, remainder three. On the next problem there are enough remainders to make a new group, which adds another number to the first part of the quotient."

I said, "I agree with your reasoning for problems with a divisor of four. What about problems with divisors of two or three?" I moved on as Alexa and her partner started discussing this idea. (See Figure 2–2.)

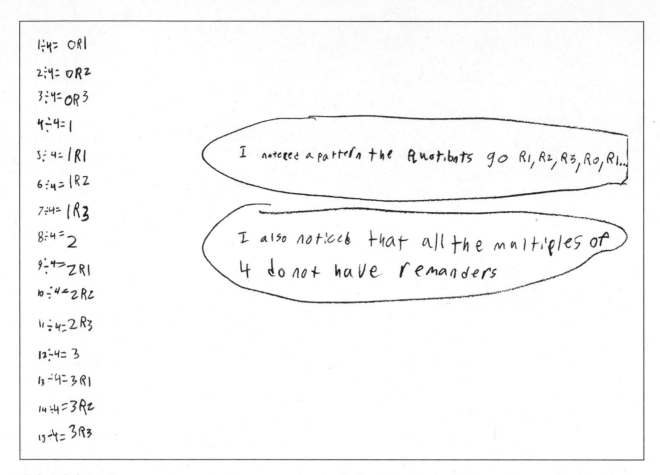

▲▲▲▲▲▲Figure 2–1 *Tim noticed two patterns, including the pattern that problems with dividends that are multiples of the divisor have no remainder.*

```
1 ÷ 4 = 0 R1
2 ÷ 4 = 0 R2
3 ÷ 4 = 0 R3
4 ÷ 4 = 1
5 ÷ 4 = 1 R1
6 ÷ 4 = 1 R2
7 ÷ 4 = 1 R3
8 ÷ 4 = 2
9 ÷ 4 = 2 R1
10 ÷ 4 = 2 R2
11 ÷ 4 = 2 R3
12 ÷ 4 = 3
13 ÷ 4 = 3 R1
14 ÷ 4 = 3 R2
15 ÷ 4 = 3 R3
```

I noticed that it goes R1, R2, R3, NR, R1, R2, R3, NR....
I noticed that every fourth number has NR.

I noticed that there are four of the same numbers before going into a new number.

▲▲▲▲▲▲Figure 2–2 *Alexa noticed three patterns.*

When I noticed that most of the students were finishing, I quickly checked Cameron's paper and asked him to write on the chart the answers for the first five problems with a divisor of four. I asked Damon to write the answers on the chart to the second five problems and then asked Amy to finish the list. I gave the rest of the students a one-minute warning to finish. At the end of one minute, I asked for the students' attention.

$1 \div 4 = 0\ R1$	$9 \div 4 = 2\ R1$
$2 \div 4 = 0\ R2$	$10 \div 4 = 2\ R2$
$3 \div 4 = 0\ R3$	$11 \div 4 = 2\ R3$
$4 \div 4 = 1$	$12 \div 4 = 3$
$5 \div 4 = 1\ R1$	$13 \div 4 = 3\ R1$
$6 \div 4 = 1\ R2$	$14 \div 4 = 3\ R2$
$7 \div 4 = 1\ R3$	$15 \div 4 = 3\ R3$
$8 \div 4 = 2$	

A Class Discussion

"What do you notice about the problems with divisors of four?" I asked.

Kaleb shared, "The remainders go up by one—one, two, three. Then there's no remainder."

Amy added, "I think there's no remainder after three because the remainder got big enough to add another group."

"Oh yeah!" several students replied aloud.

I recorded Amy's and Kaleb's ideas on the board:

Kaleb: The remainders go up by 1.

Amy: There are no remainders larger than 3 because after 3 there's enough for another group.

Alexa shared next. She said, "The quotient of every fourth problem increases by one whole number. I think it happens for the reason that Amy already said."

With the rest of the class, I checked Alexa's idea by counting every four problems, and together we verified what she said. I recorded Alexa's idea on the board:

Alexa: The quotient of every fourth problem increases by one whole number.

The students sat thinking quietly. I ended the lesson at that point.

DAY 3

I gathered the students on the floor. After the students were settled and quiet, I said, "Together we've explored patterns in division problems with divisors of two, three, and four. Today you'll work with your partner on another part of the investigation. The first task for you and your partner will be to choose a number from five to ten to use as the divisor for your division problems. Then you list the problems, but instead of stopping with the dividend of fifteen as we've done so far, continue your list up to the dividend of fifty. Solve the problems. Then search your work for patterns and write about them on your paper as you did when you investigated division problems with a divisor of four. Please work together on the same paper."

Then, to be sure that each divisor was chosen at least once, I added, "I'll list the divisors on the board and when you and your partner have decided on the divisor you want to use, tell me and I'll write your name next to that divisor. Have a couple of choices in mind in case your first choice has too many people."

"Do we have to record our work like you did?" Juan asked.

I replied, "Yes, please do. Listing the problems in order as I did will help you discover patterns in your work."

"Where do we get the paper?" Anna asked.

"When you and your partner have reported to me which divisor you would like to use, I'll give you a sheet of paper," I answered.

There were no more questions. I wrote on the board:

As you look for patterns, think about the following:

▲ *Which dividends don't have remainders? What is the pattern?*

▲ *Which dividends have R1? R2? R3 and so on? What patterns do you notice?*

▲ *What's the largest remainder you found for your divisor? Why do you think this is so?*

"Refer to these when you're ready to write," I said as I pointed to the questions I'd written on the board. The children then talked with their partners about their choices for divisors and reported them to me, and I gave each pair a sheet of paper.

Observing the Students

As I listened and observed, I noticed many pairs working through the first several problems using concrete materials, such as color tiles, pencils, books, or whatever was handy. These students made few errors in their work. When I noticed errors in students' work and the students hadn't used concrete materials, I suggested they check their work by doing so. Typically, using concrete materials helped students find and correct their errors.

Daniel and Kendrick called me over to share their discovery. Daniel explained with excitement, "Our divisor is nine and we found out that all the quotients with no remainders have dividends that are multiples of nine. For example, eighteen divided by nine is two and there's no remainder. It works with twenty-seven, thirty-six, and forty-five, so we think it will keep on working." Kendrick nodded his head in agreement.

"What about nine?" I asked. "Nine is a multiple of nine. Does it have a remainder when it's divided by nine?" The boys checked their work and shook their heads.

"Nope, it works, too," Kendrick concluded. (See Figure 2–3.)

Joaquin and Kaleb ran into difficulty. They had chosen the divisor of eight, and their list included 32 ÷ 8 = 3 R7. Kaleb explained, "I think this is wrong. I know thirty-two divided by eight, and the correct answer is four. Eight times four is thirty-two, so I know it works. But we got three remainder seven." Both boys looked at me with confusion on their faces.

"Tell me about what you were doing," I said. The boys had discovered that the quotients started with the same number for eight problems in a row, with remainders that increased by one in each of the eight quotients. The boys didn't check to see if their answers made any sense until they got to 32 ÷ 8.

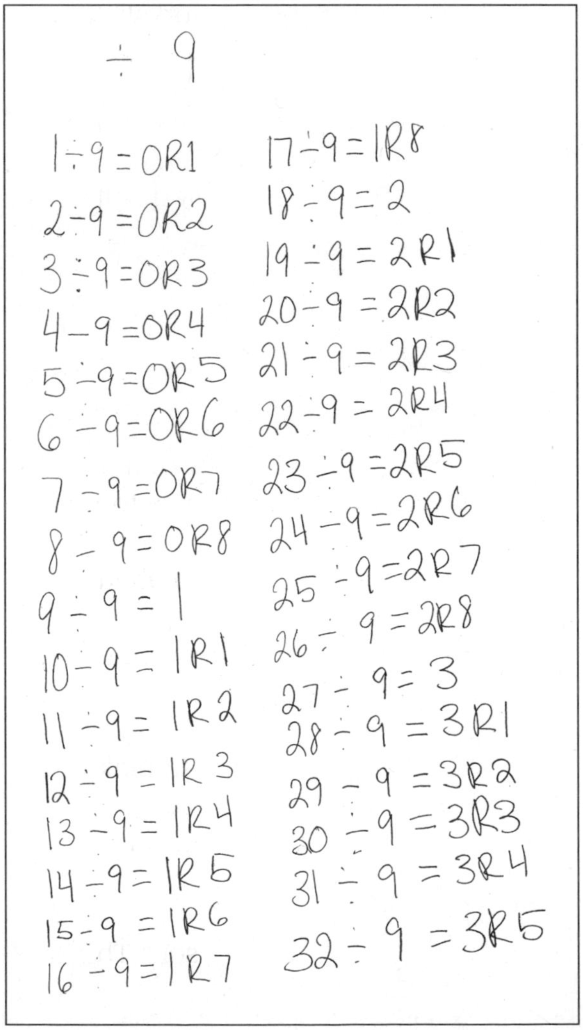

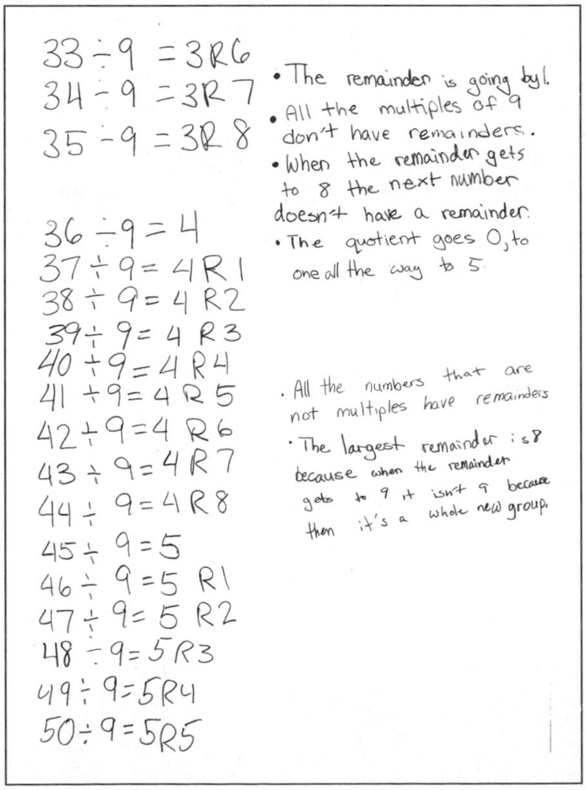

$$\div 9$$

$1 \div 9 = 0\,R1$	$17 \div 9 = 1\,R8$
$2 \div 9 = 0\,R2$	$18 \div 9 = 2$
$3 \div 9 = 0\,R3$	$19 \div 9 = 2\,R1$
$4 \div 9 = 0\,R4$	$20 \div 9 = 2\,R2$
$5 \div 9 = 0\,R5$	$21 \div 9 = 2\,R3$
$6 \div 9 = 0\,R6$	$22 \div 9 = 2\,R4$
$7 \div 9 = 0\,R7$	$23 \div 9 = 2\,R5$
$8 \div 9 = 0\,R8$	$24 \div 9 = 2\,R6$
$9 \div 9 = 1$	$25 \div 9 = 2\,R7$
$10 \div 9 = 1\,R1$	$26 \div 9 = 2\,R8$
$11 \div 9 = 1\,R2$	$27 \div 9 = 3$
$12 \div 9 = 1\,R3$	$28 \div 9 = 3\,R1$
$13 \div 9 = 1\,R4$	$29 \div 9 = 3\,R2$
$14 \div 9 = 1\,R5$	$30 \div 9 = 3\,R3$
$15 \div 9 = 1\,R6$	$31 \div 9 = 3\,R4$
$16 \div 9 = 1\,R7$	$32 \div 9 = 3\,R5$

$33 \div 9 = 3\,R6$
$34 \div 9 = 3\,R7$
$35 \div 9 = 3\,R8$

- The remainder is going by 1.
- All the multiples of 9 don't have remainders.
- When the remainder gets to 8 the next number doesn't have a remainder.
- The quotient goes 0, to one all the way to 5.

$36 \div 9 = 4$
$37 \div 9 = 4\,R1$
$38 \div 9 = 4\,R2$
$39 \div 9 = 4\,R3$
$40 \div 9 = 4\,R4$
$41 \div 9 = 4\,R5$
$42 \div 9 = 4\,R6$
$43 \div 9 = 4\,R7$
$44 \div 9 = 4\,R8$
$45 \div 9 = 5$
$46 \div 9 = 5\,R1$
$47 \div 9 = 5\,R2$
$48 \div 9 = 5\,R3$
$49 \div 9 = 5\,R4$
$50 \div 9 = 5\,R5$

- All the numbers that are not multiples have remainders
- The largest remainder is 8 because when the remainder gets to 9 it isn't 9 because then it's a whole new group.

▲▲▲▲▲▲Figure 2–3 *Daniel and Kendrick explored the divisor 9.*

I first confirmed Kaleb's observation. I said, "I agree that thirty-two divided by eight is four and it can be checked by multiplying four times eight, which equals thirty-two." I pointed to where they'd written $32 \div 8 = 3 \, R7$ and continued, "In the quotient three remainder seven, what does the three actually mean?"

Kaleb said, "The three means there are three groups and seven left over."

"Three groups of what?" I pushed.

"I'm not exactly sure," Kaleb replied.

"What do you think?" I asked Joaquin.

"I think it means three groups of eight . . . and there are seven left," Joaquin said.

"How many is three groups of eight?" I asked.

Together the boys said, "Twenty-four."

"How many would be in three groups of eight plus the seven left over?" I asked.

Kaleb said, "That would be twenty-four plus seven, which equals thirty-one."

"We're one problem off," Joaquin commented. "Look! For twenty-four we said the quotient was three with no remainder. That's right because three times eight is twenty-four. Our mistake must be between twenty-four and thirty-two." The boys examined their work carefully, found their error, made the necessary corrections, and continued on, this time checking to make sure their answers made sense.

I checked on Amy and Nalani. Both girls were consumed with their work. They were looking for patterns in the quotients with a remainder of one.

Nalani explained, "I listed all the answers with remainder one. Our divisor is six, and I noticed that the dividends with remainder one are one bigger than a multiple of six. We discovered yesterday that multiples of six don't have remainders. So for remainder one, one, seven, thirteen, nineteen, and all these other numbers are on the list." She pointed to her paper where she and Amy had listed the num-

bers. "Amy noticed that you add six to each number to get to the next number. It's like some number times six plus one gives you a number that will have remainder one."

To clarify what Nalani said, I asked, "If I take a number, for example five, multiply it by six, and add one, then are you saying that I'll get an answer that will have a remainder of one when I divide it by six?"

Both girls thought about this quietly for a moment. Then Nalani started counting by fives six times, using her fingers to help her keep track. She said, "Five times six is thirty plus one equals thirty-one." She looked on her paper, found $31 \div 6$, and verified that indeed there was a remainder of one. "It works! My idea works!"

"I wonder if it works for the dividends with remainder two," Amy said. The two girls went to work to find out. (See Figure 2–4 on the following page.)

The class period was over. I collected the students' papers to read before the next day.

DAY 4

To begin class, I said, "I noticed that some of you haven't yet had a chance to write about what you noticed. I'm going to return your papers and give you about fifteen minutes to complete your work. Be sure to refer to the questions on the board for ideas about what to write."

"What if we're done?" Brooke asked.

I said, "Check your work to make sure it's complete and accurate, make sure you've answered the questions on the board, and then bring your work to me. If we agree it's complete, you'll have time to begin exploring another divisor." There were no further questions, so I distributed the students' papers and they got to work quickly.

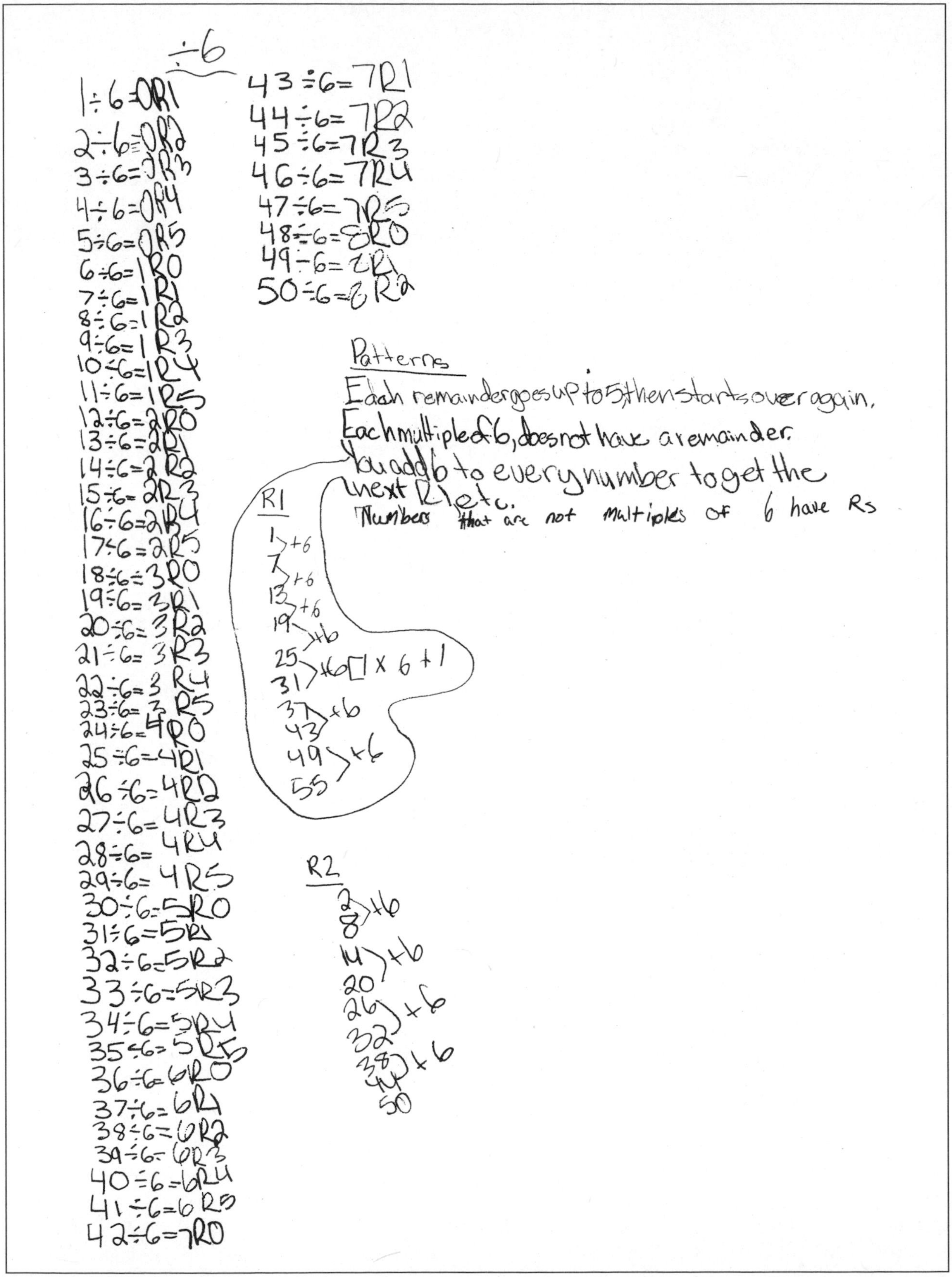

÷6

1÷6=0R1
2÷6=0R2
3÷6=0R3
4÷6=0R4
5÷6=0R5
6÷6=1R0
7÷6=1R1
8÷6=1R2
9÷6=1R3
10÷6=1R4
11÷6=1R5
12÷6=2R0
13÷6=2R1
14÷6=2R2
15÷6=2R3
16÷6=2R4
17÷6=2R5
18÷6=3R0
19÷6=3R1
20÷6=3R2
21÷6=3R3
22÷6=3R4
23÷6=3R5
24÷6=4R0
25÷6=4R1
26÷6=4R2
27÷6=4R3
28÷6=4R4
29÷6=4R5
30÷6=5R0
31÷6=5R1
32÷6=5R2
33÷6=5R3
34÷6=5R4
35÷6=5R5
36÷6=6R0
37÷6=6R1
38÷6=6R2
39÷6=6R3
40÷6=6R4
41÷6=6R5
42÷6=7R0

43÷6=7R1
44÷6=7R2
45÷6=7R3
46÷6=7R4
47÷6=7R5
48÷6=8R0
49÷6=8R1
50÷6=8R2

Patterns

Each remainder goes up to 5 then starts over again.
Each multiple of 6, does not have a remainder.
You add 6 to every number to get the next R1 etc.
Numbers that are not multiples of 6 have Rs

R1
1 ⟩+6
7 ⟩+6
13 ⟩+6
19 ⟩+6
25 ⟩+6 [] x 6 + 1
31 ⟩+6
37 ⟩+6
43
49 ⟩+6
55

R2
2 ⟩+6
8 ⟩+6
14 ⟩+6
20 ⟩+6
26 ⟩+6
32 ⟩+6
38 ⟩+6
44
50

▲▲▲▲▲▲Figure 2–4 *Nalani and Amy explored the relationship between the dividend and quotients with remainders of 1 and 2.*

After fifteen minutes, I made a quick visual check to see how many students were finished. Most were. I asked for their attention. When everyone quieted, I asked the students to bring their papers and sit with their partners on the floor where they could see the board. I reminded them to put their papers on the floor in front of them where they could still see their work, but wouldn't be tempted to play with their papers, creating noise and a distraction for others. Also, I made sure they all could see the lists of problems with divisors of two, three, and four.

A Class Discussion

For this discussion, I intended to choose one divisor to discuss in depth, then give students time to let the ideas settle. Then on other days, I planned to discuss other divisors, each time discussing the problems with a particular divisor in depth, then allowing students time to absorb what had been discussed. I chose to begin this class discussion with nine because more students had expressed interest in exploring nine than any of the other numbers. To ensure that all numbers were investigated, I had to ask some students to choose a number other than nine.

"Several of you used the divisor nine for this investigation," I said to begin the discussion. "Let's all look at patterns for the divisor of nine." Allani, Jan, and Anna had worked as a trio and were eager to share. I asked them to read aloud the first nine problems on their paper and reminded the rest of the class to look for patterns as I recorded the problems on the board:

$$1 \div 9 = 0 \ R1$$
$$2 \div 9 = 0 \ R2$$
$$3 \div 9 = 0 \ R3$$
$$4 \div 9 = 0 \ R4$$
$$5 \div 9 = 0 \ R5$$
$$6 \div 9 = 0 \ R6$$

$$7 \div 9 = 0 \ R7$$
$$8 \div 9 = 0 \ R8$$
$$9 \div 9 = 1$$

"I notice something about the remainders," Natalia volunteered. "They only go up to eight."

"That's because if they went to nine, that would be enough for another group," Toshi responded. "Jodi and me think that the remainder always has to be smaller than the divisor; otherwise, you have enough for another group."

"That's what we think, too," Joaquin said.

"Robyn and I went around and looked at some people's work and we noticed the remainders were always less than their divisors, too," Tanner shared.

"It seems that you agree that the remainder should be less than the divisor," I said. "Does anyone have a remainder that's larger than the divisor?" The students studied their papers, then gave a thumbs-down to show they didn't have remainders larger than their divisors.

"Remainders should be less than the divisors, or, as Toshi said, you'd have enough for another group," I said.

"I have an idea," Kendrick said. "Daniel and I used nine as the divisor, and we discovered that the dividends that are multiples of nine don't have remainders."

"Give me some examples," I encouraged Kendrick. "Allani, Jan, and Anna, check your paper to see if you agree with Daniel and Kendrick since all of you used the divisor of nine."

As Kendrick read the dividends that were multiples of nine, I listed them on the board:

R0 (no remainder)

9

18

27

36

45

When I asked Allani, Jan, and Anna if they agreed that dividends on the list didn't have remainders, they nodded their agreement.

"Each of the numbers on the list goes up by nine," Jacob commented.

"Oh yeah!" responded several other students.

I explained to the students that I was going to continue the list of division problems from $9 \div 9 = 1$ to $19 \div 9 = 2$ R1 to give us the opportunity to discover other patterns. I quickly added the problems to the list.

$1 \div 9 = 0$ R1	$11 \div 9 = 1$ R2
$2 \div 9 = 0$ R2	$12 \div 9 = 1$ R3
$3 \div 9 = 0$ R3	$13 \div 9 = 1$ R4
$4 \div 9 = 0$ R4	$14 \div 9 = 1$ R5
$5 \div 9 = 0$ R5	$15 \div 9 = 1$ R6
$6 \div 9 = 0$ R6	$16 \div 9 = 1$ R7
$7 \div 9 = 0$ R7	$17 \div 9 = 1$ R8
$8 \div 9 = 0$ R8	$18 \div 9 = 2$
$9 \div 9 = 1$	$19 \div 9 = 2$ R1
$10 \div 9 = 1$ R1	

"If we look at the problems that have a remainder of one, what are the dividends?" I asked.

Several students suggested one, nineteen, and ten.

I listed these on the board:

R1

1

10

19

"I think twenty-eight would come next," Nalani said. "The numbers are adding by nine again, just like they did on the Remainder Zero list."

Toshi waved her hand with excitement. "I think I know why that happens! It's because you multiply a number by nine and add one and you get a number that's a multiple of nine plus one and the one is the remainder when you go backward and divide. Oh, that's cool!"

"I think Toshi's idea works," Damon said thoughtfully. "I tested it with nineteen. Two times nine is eighteen; add one and it's nineteen. You divide nineteen by nine and it's two with a remainder of one!"

"It works with twenty-eight, too," Nalani said. "Nine times three is twenty-seven and one more is twenty-eight. If you divide twenty-eight by nine, that's three groups of nine with one remainder."

"What other numbers could go on the Remainder One list?" I asked.

"Thirty-seven, then forty-six, then fifty-five, sixty-four, seventy-three," the children chorused as they continued to add nines. I listed these numbers on the board. I asked Daniel and Kendrick, who had used the divisor of nine to divide all the numbers to fifty, to verify that the dividends on the list that were fifty or less had remainders of one. The boys checked and agreed.

"I have a prediction," Kaleb announced. "I predict that if you add two to all the numbers on the Remainder Zero list or add one to all the numbers on the Remainder One list, you'll get all the dividends that will have remainders of two when you divide by nine."

"Which numbers have remainder two so far?" I asked.

Daniel read them off as I recorded them on the board:

R2

2

11

"Oh my gosh! Look!" Natalia said with excitement. "So far the numbers are nine apart, just like the other two lists."

"And look," Brooke said, "if you add two to nine, the first number on the Remainder Zero list, it's eleven, which is on the Remainder Two list."

"I looked at our list," Daniel said, "and the next dividend with remainder two is twenty. If you add nine to eleven, you get twenty. Then the next remainder two number after that is twenty-nine."

Nalani said, "It makes sense! If you divide eleven by nine, it's one with a remainder of two. This is very cool!" Many agreed with Nalani.

"What do you think the remainder would be if the dividend was ninety-one and the divisor was nine?" I asked. "Talk it over with your partner." After a few moments, I asked for the students' attention. Hands danced in the air, indicating the students' eagerness to share.

"Show me with your fingers what the remainder would be," I said. Immediately each student held up one finger. "Who would like to explain why the remainder is one?" I called on Maria.

"It's easy when you think about it," Maria began. "Ten times nine is ninety. Ten's the most groups of nine you can get in ninety-one. That leaves one. So that means the remainder is one."

I gave the class another problem. "What about forty-seven divided by nine?" I asked.

"There's a remainder of two because nine times five is forty-five and it's two from forty-five to forty-seven," Chris explained. The students showed their agreement with thumbs up. Kendrick and Daniel checked their work, confirming that forty-seven divided by nine was five remainder two.

"I made up my own problem," Kaleb said. "I picked forty-one. I think it has a remainder of five because four times nine is thirty-six. Forty-one minus thirty-six is five." Kendrick confirmed that Kaleb was right.

I ended the discussion there, promising the students we would have additional discussions about other divisors. I collected their papers for future use.

For students to get the full benefit of this activity, it's important to lead discussions about all of the divisors from five to ten. These discussions can be spread out over several weeks.

Questions and Discussion

▲▲▲

▲ *Why did you make the decision for students to work in pairs rather than individually?*

Each pair of students completed at least thirty problems during this investigation. Working alone, this would be an overwhelming prospect for many students, and some would give up before starting. Working with partners makes the task seem less daunting while still giving students ample practice with division. In addition, the partners have the benefit of discussing ideas and checking each other's work for accuracy.

▲ *What's the value of students restating one another's ideas? Why do you encourage this?*

I encourage students to share all their ideas, which sometimes results in ideas being shared more than once. Often when students hear an idea different from their own, they need a few moments to think about it. After some thought, they will restate the idea using different words, making it their own. Other students have the benefit of hearing the same idea presented in different ways, which increases the chances for more children to understand and deepen their own learning.

CHAPTER THREE
INVESTIGATING FACTORS

Overview

In this lesson, students strengthen their understanding of the connection between division and multiplication by exploring the factors of the numbers from one to fifty. Students use their knowledge of division, multiplication, and divisibility rules to find all factors for each number. Students learn which numbers are prime and which are composite, think about why some numbers have an odd number of factors and others have an even number of factors, and investigate what happens to the number of factors when a number doubles. The lesson provides students with practice using the basic division and multiplication facts.

Materials

▲ chart paper, several sheets ruled into five columns, each 5 inches wide, or butcher paper posted sideways

▲ *Investigating Factors,* on an overhead transparency or 1 per pair of students (see Blackline Masters)

Time

▲ four class periods

Teaching Directions

1. Write *6* on the board. Ask: "What numbers can you divide into six with no leftovers?" List under the 6 the divisors the students suggest and ask them to justify their suggestions. (Students should identify one, two, three, and six.)

2. Ask students to explain why four, five, and seven do not belong on the list. (Asking about seven is useful for establishing that dividing a smaller number by a larger number is possible and that the division results in a fraction less than one.)

3. Explain that for this lesson, students will investigate divisors that are whole numbers and divide exactly into other numbers to result in whole number quotients with no remainders. Tell them that these special divisors are called factors.

4. Draw on the board the following chart:

Number	Factor	Division Sentence	Number of Factors	Multiplication Check

5. Write *6* under the columns titled Number and Factor. Ask students for a division sentence to show that six is a factor of six. Record under the column Division Sentence.

Number	Factor	Division Sentence	Number of Factors	Multiplication Check
6	6	6 ÷ 6 = 1		

6. Ask students for a multiplication sentence to show that six divided by six equals one. Record under the Multiplication Check column. Repeat for the other factors of six—one, two, and three. Write the total number of factors under the column Number of Factors.

Number	Factor	Division Sentence	Number of Factors	Multiplication Check
6	6	6 ÷ 6 = 1	4	1 × 6 = 6
	3	6 ÷ 3 = 2		2 × 3 = 6
	2	6 ÷ 2 = 3		3 × 2 = 6
	1	6 ÷ 1 = 6		6 × 1 = 6

7. Repeat Steps 5 and 6 for the number seven.

8. Lead a class discussion in which students can share what they notice about the information shown on the chart thus far.

9. Repeat Steps 5 and 6 for the numbers eight through twelve.

10. Copy the chart from the board onto chart paper, leaving room above 6 for the numbers 1 to 5.

11. On Day 2, ask students to work in pairs to make a chart as you did the previous day, fill it in for the factors for the numbers one through five, and show one way to prove each factor is correct.

12. When students have finished, record on the class chart.

13. Use the following for a class discussion:
▲ *Which numbers from one to twelve have exactly one factor? Exactly two factors? More than two factors? (Introduce the ideas of prime and composite numbers.)*
▲ *Which number from one to twelve has the most factors? The least?*

14. With the class, complete the chart for thirteen and fourteen.

15. On Day 3, list the numbers from 15 to 50 on the board. Ask each pair to choose a number, mark it with their initials, and complete the chart for it on their paper. When you've checked their work, they can record on the class chart.

16. On Day 4, after the class chart is completed, use the following questions for a class discussion (see *Investigating Factors* in Blackline Masters). Either project an overhead transparency of the questions or duplicate and distribute a copy to each pair.

Investigating Factors

1. Which numbers from one to fifty have exactly two factors? What do you notice about them?

2. What is the largest prime number from one to fifty? What is the smallest?

3. Which number from one to fifty has the most factors? Which has the fewest?

4. What happens to the number of factors when a number doubles?

5. Which numbers from one to fifty have an odd number of factors? What do you notice about them?

Teaching Notes

The students in the following vignette had prior experience with representing division and multiplication using arrays as a model. For additional information about arrays, see *Teaching Arithmetic: Lessons for Introducing Multiplication, Grade 3,* by Marilyn Burns (Math Solutions Publications 2001). This experience provided students with a helpful tool that they relied on throughout the lesson.

The term *factor* is used throughout the chapter. *Factor* is a word most often associated with multiplication. However, in the context of division, a factor is a particular kind of divisor, one that divides exactly into a number so that the quotient is a whole number with no remainder. For example, six can be divided by three, resulting in a quotient of two with no remainder, so three is a factor of six. Students can check this by using multiplication—two times three equals six—which strengthens their understanding of the relationship between division and multiplication and provides practice with the multiplication and division facts.

During the lesson, students have the opportunity to discover that factors usually come in pairs. For example, the number three has two factors—one and three. One and three, in this case, are a factor pair. The number ten has four factors—one, two, five, and ten. We can think of these as two sets of factor pairs—one and ten, and two and five. Some students find thinking about factor pairs to be a useful strategy for finding all the factors of a number.

In this class, many students made the connection that factor pairs relate to the shape of arrays. For the number ten, for example, the factor pair two and five can be represented by a 2-by-5 array.

In this lesson, students have the opportunity to learn about and explore prime and composite numbers. A prime number is any number with exactly two factors, one and itself. A composite number is any number with more than two factors. Because the number one has only one factor, itself, it is neither prime nor composite.

Students also investigate which numbers from 1 to 50 have an odd number of factors—1, 4, 9, 16, 25, 36, and 49. Numbers with an odd number of factors are all square numbers; one of their factors pairs with itself. For example, 9 is a square number. One and 9 are a factor pair and can be represented by a 1-by-9 array. The other factor of 9 is 3, for which 3 is its partner; 9 can also be represented with a 3-by-3 square array.

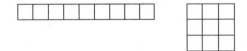

As students explore the idea of what happens to the number of factors when a number doubles, they discover different patterns depending on which number they use as their beginning number. For example, 2 has two factors. Double 2 to 4, and 4 has three factors, an increase of one factor. Double 4 to 8, and the number of factors increases from three to four, again an increase of one factor. However, if you start with 5 and double it to 10, the number of factors increases from two to four factors, an increase of two. Double 10 to 20, and the number of factors increases from four to six, again an increase of two. Starting with 7 results in the same pattern as starting with 5. The reason for this is that the only time the number of factors can increase by one is if the number of factors is going from an even number to an odd number, or vice versa. And an odd number of factors only occurs when a number is a square number—1, 4, 9, 16, and so on. When you start with a square number, double it, and continue to double it, every other number will be square. For example, starting with 1 and doubling produces 1, 2, 4, 8, 16, 32, 64, and so on; every other number is a square number and, therefore, has an odd number of factors. Thinking about numerical relationships such as these helps us as teachers prepare for what students might observe during class investigations and discussions.

The "Extension" section suggests an investigation of twin primes. Twin primes are odd prime numbers that are consecutive. Another way of saying this is twin primes are odd prime numbers with a difference of two. For example, three and five are twin primes. They are both odd and they have a difference of two. Two and three are not twin primes. Two is an even number and the difference between two and three is only one, not two. Nineteen and twenty-three aren't twin primes. They're both odd, but they are not consecutive odd numbers and their difference is four, not two.

In the lesson, students create a class chart. On the first day, I suggest creating the chart on the board. Students typically make errors early in the lesson, and having the chart on the board makes it easy to erase and correct errors. At the end of the first day, I copy the chart onto chart paper, using butcher paper turned sideways, which I rule into several sections of five 5-inch columns, labeled as shown:

Number	Factor	Division Sentence	Number of Factors	Multiplication Check

The Lesson

▲▲▲

DAY 1

I wrote 6 on the board, turned to the students, and asked, "What numbers can you divide into six with no leftovers?" I waited until about half the students had their hands up. I called on Samara.

"Six can go into itself evenly. It's one group of six," she explained. Under the 6 I wrote 6 again to list six as a divisor of six.

Terrell said, "Three works. I know because you can count by threes and land on six. Three, six. Also, six is a multiple of three, so it's divisible by three." I added a 3 to the list.

Katie shared next. "Two works. Six is an even number, so it's divisible by two because all even numbers are divisible by two."

Yolanda said, "One goes into six with no remainders. One goes into any whole number with no remainders." I added 2 and 1 to the list.

6
—
6

3

2

1

The students were quiet. I asked, "Will four go into six without a remainder? Put your thumb up if you think yes, down if you think no, and sideways if you're not certain or confused." All thumbs were down.

Neil said, "If you count by fours, you jump right over six: four and then eight."

"What about five? Can six be divided into groups of five with no leftovers?" I asked. The students showed thumbs down.

Rachel said, "For a number to be divisible by five, it has to end in a zero or five, and six doesn't."

"What about seven?" I asked next.

"No way!" "Won't work!" responded some of the students.

"Why do you think seven won't work?" I probed.

Celena explained, "Draw a number line and show the numbers from zero to seven." I did as Celena instructed and she nodded her approval. "You start at zero and hop to seven when you count by sevens. You hop right over six. Six isn't even big enough to have one group of seven. It's too small." Starting at 0, I hopped to 7 to reinforce visually what Celena had said.

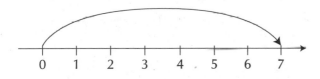

Shawn raised his hand and asked, "Does that mean a bigger number can't go into a smaller number?" I was glad Shawn raised this question. The idea that a smaller number can't be divided by a larger number is a common misconception among students studying division.

I paused for a moment to consider how best to answer Shawn's question. I said, "You can divide a smaller number by a larger number. It results in a fraction less than one. For example, if I have one cookie and I want to divide it between you and me, we divide one by two, one cookie divided by two people. We each get one-half of the cookie, which is less than one

whole cookie. If I have one marker and I want to divide it between you and me, we would also divide one by two. But it wouldn't make sense for each of us to get one-half of the marker. That means we'd each get zero markers with one marker left over. In that case, one divided by two would equal zero remainder one. One divided by two can be thought of as either one-half or zero remainder one, depending on what we're dividing."

Shawn nodded and said, "So it's possible to divide six by seven, but the answer is less than one and not a whole number, right?" I nodded.

"Today we're looking for divisors that are whole numbers and result in whole number answers, or quotients, with no remainders. Divisors that result in whole number answers with no remainders have a special name. They are called factors," I explained. As a quick check for understanding, I asked, "Who would like to explain in your own words what a factor is?"

Katie said, "A factor is a number that goes into another number with no leftovers. For example, three is a factor of six, but four isn't. Four has leftovers if you divide it into six." The students showed their agreement with thumbs up.

I wrote on the board:

Factor: a whole number, or divisor, that divides into another whole number with no leftovers.

Although Katie didn't use the terms *divisor* or *dividend* in her explanation, this was a good opportunity to paraphrase slightly and introduce the notion that a factor is a specific type of divisor, a whole number that divides exactly into a number so the quotient is a whole number with no remainder. I explained this to the students.

To change the direction of the conversation, I said, "We're going to be gathering some other information so I'm going to draw a chart on the board to help us organize it." I drew on the board the first chart, below.

I pointed to the first factor on the list of factors of six and asked, "What's a division sentence we could write to show six is a factor of six?"

Neil said, "Write six, then a division sign, then six again, an equals sign, and one because there is one group of six in six." I recorded as shown in the second chart below.

"What's a multiplication sentence that proves six divided by six equals one?" I asked.

Jina said tentatively, "One times six equals six. Is that right?"

I said to the other students, "What do the rest of you think about Jina's idea? Does one times six equal six?"

Cody said with surprise, "She's right, and I notice that one times six equals six is the division problem turned around!"

I asked the students, "Why do you think that is?" The students started to chat among themselves. After a few moments, I asked for their attention. Many had their hands up, eager to explain ideas.

Rachel said with confidence, "Six divided by six means 'How many groups of six are in six?' Well, there is one group of six in six. The multiplication sentence, one times six equals six, means one group of six equals six. That's what I think!"

Binh added, "It's like they're related, like cousins or something like that."

"Yeah!" replied several other students.

"They're sort of opposites, too," Ali said. "With division, you know how many altogether. You don't know how many altogether with multiplication. So it's like you're trying to figure out different parts of the same thing, you know what I mean? It's hard to explain!"

I added $1 \times 6 = 6$ to the chart under the column labeled Multiplication Check.

Next I asked the students to tell me a division sentence for the next factor on the list, 3.

Kaylee suggested, "Three divided by six equals two." I wrote what Kaylee said on the chart. Several hands shot into the air.

Number	Factor	Division Sentence	Number of Factors	Multiplication Check

Number	Factor	Division Sentence	Number of Factors	Multiplication Check
6	6	$6 \div 6 = 1$		

Shawn said, "I disagree! We said before that dividing a larger number into a smaller number makes a fraction that's less than one. Two is your answer, and it's not less than one!"

Kaylee's error is common and I knew other students were likely to make the same mistake. I said to Kaylee and the others, "If I have three cookies and I want to share them equally among Neil, Kaleb, Jina, Kaylee, Elise, and Joby, would each person receive two cookies?"

"No," the students chorused.

Kaylee got a look of relief on her face. She said, "I know what to do. The division sentence should be six divided by three equals two. That works!" The students nodded their heads in agreement. I erased the division sentence Kaylee originally suggested and replaced it with her corrected one, $6 \div 3 = 2$.

Nariko raised her hand and said, "I think you'll ask for the multiplication sentence next to prove that six divided by three equals two. But I'm confused. Should the multiplication be two times three equals six, or three times two equals six? They both equal the same amount, but I'm not sure which should go with the division sentence."

While both multiplication sentences yield the same product, there are different ways to interpret them and also the division sentence. To help me understand Nariko's thinking about division, I asked, "Tell me what you think six divided by three equals two means."

Nariko explained, "It means there are six things. You want to put them into groups of three. How many groups of three in six? There are two groups of three in six."

I said, "What does the multiplication sign mean?"

"Groups of," Nariko replied.

I said, "Would it make the most sense to say two groups of three equal six or three groups of two equal six?"

"Uhmmm, two groups of three equal six," Nariko said after some thought.

"So we write that as two times three," I said. Nariko interpreted $6 \div 3$ as dividing six into groups of three, instead of into three groups to produce three groups of two, which relates to 3×2. Either interpretation is correct, as is either multiplication sentence.

We repeated this process for the factors two and one, adding the appropriate information to the chart as we proceeded. The chart now looked like the one below.

Finding the Factors of Seven
"What are the factors of seven?" I asked. Hands were up quickly.

Joby explained, applying what he already knew about the divisibility rules, "Seven is easy. Two won't work because seven's not even, five won't work because there's a seven in the ones place, not a five or a zero. Three won't work because you go three, six, nine, and skip seven. Six won't work, either. That leaves one, four, and seven. If I use a number line to

Number	Factor	Division Sentence	Number of Factors	Multiplication Check
6	6	$6 \div 6 = 1$	4	$1 \times 6 = 6$
	3	$6 \div 3 = 2$		$2 \times 3 = 6$
	2	$6 \div 2 = 3$		$3 \times 2 = 6$
	1	$6 \div 1 = 6$		$6 \times 1 = 6$

skip-count, I hop from zero to four and then to eight. I hop right over seven. Four doesn't work. That leaves one and seven."

Yolanda added, "What Joby says about one and seven has to be right because all whole numbers are divisible by one and all numbers are divisible by themselves."

I said to the rest of the class, "Are there any other factors of seven besides one and seven?"

"No!" the students responded.

I asked, "What division sentence can we write to show that one is a factor of seven?"

Elise volunteered, "Seven divided by one equals seven." The students showed their agreement with thumbs up.

"I know a multiplication sentence that proves that," Justin said. "Seven times one equals seven." I recorded both number sentences on the chart.

"I know the division sentence for seven," Terrell said. "It's seven divided by seven equals one. I just have to turn around the last two numbers from the first division sentence."

"The factors seem to come in pairs, like one and seven," Nariko commented.

Neil said, "I think Nariko's right. With six, one and six go together and so do two and three. That's cool." I was pleased that Nariko and Neil noticed that factors come in pairs. This was an idea I'd planned to explore with the students during the lesson.

To return the focus of the lesson to writing the division and multiplication

sentences for seven, I said, "What multiplication sentence can we write to show that seven divided by seven equals one?"

Samara said, "One times seven equals seven." The students agreed and I wrote on the chart *7 ÷ 7 = 1* and *1 × 7 = 7*.

I asked, "How many factors of seven are there? Show me with your fingers." The students held up two fingers each and I completed the chart for seven (see below).

"What do you notice about the information on the chart so far?" I asked.

Cody shared, "At first I didn't understand what Nariko and Neil were talking about when they said the factors came in twos. Then when I saw both seven divided by one equals seven and seven divided by seven equals one, I got it. The factors of seven are one and seven, and they just switched places. Seven was the answer in the first problem and the factor, or divisor, in the second problem, so the seven went from the answer to the factor, and the one went from the factor to the answer. Six does the same thing with its factors."

To paraphrase what Cody said with the terminology of division, I said, "I agree with what Cody noticed. The quotient of seven from the first division sentence becomes the divisor in the second division sentence, and the divisor of one in the first sentence becomes the quotient of one in the second."

Celena said, "I think you can prove whether a factor is a factor or not with arrays. Can I show?" I nodded and Celena

Number	Factor	Division Sentence	Number of Factors	Multiplication Check
6	6	6 ÷ 6 = 1	4	1 × 6 = 6
	3	6 ÷ 3 = 2		2 × 3 = 6
	2	6 ÷ 2 = 3		3 × 2 = 6
	1	6 ÷ 1 = 6		6 × 1 = 6
7	1	7 ÷ 1 = 7	2	7 × 1 = 7
	7	7 ÷ 7 = 1		1 × 7 = 7

came to the board and drew a 1-by-7 array. She explained, "The total number of squares in the array is seven. That's like the number we're starting with. One side is one square long, which is like the divisor in the first division sentence, and the other side is seven squares long, which is like the quotient in the first division sentence."

"I wonder if Celena's idea works for six, too?" I mused aloud. The students talked among themselves. Soon hands were up.

Rachel said, "I think it does. Can I show?" I nodded and Rachel came to the board quickly and drew a 1-by-6 array and then a 2-by-3 array. She labeled the sides and explained how the number on each side of each array related to the factors of six.

For the rest of the class, we found the factors of the numbers from eight to twelve as we had done with six and seven. After class I copied the chart from the board onto chart paper, leaving space for recording the numbers 1 through 5 above the 6. (I made the chart on the board first rather than on chart paper so errors and false starts could be erased easily.)

DAY 2

I showed the students the chart I copied from the board, pointing out the large empty space I had left for the numbers 1 through 5. I explained, "Today you'll work with your partner. Together you will find the factors for the numbers one through five and record on a chart as I did yesterday. Be sure to write a division sentence to show each factor of a number and a way to test that a number is a factor. What are some ways you could test that a number is a factor of another number?"

Samara said, "You could skip-count by the factor, and if you land on the number you're supposed to, then it's a factor. For example, five is a factor of ten. I can skip-count by fives, five, ten, and land on ten."

I said, "Skip-counting is a way to verify whether or not a number is a factor." I wrote on the board:

testing factors

skip-counting

Katie said, "Samara used ten as an example. With ten, if you know the divisibility rules, you know that ten is divisible by two because it's even and by five because it ends with a zero or five. You can use divisibility rules." I added this to the list.

Celena suggested, "You can use a number line. Like with ten, if you want to prove that five is factor of ten, draw a number line and hop by fives. You land on ten, so five is a factor of ten." I wrote *number line* on the list.

Neil said, "You can use multiplication to prove if a number is a factor, like we were doing yesterday. For ten, if you want to see if two is a factor of ten, think, 'Two times what number equals ten?' Two times five equals ten. That means both two and five are factors." I wrote *multiplication* on the list.

Justin asked, "Could you use a calculator?"

I replied, "Tell me more about what you would do with a calculator."

"I'd skip-count. If I wanted to see if two was a factor of ten, I'd press two, plus, equals, equals, equals, like that. If the calculator showed ten, then I'd know two was a factor." I added *calculators* to the list.

Nariko made another suggestion. "I think you could draw arrays. The sides of arrays are factors of the total number of squares in the array." I wrote Nariko's idea on the list. The students were quiet. The final list looked as follows:

testing factors

skip-counting

divisibility rules

number line

multiplication

calculators

arrays

I said, "There are many good ways on the list to show a number is a factor of another number. You need to choose at least one way to verify a number is a factor." To reinforce for the students what they were to do, I wrote on the board the following instructions:

▲ *Make a chart for the factors of the numbers from one to five.*

▲ *Test each number to be sure it is actually a factor.*

Kaleb asked, "Should we share a paper or each have our own?"

I said, "You may share a paper." There were no other questions. The students went to work quickly, discussing first how to organize their papers and then how to prove numbers were factors.

As the students worked, I observed. The assignment was easy for them to do. (See Figure 3–1 for one example.)

As the students finished their work, I checked it and asked them to make any needed corrections or revisions. I also asked Binh and Nariko to record neatly their information on the class chart I'd copied the day before. Then I asked the students to sit where they could see the chart and together with their partners search the chart for patterns.

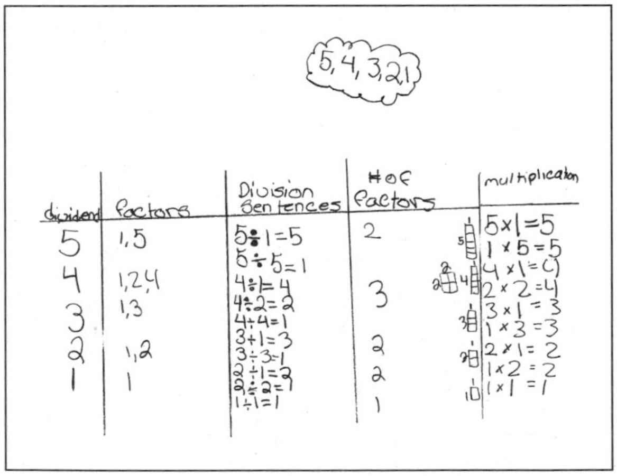

▲▲▲▲▲▲Figure 3–1 *Although Celena and Katie forgot 1 × 4 as a multiplication check, they showed good understanding. Also, they used arrays as a way to check.*

A Class Discussion

When all the students were finished with the assignment, I began a class discussion. "What do you notice about the information we have so far?"

Yolanda said, "There's only one number with one factor—one."

Shawn noticed, "A lot of numbers have two factors."

"Let's list them together," I suggested as I wrote on the board:

numbers with exactly 2 factors

"Two has two factors," Kaylee said.

"What are the two factors of two?" I asked.

"One and two," Kaylee responded.

I wrote on the board:

numbers with exactly 2 factors	*factors*
2	1, 2

Students continued to suggest numbers and give the factors while I recorded on the board. The completed list looked as follows:

numbers with exactly 2 factors	*factors*
2	1, 2
3	1, 3
11	1, 11
5	1, 5
7	1, 7

Katie said, "They all have one as a factor. I heard someone say that before, but I didn't exactly get it. Now I see it."

Rachel said, "They all have themselves as factors, too."

To introduce the vocabulary *prime* and *composite,* I said, "Mathematicians have a special name for numbers with exactly two factors. They call them prime numbers." I pointed to the list and said, "These numbers are all examples of prime numbers." I wrote on the board above the list *prime numbers.* "Numbers with more than two factors are called composite numbers. Four and eight are examples of composite numbers." I wrote on the board *composite numbers* and listed *4* and *8* beneath.

I recorded on the board under the list of numbers with two factors Katie's and Rachel's ideas (see below). The pause created as I wrote gave the students time to search for other patterns.

Neil raised his hand. He said, "It's weird, but the prime numbers are all odd numbers except for two. At first I thought two must be a mistake because it's even, but it really has two factors like the others. Then I thought maybe we missed an even number that should be there, but I don't think so. Four has three factors, six has four, so do eight and ten, and twelve has six factors."

I asked, "Which number has the most factors?"

"Twelve," the students replied.

"How many factors does twelve have?" I asked.

Justin said, "Six. One goes with twelve, two goes with six, and three goes with four. That's six factors."

"Which number has the least number of factors?" I continued.

Samara replied, "One has the least. It only has one factor."

"How many factors do you think thirteen has?" I asked. "Show me by holding up your fingers." All students held up two fingers.

Terrell explained, "It's not divisible by two because it's odd. Three doesn't work because if you add the digits, one and three, the sum is four and that's not a multiple of three. Five won't work because thirteen doesn't end in a zero or a five. Ten doesn't work because thirteen doesn't end with zero. Six doesn't work because if you count by sixes, you skip thirteen—same with seven, eight, nine, eleven, and twelve. That leaves one because all whole numbers are divisible by one and thirteen because all numbers are divisible by themselves."

"Does anyone have anything to add to what Terrell said?" I asked. No one did. I added 13 to the chart and filled in the other columns with the students' help. We then did the same for fourteen.

I asked, "What do you think the next prime number will be?" I was curious to see if the students would predict fifteen since it is odd. Typically, students do, but none of these students did. Their predictions included seventeen, nineteen, twenty-three, and twenty.

"Why not fifteen?" I asked. Hands shot into the air.

Rachel explained, "It has at least four factors I can think of. One and fifteen, three and five." The students indicated their agreement by putting their thumbs up. I ended the lesson for the day.

DAY 3

Finding the Factors of Fifteen to Fifty

I listed the numbers from 15 through 50 on the board. I explained to the students, "You and your partner will work as you

prime numbers			
numbers with exactly 2 factors	factors	composite numbers	factors
2	1, 2	4	1, 2, 4
3	1, 3	8	1, 2, 4, 8
11	1, 11		
5	1, 5		
7	1, 7		

All numbers have one as a factor.

All numbers have themselves as a factor.

did before to find the factors of numbers. The list of numbers to investigate is on the board and you'll each do some of them. Together decide which number you'd like to investigate and then put your initials next to it so we all know someone has that number. For your number, you need to figure out the information for all the columns in our chart. When you are finished with your number, bring your paper to me. I'll check it and ask you to make needed corrections, and then you'll record the information from your paper onto our class chart. Then you may choose another number." There were no questions, as the students were familiar with the procedure from earlier in the lesson. As a visual reminder for those who might need it, I wrote the following directions on the board:

▲ *Choose a number and initial it.*
▲ *Find all the factors and record in the columns on your paper.*
▲ *Bring your paper to me to check.*
▲ *Record the information from your paper onto the class chart.*
▲ *Choose a new number. (If none are left, pick one that's been recorded and check that is was done correctly.)*

As the students worked, I circulated through the room, taking note of the approaches they took to find all the factors. Katie and Celena chose thirty-two. Katie explained to Celena, "We know one and thirty-two are factors of thirty-two."

Celena picked up the conversation. "And thirty-two is even, so we have to figure out how many times two goes into thirty-two."

Katie commented, "Just count by twos and see how many times you counted." Together the girls counted by twos and found there were sixteen.

Celena said, "I know four times eight is thirty-two, so four and eight have to go into thirty-two with no leftovers." I left the

girls to complete their work. When they brought it to me to check, it was correct.

Shawn and Cody were working together. The boys had chosen thirty-six and were having difficulty. Their frustration resulted in arguing and an inability to make progress on the task.

I said, "I can see you two are having some difficulties. Tell me about them."

Cody said, "We can't agree on how to write the division sentences."

"I'm not exactly sure I understand. Can you give me an example or show me?" I asked.

Cody explained, "I think the thirty-six should come first, and Shawn won't write it that way."

I said to Cody, "Why do you think the division sentence should begin with thirty-six?"

"Because there are thirty-six things altogether," Cody said.

I said to Shawn, "Tell me what you're thinking."

Shawn shrugged. I waited quietly for a moment. Shawn explained, "You can write a division sentence for thirty-six that doesn't start with thirty-six, but Cody wouldn't listen." Shawn picked up his pencil and to prove his point, he wrote: $1\overline{)36}$.

"But you can write it like this, too," Cody said as he wrote $36 \div 1 = 36$.

Both boys became quiet and looked to me. I said, "You're both right. It's correct to write thirty-six divided by one both ways. I've been writing it the way Cody is suggesting because it's easier to fit on the class chart and easier to see patterns. You boys may write it either way or both ways. It's your choice." The boys decided to use Cody's way.

Cody said, "We know thirty-six is divisible by three because if you add the digits, three and six, the sum is nine. Nine is divisible by three. But we don't know what the factor partner is."

Shawn asked, "Can we use a calculator?"

I replied, "You may, but first tell me what you're going to do with it."

Shawn and Cody talked quietly to one another and then Shawn said, "I think you can press three then plus, equals, equals, equals, and count how many times it takes to get to thirty-six." I nodded my agreement and Shawn went to get a calculator.

I checked back with Shawn and Cody a while later. "We discovered something really cool," the boys chorused.

"We figured out we could write the division and multiplication sentences in pairs to help us keep track," Shawn said. "And thirty-six has the same factor twice, so that's why it doesn't have a partner." (See Figure 3–2.)

As students finished working on a number, I checked their work and asked them to make needed corrections. Then they would record on the class chart, choose a new number, initial it on the board, and repeat the investigation.

To find the factors of their numbers, most students relied on division facts, multiplication facts, or divisibility rules, although some drew arrays or built them with tiles, used calculators, skip-counted, or drew number lines. Elise and Joby's paper was typical of the students' work. (See Figure 3–3.)

When all the numbers had been checked off, I asked for the students' attention. I said, "After you finish investigating

the number you're working on now, and I've checked it, and you've recorded on the class chart, please sit with your partner where you both can see the chart. Study the chart for information about these questions." I projected the questions on an overhead transparency (see *Investigating Factors* in Blackline Masters and page 34). The first question reviewed what we had already discussed; the others posed new ideas to explore.

The chart was completed just before math class was over for the day. Many of the students had had time to discuss the questions I listed with their partners. I told the students we'd discuss the questions as a class the following day.

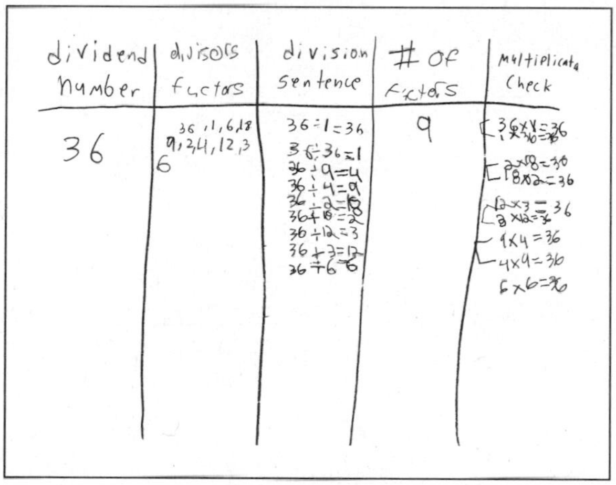

▲▲▲▲▲▲**Figure 3–2** *Shawn and Cody used brackets to show factor pairs.*

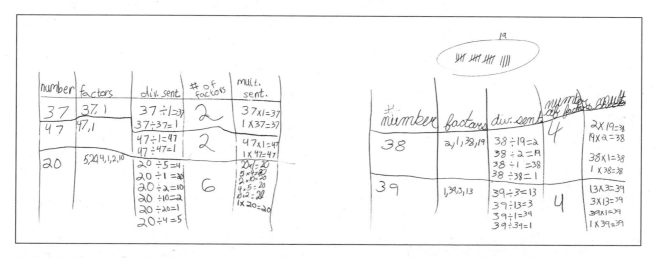

▲▲▲▲▲▲**Figure 3–3** *Elise and Joby used tally marks to help figure how many 2s are in 38.*

DAY 4

As I had done the day before, I asked the students to sit with their partners where they could see the chart and the questions I projected. To begin I asked a question to review what we had already discussed: "Which numbers on our chart have exactly two factors?" I recorded on the board the first several numbers the students suggested—*2, 13, 7, 11,* and *23.* "What did you notice about these numbers?" I then asked.

"They're all odd except for two," Neil said.

"Is there any other even number on the list that has exactly two factors?" I asked.

"No," the students said.

"Can anyone think of another even number not on the list that has exactly two factors?"

Nariko suggested, "One hundred two."

Several hands went up immediately. Rachel explained, "I don't know how many factors are in one hundred two, but I know both one and one hundred two are factors of one hundred two. And, because it's even, so is two. That's three factors right there."

Nariko said, "Hmm, I just had an idea. Rachel made me think of it. I don't think any other even numbers can be on the list because they all have at least three factors, one, themselves, and two, because all even numbers are multiples of two."

"I think I agree with that," Justin chimed in.

"What are numbers with exactly two factors called?" I asked.

"Prime," Joby responded.

"All the rest are called compulsory," Yolanda said.

"I think you mean composite," Kaleb corrected.

Yolanda giggled and smiled and said, "Oh yeah, you're right."

"Which number is neither prime nor composite?" I asked. I gave the students a

moment to study the chart. When most hands were up, I called on Samara.

"One," she replied. "It only has one factor. No other number has only one factor, just one." I nodded my agreement.

"I know what the largest prime number is on the chart," Cody said, referring to the next question on the list. "It's forty-seven. And the smallest is one."

Elise said, "I agree forty-seven is the largest, but I disagree that one is the smallest. A number has to have two factors to be a prime number. One only has one factor."

"Oh yeah," Cody said quietly. Then he added quickly, "Three is the smallest prime number."

"I think two is the smallest prime number," Kaylee said.

"But two's not an odd number," Katie replied.

"But it does have exactly two factors and two was on the list of prime numbers before," Kaylee said in defense. "It's the only even prime number."

The students were quiet. I said, "Do you agree two is the smallest prime number on our chart and forty-seven is the largest?" The students showed their agreement with thumbs up.

I returned to the list of questions and focused the class on Question 3: Which number from one to fifty has the most factors? Which has the fewest? The students quickly identified forty-eight and one. No one had more to say.

I moved on to the fourth question: What happens to the number of factors when a number doubles?

Neil shared, "I noticed a pattern when I doubled two to four. The number of factors went up by one. The same thing happened when I doubled four to eight. The number of factors went up by one again."

"Do you think that always happens?" I asked Neil and the others.

"Maybe," "Yes," and shrugs were some of the responses.

I wrote 5 on the board. Next to it I wrote 2. I turned to the students and explained, "Five has two factors. I get ten when I double five. If five follows the same pattern as Neil found, how many factors should ten have?"

"Three," the students responded.

"Look on the chart to see how many factors ten has," I said.

"Hey, it has four!" Celena said.

"It's a different pattern!" Justin added. "I wonder how many different patterns there are."

I then asked, "Let's double ten to twenty. How many factors does twenty have?"

Nariko answered, "Twenty has six. The pattern goes two, four, six."

Binh waved his hand in the air excitedly. He said, "I started with seven and it works the same. Seven has two factors. I doubled it to fourteen. That's four factors. Then I doubled fourteen to twenty-eight and that's six factors. It's like five."

Rachel said, "I think some starting numbers will have the same pattern, like two and four and eight. If you start with each of those numbers, it'll be the same pattern because four and eight are really part of the two pattern when you double two."

The students were quiet, so I decided to move on to the last question on the list: Which numbers from one to fifty have an odd number of factors? As students identified them, I recorded on the board:

16
4
9
25
1
36
49

"What do you notice about the numbers on this list? Why do they have an odd number of factors?" The students sat quietly, many with perplexed looks.

I said, "It might be helpful to list the numbers with an odd number of factors from the smallest to the largest and make a chart as a way to organize information to help us make sense of what's going on." With the help of the students, I did this quickly and set up a chart as follows:

Numbers with Odd Number of Factors	Factor	Arrays
1		
4		
9		
16		
25		
36		
49		

"What are the factors of one?" I asked.

"One," the students replied.

I said, "You could show one as an array like this." I drew one square on the chart.

Numbers with Odd Number of Factors	Factors	Arrays
1	1	
4		
9		
16		
25		
36		
49		

"What are the factors of four?" I asked. Hands were up quickly.

Kaleb said, "One is a factor of four."

I asked, "What's the factor partner for one?"

"It's four," Celena said. I listed 1 and 4 on the chart as a pair. This way students would have a better chance of seeing that some numbers have an odd number of factors because in some factor pairs, both factors are the same. For the number four, for example, two's factor partner is two.

These numbers are square numbers, and one of their arrays is a square.

"How can I draw an array to show one and four are factors of four?" I asked.

Samara said, "It can have one going down and four going across. That's the one and four."

Ali said, "I know another way. Two is a factor of four. You can make a square with two going down and two going across." I added the information from Samara and Ali to the chart.

Joby said, "Nine has three factors; one goes with nine and three goes with itself. You can draw a rectangle that's one down and nine across for the factors one and nine, and then draw a square that's three down and three across." I recorded this on the chart:

Numbers with Odd Number of Factors	Factors	Arrays
1	1	(1×1 array)
4	1, 4	(1×4 array)
	2, 2	(2×2 array)
9	1, 9	(1×9 array)
	3, 3	(3×3 array)
16		
25		
36		
49		

The students were starting to talk among themselves. I said, "Talk with your partner for thirty seconds about what you notice. First one of you talks for thirty seconds while the other listens. At the end of thirty seconds I'll give you the signal to switch so the first talker gets to listen and the first listener gets to talk. Remember not to interrupt the talker." I gave the signal to begin. After thirty seconds, I gave the signal to switch roles, and at the end of the second thirty seconds, I asked for the students' attention. The students were eager to share.

Elise said, "So far all the numbers can be made into squares."

Neil said, "They all have a factor pair with both numbers the same."

Terrell added, "They have to have a factor pair that's the same if you can make it into a square. The factors are the sides and a square has equal sides, so both parts of the factor pair have to be the same."

I said, "In mathematics, numbers like these are called square numbers for just the reasons you've shared. Why do you think these numbers have an odd number of factors?"

Yolanda said, "I get it now. They have an odd number of factors because two of the factors are the same, so the ones that are the same get counted as one." The students showed their agreement with Yolanda's thinking with thumbs up.

This discussion ended the lesson for the day. During the days that followed, we revisited some of the ideas. For example, students continued to think about what happens to the number of factors when a number doubles and then we talked about what happens to the number of factors when a number triples. Also, we talked about why forty-eight has so many factors, and which number up to hundred has the most factors.

EXTENSION

For another discussion, introduce students to twin primes. Two prime numbers that are consecutive odd numbers are called twin primes. Another way of saying this is twin primes are prime numbers with a difference of two. For example, five and seven are twin prime numbers; two and three are not. An appropriate assignment is for students to identify all pairs of twin primes from one to fifty. Figures 3–4 and 3–5 show two examples of how students approached this assignment.

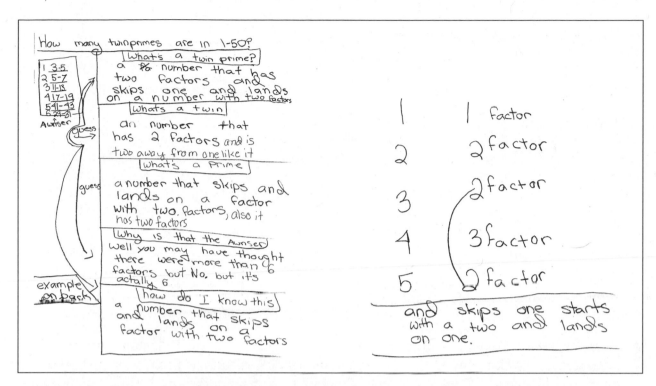

▲▲▲▲▲▲Figure 3–4 *As a way of making sense of the problem, Kaylee restated what she knew. Although there were some errors in her usage of the word* factor, *she was able to make sense of the problem, give an example of her thinking, and arrive at the correct answer.*

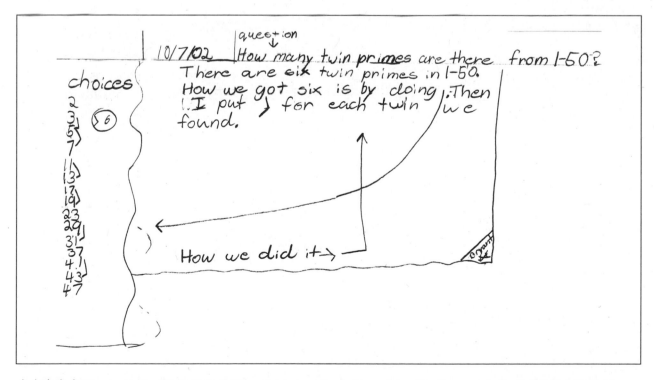

▲▲▲▲▲▲Figure 3–5 *Binh listed the prime numbers from 1 to 50, then searched the list for twin primes.*

Questions and Discussion

▲▲▲

▲ *Isn't a lesson about factors more appropriate when we are teaching students about multiplication? How does it help students with division?*

Too often, students learn mathematical ideas as separate, unrelated concepts that do not have a connection to other ideas they study. However, as stated in the NCTM's *Principles and Standards for School Mathematics,* "When students can connect mathematical ideas, their understanding is deeper and more lasting" (2000, 64). Our instructional programs should help students recognize and use connections among ideas and see how interconnecting ideas build on one another. Incorporating an activity such as this one that links factors and divisors builds on students' previous learning about multiplication to address divisibility, an important aspect of division.

▲ *Why is it important for students to investigate the number of factors, or the patterns in factors, that result when numbers are doubled?*

There are several reasons for having students investigate patterns in factors. Investigating these patterns, as well as investigating other numerical ideas such as prime, composite, and square numbers, gives students experience that builds their numerical intuition, an important component for developing their number sense. Also, thinking about these ideas provides students with practice with basic number facts as they apply those facts to numerical investigations. In addition, exploring numbers in these ways helps develop students' understanding of important properties of numbers. Finally, the investigations give students opportunities to make conjectures about properties of numbers and then find ways to justify or disprove their conjectures, important aspects of mathematical thinking.

▲ *Do you allow students to use calculators at their discretion?*

Typically, I allow children to decide when to use a calculator. A calculator is a tool, like paper and pencils or manipulatives. Answers do not lie in the materials or tools used; rather, materials and tools are means to support the students as they search for meaning and the answer. The child must understand what to do with a calculator before it can generate a meaningful answer. This is the reason I asked Shawn and Cody how they planned to use the calculator during the vignette. Their answer made sense and described a valid use of the calculator.

There are times I ask students to do their work without a calculator, as I need to know what they can do unassisted. Also, I find students often ignore calculators and are more interested in finding solutions in other ways.

CHAPTER FOUR
AN INTRODUCTION TO DIVISION COMPUTATION
IF YOU HOPPED LIKE A FROG

Overview

This lesson uses the book *If You Hopped Like a Frog*, by David M. Schwartz, as a context for introducing a division algorithm that is an alternative to the standard "divide, multiply, subtract, bring down" method. The book states that a chameleon's tongue is half its body length. Students figure the length the teacher's tongue would be if the teacher had a tongue like a chameleon. After students share their strategies, they are introduced to a division algorithm that builds on their number sense and knowledge of multiplication of ten and multiples of ten. Later in the lesson, students work independently to find the length of their own tongues if they had tongues like a chameleon.

Materials

▲ *If You Hopped Like a Frog*, by David M. Schwartz (Scholastic 1999)

Time

▲ one to two class periods

Teaching Directions

1. Read aloud to the students the book *If You Hopped Like a Frog*, by David M. Schwartz. After sharing the story, read aloud the section at the back about chameleons, stopping after the sentence about the chameleon's tongue being one-half as long as its body length.

2. Pose the following question to the class: "If I had a tongue like a chameleon, how long would my tongue be?"

3. Measure yourself in centimeters. Affix two meter sticks vertically on the wall, one above the other, with the lower one resting on the floor. Have a student mark where the top of your head reaches. Doing this models for students a procedure they can later use to measure their own heights.

4. Give students a few moments to consider how long your tongue would be if you had a tongue like a chameleon. Then have students share their strategies for figuring. Record their strategies on the board.

5. Introduce a procedure for dividing. This procedure is different from the typical algorithm introduced in textbooks. See the "Teaching Notes" section for an explanation.

6. Tell students they are to find out how long their tongues would be if they had tongues like a chameleon. Have them find their heights in centimeters. See "Teaching Notes" for a suggestion about how to manage this. Remind students to show at least two ways to solve the problem.

7. Circulate through the class, observing and asking students questions about their work.

Teaching Notes

If You Hopped Like a Frog, by David M. Schwartz, begins: "If you hopped like a frog . . . you could jump from home plate to first base in one mighty leap! If you were as strong as an ant . . . you could lift a car!" The book continues by describing the amazing things you could do if you were like other animals—brachiosaurus, snake, shrew, flea, chameleon, crane, eagle, pelican, and spider. The section at the back of the book suggests problems for children to solve based on the facts provided, all of which engage students with ideas of ratio and proportion and lead to division problems. Students find the book fascinating and are eager to explore and discuss the problems presented.

The division algorithm introduced in this lesson is different from the standard "divide, multiply, subtract, bring down" algorithm. This alternative makes use of students' number sense and their knowledge about multiplying by 10 and multiples of 10. Introducing students to this procedure makes sense for several reasons. Most students in fourth and fifth grade multiply easily by 10 and multiples of 10—20, 30, 40, 50, and so on. The procedure introduced in this chapter takes advantage of this knowledge and helps students apply what they already know to a new situation. Also, this alternative algorithm keeps students' number sense intact because students are always considering the whole dividend rather than focusing on the individual digits in the dividend, thus preventing many common errors that occur when students are learning to use the traditional algorithm. Most students can learn this alternative method quickly and use it accurately from the beginning, preventing many unhappy episodes of practicing something incorrectly only to face the frustration of relearning it. Also, this algorithm looks similar enough to the traditional algorithm and is easy enough for students to learn that students can help their parents understand it.

The problem the class solved together in the vignette was to find the length of the teacher's tongue if the teacher had a tongue like a chameleon, that is, if the teacher's tongue were half the teacher's height. This problem is an example of the sharing, or partitioning, model of division. The total number of centimeters is known, the number of groups is known, and the unknown is the number of centimeters in each of the two groups. Specifically, the students were to divide my height of 164 centimeters by two. To introduce the alternative algorithm, begin by asking the students if 164 (or whatever your height) is large enough so that if you split it into two groups, there would be at least 10 in each group. The students should quickly recognize that because two groups of 10 equals 20, the answer is yes. Next, ask students to figure how much is left if two groups of 10, or 20, are removed from the dividend of 164. They should respond that 144 remain. Record on the board as follows:

$$
\begin{array}{r}
10 \\
2\overline{)164} \\
-20 \\
\hline
144
\end{array}
$$

Continue by asking the students if 144 is large enough to put 10 more in each of two groups, or 20. The students will recognize it is. Subtract 20 from 144 and record as follows:

$$
\begin{array}{r}
10 \\
10 \\
2\overline{)164} \\
-20 \\
\hline
144 \\
-20 \\
\hline
124
\end{array}
$$

Continue in this way until the problem is completed. Add the list of partial quotients to find the answer (see the first column, next page). Some teachers introduce this same algorithm with a variation, recording the partial products on the side, next to a vertical line, and recording only the final answer above the dividend. The same problem done this way would like that in the second column, next page. You can see student work using this format in Chapter 13.

```
   2 ⌉
  10 |
  10 |
  10 |
  10 | 82
  10 |
  10 |
  10 |
  10 ⌋
 2)164
  -20
  ———
  144
  -20
  ———
  124
  -20
  ———
  104
  -20
  ———
   84
  -20
  ———
   64
  -20
  ———
   44
  -20
  ———
   24
  -20
  ———
    4
   -4
  ———
    0
```

```
       82
    2)164
     -20 | 10
     ———
     144
     -20 | 10
     ———
     124
     -20 | 10
     ———
     104
     -20 | 10
     ———
      84
     -20 | 10
     ———
      64
     -20 | 10
     ———
      44
     -20 | 10
     ———
      24
     -20 | 10
     ———
       4
      -4 | 2
     ———
       0
```

Like the students in the vignette, your students will discover that using multiples of 10 can improve the efficiency of this method. For example, when you first think about splitting 164 into two groups, there would be at least 50 in each group. Subtracting two groups of 50, or 100, results in 64 still to be divided.

```
      50
   2)164              2)164
                      -100 | 50
   -100      or       ————
   ————                 64
     64
```

Suggest using multiples of 10 when you think the students are ready.

For the students in the following vignette, this was an introductory experience to the algorithm just described. The students had a strong conceptual understanding of division and multiplication and the relationship between the two. They had experienced many of the lessons in the book *Teaching Arithmetic: Lessons for Introducing Division*, Grades 3–4, by Maryann Wickett, Susan Ohanian, and Marilyn Burns (Math Solutions Publications 2002), and *Teaching Arithmetic: Lessons for Introducing Multiplication*, Grade 3, by Marilyn Burns (Math Solutions Publications 2001). The students could easily multiply by ten and multiples of ten.

The students also had recently measured their heights using centimeters, so they didn't need to do this step in the lesson. To help them measure their heights accurately and efficiently, I affixed to the back wall of the classroom several pairs of meter sticks placed vertically one above the other, with one meter stick resting on the floor and the second directly above it. I spaced the pairs of meter sticks several feet apart. Working in pairs, one student stood with his or her back against the wall next to the meter sticks while the other student placed a pin into the wall where the top of the student's head touched. Together the two students figured the height. Then the students switched roles. If you have students measure their heights as part of this lesson, allow two days for the lesson. If you have the students find their heights prior to the lesson, the lesson can be done in one day, as described in the vignette.

In the vignette the students used their heights as measured in centimeters. I made this decision because height in centimeters gives larger numbers than height in inches. If you have an inexperienced class, using height in inches may make more sense for your students, as the numbers will be smaller.

The Lesson

▲▲

I gathered the students on the floor and asked, "If you were playing baseball and you could hop like a frog, do you think you could leap to first base in one hop?"

"Wow! That would be cool if I could do that!" Dante exclaimed.

"No one could get me out," Celena commented.

Skylar speculated, "I think if I could get to first base in one hop, I could get a lot more home runs because I could go around all the bases in less time than I can run to first base now."

I said, "I have a book to share with you that will answer this question and present you with other interesting ideas to consider." I held the book so the students could see the cover. "The book is called *If You Hopped Like a Frog,* and it's written by David M. Schwartz." I began reading the book aloud, starting with the author's introductory letter. As I read, the students were interested in discussing their thoughts about the information in the book, for example, how it would be to have a brain like a brachiosaurus, which would make their brains the size of a pea, or the idea that they could gulp a hot dog thicker than a telephone pole if they could swallow like a snake.

At the end of the book there is additional information about each of the situations presented. I read the first part of the section about chameleons, stopping after the sentence about a chameleon's tongue being one-half as long as its body length. The students were fascinated with the idea. I asked, "If I were a chameleon, how long would my tongue be?"

The students talked among themselves about my question. After a few moments, I called them back to order. I asked, "What information do we need to know to answer the question about how long my tongue would be if I were a chameleon?"

Amaya suggested, "We need to know how tall you are."

There were no other comments. I asked Amaya to help me measure myself. I taped two meter sticks to the wall, one placed vertically on top of the other, with the lower one resting on the floor. I stood against the sticks with my back to the wall while Amaya carefully marked my height by pushing a pin into the wall to mark where the top of my head touched. We found out I was 164 centimeters tall.

I recorded my height on the board two ways to model using the abbreviation: *164 centimeters or 164 cm.* After explaining the standard abbreviation of cm for centimeters, I said, "If I had a tongue like a chameleon, how long would my tongue be?" I paused while the students thought about this. Then I continued, "Is my height an even or an odd number?"

"Even," the class chorused.

I asked next, "If my height is an even number, will there be a remainder?" The students began to talk among themselves. After a few moments, hands began to go up.

Dante shared, "I don't think there can be a remainder because finding half is like dividing by two, and all even numbers are divisible by two."

"He stole my idea!" Emmi said.

"Are you saying that you and Dante had the same idea?" I asked Emmi. She nodded. I said to the rest of the class, "Show me with your thumb if you had Dante and Emmi's idea." Most thumbs went up immediately.

I asked, "What if my height were odd? Would there be a remainder?"

Adam said, "An odd number divided by two always has a remainder."

Amaya added, "An odd number divided by two always has a remainder, like Adam said, and the biggest the remainder can be is one."

"Why is that?" I probed.

Amaya explained, "If the remainder is two or bigger, then there's enough for more groups of two." No one had anything to add.

"How could I figure out my tongue length if I had a tongue like a chameleon?" I asked. The students talked among themselves. I waited until about half the students had raised their hands. I called on Bonnie.

"I figured it by doing this: First I added sixty and sixty, and that was one hundred twenty," Bonnie explained. "Too small! So I tried seventy and seventy, which was one hundred forty. Still too small! I did eighty plus eighty, and that was one hundred sixty. That's close. That left four. Four divided by two is two. Eighty plus two equals eighty-two."

I recorded Bonnie's thinking on the board:

Bonnie: 60 + 60 = 120 too small
            70 + 70 = 140 too small
            80 + 80 = 160 that's close
            4 ÷ 2 = 2
            80 + 2 = 82

Jackson waved his hand in the air with excitement. He explained, "I know a way to check Bonnie's idea. Add up eighty-two and eighty-two and if it comes out to one hundred sixty-four, then it's right. I added it and it works."

I recorded on the board next to Bonnie's idea:

Jackson's check: 82 + 82 = 164

"I know another way to check," Reilly said. "You can multiply eighty-two times two and it should equal one hundred sixty-four."

Jaime said, "If you think the answer is eighty-two, then you can subtract eighty-two from one hundred sixty-four and the answer should also be eighty-two."

I recorded Reilly's and Jaime's checks alongside Jackson's:

Reilly: 82 × 2 = 164

Jaime: 164 − 82 = 82

"I have another way," Alika said. "I know that half of one hundred sixty is eighty."

"How did you figure that out?" I asked Alika.

"I knew that half of sixteen was eight, so half of one hundred sixty is eighty," she explained. "I figured out half of one hundred sixty, and that leaves four. Half of four equals two. Eighty and two equals eighty-two."

I recorded on the board Alika's thinking:

Alika: $\frac{1}{2}$ of 16 = 8
           $\frac{1}{2}$ of 160 = 80
           $\frac{1}{2}$ of 4 = 2
           80 + 2 = 82

Amaya shared next. "My way is sort of like Alika's, but different too. I split apart one hundred sixty-four. I made it into one hundred plus sixty plus four. Then I figured out half of one hundred, which is fifty; half of sixty, which is thirty; and half of four, which is two. Add them up. Fifty plus thirty is eighty and two more equals eighty-two."

I recorded on the board:

Amaya: $164 = 100 + 60 + 4$

$\frac{1}{2}$ of $100 = 50$

$\frac{1}{2}$ of $60 = 30$

$\frac{1}{2}$ of $4 = 2$

$50 + 30 = 80$

$80 + 2 = 82$

No one else had an idea about how to figure out how long my tongue would be if I were a chameleon. I asked, "What kind of a problem have we been solving?"

Jaime responded, "Multiplication."

I asked Jaime and the rest of the students, "Can you give me a multiplication sentence that would show what we're trying to figure out?" Jaime looked perplexed.

"I'm not sure," Jaime said after a few moments. "Can I call on someone to help?" I nodded. He called on Alberto.

Alberto said, "It's some number times two equals one hundred sixty-four."

I said, "Is it OK if I draw a box to represent 'some number'?" Alberto nodded. I recorded on the board:

$\square \times 2 = 164$

Bonnie said, "I think the problem could be addition, subtraction, multiplication, division . . . or even fractions." Several students nodded their agreement.

CONNECTING TO DIVISION

Because my goal was to introduce a way of solving the problem using division, I asked, "If I wanted to think of the problem as a division problem, what division sentence could I write? Talk this over with your neighbor." After a few moments, I settled the class again. Most hands were up. I called on Kristin and asked her to come to the board to write her division sentence. She wrote:

$164 \div 2 = 82$

Reilly had a different way. He came to the board and wrote:

$$2\overline{)164}^{\,82}$$

Celena had a third way to represent the division problem symbolically. She came to the board and wrote:

$\frac{164}{2} = 82$

No one had anything to add.

INTRODUCING LANDMARK NUMBERS

To change the direction of the conversation, I asked the class, "What is a landmark?"

Jaime explained, "It's something you recognize."

Amelia added, "It can help you find your way."

Skylar said, "It's familiar and helps you know where you are."

I said, "I agree with all of your ideas. What do you suppose a landmark number is?"

Alika said with uncertainty, "A number that's easy to think about."

"Tell us more about your idea," I encouraged.

"Well, like ten and five are easy numbers," Alika explained. Several students nodded their agreement with Alika's thinking.

Gabe added, "It's a number you can use to help you. I think one hundred would be a landmark number, too."

I started a list on the board of the numbers students suggested as landmark numbers:

5

10

100

Amelia had another thought. "I think a landmark number can help you know where you are in the number world. Like, if you have seventeen of something, are you closer to having twenty or ten?" A few students nodded.

The students were quiet. I asked, "Do you think a number like thirteen would be a landmark number?"

Belinda said, "I don't think thirteen is a landmark number. It's hard to think about thirteen. I can think about two tens and know really fast it's twenty, but two thir-teens is harder. I can think ten plus ten plus three plus three, but it's not as easy as thinking about tens."

Adam added, "I think a landmark num-ber is a friendly number. Ten is a friendly number and thirteen isn't. I agree with Belinda." Most students nodded their agreement.

"I have another way of figuring out how long my tongue would be if I were a chameleon," I said. "My way involves using the landmark numbers ten and multiples of ten. Multiples of ten are numbers like twenty, thirty, forty, and so on. Raise your hand if you think multiplying by ten is easy." Hands flew into the air. I continued, "Raise you hand if you think multiplying by multiples of ten, like twenty, is easy." Most hands were up again. "I'm pleased to see so many of you are comfortable multiplying by ten and multiples of ten, because we're going to use that knowledge in just a few moments. We're going to be finding half of something by thinking about splitting it equally it into two groups. See if you can follow my thinking."

I wrote on the board:

2)164

I asked the students, "Do you think if you split one hundred sixty-four into two groups that there will be at least ten in each group? If you think yes, put your thumb up. If you think no, put your thumb down. If you're not sure, put your thumb sideways." All thumbs were up.

I wrote 10 above the 164 and asked, "If we put ten in each group, how much of the one hundred sixty-four did we use up?" As I said this, I pointed to the divisor of 2 and the partial quotient of 10.

$$\frac{10}{2)164}$$

"Twenty," the students responded quickly. I recorded the 20 beneath 164.

$$\begin{array}{r} 10 \\ 2)\overline{164} \\ -20 \end{array}$$

"When I put ten in each of two groups, I used twenty," I said. "If I subtract the twenty I just used, how many are left to divide into two groups?"

"One hundred forty-four," the students chorused. I recorded this on the board.

$$\begin{array}{r} 10 \\ 2)\overline{164} \\ -20 \\ \hline 144 \end{array}$$

I continued, "Is one hundred forty-four large enough to put ten more into each of two groups?" The students nodded. I wrote another 10 above the first and said, "Two tens equal twenty. One hundred forty-four minus twenty equals one hundred twenty-four." I recorded on the board as follows:

$$\begin{array}{r} 10 \\ 10 \\ 2)\overline{164} \\ -20 \\ \hline 144 \\ -20 \\ \hline 124 \end{array}$$

Alberto raised his hand and asked, "Why don't you use a larger number? Like instead of ten, why don't you put twenty in each group?" A couple of students nodded.

I asked the class, "What is two times twenty?"

"Forty," the students responded together. I recorded on the board:

```
       20
       10
       10
    2)164
     −20
      144
     −20
      124
     −40
       84
```

Several students put their hands up. I called on Bonnie. Bonnie said, "You have eighty-four left. I think you should multiply two times forty, because that's eighty." I did as Bonnie suggested and with the students' help recorded the following on the board:

```
       40
       20
       10
       10
    2)164
     −20
      144
     −20
      124
     −40
       84
     −80
        4
```

All hands were up. The students were eager to tell me how to finish the problem. I called on Reilly.

Reilly said, "There are four left. You can put two in each group. You need to write a two at the top of the numbers and then you need to subtract four from four, and it's zero so you're all done!" I did as Reilly instructed me to do.

```
        2
       40
       20
       10
       10
    2)164
     −20
      144
     −20
      124
     −40
       84
     −80
        4
       −4
        0
```

"The next thing I'm going to do is add up these numbers to figure out how much is in each group," I said as I pointed to the partial quotients. I added the numbers aloud, figuring the quotient to be eighty-two.

```
        2 ⌉
       40 |
       20 | = 82
       10 |
       10 ⌋
    2)164
     −20
      144
     −20
      124
     −40
       84
     −80
        4
       −4
        0
```

Dante raised his hand with excitement. He said, "I think I know another way you could do it your way! You could start with fifty in each group. That would be one hundred. That's sixty-four left over. Then multiply thirty by two, and that's sixty. That leaves four. Four divided by two equals two. Fifty plus thirty plus two equals eighty-two."

I repeated the procedure, recording Dante's idea.

$$
\begin{array}{r}
2 \\
30 \\
\underline{50} \rceil 82 \\
2)\overline{164} \\
\underline{-100} \\
64 \\
\underline{-60} \\
4 \\
\underline{-4} \\
0
\end{array}
$$

Bonnie shared next. "I know an even shorter way. Start with eighty. Eighty times two equals one hundred sixty. That leaves four. Four divided by two equals two. It comes out to eighty-two, just like all the other ways. That's cool!" I recorded Bonnie's thinking on the board next to Dante's.

$$
\begin{array}{r}
2 \\
\underline{80} \rceil 82 \\
2)\overline{164} \\
\underline{-160} \\
4 \\
\underline{-4} \\
0
\end{array}
$$

There were no more comments. If Dante and Bonnie hadn't volunteered their suggestions for how to make my method more efficient, I would have asked the students for more efficient ways. If no one had had an idea, I would have presented other ways on other days to help students think about alternatives.

AN INVESTIGATION

"If I were a chameleon, my tongue would be eighty-two centimeters long," I said. I reached for a meter stick and showed the students how long 82 centimeters were.

"How long would your tongue be if you were a chameleon?"

The students began to talk among themselves. I settled the class and continued. "You measured yourself in centimeters last week and I have your papers with that information. I'll return these to you in a few moments. Your job is to figure how long your tongue would be if you were a chameleon. Write your height in centimeters on your recording sheet and show how to figure your answer in at least two ways that make sense to you. One of those ways should include division." (If the students hadn't previously measured their heights, I'd have had them do so before introducing this investigation.)

"Do we need a title?" Kristin asked.

"You do need a title and I'll let you decide what title you'd like to use," I said.

"How do you spell *chameleon?*" Skylar asked. I wrote *chameleon* on the board.

"Can we use the ideas on the board to figure out how long our tongue would be?" Belinda asked.

"You may use the ideas on the board as long as they make sense to you and you can explain them," I replied. "You may also use other ideas you have as long as they make sense to you." There were no more questions. I handed back the students' papers with their heights, then reminded each of them to get a blank sheet of paper to use as a recording sheet.

OBSERVING THE STUDENTS

I was interested to find out what approaches the students would use to solve this problem and whether any of them would try the method I'd introduced. Within a few minutes, all students were engaged. Some talked quietly with their table partners about their methods while others worked silently. I circulated, looking over shoulders and noting what the students were doing.

As I looked over Alberto's shoulder, I noticed he was using decimals. "What does this mean?" I asked, pointing to the .5 in the 6.5 he'd written on his paper.

Alberto replied, "It's point five. It means five-tenths and that's the same as one-half." I nodded.

"Why did you figure one-half of thirteen?" I asked Alberto.

Alberto explained, "Oh, I used one-half of thirteen to figure out one-half of one hundred thirty. One-half of thirteen is six and five-tenths. Ten times thirteen is one hundred thirty, so ten times six and five-tenths is sixty-five." I moved on, leaving Alberto to complete his work. When I checked back later, I noticed he had also used the procedure of dividing that I had presented to the class earlier. (See Figure 4–1.)

I paused to look over Bonnie's shoulder next. I noticed that she was trying the procedure I introduced. Bonnie said, "I'm a little stuck. I'm one hundred thirty-three centimeters tall. That's an odd number, so I have one left over. My tongue would be sixty-six centimeters, but I'm not sure what to do with the one centimeter that's left."

I paused a moment and then asked Bonnie, "If I were dividing cookies between two people and I had one left, what could I do with it?"

"Oh, I know," Bonnie said, her face lighting up. "You could divide it into half. So I could divide the leftover centimeter into half. My tongue would be sixty-six and one-half centimeters long if I were a chameleon." Bonnie used the guess-and-check method she had shared during the class discussion as her second method. (See Figure 4–2.)

Mark's height was also an odd number, 141 cm. He explained he'd rather have an even number, so he subtracted 1 to get 140. Then he found half of 140 and finally half of the 1 he subtracted earlier and combined these amounts. (See Figure 4–3.)

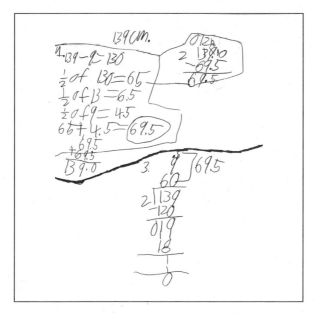

▲▲▲▲▲▲Figure 4–1 *Alberto began first by finding a more friendly number than 39.*

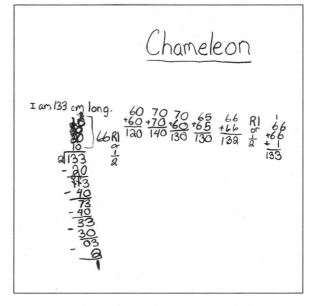

▲▲▲▲▲▲Figure 4–2 *Bonnie used the alternative algorithm and her own method.*

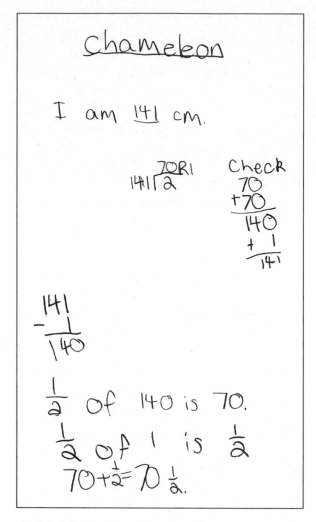

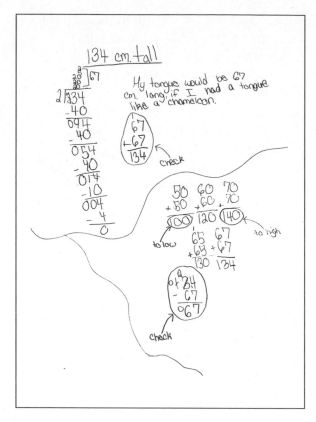

▲▲▲▲▲▲Figure 4–3 *Mark subtracted 1 to get an even number, then solved the problem, remembering to include the 1 he initially subtracted out. Mark reversed the dividend and divisor when he wrote $141\overline{)2}\,^{70\ R7}$, an error common at this stage.*

Just over half the students used the method I introduced as one of their strategies. All who tried it did so accurately. (See Figures 4–4 through 4–6.) Alika commented, "I tried the new way and it was fast and easy. It was cool! I thought big division problems would be harder than that." I collected the students' papers and ended the lesson for the day.

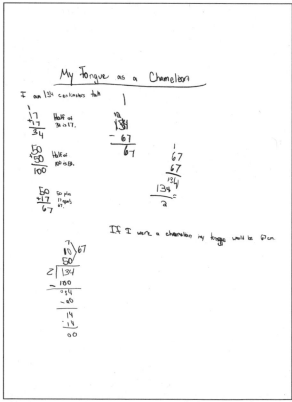

▲▲▲▲▲▲Figures 4–4, 4–5, 4–6 *Figures 4–4, 4–5, and 4–6 show varying ways to use the alternative algorithm efficiently and accurately.*

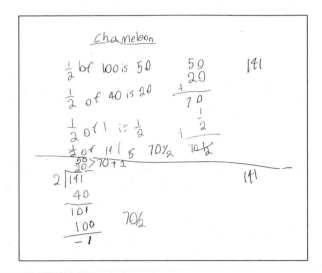

▲▲▲▲▲▲Figures 4–4, 4–5, 4–6 *(continued)*

EXTENSIONS

I gave students many additional experiences similar to this one—presenting an-

other division problem, talking about ways to solve it, modeling again the procedure I introduced, then having them work on a similar, related problem and show at least two ways to solve it. I used another problem from the book. The book states that a crane's neck is one-third of its height. Students figured out how long their necks would be if they had necks like a crane.

I also presented problems in different contexts. For example: *There are 300 seats in the school theater. If 24 students each got the same number of tickets for the class play to give to families and friends, how many tickets would each student get?*

At other times, I presented problems numerically, without a context, choosing numbers that were appropriate for the students. For example, 4)$\overline{175}$ and 15)$\overline{1,000}$.

Questions and Discussion

▲▲

▲ *This algorithm looks similar to yet different from the one I learned in school. Won't parents object to their students learning division this way?*

It's true, the algorithm presented in this chapter looks similar to but is different from the algorithm most of us learned when we were in school. However, it takes most children only a short time to understand and learn it. Students use a skill they already know well, multiplying by ten and multiples of ten, and apply it successfully and accurately to solve a new kind of problem. This builds confidence and strengthens previous understanding. Because students understand what they're doing, they can explain it to their parents. Also, as students gain experience with this method, they learn that using multiples of ten is a shortcut, making this method a very quick and accurate way to solve division problems. Additionally, this method works with two- and three-place divisors as well as larger dividends.

▲ *Because the algorithm presented in this chapter is different, won't teachers who receive my students next year or the year after complain?*

Few teachers object to a student's methods when those methods consistently produce accurate answers in an efficient manner. Most likely those teachers receiving your students will ask about the method you taught. When you share the algorithm you taught, you are giving those teachers a different tool to try with their students.

▲ *Will students who use the algorithm presented in this chapter be hampered on standardized, timed tests?*

Absolutely not. If anything, they will have an advantage. This is because they understand what they are doing; their number sense is intact, so they can determine reasonable and unreasonable answers quickly; computing using this method is efficient and accurate; and they don't make the mistakes many students of this age make when zero is involved in the quotient.

▲ *Some of my students have already learned the standard algorithm. Won't introducing them to a new way confuse them?*

The students in the vignette were new to long division, with little or no prior experience using the standard algorithm. As a first experience using a division algorithm, this method made sense to them, so many chose to use it. In other classes, where I've taught this lesson to students with prior experience with the standard algorithm, some preferred to continue with the method they knew while others eagerly tried the alternative algorithm. Often the students who benefited the most were those who didn't understand the standard algorithm. When the algorithm presented in this chapter is presented several times as another way to solve a division problem, those who have trouble with the standard algorithm are given an alternative. What's important here is not to ask students to learn a different algorithm by rote memory, but to present them with ideas that will help them make sense of division.

CHAPTER FIVE
THE DIVIDEND STAYS THE SAME

Overview

In this lesson, students interpret and solve several series of division problems in which the dividend stays the same and the divisors go from one to ten. Students investigate the different ways to represent quotients for division problems in which the divisor is larger than the dividend. The structure of this lesson is similar to that of *The Divisor Stays the Same* (see Chapter 2). Initially, the class works together to find the quotients for problems with a dividend of one and divisors from one to ten and then discuss the patterns they notice. Next, working in pairs, students choose a dividend from two to ten, divide their chosen dividend by the divisors one to ten, and write about the patterns they notice. In a whole-group discussion, students examine one another's work, share patterns they notice, and make generalizations based on their observations.

Materials

▲ optional: chart paper

Time

▲ two class periods

Teaching Directions

1. Write on the board the following list of division problems, occasionally stopping to ask students to predict the problem you'll write next:

$1 \div 1 =$ $1 \div 6 =$

$1 \div 2 =$ $1 \div 7 =$

$1 \div 3 =$ $1 \div 8 =$

$1 \div 4 =$ $1 \div 9 =$

$1 \div 5 =$ $1 \div 10 =$

2. When the list is completed, discuss the vocabulary *dividend, divisor,* and *quotient.* Write above the list of division problems: *dividend ÷ divisor = quotient.*

3. Students are often confused when the dividend is smaller than the divisor, so talk with students about how to represent the answer to 1 ÷ 2 in two ways. Use concrete materials to model the solution. For example, use markers, pencils, tiles, or some other material that can't be broken apart to model dividing one object between two students. By using an object that can't be broken, you can show students why the answer 0 R1 makes sense in this situation. Then, to help students understand that $\frac{1}{2}$ is also a correct answer to 1 ÷ 2, present a situation in which you can divide what is being shared: How much would each person get if one brownie were shared between two people?

4. Ask for students to volunteer to choose another problem to solve, come to the board to write the quotient for that problem in two ways, and explain the solutions. Have the rest of the students indicate their agreement with the answer by putting their thumbs up if they agree, down if they disagree, or sideways if they're unsure or don't know. The final list will look as follows:

dividend ÷ divisor = quotient

	Markers	Brownies
1 ÷ 1 =	1	1
1 ÷ 2 =	0 R1	$\frac{1}{2}$
1 ÷ 3 =	0 R1	$\frac{1}{3}$
1 ÷ 4 =	0 R1	$\frac{1}{4}$
1 ÷ 5 =	0 R1	$\frac{1}{5}$
1 ÷ 6 =	0 R1	$\frac{1}{6}$
1 ÷ 7 =	0 R1	$\frac{1}{7}$
1 ÷ 8 =	0 R1	$\frac{1}{8}$
1 ÷ 9 =	0 R1	$\frac{1}{9}$
1 ÷ 10 =	0 R1	$\frac{1}{10}$

5. Discuss and record on the board patterns students notice about the division problems and quotients.

6. Organize the students into pairs and ask each pair to choose a dividend from two to ten. Using the divisors from one to ten, they should write a list of division problems as you did for the dividend of one and solve the division problems using both contexts—markers and brownies. Then they should write about the patterns they discover. Have students who finish early post their work on the board or chart paper so that you have a list for each of the dividends from two to ten. If there is still time after students have completed the assignment, ask them to select another dividend to explore.

7. Lead a class discussion. Discussion questions could include the following:

▲ Why do you represent answers differently when thinking about dividing markers or dividing brownies?

▲ When a quotient is represented as zero with a remainder, why are the remainder and the dividend the same?

▲ When problems have the same dividend but different divisors, all of which are greater than that dividend, why do they all result in the same quotient—zero with a remainder that is the same as the dividend?

▲ When a quotient is expressed as a fraction, for example, $5 \div 7 = \frac{5}{7}$, why are the dividend and the numerator the same? Why are the divisor and denominator the same?

Teaching Notes

This lesson provides students the opportunity to investigate division problems for which the divisor is larger than the dividend, for example, $1 \div 2$, $5 \div 8$, $3 \div 4$, and so on. They interpret problems like these in two different situations, one in which they are dividing objects that cannot be broken apart to be shared, such as markers, tiles, or balloons, and the other in which they are dividing objects that can be broken apart to be shared, such as brownies or cookies. Relating division problems to familiar contexts, or using concrete materials to solve them, helps students bring meaning to the problems and their solutions.

For example, $1 \div 2$ could be interpreted as dividing one marker between two people. There aren't enough markers to share, and it doesn't make sense to break a marker into two parts. Therefore, each person gets zero markers, and the marker is still remaining. The answer to the problem in this context is $1 \div 2 = 0$ R1. However, if you think about $1 \div 2$ as dividing one brownie between two people, you *can* break apart the brownie into two equal parts and give each person one-half. It makes sense to express the answer to the problem in this context as $1 \div 2 = \frac{1}{2}$. Similarly, the answer to $5 \div 8$ can be expressed as either 0 R5 or $\frac{5}{8}$, depending on the interpretation of the problem. And the answer to $3 \div 4$ can be expressed as 0 R3 or $\frac{3}{4}$.

In the lesson, after the class solves the list of problems with one as the dividend and divisors from one to ten, interpreting the problem both as dividing markers and as dividing brownies, pairs of students solve lists of problems for other dividends, also with divisors from one to ten. For example, for a dividend of three, students would list ten problems, solve them for the interpretations of sharing markers and then brownies, and write about the patterns they notice. Solving a set of problems like this helps students gain a deeper understanding of the meaning of each of the parts of a division problem.

	Markers	Brownies
$3 \div 1 =$	3	3
$3 \div 2 =$	1 R1	$1\frac{1}{2}$
$3 \div 3 =$	1	1
$3 \div 4 =$	0 R3	$\frac{3}{4}$
$3 \div 5 =$	0 R3	$\frac{3}{5}$

$3 \div 6 =$	0 R3	$\frac{3}{6}$
$3 \div 7 =$	0 R3	$\frac{3}{7}$
$3 \div 8 =$	0 R3	$\frac{3}{8}$
$3 \div 9 =$	0 R3	$\frac{3}{9}$
$3 \div 10 =$	0 R3	$\frac{3}{10}$

Once lists are posted for all of the dividends from one to ten, students look for patterns and discuss what they notice. The goals for the lesson include students gaining understanding of the following ideas:

▲ Contexts are important when determining an appropriate way to represent the answer to a problem.

▲ When the quotient of a division problem is zero with a remainder, the dividend and the remainder are the same number.

▲ For division problems with the same dividend but different divisors, those problems with divisors larger than the dividend all have the same answer—zero with a remainder the same as the dividend.

▲ When the quotient to a division problem with a divisor larger than the dividend is expressed as a fraction, the dividend and numerator are the same, and the divisor and denominator are the same.

In the following vignette, some students didn't clearly understand the meaning of the dividend and the divisor. As a result, some students switched the numbers to make a problem more manageable for them and then solved it. For example, they would think of $5 \div 7$ as $7 \div 5$ and arrive at an answer of 1 R2 instead of 0 R5 or $\frac{5}{7}$. When asked to explain their thinking, they typically explained that they could simply switch the order of the numbers. (They approached division as if it were commutative, as are addition and multiplication.) However, when asked to explain their thinking in the context of markers or brownies, they typically realized their error. And for students who were still confused, I again modeled the problem for them to help them bring meaning to what the dividend and divisor represented.

The Lesson

▲▲

DAY 1

As the students settled, I began listing the following division problems on the board:

$1 \div 1 =$

$1 \div 2 =$

$1 \div 3 =$

After I wrote $1 \div 3 =$, Alan said, "I know what you're going to write next."

I stopped writing, turned to the class, and said, "Who else thinks you know what problem I'm going to list next?" Hands flew into the air. I paused just a moment longer to give the few students who didn't have their hands up additional time to think. "Tell me in a whisper voice," I said.

"One divided by four," the students chorused.

"You're absolutely correct!" I replied as I wrote on the board $1 \div 4 =$. Jason waved his hand, eager to share a thought.

"The first number is staying the same. It's always a one," he observed.

"What's the first number called?" I asked Jason. He shrugged and asked if he could call on someone else. I nodded and he called on Veda.

"I think it's the dividend," Veda said. I nodded my agreement.

Next I asked what the numbers in the second column are called and then what the answers are called. I wrote above the first problem in the list: *dividend ÷ divisor = quotient*. Providing terminology for students in this way reinforces correct mathematical vocabulary, gives students a reference that uses the correct terms, and facilitates clear communication about ideas during discussions.

"I see another pattern different than Jason's," Alycia said. "The divisor is getting bigger by one each time you write a new problem. First it's one, then two, and like that." Several students nodded their agreement with Alycia.

The students had no more ideas they wanted to share. With their assistance, I continued to list the problems, stopping with a divisor of ten.

dividend ÷ divisor = quotient

1	÷	1	=	
1	÷	2	=	
1	÷	3	=	
1	÷	4	=	
1	÷	5	=	
1	÷	6	=	
1	÷	7	=	
1	÷	8	=	
1	÷	9	=	
1	÷	10	=	

"Who would like to choose from the list a division problem to solve, then come to the board and write the quotient?" I asked. Students were eager and quickly had their hands up. I called on Isiah, who came to the board and wrote *1* as the answer to $1 \div 1$.

"If you agree that one divided by one equals one, put your thumb up; if you're not sure, put your thumb sideways; and if you disagree, put your thumb down," I said to other students. Thumbs went up immediately. I continued, "It looks like we all agree that one divided by one equals one. Raise your hand if you'd like to choose a different division problem to solve and Isiah will choose someone else to come to the board." I paused a moment. Few students raised their hands. This didn't surprise me, as the students had little experience solving division problems with a divisor larger than the dividend.

To give more students a way to think about the remaining problems listed on the board, I decided to present a concrete model to support their understanding. I held up a marker and posed the following situation to the students: "Suppose I have one marker and I want to divide it between two students, Abbie and Kenny. How many markers would each student get?"

Wendi commented, "That's tricky."

"Why is it tricky?" I asked her.

"If it were a cookie or something like that, you could divide it into two parts and give each person a part. You can't divide a marker in two."

Before going on, I wanted to reinforce a key idea of division. I said to the students, "When dividing something into parts, all of the parts must have the same amount, that is, they have to be equivalent. So, while dividing a cookie or a sheet of paper is possible, dividing a marker into two equivalent parts doesn't make sense. Since I can't break the one marker I have into two parts, how many markers do Abbie and Kenny each get?"

"Zero!" the students replied confidently in unison.

"How many are left over?" I asked.

"One," they replied together, but not as confidently.

I explained, "For this problem of dividing one marker between two people, I can record the quotient as zero remainder one." I recorded to complete the problem on the board: $1 \div 2 = 0\ R1$.

Because $\frac{1}{2}$ is a valid quotient for $1 \div 2$, I wanted to present the children with a situation for which this would be an appropriate answer. My intent was to help them to see that it's important to consider the context when deciding how to represent a quotient. I said, "While it doesn't make sense to divide a marker into two parts, it could make sense to divide a brownie between two students. How much would each student get if Abbie and Kenny divided a brownie?"

Brianna explained, "You would have to make sure they each got the same amount and that would be one-half." The other students nodded their agreement. I wrote on the board:

	Markers	Brownies
$1 \div 2 =$	$0\ R1$	$\frac{1}{2}$

Before asking students to solve other problems, I decided to do one more problem together.

I said to the students as I pointed to the list of division problems, "Which problem should we solve next?" Students called out a variety of suggestions. After settling them, I called on Cassi.

"Let's do one divided by six," she suggested.

"Are we dividing markers or brownies?" Emily asked.

"First, let's think about the problem with markers and then with brownies. Who can interpret the problem using the context of markers?"

Joaquin responded, "With markers, the problem would be one marker divided among six kids. Is that right?"

"What do the rest of you think?" I asked the others. Most students gave Joaquin's idea a thumbs-up. "I agree with Joaquin's idea about the problem, one marker divided among six students. What would the answer be?" When most of the students had their hands raised, I called on Karalynn.

"I think no one would get a marker and the marker would be left over, so zero remainder one," she said. I recorded Karalynn's answer of $0\ R1$ on the list next to $1 \div 6$:

	Markers	Brownies
$1 \div 1 =$	1	1
$1 \div 2 =$	$0\ R1$	$\frac{1}{2}$
$1 \div 3 =$		
$1 \div 4 =$		
$1 \div 5 =$		
$1 \div 6 =$	$0\ R1$	

"Hey! That's the same answer as one divided by two!" said Pesach with great surprise.

"Oh yeah!" several others agreed.

"I don't see how two different problems can get the same answer," Jamal said, perplexed. I allowed the students to talk among themselves for a moment, then called them back to order. As they settled, hands went up.

"I'm confused," Jael said. Several others nodded.

"Are you confused because the quotients are the same?" I asked. Jael nodded. "Can you think of any other situation when different problems result in the same answer?" My question met with blank stares initially. After a couple of moments, a few hands went up. I waited a little longer, and a few more hands went up. I called on Latonya.

"When you divide one by one and two by two, you get the same answer. They both equal one," Latonya shared.

"You can multiply any number by zero and the answer will always be zero," Jason said. No one had anything to add.

"How about adding five plus five and then adding six plus four?" I asked.

"They're both ten," Cassi answered.

"So, it's possible for two different problems to have the same answer," I summarized.

I then asked, "What if instead of one marker, I was dividing one brownie among six people? How much would each person get? Talk with your neighbor about this." The room came alive with conversations. I circulated through the room, listening to the discussions. Most students recognized that the brownie would need to be divided into six equal pieces and each person would get one of the pieces, or one-sixth. Jewell, who liked to play with ideas and think outside the box, was trying to convince her partner that the brownie could also be divided into twelve equal pieces. "Each of the six people could get two of the twelve pieces, or two-twelfths, and that's the same as one-sixth," she said. Jewell's partner was skeptical. I called the class back to order. Students quickly raised their hands, eager to share their ideas.

Jacinto said, "If you're sharing a brownie, you would have to divide it into equal pieces, one for each person. That's six pieces. Each person would get one-sixth of the brownie. Can I show it on the board?" I nodded and Jacinto came to the board, drew a rectangle, and divided it into sixths. "Six people, six pieces of brownie, one-sixth for each."

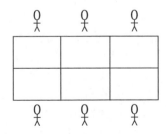

"I noticed something about the last two problems we did, one divided by two and one divided by six," Jael shared. "They both have the same answer for dividing markers, zero remainder one, but they have different answers for dividing brownies."

"Tell us more about your thinking," I encouraged Jael. He was making an important point about how the context of a problem determines what makes a sensible, appropriate answer. Had he or another student not brought this point up, I would have asked the class about it.

Jael paused to collect his thoughts and then continued. "Well, one brownie divided between two people could be one-half. One brownie divided among six people could be one-sixth. Those are different answers. But with markers, the answer to both problems is zero remainder one. The answer depends on what you're dividing." Several students nodded. No one wanted to add any other ideas.

"Who would like to choose a problem and come to the board and write the quotient?" I asked. "First, solve the problem as if you were dividing markers, then solve the problem as if you were dividing brownies." Hands flew into the air.

I handed the chalk to Kelsey. She came to the board and wrote *0 R1* under the column for markers for the division problem $1 \div 4$. Kelsey explained, "If there were four people and I wanted to divide one marker among them, no one would get one. Each person would get zero and the marker would still be left." Next, Kelsey turned back to the board and wrote $\frac{1}{4}$. She said, "With brownies, I would have to cut one brownie into four equal parts. Each person would get one out of the four parts, which is one-fourth." The other students indicated their agreement with thumbs up. Kelsey handed the chalk to Jason.

Jason chose the problem $1 \div 10$. "Ten people can't divide one marker. So they each get zero with one marker left. But with brownies, even though the pieces would be very small, like crumbs, I think, it could be cut into ten pieces and each person would get one out of ten pieces." Jason wrote *0 R1* under the Markers column and $\frac{1}{10}$ under the Brownies column.

We continued in this way until all the problems had been solved. The completed list looked as follows:

	Markers	Brownies
$1 \div 1 =$	1	1
$1 \div 2 =$	0 R1	$\frac{1}{2}$
$1 \div 3 =$	0 R1	$\frac{1}{3}$
$1 \div 4 =$	0 R1	$\frac{1}{4}$
$1 \div 5 =$	0 R1	$\frac{1}{5}$
$1 \div 6 =$	0 R1	$\frac{1}{6}$
$1 \div 7 =$	0 R1	$\frac{1}{7}$
$1 \div 8 =$	0 R1	$\frac{1}{8}$
$1 \div 9 =$	0 R1	$\frac{1}{9}$
$1 \div 10 =$	0 R1	$\frac{1}{10}$

By the time we finished the list, math time was over. I said, "I'll copy the list of division problems onto a piece of chart paper and post it so you can study them. Tomorrow we'll discuss what you notice." It has been my experience that giving students time to consider information deepens their thinking and understanding, thus enriching later class discussions.

DAY 2

I asked the students to discuss with their partners what they noticed about the list of problems from the day before. After a few moments, I called the class to order.

I began a class discussion by asking, "Who would like to share something you noticed?" Many hands were up quickly. I called on Alycia.

"I noticed that once the divisor was bigger than the dividend, either the answer was zero with a remainder or a fraction," she shared.

I recorded Alycia's idea on the board:

Alycia: When the dividend is bigger than the divisor, the answer is zero with a remainder, or a fraction.

Alycia nodded her agreement with what I wrote.

Abbie added, "Something I noticed about the fractions is the lower number is the same as the divisor."

To encourage the use of correct mathematical vocabulary and to verify that I understood Abbie's idea, I asked as I pointed to the denominator in one of the fractions, "Are you saying that the denominator is the same as the divisor?"

Abbie nodded.

I recorded Abbie's idea on the board beneath Alycia's:

Abbie: When a quotient is a fraction, the denominator is the same as the divisor.

Emily built on Abbie's idea. She said, "The numerator is the same as the remainder and the dividend."

I added Emily's idea to the others:

Emily: When the quotient is a fraction, the numerator is the same as the dividend. It is also the same as the remainder in the other answer.

"It's like that for all of them," Eduardo said with surprise.

Jael said, "My pattern is one we said yesterday. All the dividends are the same and the divisors get bigger by one each time as you go down the list." I recorded Jael's idea on the board.

"And one more thing: For the marker problems, the remainders are all the same, one, and all the dividends are the same as the remainders," Kiley shared. I recorded Kiley's idea.

Introducing an Exploration

Next I asked, "What if I changed the dividend from one to two, or some other number, and again wrote problems with all the divisors from one to ten? What do you think would happen?" I paused while the students thought for a moment. Hands started to go up as the students talked among themselves.

Jewell shared, "I think some of the problems will have remainders, like on the list we did, but I'm not sure what the remainder will be. And I think if we're dividing markers, then some of the problems will have zero in the answer."

Jamal added, "I think I agree with what Jewell said, but I think maybe if the dividend is two, then the remainder will be two, but I don't know why."

"I think the remainder will be two because you start with two markers and if you can't give one to each person, then the two markers you started with will be leftovers," Jael explained.

I then explained to the students, "In a few moments, you and your partner will choose one number between two and ten to use as the dividend for a list of problems, just as I used one as the dividend for all the problems we solved together." I pointed to the dividends on the list of problems we'd completed. "Then you'll write a list of ten problems, using the numbers one to ten as the divisors and the number you chose as the dividend." Again I pointed to the list, this time indicating the divisors. "Then you will solve the problems together, thinking about each in two ways: first as if you were dividing markers and then as if you were dividing brownies. Finally, you'll write about patterns you notice."

"Do we use one paper for both of us or do we each get our own?" Eduardo asked.

I replied, "Either is fine. If you both use the same piece of paper, remember to put both of your names on it."

"Can we do more than one number?" Dennie asked.

"If there is still time after you've explored one number and written about the patterns you notice, you may choose another number," I said.

"Can we use markers or crayons or color pencils or draw brownies to help us?" Abbie asked.

"That's an excellent idea if it helps you make sense of the problems," I said. There were no more questions. I gave one last direction. "With your partner, decide which number you'd like to use as your dividend and raise a hand when you're ready to report it to me. Have a second choice in mind in case too many people are exploring your first choice. I'll record your number on the board so I can keep track of who's doing what number and to make sure at least one pair investigates each number." After the students reported their choices, they quickly got to work.

Observing the Students

As the students worked, I circulated through the class, listening to conversations, answering occasional questions, and asking a few of my own.

Wendi and Emily were excited to show me their work. They had written their division problems correctly, but rather than divide, they multiplied.

"Let's look at your first problem," I said. "Five is the dividend. What does it tell you?"

"We have five markers," Emily replied. Wendi nodded her agreement.

"What does the divisor of one mean?" I continued.

"It means there is one person to share the markers," Wendi replied somewhat tentatively.

"How many markers will the one person get?" I asked.

"Five," the girls responded, indicating where they had written 5 for their answer.

I nodded and continued, "Explain to me what the second problem is about."

"Well, there are five markers and two people to share them," Wendi said.

"That's ten," Emily chimed in.

Wendi had a look of confusion on her face. I suggested she gather five markers and then divide them between herself and Emily. "Oh, I think I see now!" Wendi responded with surprise. "We each get two markers and there's one left over." The girls began talking about what to do next, asked for a new sheet of paper, and began again. I moved on, making a note to myself to check on their progress later.

Kenny and Alan were working hard. They had chosen ten as their dividend and were writing about the patterns they noticed in the quotients when they solved the problems as if they were dividing markers. They hadn't yet considered how to solve the problems as if they were brownies. Kenny commented, "I notice that none of our problems had a zero in the quotient."

"Why do you think that is?" I questioned.

Kenny and Alan talked this over a moment, then looked across the table at Cassi and Latonya's paper. Cassi and Latonya had chosen three as their dividend. After talking with Kenny for a few moments, Alan responded to my question.

He explained, "We think maybe you can't have zero in the quotient unless the divisor is bigger than the dividend. On Cassi and Latonya's paper there was a zero in the quotient when the divisor was four and bigger but not when the divisor was less than four. On ours, the dividend was ten, so the divisor never got bigger than ten." (See Figure 5–1.)

Jael and Jamal extended their work to include divisors up to seventeen. Jael said, "I think I can predict the answer for any division problem with a dividend of seven and a divisor larger than seven!"

"Me too!" Jael said.

"Give us a problem," the boys said together. I wrote on the back of their paper: $7 \div 3,006,972 =$.

"That's easy!" the boys said. "It's zero remainder seven!"

"How do you know?" I pushed.

Jamal said, "There are seven of something to share and way more people than seven to share it. No one gets anything, and that means the seven things are leftovers."

"Do you agree, Jael?" I asked.

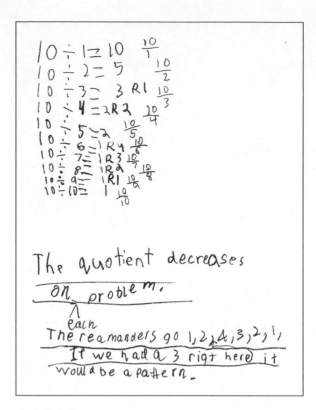

▲▲▲▲▲**Figure 5–1** *Alan and Kenny's completed work.*

He nodded. "It doesn't matter how many people there are if the number of people is bigger than the number of things to share. If it's markers or something that can't be broken apart to share, then no one gets anything."

I nodded my agreement, then said, "And what if it's brownies instead of markers?"

Jael said tentatively, "It would be a fraction. I think the seven would be the top number and the bottom number would be that number." He pointed to 3,006,972.

Jamal commented, "That seems like a really small, weird amount of a brownie, like maybe a speck or something."

"Can we try it with eleven as the dividend?" the boys asked. I nodded and they quickly got to work. (See Figure 5–2.)

I checked back with Wendi and Emily. They had solved correctly the first five problems. When they got to $5 \div 6$, they incorrectly wrote 0 R6 as the quotient.

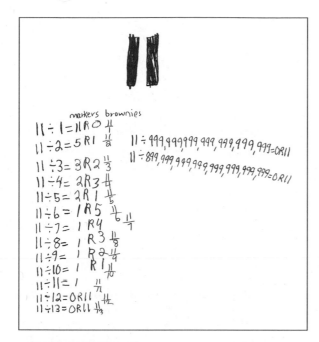

▲▲▲▲▲▲Figure 5–2 *Jamal and Jael went beyond the assignment to explore the dividend 11.*

▲▲▲▲▲▲Figure 5–3 *Wendi corrected her work after discovering her mistakes when asked to explain her thinking. She also used pictures to help make sense of the problems, although she was unable to complete the assignment.*

They had stopped using markers to help them make sense of the problems and, as a result, made a mistake and used the divisor as their remainder rather than the dividend.

I asked them to use markers to show me how they got their answer. As they modeled their solution with markers, Wendi paused, then said, "Oh, the remainder can't be six! That's how many people are sharing! Five is the number of markers. There aren't enough for each person to get one, so all the markers are left over! I get it!" She and Emily corrected their paper. (See Figure 5–3.)

I next noticed that Karalynn and Kelsey had written 1 R1 for the division problem 2 ÷ 3. For the division problem of 2 ÷ 4, they'd written the quotient of 2. I asked the girls to explain their solutions. Kelsey pointed to 2 ÷ 3 and explained, "We turned the numbers around and solved the problem three divided by two." I asked her to explain the problem using markers. As she did, she realized the 2 represented the number of markers

while the 3 represented the number of people, and that switching the numbers changed the problem and wouldn't work.

Wendi and Emily came to me, explaining they were uncertain about how to solve the division problems when thinking about brownies. They had chosen five for their dividend. As before, I asked the girls to interpret the first problem using the context of brownies. Emily explained, "There are five brownies and only one person to share them."

"How do you know?" I asked.

Emily referred to the problems listed on the board, then explained, "Well, the dividend tells how many there are to share and the divisor tells how many people have to share." Both Wendi and I nodded our agreement with Emily.

Wendi thought hard, then came to life. "I know! The numerator tells how many to share and the denominator tells how many people. I get it!"

"Oh! So the fraction answer for the first problem would be five on top and one on the bottom," Emily said as she wrote this on her paper.

"What about the second problem?" I asked.

Wendi explained, "There are five brownies and two people share them. So it's five halves, or five over two."

While Wendi was talking, Emily quickly drew five brownies, then stopped. I said, "Tell us about what you're doing and thinking."

"I wanted to draw a picture, but I'm not sure what to do next," Emily explained.

I said, "Wendi's answer says each person gets five halves. How could you show this with your picture?"

"Divide the brownies in half?" Emily said with hesitation.

"Try it and see what happens," I encouraged. Emily quickly divided each brownie into halves as Wendi and I watched. Then she counted the halves and commented there were ten halves, which meant each of two people would get five of the ten halves.

After fifteen minutes or so, most students were finishing their first number and beginning a second exploration. I asked the students who completed the task correctly to list their work on the board for a class discussion. The lists appeared as follows.

	Markers	Brownies		Markers	Brownies
$2 \div 1 =$	2	2	$3 \div 1 =$	3	3
$2 \div 2 =$	1	1	$3 \div 2 =$	1 R1	$\frac{3}{2}$ $(1\frac{1}{2})$
$2 \div 3 =$	0 R2	$\frac{2}{3}$	$3 \div 3 =$	1	1
$2 \div 4 =$	0 R2	$\frac{2}{4}$	$3 \div 4 =$	0 R3	$\frac{3}{4}$
$2 \div 5 =$	0 R2	$\frac{2}{5}$	$3 \div 5 =$	0 R3	$\frac{3}{5}$
$2 \div 6 =$	0 R2	$\frac{2}{6}$	$3 \div 6 =$	0 R3	$\frac{3}{6}$
$2 \div 7 =$	0 R2	$\frac{2}{7}$	$3 \div 7 =$	0 R3	$\frac{3}{7}$
$2 \div 8 =$	0 R2	$\frac{2}{8}$	$3 \div 8 =$	0 R3	$\frac{3}{8}$
$2 \div 9 =$	0 R2	$\frac{2}{9}$	$3 \div 9 =$	0 R3	$\frac{3}{9}$
$2 \div 10 =$	0 R2	$\frac{2}{10}$	$3 \div 10 =$	0 R3	$\frac{3}{10}$

	Markers	Brownies		Markers	Brownies
$4 \div 1 =$	4	4	$5 \div 1 =$	5	5
$4 \div 2 =$	2	2	$5 \div 2 =$	2 R1	$\frac{5}{2}$ $(2\frac{1}{2})$
$4 \div 3 =$	1 R1	$\frac{4}{3}$ $(1\frac{1}{3})$	$5 \div 3 =$	1 R2	$\frac{5}{3}$ $(1\frac{2}{3})$
$4 \div 4 =$	1	1	$5 \div 4 =$	1 R1	$\frac{5}{4}$ $(1\frac{1}{4})$
$4 \div 5 =$	0 R4	$\frac{4}{5}$	$5 \div 5 =$	1	1
$4 \div 6 =$	0 R4	$\frac{4}{6}$	$5 \div 6 =$	0 R5	$\frac{5}{6}$
$4 \div 7 =$	0 R4	$\frac{4}{7}$	$5 \div 7 =$	0 R5	$\frac{5}{7}$
$4 \div 8 =$	0 R4	$\frac{4}{8}$	$5 \div 8 =$	0 R5	$\frac{5}{8}$
$4 \div 9 =$	0 R4	$\frac{4}{9}$	$5 \div 9 =$	0 R5	$\frac{5}{9}$
$4 \div 10 =$	0 R4	$\frac{4}{10}$	$5 \div 10 =$	0 R5	$\frac{5}{10}$

	Markers	Brownies			Markers	Brownies
$6 \div 1 =$	6	6		$7 \div 1 =$	7	7
$6 \div 2 =$	3	3		$7 \div 2 =$	3 R1	$\frac{7}{2}$ $(3\frac{1}{2})$
$6 \div 3 =$	2	2		$7 \div 3 =$	2 R1	$\frac{7}{3}$ $(2\frac{1}{3})$
$6 \div 4 =$	1 R2	$\frac{6}{4}$ $(1\frac{2}{4})$		$7 \div 4 =$	1 R3	$\frac{7}{4}$ $(1\frac{3}{4})$
$6 \div 5 =$	1 R1	$\frac{6}{5}$ $(1\frac{1}{5})$		$7 \div 5 =$	1 R2	$\frac{7}{5}$ $(1\frac{2}{5})$
$6 \div 6 =$	1	1		$7 \div 6 =$	1 R1	$\frac{7}{6}$ $(1\frac{1}{6})$
$6 \div 7 =$	0 R6	$\frac{6}{7}$		$7 \div 7 =$	1	1
$6 \div 8 =$	0 R6	$\frac{6}{8}$		$7 \div 8 =$	0 R7	$\frac{7}{8}$
$6 \div 9 =$	0 R6	$\frac{6}{9}$		$7 \div 9 =$	0 R7	$\frac{7}{9}$
$6 \div 10 =$	0 R6	$\frac{6}{10}$		$7 \div 10 =$	0 R7	$\frac{7}{10}$

	Markers	Brownies			Markers	Brownies
$8 \div 1 =$	8	8		$9 \div 1 =$	9	9
$8 \div 2 =$	4	4		$9 \div 2 =$	4 R1	$\frac{9}{2}$ $(4\frac{1}{2})$
$8 \div 3 =$	2 R2	$\frac{8}{3}$ $(2\frac{2}{3})$		$9 \div 3 =$	3	3
$8 \div 4 =$	2	2		$9 \div 4 =$	2 R1	$\frac{9}{4}$ $(2\frac{1}{4})$
$8 \div 5 =$	1 R3	$\frac{8}{5}$ $(1\frac{3}{5})$		$9 \div 5 =$	1 R4	$\frac{9}{5}$ $(1\frac{4}{5})$
$8 \div 6 =$	1 R2	$\frac{8}{6}$ $(1\frac{2}{6})$		$9 \div 6 =$	1 R3	$\frac{9}{6}$ $(1\frac{3}{6})$
$8 \div 7 =$	1 R1	$\frac{8}{7}$ $(1\frac{1}{7})$		$9 \div 7 =$	1 R2	$\frac{9}{7}$ $(1\frac{2}{7})$
$8 \div 8 =$	1	1		$9 \div 8 =$	1 R1	$\frac{9}{8}$ $(1\frac{1}{8})$
$8 \div 9 =$	0 R8	$\frac{8}{9}$		$9 \div 9 =$	1	1
$8 \div 10 =$	0 R8	$\frac{8}{10}$		$9 \div 10 =$	0 R9	$\frac{9}{10}$

	Markers	Brownies
$10 \div 1 =$	10	10
$10 \div 2 =$	5	5
$10 \div 3 =$	3 R1	$\frac{10}{3}$ $(3\frac{1}{3})$
$10 \div 4 =$	2 R2	$\frac{10}{4}$ $(2\frac{2}{4})$
$10 \div 5 =$	2	2
$10 \div 6 =$	1 R4	$\frac{10}{6}$ $(1\frac{4}{6})$
$10 \div 7 =$	1 R3	$\frac{10}{7}$ $(1\frac{3}{7})$
$10 \div 8 =$	1 R2	$\frac{10}{8}$ $(1\frac{2}{8})$
$10 \div 9 =$	1 R1	$\frac{10}{9}$ $(1\frac{1}{9})$
$10 \div 10 =$	1	1

A Class Discussion

I asked the students to bring their papers and sit on the floor where they could see the work that had been written on the board a few minutes earlier. As the students settled, I reminded them to put their papers on the floor in front of them. This allows students visual access to their work while reducing distractions and the noise from rustling papers.

To begin the conversation, I asked students what they noticed about the problems on the board. After a few moments, hands began to go up. I called on Brianna.

"In all the groups of problems, the divisors always go up by one," she shared.

Latonya shared next. "Cassi and I did threes and tens. We noticed that when the divisor and dividend were the same, the answer was one. Then after that, when the divisors got bigger and the dividend stayed the same, for the markers the quotient was always zero with a remainder."

I said to the other students, "Look at your papers. Does the information on your paper match Latonya and Cassi's? That is, is the quotient one when the dividend and divisor are the same? Show me with your thumb if you agree, disagree, or aren't sure." The students studied their papers for a few moments and thumbs then went up. Samir waved his hand madly in the air.

"Hey, I think the other part of what Latonya said is right, too. In all the groups of problems on the board and on my paper, after the problem with the dividend and divisor being equal, the quotient becomes zero and the remainder matches the first number."

"What do you call the first number?" I asked Samir.

"Um, it's the dividend," he said. I nodded.

"That's the way it is on my paper and Jacinto's," Miguel added.

"How many notice this pattern on your papers?" I asked. Again thumbs went up

quickly as students checked their work. "Why do you think this happens?" I asked. "Talk with your partner. One of you speaks for thirty seconds while the other listens. At the end of thirty seconds, I'll give you a signal to switch roles so that the first listener gets to speak and the first speaker gets to listen. Remember, no interruptions." The students began sharing their ideas. After thirty seconds, I reminded the students to switch roles. At the end of another thirty seconds, I asked for the students' attention. Hands were up immediately.

Jael explained, "I think it's because there isn't enough for each group to get one, so all the ones you started with, which is the dividend, become leftovers." Several students nodded their agreement.

"I think whenever the divisor is bigger than the dividend, the quotient is zero because there isn't enough for each person," Dennie said.

"I think I just said that," Jael said sarcastically.

I intervened. "I do think you both stated the same idea, although you used different words. That's OK. Sometimes restating an idea in one's own words helps a person understand more clearly. Also, sometimes different words make sense to different people. Saying the same idea in more than one way is a good thing."

To change the direction of the discussion, I asked, "What do you notice about the quotients from here down?" I pointed to the quotients for the problems with dividends of three and divisors greater than three.

"They're all the same," the students chorused.

Jewell added, "That's true when the dividends are the same and the divisors are bigger. It works for dividends of five and six and all of them."

"But what if it was brownies or cookies or something like that?" Miguel asked.

"We haven't talked about that part of our information yet," I replied to Miguel. "What do you notice about the information when we thought about these problems as if we were dividing brownies?"

Alycia raised her hand. She said, "I notice that with the fractions, the numerator is the same as the dividend and the denominator is the same as the divisor."

Pesach commented, "When we were working on our paper, we kind of kept getting confused when we tried to divide brownies and got fractions. We had a hard time remembering where the numbers went. We weren't sure if the number of people sharing or the number of brownies went on top of the fraction."

Dennie explained, "We sort of had trouble with that, too. Then we looked on the board at one divided by two and remembered that meant there was one brownie for two people to share, and each got one-half. How many brownies you have to share goes on the top of the fraction and how many people sharing goes on the bottom of the fraction."

Jamal added, "I think you have to really think about what you're doing before you choose which answer to use. That's what I think. And what answer you choose has to do with what you can break apart and what you can't." Most students nodded their agreement.

Eduardo raised hand and shared, "I think because we did this I really understand better what the numbers mean in a division problem. I didn't really get that before."

Dennie added, "The same thing Eduardo just said, and I think I get what the numbers in fractions mean and I'm sort of getting how fractions are another way to say division."

"I didn't really think you could do problems like three divided by nine until now," Abbie said.

There were no more comments, so I ended the lesson there.

Questions and Discussion

▲ *Some students were confused about* **dividend** *and* **divisor** *and what they mean in a division problem. Why didn't you teach this before beginning the lesson?*

I did not specifically teach the meaning of *dividend* and *divisor* before beginning the lesson because I knew that struggling to make sense of these ideas within the context of the lesson would deepen students' understanding. The lesson gave them a reason to carefully consider the meaning of the numbers and a way to understand and remember.

▲ *During the class work time you spent time listening to students explain their incorrect answers. Wouldn't it have been more efficient to tell them their answers were wrong and why?*

Perhaps in terms of saving time at that particular moment, it would have been more efficient. However, I don't think this is so in the long run. Rarely do people learn by being told. Simply telling a child that an answer is wrong and why when there is an opportunity for the child to discover this herself deprives that child of the opportunity to learn on her own. Having a student explain her solution is a way for both of us to gain insight into errors. Often as a child explains, the error becomes apparent to her. The child gains new understanding and is able to make the correction and move on. As a result, the child is more likely to remember and learn from the error. Additionally, this process builds confidence in that child.

▲ *Won't children become confused when they write answers to division problems both with whole number remainders and with fractions?*

Confusion often results when children have no context for thinking about a problem. Providing students with contexts to which they can easily relate, such as markers and brownies, gives them a way to think about the problems and also a way to verify their thinking. The students had markers, crayons, and color pencils readily available to them, and they could draw brownies to help them consider reasonable answers.

If you feel your students might become too confused by exploring both contexts for these problems in one day, present the investigation to them on one day using the context of markers, then on the next day, present the lesson using brownies as a context. Finally, lead a class discussion focusing on the importance of the context when representing an answer either as a quotient with a whole number remainder or as a fraction.

CHAPTER SIX
THE QUOTIENT STAYS THE SAME

Overview

In this chapter, students use the lists of division problems from the lesson in Chapter 2, "The Divisor Stays the Same," to search for division problems with the same quotient. They explore the relationships between different dividends and divisors that produce the same quotient. For this lesson, students focus on quotients represented with whole number remainders. Later, students figure out, share, and compare division problems that result in the same quotient.

Materials

▲ class chart from *The Divisor Stays the Same*

Time

▲ one class period; lesson can be repeated multiple times for other quotients (see "Extensions")

Teaching Directions

1. Using the chart from *The Divisor Stays the Same,* ask students to find different division problems with quotients that are the same. For example, a quotient of one, two, one remainder one, and so on.

2. Write on the board *quotient of 1*. Ask students to report different division problems with the quotient of one and list them on the board. Lead a class discussion by asking: "What do you notice about the dividends and divisors when the quotient is one?"

3. Repeat Step 2 for problems with a quotient of two.

4. Repeat Step 2 for problems with a quotient of one remainder one.

5. Have students work in pairs to write division problems resulting in a quotient of one remainder one. For students who finish early, suggest a second, challenge problem: *List problems with a quotient of two remainder one.* Next, have students share with the class their problems with a quotient of one remainder one. List on a chart the problems shared. Encourage students to add to the list as they think of other division problems that have a quotient of one remainder one.

Teaching Notes

Before teaching this lesson, be sure to teach the lesson in Chapter 2, "The Divisor Stays the Same." The chart from that lesson along with the experience and understanding that students gain are important prerequisites of this lesson.

In this lesson, the focus is on representing and interpreting remainders as whole numbers rather than as fractions or decimals. It helps to think about division in contexts to explore the difference. If we think about sharing four markers among three people, for example, we can represent that as $4 \div 3 = 1$ R1 and interpret that as each person gets one marker and there is one marker left over. Sharing five markers among four people results in the same answer: each gets one marker and there is one left over, or $5 \div 4 = 1$R1. The same answer holds for $3 \div 2$, sharing three markers between two people.

However, if we think about division in the context of sharing cookies, we can represent the remainders in the quotients as fractions, and the answer to each of the three problems—$4 \div 3$, $5 \div 4$, and $3 \div 2$—is different. Four cookies shared among three people is one and one-third cookies per person: $4 \div 3 = 1\frac{1}{3}$. Five cookies divided among four people is one and one-fourth cookies per person: $5 \div 4 = 1\frac{1}{4}$. Three cookies shared between two people is one and one-half cookies per person: $3 \div 2 = 1\frac{1}{2}$. When sharing something that can be broken apart, such as cookies, the answers are different.

In this lesson, the focus is on the quotient and how to keep it constant. Representing the remainder as a whole number helps students more easily see relationships between divisors and dividends. In order for a quotient to be larger than 1, the dividend must be larger than the divisor. More specifically, problems with a quotient of 1 R1 must have a divisor that is one less than the dividend. For example, $5 \div 4 = 1$ R1, $9 \div 8 = 1$ R1, and so on. If a quotient is exactly 1, then the divisor and dividend must be the same. For example, $5 \div 5 = 1$, $9 \div 9 = 1$, and so on. If a quotient is 2, the dividend must be twice the divisor. For example, $10 \div 5 = 2$, $18 \div 9 = 2$, and so on. If a quotient is 2 R3, then the dividend must be two times the divisor plus three. For example, $13 \div 5 = 2$ R3, $21 \div 9 = 2$ R3, and so on. This lesson helps students understand that for any quotient, there are many possible division problems.

The Lesson

▲▲▲

Before class I posted the following chart from the lesson *The Divisor Stays the Same*.

$1 \div 2 = 0\ R1$	$1 \div 3 = 0\ R1$	$1 \div 4 = 0\ R1$
$2 \div 2 = 1$	$2 \div 3 = 0\ R2$	$2 \div 4 = 0\ R2$
$3 \div 2 = 1\ R1$	$3 \div 3 = 1$	$3 \div 4 = 0\ R3$
$4 \div 2 = 2$	$4 \div 3 = 1\ R1$	$4 \div 4 = 1$
$5 \div 2 = 2\ R1$	$5 \div 3 = 1\ R2$	$5 \div 4 = 1\ R1$
$6 \div 2 = 3$	$6 \div 3 = 2$	$6 \div 4 = 1\ R2$
$7 \div 2 = 3\ R1$	$7 \div 3 = 2\ R1$	$7 \div 4 = 1\ R3$
$8 \div 2 = 4$	$8 \div 3 = 2\ R2$	$8 \div 4 = 2$
$9 \div 2 = 4\ R1$	$9 \div 3 = 3$	$9 \div 4 = 2\ R1$
$10 \div 2 = 5$	$10 \div 3 = 3\ R1$	$10 \div 4 = 2\ R2$
$11 \div 2 = 5\ R1$	$11 \div 3 = 3\ R2$	$11 \div 4 = 2\ R3$
$12 \div 2 = 6$	$12 \div 3 = 4$	$12 \div 4 = 3$
$13 \div 2 = 6\ R1$	$13 \div 3 = 4\ R1$	$13 \div 4 = 3\ R1$
$14 \div 2 = 7$	$14 \div 3 = 4\ R2$	$14 \div 4 = 3\ R2$
$15 \div 2 = 7\ R1$	$15 \div 3 = 5$	$15 \div 4 = 3\ R3$

I asked the students to sit on the floor so they could easily see the chart. As they settled, Tanya commented, "I bet we're going to look for more patterns."

"I wonder what kind this time?" Arianna replied to Tanya. Both girls shrugged.

I asked for the students' attention. I began by saying, "I'm sure you recognize the chart I've posted."

"It's the chart from a couple of weeks ago," Jarrell responded.

"You're right, Jarrell," I said. "Today we're going to revisit the chart. This time we're going to look for division problems that result in the same quotient. Please take a few moments to study the chart quietly and look for quotients that appear more than once." I paused to give students time to study the chart. After a few moments, I continued. "Please talk with your neighbor about the division problems you found that have the same quotients and talk about what you think causes different problems to have the same answer." The room erupted in animated conversations as students shared and discussed ideas. As the students talked, I listened in on various conversations. After several minutes, I called the class to order.

I asked, "Did anyone find two or more division problems with a quotient of one?" Hands leaped into the air. I called on Ada.

She said, "Three divided by three has a quotient of one, and so does four divided by four."

"Why does that make sense?" I asked Ada.

Ada explained, "Well, in the problem three divided by three, that means 'How many threes in three?' There's one group of three in three. It's the same thing with four divided by four. There's one group of four in four." Several students nodded, indicating their agreement.

On the board I wrote *Quotient of 1* and listed Ada's suggestions beneath it.

Quotient of 1

$3 \div 3 = 1$

$4 \div 4 = 1$

Nori added, "There's another one that has a quotient of one. It's two divided by two." The students indicated their agreement by showing thumbs up. I added $2 \div 2 = 1$ to the list.

I asked, "What do you notice that's the same about these problems?" I paused a moment to give students time to consider my question. Hands began to go up.

Jadon shared, "One thing that I notice about the dividend and divisor is that they're the same in each problem."

"I think that means that there are the same number of things to be divided as there are groups," Derrek added.

"Or it could be that there's one group of that number, like three divided by three could mean one group of three in three," Dana explained.

I responded, "I agree with both interpretations of the problem. Based on what you've shared, can you predict what other division problems could be included in the list?"

Josie said, "Five divided by five."

I said to the other students, "If you agree that five divided by five belongs on the list, put your thumb up; if you disagree, put your thumb down; and if you're not sure, put your thumb sideways." All thumbs were up. I added to the list $5 \div 5 = 1$. "Who would like to explain why five divided by five belongs on the list?"

Thomas explained, "It's like the other problems on the list because the dividend and divisor are the same. Also, if you have five things to divide among five people, then each person will get one thing. The answer is one."

Dana said, "You could also think of it as putting cookies into groups of five and how many groups of five are in five? There's one group of five in five." I nodded my agreement with Dana's thinking. If Dana or another student hadn't pointed this out, I would have done so to remind the class about the other interpretation of division.

"I know another problem," Rasheeka said with a sly smile. I nodded to encourage Rasheeka to go on. "Ten million, one hundred fifty-two thousand, five hundred ten divided by ten million, one hundred fifty-two thousand, five hundred ten. They're big numbers, but they're the same, so that means when you divide them, the answer will be one." The rest of the class giggled at Rasheeka's large number, then put their thumbs up to show their agreement with her idea. I asked Rasheeka to tell me how to write such a large number. As she did so, I recorded her problem on the list of division problems with a quotient of one. I called on two more students to suggest

problems to add to the list. The rest of the students indicated their agreement with thumbs up. I added the suggestions to the list:

Quotient of 1

$3 \div 3 = 1$

$4 \div 4 = 1$

$2 \div 2 = 1$

$5 \div 5 = 1$

$10,152,510 \div 10,152,510 = 1$

$25 \div 25 = 1$

$963 \div 963 = 1$

I then wrote *Quotient of 2* on the board next to the first list and said, "Are there different division problems on the chart that have a quotient of two?" Again hands shot into the air.

"Four divided by two has a quotient of two," Becky said. "So does six divided by three. I know because two times two equals four and three times two equals six."

"There's also eight divided by four," Cameron added. I recorded these suggestions on the board as follows:

Quotient of 2

$4 \div 2 = 2$

$6 \div 3 = 2$

$8 \div 4 = 2$

"I know why that happens," Amelie said with excitement. "It's easy once you get it. One of the numbers is twice as big as the other."

"Which number is bigger?" I asked.

"I think it's the dividend," Amelie said.

"Hey, that's right!" Jarrell replied along with a few others. I nodded my agreement.

"What's another problem that could go on our list of division problems with a quotient of two?" I asked.

"Ten divided by five," Naomi suggested. "I know because if I count by fives to ten, there are two fives in ten." The students showed their agreement with Naomi's idea with their thumbs. I added her division problem to the list.

"How about fifty divided by twenty-five?" Bo volunteered.

"Why do you think your problem belongs on the list of division problems with a quotient of two?" I asked.

Bo explained, "If you think of it as money, there are two quarters in fifty cents. One quarter is half of fifty cents, so there are two quarters, or two groups of twenty-five cents, in fifty."

Brooke added, "Just multiply two times twenty-five and it equals fifty."

The students gave a thumbs-up to Bo's suggestion and I added it to the list.

Several other students shared problems to add to the list along with their justification for why each problem should be included.

Quotient of 2

$4 \div 2 = 2$

$6 \div 3 = 2$

$8 \div 4 = 2$

$10 \div 5 = 2$

$50 \div 25 = 2$

$100 \div 50 = 2$

$40 \div 20 = 2$

$80 \div 40 = 2$

I then posed a new challenge. "Find different division problems with a quotient of one remainder one." The students talked among themselves for a few moments and then hands went up.

Tanya was excited to share what she noticed. She began, "I don't quite know why this works yet, but I did find two problems with an answer of one remainder one. One problem is four divided by three and the other is five divided by four. Both of them have the answer one remainder one. I think that's amazing!"

I recorded Tanya's idea on the board as follows:

Quotient of 1 R1

$4 \div 3 = 1 R1$

$5 \div 4 = 1 R1$

Ada said, "I notice something about the problems Tanya shared. The first number goes up by one each time and so does the second number."

I asked Ada, "What do you call the first numbers?" She shrugged. I pointed to the labels on the chart.

"Oh yeah," she said, "the first numbers are the dividends and the second ones are the divisors. The dividends are getting bigger by one and so are the divisors."

Kumar said, "I agree with what Ada said, but I don't think that's why it works. The problems could have been listed in a different order, and then the pattern she sees wouldn't be there." I rewrote the problems in reverse order for those students who needed visual evidence to understand what Kumar was saying.

"Oh yeah, I didn't think of that," Ada said.

If Kumar hadn't pointed this out, I would have done so. There were no other comments, so I asked, "Are there any other problems on the chart we can put on the list of quotients of one remainder one?"

"Three divided by two," several students replied. I added this problem to the list.

Quotient of 1 R1

$4 \div 3 = 1 R1$

$5 \div 4 = 1 R1$

$3 \div 2 = 1 R1$

"Does this new problem help you see anything new?" I asked the students. "Remember to consider both the dividend and the divisor to help you figure out what is going on to produce a quotient of one remainder one." Several hands went up. When about half the students had their hands up, I called on Arianna.

She explained, "I think I figured it out! The dividend is one bigger than the divisor. For example, four is one bigger than three, and five is one bigger than four, and three is one bigger than two." Most students nodded their agreement with what Arianna noticed.

I responded, "I agree that the dividends are one larger than the divisors. Why does this result in a quotient that is one remainder one?"

Thomas explained, "In the first problem, it could mean you have four of something to share with three people. Each person would get one thing and there would be one of those things left over. That means the answer is one remainder one."

"Does that mean anytime the dividend is one bigger than the divisor, the answer is automatically one remainder one?" Juan said with surprise and uncertainty. He continued, "Yeah, I think it is! Ten divided by nine would be one remainder one, and twenty divided by nineteen is one remainder one. Wow! That's cool. All I have to do is find a bunch of problems like that and I already know the answer!"

I asked the students, "What's another problem that could go on the list?" Most hands went up quickly.

Nori shared, "Eleven divided by ten. There is one group of ten in eleven and there's one left. That's one remainder one." The class agreed and I added Nori's idea to the list.

Rasheeka had another idea. "I think thirty-six divided by thirty-five would work. If I brought thirty-six cupcakes for my birthday and there were thirty-five kids here, that would be one for each kid and one left over." I added Rasheeka's suggestion to the list.

Quotient of 1 R1

$4 \div 3 = 1 R1$

$5 \div 4 = 1 R1$

$3 \div 2 = 1 R1$

$11 \div 10 = 1 R1$

$36 \div 35 = 1 R1$

I said, "You all have ideas to share about problems that would result in quotients of one remainder one. I'd like you to work with your partner and list at least three division problems that have quotients of one remainder one."

"Do we need our own paper or can we share?" Kevin asked.

I replied, "You may share one sheet, but make sure both of you have ideas on the paper." There were no more questions and the students got to work.

OBSERVING THE STUDENTS

The students worked quickly and eagerly. The previous class discussion had provided good support for success with this experience. For those students that completed the assignment quickly and accurately, I assigned a second, challenge problem: *List at least three division problems with quotients of two remainder one.* Most students were quick to use the ideas we'd discussed to recognize that the dividend would have to be two times the divisor plus one for a quotient of two remainder one. After five minutes or so, I asked for the students' attention.

A CLASS DISCUSSION

I began by saying, "Share the division problems you created with quotients of one remainder one with your group. Then as a table group, decide on one problem to share with the class. Don't worry if your problem doesn't get chosen because after class, I'll copy onto a sheet of chart paper all the problems you've written on your papers with one remainder one as a quotient. If you think of more problems after today, you may continue to add them to the list." I gave the table groups a couple of moments to share and choose their problems, then called for the students' attention. I went around the class, asking a student from each table group to share a problem. As each student shared, I recorded the problem on the list and then I asked the others to indicate whether they agreed that the quotient for the problem was one remainder one.

Then I asked, "Should one hundred divided by ninety-nine be on the list?" All thumbs were up. "What about ninety-nine divided by one hundred?" The students were much less confident about this question. To help them think about the problem, I put it in a context: "I have ninety-nine pencils and one hundred students. How many pencils will each student get?"

"None," the students chorused.

"Why not?" I asked.

Jarrell explained, "There's one more pencil than people . . . no wait, that's not right! Oh, I don't know." Jarrell's confusion is not uncommon, which is why I raised the question. I wanted to give the students the opportunity to make sense of the situation.

To help Jarrell, and others who were also confused, I said, "In the situation I described, I said I had ninety-nine pencils and one hundred people. The ninety-nine is the dividend and it tells how many things to be divided. The one hundred people tells us that the pencils must be divided equally among all those people."

Jarrell commented, "That would be hard because there aren't enough pencils for everyone to get one unless you break them up."

I asked, "So how many pencils will each person get?"

Jeb replied, "Zero, and all ninety-nine would be leftovers."

"That's weird," Bo added.

I said to the class, "In order to get a quotient of one remainder one, it's important to consider which number, the dividend or the divisor, is bigger. Ninety-nine divided by one hundred doesn't belong on the list." I knew some students were clear

about this point while others were still uncertain. I decided to move on, knowing that they would have additional opportunities to explore this idea.

Amelie said, "I don't exactly get why so many problems can have the same answer, but it's cool."

Tanya responded, "With the quotient one remainder one, it really means that the dividend is one more than the divisor. The whole amount is one more than the group size or the number of groups. I think there's an endless amount of problems with the answer one remainder one." The students were quiet as they considered what Tanya said along with their own thoughts. Math time was up. I collected the students' papers to later record on chart paper their problems with a quotient of one remainder one. (See Figures 6–1 through 6–3.)

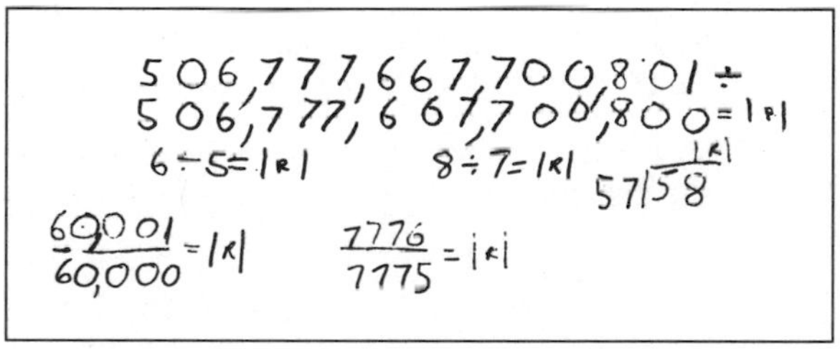

▲▲▲▲▲▲**Figure 6–1** *Rasheeka's understanding of the relationship between the dividend and divisor to produce a quotient of 1 R1 was apparent in her use of both large and small numbers.*

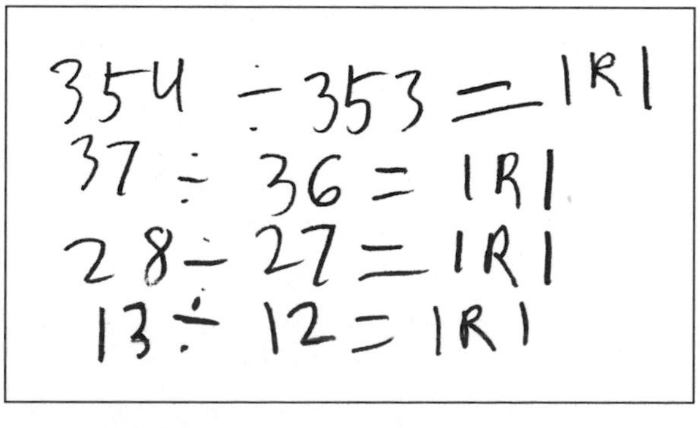

▲▲▲▲▲▲**Figure 6–2** *Becky's work was typical of many students.*

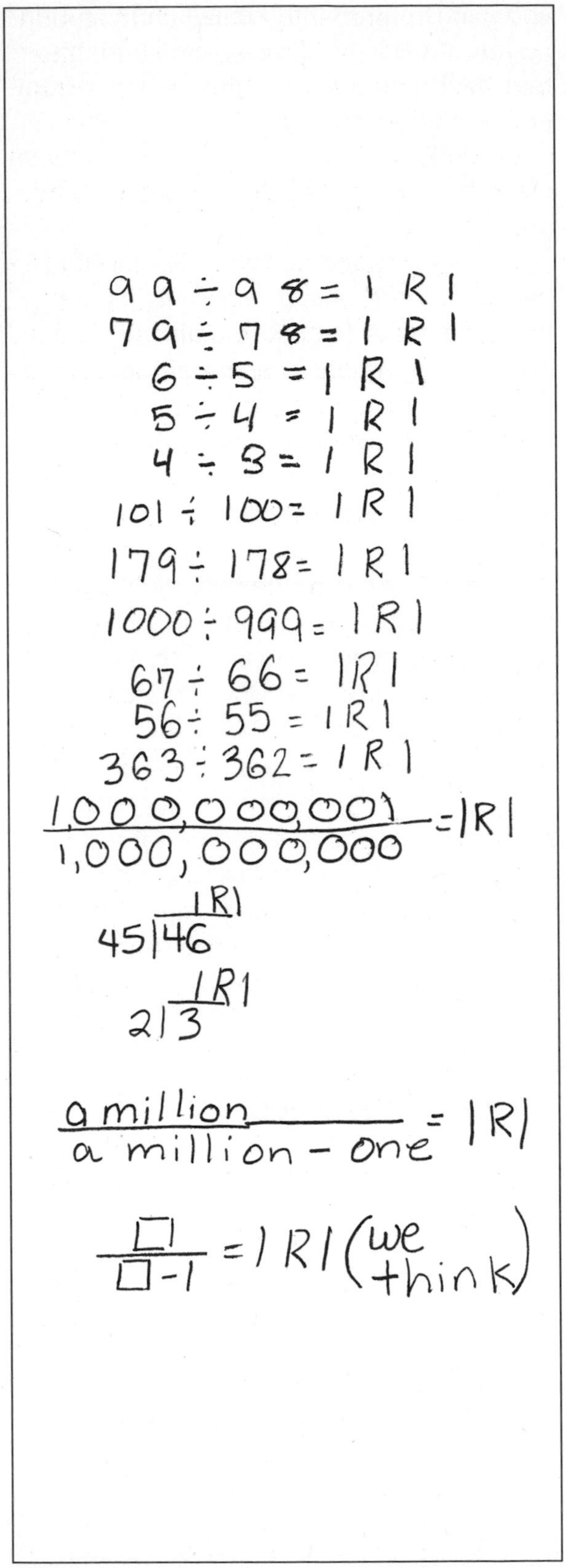

$$99 \div 98 = 1 \; R \; 1$$
$$79 \div 78 = 1 \; R \; 1$$
$$6 \div 5 = 1 \; R \; 1$$
$$5 \div 4 = 1 \; R \; 1$$
$$4 \div 3 = 1 \; R \; 1$$
$$101 \div 100 = 1 \; R \; 1$$
$$179 \div 178 = 1 \; R \; 1$$
$$1000 \div 999 = 1 \; R \; 1$$
$$67 \div 66 = 1 \; R \; 1$$
$$56 \div 55 = 1 \; R \; 1$$
$$363 \div 362 = 1 \; R \; 1$$
$$\frac{1,000,000,001}{1,000,000,000} = 1 \; R \; 1$$
$$45 \overline{)46} = 1 \; R \; 1$$
$$2 \overline{)3} = 1 \; R \; 1$$

$$\frac{a \; million}{a \; million - one} = 1 \; R \; 1$$

$$\frac{\square}{\square - 1} = 1 \; R \; 1 \; \left(\begin{array}{c} we \\ think \end{array} \right)$$

▲▲▲▲▲▲Figure 6–3 *The openness of the assignment allowed Juan to explore a variety of problems, including representing his understanding algebraically.*

EXTENSIONS

This same activity can be repeated many times spread out over several weeks or even throughout the year. Each time, present a different quotient. Ask students to figure out the relationship between the dividend and divisor that produces that quotient, and then have them generate division problems with that quotient. Figures 6–4 through 6–6 show three students' work on this activity.

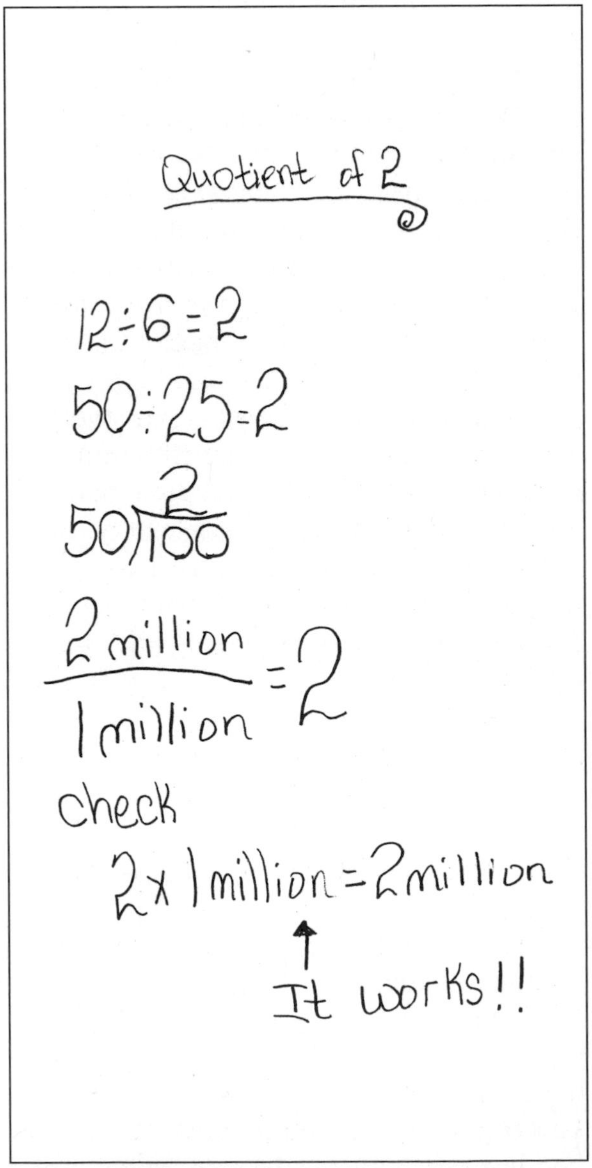

Quotient of 2

$$12 \div 6 = 2$$
$$50 \div 25 = 2$$
$$50 \overline{)100} = 2$$

$$\frac{2 \; million}{1 \; million} = 2$$

check
$$2 \times 1 \; million = 2 \; million$$

It works!!

▲▲▲▲▲▲Figure 6–4 *Derrek showed an understanding of how to get a quotient of 2.*

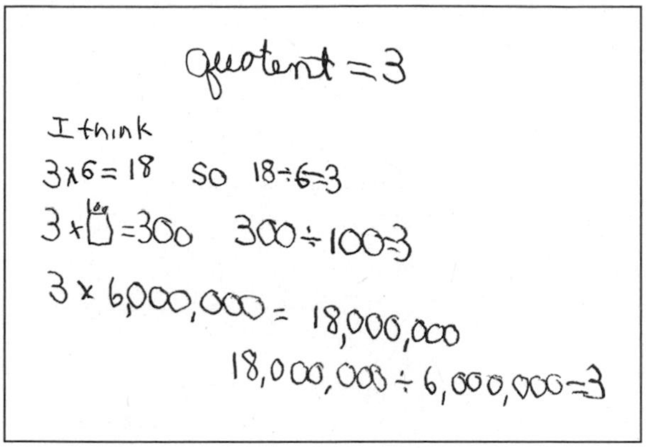

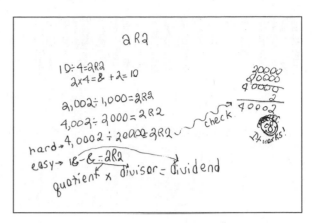

quotient = 3

I think

3 × 6 = 18   So   18 ÷ 6 = 3

3 × □ = 300   300 ÷ 100 = 3

3 × 6,000,000 = 18,000,000

18,000,000 ÷ 6,000,000 = 3

▲▲▲▲▲▲**Figure 6–5** *Brooke used multiplication to help her complete the assignment for quotients of 3.*

2 R 2

10 ÷ 4 = 2 R 2
2 × 4 = 8 + 2 = 10

2,002 ÷ 1,000 = 2 R 2

4,002 ÷ 2,000 = 2 R 2

hard → 4,0002 ÷ 20000 = 2 R 2 ✓ ← check

easy → 16 ÷ 8 = 2 R 2

quotient × divisor = dividend

20000
80000
40000
          2
       40002

It works!

▲▲▲▲▲▲**Figure 6–6** *Amelie proved two of her problems using multiplication.*

Questions and Discussion

▲▲▲

▲ *Some of the topics discussed in this lesson have come up before in some of the other lessons. Why is it worthwhile for my students to do this lesson as well as the others?*

While many of the ideas explored and discussed in this lesson are brought up in other lessons as well, this lesson focuses students' attention specifically on the relationship between dividends and divisors that create like quotients. Multiple opportunities to explore ideas increase the chances that students will learn and understand a concept or idea. Those who already understand deepen that understanding each time they encounter the same idea.

CHAPTER SEVEN
EXPLORING DIVISIBILITY RULES FOR TWO, FIVE, AND TEN

Overview

In this lesson, students generate lists of multiples for two, five, and ten and learn that all multiples of a number are divisible by the number, thus strengthening their understanding of the relationship between multiplication and division. To begin, students generate a list of multiples for two and search the list for patterns. In a class discussion, students share the patterns they notice and generalize a divisibility rule to use to test other possible multiples of two not already listed. This same process is repeated for multiples of five and ten.

Materials

▲ chart paper

Time

▲ two class periods

Teaching Directions

1. Begin by writing on the board:

Divisible by 2

Multiples of 2

2. Ask students to suggest numbers that belong on the list. Record their suggestions. If students are unable to make appropriate suggestions, help them get started by listing the first three or four multiples of two. Ask students what they notice about the numbers on the list. (All the numbers are even.)

3. With the help of the students, continue to list the multiples of two in sequential order from 0 to 30.

4. Ask students: "What patterns do you notice?" Record their ideas on the board. Have students suggest additional numbers to add to the list. Then suggest numbers to students and ask if they belong on the list. For example, seventy-seven, ninety-nine, and forty-two. Students should explain their reasoning about why a number does or does not belong on the list. Next ask: "What rule were you using when you suggested numbers?" Help students generalize the patterns and rules they used to suggest numbers into a rule for divisibility by two. Record the divisibility rule for two.

5. Copy onto chart paper the list of multiples of two and the rule for divisibility by two to serve as a reference during other divisibility rule lessons.

6. On another day, to introduce the divisibility rules for five and ten, repeat Steps 1 through 5 twice, first for five and then for ten.

7. For a class discussion, ask questions such as "How are the lists of multiples alike? Different?" and "How are the divisibility rules for five and ten alike? How are they different?"

Teaching Notes

The focus of this lesson is to build students' understanding of the close link between multiples and divisibility. Students learn that numbers that are multiples of a number are also divisible by that number. For example, eight is a multiple of two, and eight is also divisible by two. They also learn that when you divide a number by another, and there is no remainder, then the first number is said to be divisible by the second. For example, twelve divided by six is two with no remainder; therefore, twelve is divisible by six.

Students generate lists of multiples of two, five, and ten and then search the lists for patterns. They use the information from the lists to help them generalize rules of divisibility. Because multiples and divisibility are so closely connected, the words *multiple* and *divisible* are used interchangeably throughout the lesson.

The divisibility rules used in the following vignette are as follows:

Divisibility by two: A number is divisible by 2 if it is even. Or, a number is divisible by 2 if it has a 0, 2, 4, 6, or 8 in the ones place. Examples: 34, 56, and 342.

Divisibility by five: A number is divisible by 5 if it has a 0 or a 5 in the ones place. Examples: 15, 60, 475.

Divisibility by ten: A number is divisible by 10 if it has a 0 in the ones place. Examples: 10, 210, 3,030.

This lesson is the first in a sequence of three lessons about exploring divisibility. The other two lessons follow in Chapters 8 and 9. The lessons were taught in the order they appear; however, this is not necessary, nor is it necessary to present them on consecutive days.

The Lesson

▲▲▲

DAY 1

Divisibility by Two

As the students settled, I wrote on the board:

Divisible by 2

Multiples of 2

"Who would like to give me an example of a number I could write on a list with this title?" I asked, pointing to what I'd just written. "The number should be divisible by two and should also be a multiple of two."

Katie said, "I think that six works. Two times three is six, so six is a multiple of two." Several students nodded their agreement.

Joby added, "Six is also a multiple of three."

I explained, "Yes, six is a multiple of both two and three, so we can say that six is divisible by both two and three. Six is a multiple of two, so it can also be divided by two with no remainder, and six is a multiple of three, so it can be divided by three with no remainder." The students were quiet.

"Does six fit on my list of numbers that are multiples of two and divisible by two?" I asked.

"Yes!" the students immediately chorused. I wrote *6*, leaving a space so I could later add *0*, *2*, and *4* above it on the list and keep the multiples in sequential order. This would allow students to more easily see patterns that would help them define the divisibility rule for two.

"I know another number that could be on the list," Nariko volunteered. I nodded to encourage her to continue. "I think four would work. You count by twos and you land on four. Two, four."

"So a multiple of two is like counting by twos?" Neil asked. I nodded.

Terrell said, "I know another way to prove it. You can divide four by two with no leftovers."

To reinforce Terrell's idea and make the connection between multiplication and division, I said, "Yes, you can prove that four is a multiple of two by showing that it's divisible by two and that you can get four by multiplying two times two." I added *4* to the list.

Divisible by 2
Multiples of 2

   4

   6

I continued, "What's another number that's divisible by two?"

Cody said, "Three." The others showed their disagreement with thumbs down.

Celena explained, "Three isn't a multiple of two because when you count by twos, you skip right over it."

Elise said, "I know another number. Eight. Two, four, six, eight. It works." The students indicated their agreement with thumbs up. I added *8* to the list.

Divisible by 2
Multiples of 2

   4

   6

   8

"What about two?" Ali said. "Isn't two a multiple of two? There's one group of two in two with no remainder." I added *2* to the list.

"Zero works," Shawn said. "Zero twos is zero." I added *0* to the top of the list.

Divisible by 2
Multiples of 2

   0

   2

   4

   6

   8

"What comes after eight? Tell me in a whisper voice," I said.

"Ten," the students whispered, and then, as they continued to whisper the multiples of two, I listed them on the board. We stopped at thirty. Cody raised his hand.

"One hundred works," he said matter-of-factly.

"Explain how you know," I encouraged.

"It's an even number. There are only even numbers on the list," Cody explained. "You can divide it by two and it's fifty. And if you count by twos, you land on one hundred." The other students indicated their agreement that one hundred was divisible by two with their thumbs. I put three dots on the list, then wrote *100*, explaining to the students that the dots indicated I skipped some numbers.

Divisible by 2
Multiples of 2

    0

    2

    4

    6

    8

   10

   12

   14

   16

   18

   20

   22

   24

   26

   28

   30

   •

   •

   •

  100

"What patterns do you notice in the list?" I asked.

Joby replied, "Like Cody said, all the numbers on the list are even."

I recorded Joby and Cody's idea on the board:

Joby and Cody: All numbers on the list are even.

Kaleb shared, "There's a pattern in the ones place. It goes zero, two, four, six, eight, zero, two, four, and keeps on."

I wrote Kaleb's pattern on the board beneath Joby and Cody's:

Kaleb: The numbers in the ones place go 0, 2, 4, 6, 8, 0, 2, 4 . . .

Ali noticed, "In the tens place there's a pattern, I think. There are five ones, then five twos, and I think if we made the list longer, there would be five threes, five fours, and so on."

I pointed to 0 through 8 on the list and asked Ali, "How do you think the first five numbers fit into your pattern?" She shrugged. The other students thought quietly and then hands started to go up.

Katie said, "I think you could have zero in the tens place because there are no tens in those numbers. Then Ali's pattern would be five zeros in the tens place, five ones, five twos, and I think it would keep going."

"Oh yeah!" several students responded as others nodded their agreement.

"How could we check to see if Ali's pattern continues as she predicted?" I asked.

"Just keep counting by twos," Elise suggested. "If you count the thirty that's already on the list, it goes thirty-two, thirty-four, thirty-six, thirty-eight. That's five numbers with a three in the tens place. It has to go on like that because it's also how the ones place repeats: zero, two, four, six, eight, then zero again. When it comes to zero in the ones place, the tens place adds one."

I wrote Ali's pattern under Kaleb's:

Ali: In the tens place the pattern is 5 zeros, 5 ones, 5 twos, and so on.

Rachel said, "I think Ali's idea works because it has something to do with ten. There are five numbers in a row with the same digit in the tens place. There's two between each number. Five times two is ten. When there is ten, you have to add one more to the tens place."

Neil observed, "Multiples of two are the same as skip-counting by two and multiplying by two."

No one had any other ideas to share. I asked, "Does seventy-seven belong on the list?" The students gave an immediate thumbs-down.

Katie explained, "None of the other numbers on the list have a seven in the ones place and, besides that, seventy-seven is odd. Odd numbers are not multiples of two and can't be divided by two without a remainder."

"What about ninety-nine?" I asked next. Again the students showed a thumbs-down, indicating 99 didn't belong on the list.

"I know a number that would work," Annie volunteered. "One hundred seventeen would work."

Kaylee said, "I disagree. One hundred seventeen is odd."

Annie corrected herself. "Oops! If I add one to an odd number it'll be an even number. One hundred seventeen and one is one hundred eighteen. That's even." The other students indicated their agreement. I added *118* to the list.

Justin said, "I think two hundred sixteen works. It's even like all the other numbers." The others agreed and I added *216* to the list.

After students suggested a few more numbers to add to the list, I pushed them to formulate a generalization. I said, "It seems that you each are following a rule to determine if numbers are divisible by two and are multiples of two so we can put them on our list. What rule are you using?"

"If a number is divisible by two or a multiple of two, then it has to be even," Neil said. The other students showed their agreement with thumbs up.

No one wanted to share other ideas.

I wrote Neil's rule for numbers divisible by two above the list: *A number is divisible by 2 if it is even.*

I copied onto chart paper the list of multiples of two and wrote the divisibility rule above the list. I planned to post the chart for student reference during the lessons about the other divisibility rules.

DAY 2

Divisibility by Five and Ten

Note: Because the divisibility rules for five and ten aren't difficult for children to uncover, and they are related, you can present them in the same lesson. You may choose to explore five and ten at another time, however, if you think that's more appropriate for your students.

I wrote on the board:

Divisible by 5
Multiples of 5

With the students' help, I quickly listed the multiples of five from 0 to 50. This was an easy task for the students and didn't take long.

Divisible by 5
Multiples of 5

0

5

10

15

20

25

30

35

40

45

50

The students were eager to share the patterns they noticed in the numbers listed. I called on Annie.

Annie said, "The ones place goes zero, five, zero, five, zero, five, and on and on like that forever, I think."

I recorded Annie's idea on the board, paraphrasing for clarity:

Annie: The numbers in the ones place go 0, 5, 0, 5 . . .

Annie nodded her head in agreement with what I wrote and I reminded the students, "The dots at the end of the sentence mean that the numbers go on and on in that same pattern."

Elise shared, "There's a pattern in the tens place, too. There are two zeros, then two ones, two twos, two threes, and I know it will keep going."

"How do you know it will keep going?" I asked.

"Well, because in every ten, there are two fives. After two fives there are enough for another ten. So there can't be more than two numbers in every ten because there can't be more than two fives," Elise explained.

I wrote Elise's pattern on the board beneath Annie's:

Elise: The numbers in the tens place go 0, 0, 1, 1, 2, 2, 3, 3 . . .

Yolanda noticed, "The numbers go even, odd, even, odd."

I wrote on the board:

Yolanda: The numbers go even, odd, even, odd.

Nariko said, "The even numbers go up by ten and so do the odd numbers. From zero to ten, which are even numbers, it's ten. From five to fifteen, which are both odd numbers, it goes up by ten. You can do that with any two even or any two odd numbers that are by each other." Several students studied the list a moment and then nodded their agreement.

I said to Nariko, "Another way to describe the even or odd numbers that are by each other is to say that they are consecutive."

I wrote Nariko's idea on the board:

Nariko: Consecutive even numbers increase by 10 and so do consecutive odd numbers.

Neil shared one last idea. "Counting by fives is just like multiplying by five." Starting at the top of the list he said, "Five times zero is zero and zero is the first number on the list. Five times one is five and five is the next number. Five times two is ten. Ten is next on the list. It keeps going like that."

I added Neil's idea to the list:

Neil: Counting by fives is like multiplying by 5.

The students were quiet. I asked, "How can I tell quickly if a number is divisible by five?"

Kaleb said, "That's easy. If a number ends with a zero or five, it's divisible by five."

I wrote above the list:

Kaleb: If a number ends in 0 or 5, it's divisible by 5.

To check the students' understanding, I wrote on the board: *226,050.* "Is two hundred twenty-six thousand, fifty divisible by five? Is it divisible by two? Talk with your partner." I asked the students about divisibility by two to connect their previous learning about divisibility by two with the their current learning about divisibility by five. Also, I wanted to reinforce that numbers can be multiples of more than one number. As the students talked with their partners, I quietly circulated, listening in on their conversations. After a few moments, I asked for their attention. Hands danced in the air as the students showed their eagerness to share.

I asked, "Is two hundred twenty-six thousand, fifty divisible by five?"

"Easy!" several children commented.

"Why is it easy?" I asked.

"It ends with a zero and all numbers ending with a five or zero are divisible by five," Neil explained. The others nodded their agreement.

Next, I asked the students as I pointed to the board, "Is two hundred twenty-six thousand, fifty divisible by two? Tell me in a whisper voice."

"Yes!" the students chorused.

"Who would like to explain how you know?" I asked. Again most hands were in the air.

Celena explained, "It's even. The zero in the ones place tells you that. If it's even, it's divisible by two." Her classmates showed their agreement with their thumbs.

I then moved on to divisibility by ten. I said to the students, "If numbers that end with zero or five are divisible by five, how do you think we can tell if a number is divisible by ten?" Most hands were up immediately. I paused a moment until all hands were up.

Rachel said, "Any number that ends with a zero is divisible by ten. You can prove it by counting by tens. I don't think there's any number in the universe that ends with zero that isn't divisible by ten."

Justin added, "When you multiply by ten, the answer always has a zero in the ones place. For example, twelve times ten equals one hundred twenty or twenty-seven times ten equals two hundred seventy. I can't think of an example that doesn't work." The other students nodded their agreement.

I asked next, "Do you think there's any relationship between the multiples of five and the multiples of ten?"

Katie responded quickly, "Every other number on the multiples of five list ends with zero. That means the numbers with zero in the ones place are divisible by ten." The others nodded their agreement.

"Let's list the multiples of ten and check out Katie's idea," I suggested. I wrote on the board:

Divisible by 10
Multiples of 10

With the help of the students, I listed the multiples of ten on the board from 0 to 120. I included numbers larger than 100 as I thought it important for the students to consider numbers ending in 0 and larger than 100.

Divisible by 10
Multiples of 10

0

10

20

30

40

50

60

70

80

90

100

110

120

Cody said, "They all end in zero and no other number is in the ones place. I think Katie's idea works." I wrote on the board:

A number is divisible by 10 if it ends in 0.

I pointed to the board where I had written the number 226,050 earlier in the lesson. I asked, "Is two hundred twenty-six thousand, fifty divisible by ten?"

"Yes!" the students quickly responded together.

"It ends in zero, so it has to be," Samara said.

I copied onto chart paper the two lists of numbers and wrote the divisibility rules for five and ten above the appropriate lists.

Questions and Discussion

▲▲

▲ *I notice you write everything on the board and then recopy it onto charts. Why not record on charts in the beginning?*

My experience is that students share and explore ideas more freely if false starts and errors are not permanently recorded on a chart. Recording on the board or on an overhead transparency allows for easy erasing and revision.

CHAPTER EIGHT
EXPLORING DIVISIBILITY RULES FOR THREE

Overview

In this lesson, students investigate numbers that are divisible by three. They generate a list of numbers divisible by three, search the list for patterns, then share the patterns they notice in a class discussion. They learn the divisibility test for three, that a number is divisible by three if the sum of its digits is divisible by three. The lesson also reinforces for students that numbers divisible by three are also multiples of three.

Materials

▲ chart paper
▲ lists of the multiples of two, five, and ten

Time

▲ one class period

Teaching Directions

1. Begin by writing on the board:

Divisible by 3

Multiples of 3

2. Ask students to suggest numbers that belong on the list. Record their suggestions. If students are unable to make appropriate suggestions, help them get started by listing the first three or four multiples of three. Ask students what they notice about the numbers on the list.

3. With the help of the students, continue to list the multiples of three in sequential order from 0 to 42.

4. Have students share about the patterns they notice in the numbers on the list of multiples and record their ideas on the board. (Examples: Every other number is even. Every other number is odd. The even numbers are also on the *Divisible by 2* list.)

5. Ask students if 120 is divisible by 3 and why. Ask if 117 is divisible by 3 and why. After students explain their reasoning, introduce the divisibility rule for 3. Have students use division to verify that 117 is divisible by 3 and has no remainder.

6. Ask students to figure the sum of the digits of 123. Then ask them to verify it is divisible by 3 by figuring the answer to 123 ÷ 3.

7. Have students verify that other numbers on the list have sums of their digits that are divisible by three. Have students add the digits of other numbers not on the list to verify their sums are not divisible by three.

8. Ask students to find the sum of the digits of 236 then figure the answer to 236 ÷ 3.

9. Repeat Step 8 for the number 9,615.

10. Have students apply the divisibility test for 3 by finding the sum of the digits for 56,349 and 305,927.

Teaching Notes

The focus of this lesson is to build students' understanding of the close link between multiples and divisibility. Students learn numbers that are multiples of a number are also divisible by that number. For example, twelve is a multiple of three and twelve is also divisible by three. They also learn that when you divide a number by three and there is no remainder, then the number is said to be divisible by three.

The structure of the lesson is similar to the lesson in Chapter 7, "Exploring Divisibility Rules for Two, Five, and Ten." The students generate a list of multiples of three and then search the list for patterns. Unlike the divisibility tests for two, five, and ten, however, the divisibility test for three is not readily apparent to children. The divisibility test for three follows:

> A number is divisible by 3 if the sum of its digits is divisible by 3. Examples: 63, 405, 3,015. (Note: If the digits of a number are added and it's unclear if the sum is a multiple of 3, add the digits of the sum. If the sum of the digits of the sum is divisible by 3, so is the original number. For example, the sum of the digits of 9,576 is 27. Add 2 and 7 and the sum is 9. Nine is a multiple of 3 and is divisible by 3, making 9,576 a multiple of 3 and divisible by 3.)

Children rarely think about adding the sum of the digits. For this reason, you will most likely need to introduce the rule, as was done in the vignette.

The Lesson

▲▲

To begin, I directed the students' attention to the charts with the multiples of two, five, and ten and then asked, "Do you think numbers that are divisible by three and are multiples of three will always be even, like numbers that are multiples of two? Or will they be odd? Or both? Do you think they will end in zero or five?" I paused to give students a moment to consider my question. After a few moments, the students began to share their ideas with their neighbors. I called the class to attention.

Yolanda said, "I'm not too sure about the questions you asked, but I'm pretty sure six is divisible by three and a multiple of three. Three times two is six, and six divided by three is two." Most students nodded their agreement as they put their hands up to be next to share an idea. I wrote on the board next to the charts I'd posted with the lists of multiples of two, five, and ten:

Divisible by 3
Multiples of 3

6

Together we listed other numbers that belonged on the list. Terrell suggested nine. He explained, "Count by threes. Three, six, nine. There are three groups of three in nine." I wrote *9* beneath the 6.

Elise said, "Three belongs on the list. There's one group of three in three and no remainder." I wrote *3* above 6.

Neil said, "I think zero can be on the list, too. Zero groups of three is zero. If you count by three zero times, it's zero. I also think zero can be on all lists of multiples." I nodded and added 0 to the top of the list.

The students continued to identify multiples of three in consecutive order. I stopped the list at 42.

Divisible by 3
Multiples of 3

0

3

6

9

12

15

18

21

24

27

30

33

36

39

42

I asked the students, "What patterns do you notice? Are the numbers on the list all even? Odd? Talk with your partner about what you notice. First one of you talks for thirty seconds while the other listens. At the end of thirty seconds, I'll give you a signal and you'll switch roles so the first talker can listen and the first can listener can talk. At the end of another thirty seconds, I'll ask for your attention." I gave a signal for the students to start. I reminded them to switch roles after thirty seconds, and at the end of another thirty seconds, I asked for their attention. Students were eager to share about the patterns they noticed.

Samara said, "On the two list, it was all even numbers. On the threes list, some are even and some are odd. The pattern goes even, odd, even, odd, and like that." Most students nodded their agreement.

I wrote Samara's idea on the board:

Samara: The numbers go even, odd, even, odd . . .

I explained to the students that the three dots meant the pattern continued.

"That's like on the fives list," Binh noticed.

Annie shared next. She noticed a pattern in the tens place. She explained, "It starts with three zeros in the tens place, then three ones in the tens place, three twos in the tens place, and then it changes to four threes in the tens place. I'm not sure if it's really a pattern because of what happens in the thirties."

Joby corrected Annie. "Look, there are really four zeros in the tens place at the top of the list, for zero, three, six, and nine."

"Oh yeah," Annie acknowledged.

Neil had an intense look on his face, then grinned and raised his hand. "In the forties there are only three times when there's a four in the tens place—forty-two, forty-five, and forty-eight. Maybe Annie's pattern does work, but we have to add more numbers to the list." If Neil or another student hadn't made this suggestion, I would have done so.

"Can we do it?" Ali asked.

"We'll verify Neil and Annie's idea in a moment," I replied. "But first let's predict. If Annie's pattern works, what's the next decade that will have four multiples in it, like the thirties did? An example of a decade is the twenties or the thirties."

Students guessed the fifties, the seventies, and the sixties.

Starting with 42, we continued to list multiples of three and verified that the sixties was the next decade to have four multiples of three.

Annie was pleased her pattern held. She said, "Maybe the nineties will have four multiples. It seems to happen every three decades; the first one, skip two, then the thirties, skip two, the sixties, and if you skip two you get to the nineties." We listed the multiples of three to 99 to confirm Annie's theory. She beamed.

I paraphrased Annie's idea as I recorded it on the board beneath Samara's:

Annie: In each decade, there are either three or four multiples of 3. There are four multiples of 3 in the first decade, then the 30s, 60s, 90s, and so on.

Annie nodded her agreement with what I wrote.

Joby had a different idea. He said, "All the even numbers go up by six. Like to go from six to twelve it's six, and from twelve to eighteen is six." Joby came to the board to point out his pattern. The others indicated their agreement with his pattern with thumbs up.

I said to Joby and the others, "We can use the word *consecutive* to describe the even numbers that Joby is referring to. In this case, six and twelve are consecutive even numbers."

I recorded his discovery on the board:

Joby: Consecutive even numbers increase by six.

Rachel noticed a pattern in the ones place. She said, "The ones go zero, three, six, nine, two, five, eight, one, four, seven, zero, three, and on and on like that." Several students nodded. I added Rachel's idea to the list:

Rachel: The numbers in the ones place go 0, 3, 6, 9, 2, 5, 8, 1, 4, 7, and then repeat 0, 3, 6, 9, 2, 5, 8, . . .

Neil waved his hand excitedly. He said, "I just noticed something. In the ones place, every third number decreases by one. Start with three, then skip six and nine and go to twelve. The two is one less than the three."

With my finger, I pointed to the 3 on the list, counted down three numbers to the 12, and then said, "I see your pattern with these two numbers. Does it work for others?" I paused as Neil and the others studied the list. Hands went up and several students gave other examples that followed Neil's pattern. Next I asked, "Can anyone find an example of two numbers that are three apart and the numbers in the ones place don't follow Neil's pattern?"

Elise raised her hand and said with some confusion, "I think there is one place Neil's idea might not work. If you start at zero and go down three more multiples, it's nine. I don't think nine is one less than zero." The students were silent as they considered what Elise shared.

Because the students were engaged and thinking about Elise's idea, I decided to ask a question that might help them clarify for themselves what was going on. "What causes this pattern?" I asked. When more than half the students had their hands up, I called on Neil.

Neil said, "I think it's caused because there are three groups of three between the numbers, and that's nine. If it was ten, then the ones place would stay the same. Nine is one less than ten, so the ones place is one less than the number you started with, except for Elise's idea, which sort of disproves it, but sort of proves it, too. To go from zero to nine is nine, but the confusing part is the nine and the zero."

Ali suggested, "Maybe you could just say for Neil's idea that every fourth multiple increases by nine. Then I think it works."

"Oh yeah!" "That works!" were some of the responses from the other students. Neil nodded his agreement with Ali's idea. I wrote on the board:

Neil and Ali: Every fourth multiple increases by nine.

Nariko shared next, "Joby's idea gave me an idea. He said consecutive even numbers increase by six. Well, I looked at the list, and consecutive odd numbers increase by six when you go down the list, too."

I recorded Nariko's idea on the board:

Nariko: Consecutive odd numbers increase by six.

Kaylee said, "I notice that the decades with four multiples of three always begin with a number that has a zero in the ones place. For example, thirty, sixty, ninety. I think the next one would be one hundred twenty."

Samara said, "I think Kaylee's right that the next decade to have four multiples of three would start with one hundred twenty. I started with ninety-nine and counted by threes and landed on one hundred twenty. Then I kept counting, one hundred twenty, one hundred twenty-three, one hundred twenty-six, one hundred twenty-nine. All those numbers are divisible by three and there are four of them in the same decade."

I wrote Kaylee's idea on the board:
Kaylee: Decades with four multiples of three begin with a number that has a zero in the ones place.

No one had another idea to share. Next I introduced the students to the general rule for divisibility by three. For divisibility by two, five, and ten, the students were able to generalize the rule for themselves from the patterns they had noticed in the lists. However, the rule for divisibility by three isn't one that students typically discover; students rarely think about adding the digits of the multiples and looking for a useful pattern in the sums. Before presenting the rule, I asked, "Is one hundred eighteen divisible by three?"

Katie said, "No, we know one hundred twenty is divisible by three and one hundred eighteen is only two less. It would have to be three less. One hundred seventeen is divisible by three."

Binh added, "Eighteen is divisible by three, but one hundred isn't. If you count by threes, you land on ninety-nine and skip one hundred, so I know one hundred isn't divisible by three, so I don't think one hundred eighteen is either."

I said, "Mathematicians have figured out a way to tell if a number is divisible by three by looking at a pattern you haven't thought about yet. If you add the digits in a number, and the sum of those digits is a multiple of three, then the number is also a multiple of three."

"I don't get it," Jina said.

I wrote on the board the two numbers the students had just considered:

118

117

I then said, "Let's add the digits of one hundred eighteen—one plus one plus eight." I pointed to each of the digits in 118 as I called them out. "What is the sum?" I asked.

"Ten," the students answered in unison.

"Is ten divisible by three?" I asked.

They again responded in unison, "No."

"Is one hundred eighteen divisible by three?"

"No," they answered again.

"Let's think about the digits in one hundred seventeen—one plus one plus seven," I said. Again, I pointed to the digits as I named them. I gave the students a chance to think about this, and they soon began murmuring.

"It's nine."

"Nine works, so one hundred seventeen does, too."

"That's cool."

"That's weird."

"But it works!"

I interrupted them and said, "Let's check to be sure that one hundred seventeen is divisible by three. With your partner, figure out how much one hundred seventeen divided by three is, and see if the remainder is zero." Some students reached for paper and pencil while others began to figure in their heads. After a few moments, I asked for their attention.

Ali reported first. She said, "Like Katie said before, one hundred twenty is divisible by three. It's forty. That's easy because

you can do three into twelve and just add a zero. So one hundred seventeen is three less, and that's like one group less, so the answer has to be thirty-nine." I wrote on the board:

Ali: $120 \div 3 = 40$

$120 - 117 = 3$

$40 - 1 = 39$

"Raise your hand if you also figured out that the answer was thirty-nine," I said. Most hands were up.

"I agree that thirty-nine is the answer. Now raise your hand if you reasoned the same way that Ali did," I said. Fewer hands were up.

"Raise your hand if you can explain another way to get the answer," I then said. I called on Shawn.

He said, "We took one hundred seventeen apart into smaller pieces. We were going to break it into a hundred and then seventeen, but we know that you can't divide one hundred by three evenly. So we took out ninety-nine and then we had eighteen left over. Ninety-nine divided by three is thirty-three, and eighteen divided by three is six, and thirty-three and six is thirty-nine." I recorded:

Shawn: $117 = 99 + 18$

$99 \div 3 = 33$

$18 \div 3 = 6$

$33 + 6 = 39$

Kaylee wondered aloud, "But I thought the number was one hundred seventeen, not one hundred eighteen. How come you divided eighteen by three?"

Shawn was confused for a moment, but then remembered what he had done. "We did use one hundred seventeen," he explained, "but we took out ninety-nine first, so we had one more to get to one hundred, so that's why the extra seventeen had to be eighteen." This seemed to help Kaylee.

Next I called on Celena. "We did it on paper," she said. I invited her to come up and reproduce on the board what she and her partner had done. She explained as she wrote, "We kept taking out ten threes at a time, which is thirty. After we did this three times, we realized that we didn't have enough for ten more threes because we only had twenty-seven left. And we knew that three times nine was twenty-seven, so we took out nine more threes. Altogether, we took out thirty-nine threes." Her finished problem on the board looked like this:

$$
\begin{array}{r}
9 \\
10 \\
10 \\
10 \\
\end{array}\left.\right\} 39
$$

$$
\begin{array}{r}
3\,\overline{)117} \\
-30 \\
\hline 87 \\
-30 \\
\hline 57 \\
-30 \\
\hline 27 \\
-27 \\
\hline 0
\end{array}
$$

I said, "So now we have four ways to prove that three divides into one hundred seventeen with no remainder. We have Ali's way, Shawn's way, Celena's way, and the method I gave of adding the digits and seeing if the sum is divisible by three. We have four ways to prove that one hundred seventeen is divisible by three."

I then wrote 123 on the board, and said, "With your partner, add the digits of one hundred twenty-three and see what the sum tells you about whether one hundred twenty-three is divisible by three. Then figure out the answer to one hundred twenty-three divided by three." The conversations were lively. After a few moments, hands began to go up.

Yolanda said, "I can prove that one hundred twenty-three is divisible by

three. I know one hundred twenty is divisible by three. I add three more to get one hundred twenty-three. Now I know one hundred twenty-three is divisible by three."

Elise said, "We added the digits—one plus two plus three. It equaled six. Six is a multiple of three, so it's divisible by three. That means one hundred twenty-three is, too."

I added 123 to our list and said, "Let's see if all of the numbers on our list follow the pattern. Add the digits in each number and check that the sum is divisible by three each time. Then try some of the numbers that aren't on our list to be sure that the sum of their digits is *not* a multiple of three." After a minute or so, the students were convinced that the pattern worked.

I wrote on the board 236 and again asked the students to add the digits to decide if it was divisible by 3 and then do the division to find the answer.

Cody said, "One hundred twenty is divisible by three. I think if you double it, then that number should also be divisible by three. One hundred twenty doubled is two hundred forty. Two hundred forty minus three is two hundred thirty-seven, subtract three more and it's two hundred thirty-four. It skips over two hundred thirty-six. I just don't think two hundred thirty-six works." Several students nodded. I recorded on the board:

120 is divisible by 3.

240 is divisible by 3.

240 − 3 = 237

237 − 3 = 234

Subtracting 3s skips over 236, so 236 isn't divisible by 3.

Kaleb then said, "We figured out that the answer is seventy-eight remainder two. We used paper and pencil." He came up and wrote on the board what he had recorded.

$$\begin{array}{r} 8 \\ 30 \\ \underline{40} \end{array}\Big]\ 78\ R2$$

$$3\overline{)236}$$
$$\underline{-120}$$
$$116$$
$$\underline{-90}$$
$$26$$
$$\underline{-24}$$
$$2$$

Kaleb explained, "First we took out forty threes, and subtracted one hundred twenty, and then we had only one hundred sixteen left. So we didn't have enough to take out forty more threes, so we took out thirty and minused ninety. That left twenty-six. Eight times three is twenty-four, and that's as close as you can get. We added forty and thirty and that gave us seventy, and eight more is seventy-eight, with a remainder of two."

Nariko had a different explanation. She said, "One hundred divided by three is thirty-three remainder one. So two hundred divided by three is double that, and that's sixty-six remainder two. And the thirty-six divided by three is twelve. So the answer is sixty-six plus twelve and that's . . . seventy-eight, and there's a remainder of two." I recorded on the board:

$100 \div 3 = 33\ R1$

$200 \div 3 = 66\ R2$

$36 \div 3 = 12$

$66 + 12 = 78$

$236 \div 3 = 78\ R2$

I chose a larger number for the students to consider next. I wanted them to know that if they weren't sure whether the sum of the digits of the number was a multiple of 3, they could add the digits of the sum. Then, if that sum is a multiple of 3, the first sum is also divisible by 3, and so is the original number. I wrote *9,615* on the board and said, "Is nine thousand, six hundred fifteen divisible by three? Add the digits, and then check by dividing."

When I interrupted them, I asked the children to say, in a whisper voice, what the sum of the digits was. "Twenty-one," they responded.

I said, "I agree. But if you're not sure if the sum of the digits is divisible by three, you can just add the digits in the sum and see if the new sum is divisible by three. Let's add the digits of twenty-one and see. What's two plus one?"

"Three," the students replied.

"Oh, cool!" "That's neat!" several students said. I then had Katie and Neil explain how they figured out the answer of 3,205 and I added *9,615* to the list of multiples.

"Let's try another number. This time you don't have to figure out the answer. I just want you to decide if the number is divisible by three, and to try the method of adding the digits in the sum," I said. I wrote on the board *56,349*. The students immediately started figuring the sum of the digits.

Terrell said, "The sum is twenty-seven. I can add the two and seven, and that's nine. It's divisible by three. I get it. I like this."

I continued, "We'll do one more number together." I wrote on the board *305,927*. "If it's divisible by three, put your thumb up; if not, put your thumb down. If you're not sure, put your thumb sideways." All thumbs were down.

Nariko said, "It doesn't work. The sum of the digits is twenty-six. I know that twenty-six isn't a multiple of three. It's not on our list, and also I added two and six, and it is eight. I know eight isn't a multiple of three, so I know three hundred five thousand, nine hundred twenty-seven isn't either."

Math time was coming to an end. I said to the students, "Who can state a rule determining if a number is divisible by three?" Most hands were up immediately.

Elise said, "Any multiple of three is divisible by three." I nodded.

Binh said, "Add the digits. If the digits are divisible by three, then the number is, too."

"Yep, that's my answer!" Rachel said.

"Mine, too," Katie agreed.

I wrote the rule for divisibility by three above the list of multiples of three: *A number is divisible by 3 if the sum of its digits is divisible by 3.*

As I had done on previous days, I copied onto chart paper the list of multiples of three and I posted it with the others where all students could see them for reference.

Questions and Discussion

▲▲

▲ **Why did you spend time discussing patterns in the list of the multiples of three that didn't lead students to discover the divisibility test for three?**

Although the patterns students shared did not connect directly to the divisibility test for three, the discussion allowed students to apply and reinforce their knowledge in several areas. As students searched for patterns, they used their knowledge of odd and even numbers, explored how the multiples increased when listed sequentially, explained why patterns occur, and used patterns to predict or determine if a number did or did not make sense.

Typically, students this age don't think about adding the digits to find the sum and therefore will not be able to discover for themselves the divisibility test for three. Introducing the idea of finding the sum of the digits of a number as part of a discussion about patterns gives students another source to search for patterns, and in this case, leads them to the divisibility test for three.

CHAPTER NINE
EXPLORING DIVISIBILITY RULES FOR SIX

Overview

In this lesson, working in pairs, students investigate numbers that are divisible by six. Students list the first thirteen multiples of six and search the list for patterns. Then, in a whole-class discussion, students share the patterns they notice. Next, students compare the lists of multiples of three and six to figure out the rule for divisibility by six, that the multiples of six, or numbers divisible by six, are the same as the even multiples of three, or the even numbers divisible by three.

Materials

- ▲ chart paper
- ▲ list of multiples of three
- ▲ optional: lists of multiples of two, five, and ten

Time

- ▲ one class period, plus additional time for extensions

Teaching Directions

1. Ask students to work in pairs and list the first thirteen multiples of six on their papers.

2. In a class discussion, ask students to report the first thirteen multiples of six and list them on the board.

3. Ask students: "What patterns do you notice?" Record their ideas on the board.

4. To push students to figure out the divisibility test for six, ask students to compare the lists of multiples for three and six. Ask: "What's the same about both lists? What's different? Why do you think this is so?" (The even multiples of three are the same as the multiples of six.)

Teaching Notes

Teach the lesson in Chapter 8, "Exploring Divisibility Rules for Three," prior to this lesson. Learning about the divisibility test for three provides a building block for exploring the divisibility test for six. The divisibility test for six is

A number is divisible by 6 if it is even and the sum of the digits is divisible by 3. Or, a number is divisible by 6 if it is divisible by 2 and also by 3. Examples: 36, 42, 168, 174, 96, 102.

The "Extensions" section of this chapter suggests that students explore divisibility for four, eight, and nine. The divisibility rule for nine is rather straightforward:

A number is divisible by 9 if the sum of the digits is divisible by 9. Examples: 234, 801, 3,699.

For many students this age, the rules for four and eight are difficult to understand and to apply. For your information, following are the divisibility rules for four and eight:

Divisibility by four: A number is divisible by 4 if the last two digits of the number are 00 or the last two digits of the number form a number divisible by 4. Examples: 76, 300, 532, 748.

Divisibility by eight: A number is divisible by 8 if the last three digits of the number are 000 or the last three digits form a number that's divisible by 8. Examples: 2,000, 3,888, 648.

There is a divisibility rule for seven, but it's neither simple nor efficient for children to use.

The Lesson

▲▲

"With your partner, please list the first thirteen multiples of six," I said to the students as I handed each pair a sheet of paper. Since the students had experience listing multiples of two, five, ten, and three, they knew what to do.

"Do we start with zero?" Elise asked. I nodded.

"Can we list more than thirteen?" Ali asked, always eager to go beyond. Again I nodded.

There were no more questions. The students worked together quickly. As they worked, I looked over shoulders, listened to conversations, and observed. When a pair made an error, I asked the children to check their work either by counting by sixes or using what they already knew about multiplication. The students were finished in a few minutes. I asked for their attention and, with their help, quickly listed on the board sequentially the first thirteen multiples of six.

Divisible by 6
Multiples of 6

0

6

12

18

24

30

36

42

48

54

60

66

72

"I see a pattern!" "Me, too!" "Can I share what I notice?" were some of the responses from the students when we finished the list. I settled the students, reminding them not to call out. Then I called on Rachel to share.

Rachel said, "The ones column goes six plus two equals eight, skip four and zero, then six plus two equals eight, skip the four and the zero, and it goes like that." I wasn't certain what Rachel saw, so I asked her to come to the board to show me. She pointed to the ones place of the second number on the list, which was 6. Then she pointed to the ones place of the third number, which was 2. She found the sum, which is eight, and pointed to the fourth number, which had an 8 in the ones place. "Skip the next two numbers on the list and it does the same thing again," Rachel said. I wrote Rachel's idea on the board:

Rachel: The numbers in the ones place follow a pattern—6 + 2 = 8, skip 4, and then there's a 0.

"That's a tricky pattern!" Nariko said.

Kaleb shared next, "The pattern in the ones is zero, six, two, eight, four, zero, six, and it just keeps on like that."

Celena noticed, "They're all even numbers."

I recorded Kaleb's and Celena's ideas:

Kaleb: The numbers in the ones place go 0, 6, 2, 8, 4, 0, 6 . . .

Celena: The numbers are all even.

Neil shared next. He began by stating he wasn't sure if his pattern would continue to repeat. "The tens column goes zero, zero, one, one, two, three, three, four, four, five, six, six, seven. I think there will be two sevens. The next decade without two of the same number in the tens place will be the eighties."

"Why do you think that?" I asked. Neil shrugged.

"Does anyone have an idea about why the next decade with just one number the same will be the eighties?" I asked the class. The students talked among themselves. After a few moments, I called for their attention.

Kaylee said, "It seems like it happens every three decades. From the twenties to the fifties is thirty. Add thirty to fifty and it's the eighties." There were no other ideas. Together we extended the chart, stopping with 96 to verify Neil's idea. To the delight of all, his prediction was correct. I recorded Neil's and Kaylee's ideas:

Neil: The numbers in the tens place go 0, 0, 1, 1, 2, 3, 3, 4, 4, 5, 6, 6, 7, 7, 8, . . .

Kaylee: The numbers in the tens place appear only once in every third decade— 20s, 50s, 80s . . .

"I noticed something else," Terrell said. "The pattern in the ones place starts over when there's a zero in the ones place." Several students nodded and I added Terrell's idea to the list:

Terrell: The pattern in the ones place starts over when it gets to zero.

Joby said, "The zero happens right after the decade with only one multiple. Like there is just fifty-four in the fifties and then the next multiple is sixty, which ends with a zero." I recorded:

Joby: Zero is in the ones place right after the decade with only one multiple of 6.

I asked Joby and the other students, "Why do you think that happens?" I paused several moments to give the students quiet time to think. I continued, "Talk with your partner. First one of you talks for thirty seconds while the other listens. When I give you the signal, change roles so the first listener talks and the first talker listens." I gave the students a signal to begin. After thirty seconds, I reminded them to switch roles. As they shared ideas, I listened. After the second thirty seconds, I called the students to order.

Celena shared first. "I think it goes thirty, sixty, and ninety because there's thirty in between. We're counting by sixes and thirty is counting by five groups of six. Then if you count backward by six you land on a number with four in the ones place, like fifty-four. There's no more sixes that can be in that decade." The students nodded as they sat quietly. There were no more ideas.

While the students noticed many interesting patterns in the list of multiples of six, they couldn't use these patterns to figure out a rule for determining if a number was divisible by six. I asked the students to compare the list of the multiples of six with the list of multiples of three. "What's the same about these two lists? What's different?" I asked. I paused as the students studied the lists. After a few moments, I said, "What do you notice?" Several students raised their hands quickly. I waited a few moments longer until most students had raised their hands. I called on Nariko.

Nariko said, "The odd numbers on the three list get skipped and aren't on the multiples of six list, but the even numbers are."

"I had that same idea," Ali commented.

"Did anyone else have the same idea as Nariko and Ali?" I asked. A few students raised their hands. I recorded on the board the idea Nariko shared:

Nariko: The odd numbers on the multiples of 3 list are not on the multiples of 6 list, but the even numbers are.

Rachel shared next, "All the numbers on the multiples of six list are even. On the multiples of three list, the numbers go even, odd, even, odd, and on like that." I recorded her idea:

Rachel: All multiples of 6 are even.
Multiples of 3 go even, odd, even, odd, etc.

No one had any more ideas to share. I said, "We know that the numbers on the multiples of six list are even. Are all even numbers divisible by six?" I paused a moment, then continued. "If you think all even numbers are divisible by six, put your

thumb up; if you think not all even numbers are divisible by six, put your thumb down. If you're confused or uncertain, put your thumb sideways." About one-fourth of the students showed thumbs up while about three-fourths showed thumbs down. To help those who thought all even numbers are divisible by six, I gave a counterexample. "Twelve is an even number and it's on the multiples of three list and the multiples of six list. What about fourteen? It's an even number. Is it divisible by six?"

Shawn explained, "I don't think fourteen is divisible by six because when I count by sixes, I don't land on fourteen. I would go six, twelve, and then eighteen."

Katie shared, "I notice that all the numbers on the list of multiples of six are also on the list of multiples of three. I think all multiples of six are also multiples of three." I wrote Katie's observation on the board and gave the students a moment to consider it.

Katie: All multiples of 6 are also multiples of 3.

"Does it make sense that all the multiples of six are multiples of three?" I asked.

Justin said, "It makes sense to me because there are two threes in six. So when you count by threes, you get twice as many numbers as when you count by sixes. Also, when you count by sixes, you skip every other number from when you counted by threes."

"Oh, I think I made a connection!" Rachel blurted out, and then apologized for blurting. "What Justin said about skipping every other three when you count by six is how come only the even numbers from the threes list are on the sixes list!"

"Oh, wow!" "She's right!" "I see what she means!" were some of the responses from the other students.

I settled the class. To help the students formulate a rule for divisibility by six, I suggested we find the sum of the digits of the numbers on the multiples of six list. As we found the sum of the digits for each of the numbers on the list, I recorded it beside that number.

Divisible by 6

Multiples of 6	Sum of the Digits
0	0
6	6
12	3
18	9
24	6

After writing several sums, I asked the students, "What do you notice about the sums of the digits of numbers divisible by six?"

Neil waved his hand excitedly, eager to share. He said, "All the sums are divisible by three, just like on the threes list." The students nodded their agreement with Neil.

I asked the students, "Based on our discussion, how can we tell if a number is divisible by six?"

Binh explained, "It has to be even and the sum of the digits has to be divisible by six."

Shawn disagreed and said, "The sum of the digits has to be divisible by three, not six."

"Why is that so?" I asked Shawn and the others.

Shawn said, "All of the numbers on the multiples of six list are also on the multiples of three list. They're the even numbers. That's why they have to be even, and if they are on the multiples of three list, then the sum of the digits is divisible by three. Besides, if you add the sum of the digits of twelve, that's three, and three divided by six is a fraction."

I wrote the divisibility rule for six above the list of multiples of six: *A number is divisible by 6 if it is even and the sum of its digits is divisible by 3.*

EXTENSIONS

On another day, have students work in pairs to create a list of multiples of nine. Have them search for patterns in the numbers on the list and use the information to generalize a divisibility rule for nine.

The divisibility rules for four and eight are challenging for many students this age but may provide an appropriate exploration for more capable and interested children.

Questions and Discussion

▲▲

▲ *I noticed that you presented the divisibility rule for 6 after the rules for 2, 5, 10, and 3. Why did you make this choice?*

Knowledge and understanding of the divisibility rules for 2 and 3 are the basis of the divisibility rule for 6. Numbers that are even *and* divisible by 3 are also divisible by 6. Therefore, presenting the divisibility rule for 6 after 2, 5, 10, and 3 makes sense because students can use what they learned previously to understand the divisibility test for 6. When students use information and connect ideas in this way, their understanding is deepened and seen by students as useful.

CHAPTER TEN
A REMAINDER OF ONE

Overview

A Remainder of One, by Elinor J. Pinczes, provides a context for students to relate multiples to division and think about divisibility rules. The story and illustrations lead the children to figure out that there are twenty-five bugs in squadron twenty-five. When the bugs march in two, three, and four equal lines, one bug, Soldier Joe, trails behind. Finally, when the bugs march in five equal lines, no bug is left out, pleasing their queen. Working in small groups, students make lists of the multiples from 1 to 100 for the numbers 2, 3, 4, 5, and 6, and together, students verify which squads from one to one hundred can march in 2, 3, 4, 5, and 6 equal lines. The lesson reinforces the terminology of *multiple, factor, divisor, divisible,* and *common multiple.*

Materials

▲ *A Remainder of One,* by Elinor J. Pinczes (Boston: Houghton Mifflin Company, 1995)
▲ 5 overhead transparencies of the 1–100 chart (see Blackline Masters)
▲ 5 overhead markers, in different colors if possible

Time

▲ two class periods, plus additional time for extensions

Teaching Directions

1. Show the students the cover of *A Remainder of One,* by Elinor J. Pinczes, and have them figure out the number of bugs pictured.

2. Read aloud the story.

3. Explain to students that the squadron number tells the number of bugs in a squadron. Ask students which squadrons from one to one hundred can march in two equal lines with no extra bugs. Write *2* on the board and, underneath, list several of the students' suggestions. Discuss what they notice about the list. Introduce the vocabulary *multiple, factor, divisor, divisible,* and *common multiple.* Write these on the board or a chart and use them as part of the discussion.

4. Repeat Step 3 for three, four, five, and six equal lines.

5. Organize the class into groups of five. Explain to the students that each member of the group of five should choose a number—2, 3, 4, 5, or 6—and list all the multiples of his or her number from 1 to 100. (If there are groups with fewer than five, have the student who finishes first do another number.)

6. Give an overhead transparency of the 1–100 chart and a different-colored marker to each member of the first group of five to finish listing their multiples correctly. Ask the students to mark their transparencies as follows:

▲ Student 1: Mark each multiple of two with a dot in the upper left corner of the square.

▲ Student 2: Mark each multiple of three with a dot in the lower left corner of the square.

▲ Student 3: Mark each multiple of four with a dot in the upper right corner of the square.

▲ Student 4: Mark each multiple of five with a dot in the lower right corner of the square.

▲ Student 5: Circle each number that is a multiple of six.

Collect their transparencies and papers.

7. On Day 2, ask five students to each write on the board a list for a different set of multiples. With the class's help, make any needed corrections to the lists of multiples on the board. Students should also make any needed corrections to their papers.

8. As a class, explore the following problem. *The queen has one hundred different-size bug squadrons, from a squadron with one bug to a squadron with one hundred bugs. The squadron number tells the number of bugs in it. Which squadrons can march in 2, 3, 4, 5, and 6 equal lines with no extra bugs?* List students' suggestions on the board.

9. Ask students: "If a squadron can march in two equal lines with no extra bugs, what do we know about the squadron number?" Next, ask students which squadron numbers on the list can be eliminated and then cross those numbers off the list.

10. Repeat Step 9 for squadrons that can march in five equal lines, three equal lines, four equal lines, and finally, six equal lines.

11. Project the overhead transparency of the 1–100 chart marked with the multiples of 2. Next, on top of the multiples of 2, lay the transparency marked with the multiples of 3. On top of these two transparencies, lay the transparency marked with the multiples of 4, then the one with the multiples of 5, and finally, the one with the multiples of 6. The transparencies should verify that 60 is the only number between 1 and 100 that is divisible by 2, 3, 4, 5, *and* 6.

Teaching Notes

A Remainder of One, by Elinor J. Pinczes, tells the story of Joe, a bug who wants to march in the parade but has to stand aside every time the lines are uneven. Joe is a determined bug, however, and he thinks hard about the problem, rearranging the twenty-five bugs in his squadron from two lines to three lines, then to four lines, and finally to five lines, where he fits in at last.

This lesson provides students with an opportunity to think about remainders and the characteristics of numbers that are divisible by 2, 3, 4, 5, and 6. A number (x) is divisible by another number (y) if y is a factor of x. Another way to state this is that x is divisible by y if x can be divided by y and the answer doesn't have a remainder (or has a remainder of zero).

Following are some of the common divisibility tests that we used for the numbers in this lesson, some stated in several ways:

Two: A number is divisible by 2 if it is even. Or, a number is divisible by 2 if it has 0, 2, 4, 6, or 8 in the ones place.

Three: A number is divisible by 3 if the sum of its digits is divisible by 3. (Students rarely discover this rule by themselves.)

Four: Starting with 4, every other number in the list of numbers divisible by 2 is also divisible by 4. This test makes sense for this lesson. However, for your information, the divisibility test for 4 is as follows: A number is divisible by 4 if the last two digits of the number are 00 or the last two digits of the number form a number divisible by 4. This is difficult for children to understand and isn't needed for this lesson.

Five: A number is divisible by 5 if it has a 0 or a 5 in the ones place.

Six: A number is divisible by 6 if it is divisible by both 2 and 3. Another way of saying this is numbers divisible by 6 are even *and* divisible by 3.

Using the context of the story to investigate divisibility by these numbers introduces students to some of the standard divisibility rules. When children have the chance to discover these rules and make sense of them for themselves, they are more likely to understand and remember them. The lessons in Chapter 7, 8, and 9 provide a more in-depth experience with divisibility rules.

The lesson also helps students become familiar with the following mathematical terminology: *multiple, factor, divisor, divisible,* and *common multiple.* Listing these on the board or a chart as you introduce them will provide a useful reference for students. Using correct terminology in lessons increases the likelihood that students will understand, remember, and become comfortable using it.

The Lesson

▲▲

DAY 1

I gathered the students on the rug. As they settled, I held up *A Remainder of One*, by Elinor J. Pinczes, so the students could see the cover. "Has anyone read or heard this book before?" I asked the students. Shelly raised her hand to indicate she was familiar with the book. I continued, "The title of the book is *A Remainder of One*. Based on the title, what do you suppose this book is about?"

Clay said, "Well, it must be about remainders because of the title and because of the picture. There's one bug all alone—he's the remainder—and the rest are in lines." Most of the students nodded their agreement.

Malina added, "If it's about remainders, then it's also about division."

Sierra said, "Division has equal groups, and I noticed the bugs on the cover are in equal groups."

"How many bugs are there?" I asked. I held up the book and then sketched on the board the arrangement of bugs on the cover, drawing a square, then five ants on each side, one at each corner, and one inside.

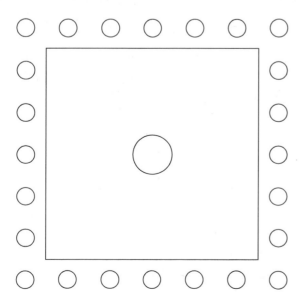

When most students had their hands raised, I called on Diego. He explained, "There are twenty-five bugs. There are five bugs on each side. Four times five is twenty. And there's a bug at each corner. That's four more. There's also one bug inside the square. Twenty and five is twenty-five."

I recorded Diego's thinking on the board:

Diego: $4 \times 5 = 20$
             $4 + 1 = 5$
             $20 + 5 = 25$

Natalie shared next. "I see four groups of six bugs. Can I show?" I nodded and Natalie came to the front and pointed out how she saw four lines with six bugs in each, starting with a corner bug each time.

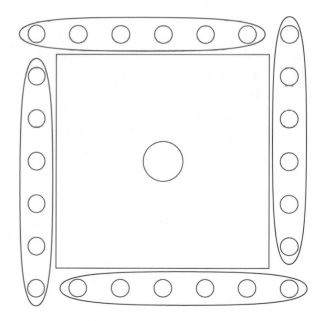

"Four times six is twenty-four, plus the one bug in the middle, who's the remainder. That's twenty-five bugs."

I recorded Natalie's idea on the board:

Natalie: $4 \times 6 = 24$
               $24 + 1 = 25$

A Remainder of One   115

Elonzo explained, "My way is sort of like Diego's but different, too. I thought of four times five, and I put that in parentheses. Four times five is twenty. Then I thought four times one and put that in parentheses. Four times one is four. Then I put a plus sign between them and then another plus sign and then a one. It still equals twenty-five."

I recorded Elonzo's thinking on the board:

Elonzo: $(4 \times 5) + (4 \times 1) + 1 = 25$
          $20 + 4 + 1 = 25$

No one had anything to add. I began reading the story aloud, stopping on page 4 to discuss the meaning of the word *squadron*. Jared explained it was a group that worked together and sometimes was in the military.

Ellyn added, "I bet it's called squadron twenty-five because there are twenty-five bugs in it." I nodded my agreement. If Ellyn hadn't made this observation, I would have elicited it by asking the students what they thought the connection was between the twenty-five bugs on the cover and the twenty-fifth squadron.

I continued reading the next page, stopping again to ask if the twenty-five bugs could divide into two equal groups with no extra bugs. All of the students indicated with thumbs down that the bugs couldn't march in two equal lines.

I read the next several pages, pausing when Joe had the idea to march in three equal lines. I said, "Joe thinks a possible solution to his problem of being a leftover bug may be solved if the bugs march in three equal lines rather than two. What do you think?" Hands shot into the air.

Katie said with assurance, "It won't work! There will still be one bug left."

"How do you know?" I asked.

"Because three times eight is twenty-four; that's one short of twenty-five," Katie said. "Or you could do it by division.

Twenty-five divided by three is eight with a remainder of one."

I recorded Katie's idea on the board:

$3 \times 8 = 24$ 1 less than 25

$25 \div 3 = 8$ R1

I turned the page of the book and the next illustration verified Katie's thinking by showing three lines of eight bugs with Soldier Joe alone at the back of the group.

"I think five lines would work," Martin conjectured. "Five times five is twenty-five, or twenty-five divided by five is five, with no remainders."

"Let's keep reading to find out," Annie said.

Kaleb said, "I bet Joe thinks to do four lines next, but it won't work. Four lines would have six bugs in each. Six times four is twenty-four. Joe is a remainder again. It's a pattern. One more line is added each time."

I continued reading the story and verified that Kaleb was right: Joe suggested four lines and he was left out once again. Martin was also right about his prediction that five lines would work.

I said, "Squadron twenty-five has twenty-five bugs. Let's say that the squadron number always tells how many bugs are in that squadron. The queen has one hundred squadrons of bugs from a squadron of one bug to a squadron of one hundred bugs. Which of those squadrons could march in two equal lines with no extra bugs?" Most students had their hands up immediately. As the students shared, I listed their suggestions on the board:

2
50
4
6
2
10
20
8
42

I asked, "What do you notice about the numbers of the squadrons that can march in two equal lines?"

"They're all even," the class chorused.

"How many of the squadrons from one to one hundred have an even number of bugs?" I asked. I waited until most hands were up and called on Roxanne.

"It's every other number, so it has to be fifty," she said.

"Yes, there are fifty," Kaleb confirmed. "I counted on my fingers and there are ten even numbers up to twenty—two, four, six, eight, ten, twelve, fourteen, sixteen, eighteen, twenty. So you do that five times to get to a hundred. And five tens is fifty."

Instead of taking the time to list all of the even numbers up to 100, I left this for a later small-group activity. Instead I said to the class, "The numbers on this list and all of the other even numbers are multiples of two. Because they are multiples of two, all these numbers have two as a factor and are also divisible by two. That means that when each of these numbers is divided by two, there's no remainder." As I gave the students time to think about what I had said, I wrote on the board *multiple*, *factor*, *divisor*, and *divisible*. Then I asked, "Do you notice anything else?" The students were quiet.

Next I asked, "Which squadrons can march in three equal lines with no extra bugs?"

Pilar replied, "Six."

"Isn't six a multiple of two and on the list for two lines?" I asked.

Momentarily, Pilar looked confused, then she brightened quickly. "Six can be on both. Two goes into six with no remainders and so does three. Six is divisible by both two and three."

I nodded and said, "I agree with Pilar." I wrote 3 on the board to head up a new list and underneath it, I wrote a 6. "Because six is divisible by both two and three, it's a multiple of both two and three."

Max said, "Nine works for three lines— three times three is nine—but nine doesn't work for two lines. Nine is odd, so two won't go into it equally."

To model correct mathematical language, I paraphrased what Max said. "Yes, nine is odd so it's not divisible by two." I wrote 9 under the 6.

Jared waved his hand with excitement. "I know another squadron that can be on both lists—twelve. It's even, so I know two works. And three goes into twelve four times."

I added 12 to the list. Again paraphrasing and modeling correct mathematical language, I said, "Yes, twelve is even, so it's a multiple of two and divisible by two. Twelve is divisible by three because three times four equals twelve. Both two and three are factors of twelve. Twelve is a common multiple of two and three, as is six." I added *common multiple* to the list of vocabulary I had started a few minutes earlier.

Joelle said, "If you add three more to twelve, it's fifteen, so I think fifteen is divisible by three. Fifteen divided by three is five. Fifteen is a multiple of three." The list of squadrons that could march in three lines looked as follows:

3

6

9

12

15

Kaleb noticed, "There's a pattern. The multiples on the list are increasing by three: six, nine, twelve, fifteen. The even numbers on the list are six apart and they are also divisible by two."

"Oh, cool!" Myles responded.

"Hey, I tried Kaleb's idea," Natalie said. "If we go in order, the next number is eighteen; it's six more than twelve and it's divisible by both two and three. That's neat!"

Shelly tried out the new mathematics vocabulary and said, "Eighteen is a common multiple of two and three."

Victoria added, "The odd numbers are six apart, too." Several students nodded.

"Which squadrons could march in four equal lines with no extra bugs?" I asked, writing a 4 to start a new list.

"Eight works," Roxanne suggested. "Four times two is eight, and eight divided by four is two."

"Twelve works for four lines and for two and three lines!" Elonzo said. "Squadron twelve could march all three ways. It's a common multiple of three numbers!"

"Squadron four could march in four lines of one," Chico shared.

Pilar said, "Sixteen works for four and for two, but not for three."

I recorded the students' suggestions on the board as they shared. The lists looked as follows:

2	3	4
50	6	8
4	9	12
6	12	4
2	15	16
10		
20		
8		
42		

Kaleb said, "I have an idea. I think any number that's divisible by four is also divisible by two. I also think that if you put all the squadron numbers in order for two lines, every other one will be divisible by four. For example, two is divisible by two but not four, four is divisible by both two and four, six is only divisible by two, and eight is divisible by two and four. It goes on like that into infinity."

"I wonder if every twelve numbers are divisible by two, three, and four," Shelly mused. "Twelve works, and so does twenty-four."

"I think you're right," Carson said. "Thirty-six would be next, and two goes into it eighteen times, three goes into

thirty-six twelve times, and four goes into thirty-six nine times." There were no other comments.

"Which squadrons could march in five equal lines with no extra bugs?" I asked, starting a new list with a 5 at the top.

Students suggested squadrons ten, twenty-five, thirty, one hundred, and fifteen. I listed these on the board.

"They all end in zero or five," Jessi noticed. "I think the numbers that end in zero can march in two lines. They're even, so they're divisible by two." Many students nodded their agreement.

"I think one hundred could go on the twos list and the fours list, but not on the threes list," Chico said. No one had anything else to add.

"Which squadrons could march in six equal lines with no extra bugs?" I asked, writing a 6 to start the list.

"Twelve works!" Roxanne announced. "And twelve is also a multiple of two, three, and four, but not five."

Ashton said, "I think squadron thirty-six works. Six times six is thirty-six."

"Thirty is a multiple of six," Ellyn said. "Thirty divided by six is five with no remainders, so it's a multiple of six."

Our lists now looked as follows:

2	3	4	5	6
50	6	8	10	12
4	9	12	25	36
6	12	4	30	30
2	15	16	100	
10			15	
20				
8				
42				

A Further Investigation of Multiples

"There are more squadron numbers that we could add to each of these lists," I said. "In just a few moments, I'll organize you into groups of five. Each member of your group will choose one number: two, three, four, five, or six. For your number, write all the multiples from one to one hundred. For example, if I chose two, then my job would be to list all the multiples of two on my paper from one to one hundred. Another way to say this is that two must be a divisor of all the numbers on my list. While I am listing all the multiples of two, someone else in my group works on listing the multiples of three. Another member of my group lists the multiples of four, someone else lists the multiples of five, and the last person in my group lists the multiples of six. Each person needs his or her own sheet of paper to list the multiples."

"How do we choose who does which number?" Malina asked.

"I'll let you and your group decide," I responded. "If you can't decide, then let me know and I'll decide for you."

As I organized the students into groups of five, I handed one member of each group five sheets of paper. Two groups had only four members, but I still gave them five sheets. "Whoever finishes first should start the last list. Others can help as they finish, too." In just a few minutes, the students were fully engaged in the task. I checked with each group, asking who was working on which number. In all cases the groups quickly told me and showed me their work up to that point.

Ashton commented, "Twos have a lot of multiples, but they're easy."

Shelly chimed in, "Sixes have a lot less, but it's harder to think of the multiples of six."

I continued to circulate through the class. Before long, Martin announced to me that he was finished. "Which number are you working on?" I asked.

"Twos," Martin replied.

"How many numbers should be on your list?" I asked.

Martin shrugged, then was quiet for a moment. Even though Kaleb had explained earlier that there were fifty multiples of two, I've learned that not all of the other students necessarily understand when a classmate explains an idea. Martin finally said, "I think fifty, because every other number from one to one hundred is a multiple of two, so that's half the numbers. Half of one hundred is fifty. Also, I think the numbers on my list should be even." I nodded my agreement with his thinking.

"Count how many numbers are on your list and let me know what you find out," I said. I noticed that Martin hadn't included a 2 on his list.

After a few moments, Martin reported that there were only forty-nine numbers on his list. He studied the list a bit, noticed the 2 was missing, and quickly added it to the list. I suggested he help another member of his group.

Before long, Katie's entire group finished. I suggested they exchange papers to check for accuracy. After they did so, I gave each of them an overhead transparency of the 1–100 chart and a different-colored overhead marker. Hayley had found the multiples of two, so I asked her to use an overhead marker to indicate each multiple of two on her transparency by putting a dot in the upper left corner of each square with a multiple of two. Krystal had worked on threes, so I asked her to use an overhead marker to indicate the multiples of three on her transparency by marking a dot in the lower left corner of each square with a multiple of three. Natalie had worked on multiples of four. On her transparency, she marked a dot in the upper right corner of each square with a multiple of four. Katie marked her transparency with a dot in the lower right corner of each square with a multiple of five, and Chico circled on his transparency each number that was a multiple of six. When they were finished, I collected the five transparencies along with the markers for use later in the lesson.

When most of the groups were finished with their lists, I gave a two-minute warning. Then I asked for the students' attention and said, "Math time is almost over for today. Be sure to put your name on your paper. Then I'd like one person from each group to collect the papers from his or her group and bring them to me. I'll keep them for tomorrow."

DAY 2

To begin class, I handed back to the students their lists of multiples from the previous day. I asked five students each to write on the board a list for a different set of multiples. As the five students wrote their lists on the board, I asked the others in the class to check their own lists to see if they agreed with the lists on the board. When the five students were finished writing their lists of multiples, I led a brief discussion and we made a few needed corrections to the lists on the board. I also instructed the students to make any needed corrections on their papers. This provided a way for all groups to have an accurate and complete list of multiples to 100 for the numbers 2, 3, 4, 5, and 6.

I then posed a question. "Which squadrons could march in two equal lines, three equal lines, four equal lines, five equal lines, *and* six equal lines with no extra bugs?" I made sure to emphasized the word *and*. I wrote the question on the board, underlining the word *and*:

Which squadrons could march in 2, 3, 4, 5, <u>and</u> 6 equal lines with no extra bugs?

I gave the students a moment to think about this question quietly. "Talk it over with your neighbor," I then suggested. After a few moments, I asked for the students' attention. "Who would like to share?"

Jared said, "I think squadron twenty could march in all those ways."

Martin said, "It's sixty, I'm sure of it." I listed Jared's and Martin's suggestions on the board.

"Who has a different idea?" I asked.

"I think one," Diego said. I added 1 to the list and continued recording as students suggested other numbers.

"One hundred," Malina said.

"How about fifty?" Krystal suggested.

"Maybe ten," Mark said.

"I think sixty, even though it's already up there," Joelle said.

"I think sixty, too," Clay volunteered.

"Twenty-five," Roxanne said.

"I have another guess: fifteen," Diego said.

"Two," Ashton suggested.

The list of suggestions on the board now looked like this:

> 20
>
> 60
>
> 1
>
> 100
>
> 50
>
> 10
>
> 25
>
> 15
>
> 2

"If a squadron can march in two equal lines with no remainders, what do we know about the number?" I asked.

"It has to be even," Shelly said. Many students nodded.

"If we know the number has to be even for the squadron to march in two lines, can we eliminate any of the guesses?" I asked.

Elonzo said, "You can cross off the twenty-five and the fifteen because they're odd." I did as Elonzo suggested.

"Are there any others?" I asked.

"One is odd, so you can cross it off," Sierra said. I crossed off the 1.

"Are there any other odd numbers?" I pushed. The students shook their heads "no."

"What about squadrons that can march in five lines? What do we know about their numbers?" I asked.

Joelle said, "They have to have a zero or a five in the ones place."

Clay jumped in, "I disagree with Joelle. She said the number has to end with a zero or a five. But it has to end with a zero because we know it has to be even if it's also divisible by two."

I said, "You're both right. Joelle gave a correct answer to my question about how we know when numbers are divisible by five. They have to have a zero or a five in the ones place. But Clay is also correct as far as this problem goes. Because we know the number has to be even to be divisible by two, it can't have a five in the ones place." Both students nodded.

"Can we eliminate any other guesses?" I asked.

Ellyn said, "Two won't work." I crossed off the 2. The list now looked like this:

20

60

~~1~~

100

50

10

~~25~~

~~15~~

~~2~~

"Hey, they all end in zero," Kaleb noticed.

"They can't end in anything else," Myles added.

"So the squadrons on the list can march in two lines and five lines," I said. "Are there any other squadron numbers we could add to the list that also can march in two lines and in five lines?"

Krystal said, "Any number that ends with zero as long as it's no bigger than one hundred. All numbers that end with zero are even, so they can be divided by two, and they can be divided by five." Most students nodded their agreement.

"So what other numbers could I add to the list?" I pushed.

Rae Ann said, "You can add thirty, forty, seventy, eighty, and ninety." The rest of the students indicated their agreement with thumbs up. I added *30, 40, 70, 80,* and *90* to the list. The list now looked as follows:

20

60

~~1~~

100

50

10

~~25~~

~~15~~

~~2~~

30

40

70

80

90

I asked next, pointing to the list, "Can all these squadrons also march in three lines?" I paused a moment to give the students time to think, then said, "Talk this over with your neighbor." After a few moments, I asked for the students' attention.

Diego shared, "Thirty works. Three lines of ten equals thirty. Ten, twenty, thirty. Sixty works, too. It's twice as big as thirty, so there would be three lines of twenty. Check it by counting twenty, forty, sixty. Ninety is like three thirties. Three lines of thirty makes ninety. Thirty, sixty, ninety."

I recorded on the board:

30 = 3 × 10	*10, 20, 30*
60 = 3 × 20	*20, 40, 60*
90 = 3 × 30	*30, 60, 90*

"Can any of the other squadrons on the list march in lines of three?" I asked. The students shook their heads "no" and I crossed off the remaining numbers, leaving only 30, 60, and 90. Before moving forward, I asked, "Are there any squadron numbers we could add to the list?"

Natalie said, "I think we've eliminated all the numbers but these three. Marching in two lines gets rid of all the odd numbers. Marching in five lines means the squadron numbers have to end in zero or five, and we know it has to be even, so that means only numbers with zero in the ones place are left."

"Which of these three squadrons can march in four lines?" I asked.

"Not thirty," Katie said.

"How do you know?" I asked.

"Because four doesn't go into thirty evenly. You get seven, but there's two left over," Katie explained. I recorded on the board: *30 ÷ 4 = 7 R2*. Then I crossed 30 off the list.

"I don't think ninety works, either," Chico said.

"Please explain your thinking," I replied to Chico.

"Well, four times twenty-five is one hundred. If I start at one hundred and count back by fours, I don't land on ninety. I go one hundred, ninety-six, ninety-two, eighty-eight," Chico explained. I recorded *100, 96, 92, 88* on the board and crossed off 90.

"Sixty works!" Martin said. "Sixty divided by four is fifteen. You can check by counting by fifteens: fifteen, thirty, forty-five, sixty." I wrote on the board:

60 ÷ 4 = 15

15, 30, 45, 60

Martin continued, "And sixty is divisible by six. Sixty divided by six is ten with no remainder. Sixty works for two, three, four, five, and six!"

Natalie restated Martin's thinking with awe, "So the only squadron that could march in two lines, three lines, four lines, five lines, and six lines is sixty. Wow!" The students were quiet.

Patterns on the 1–100 Chart

"Yesterday, I asked Krystal's group to record their multiples on transparencies of the hundreds chart. Hayley put a dot in the upper left corner of each multiple of two," I explained as I projected Hayley's transparency.

1–100 Chart

1	2	3	4	5	6	7	8	9	10
11	12	13	14	15	16	17	18	19	20
21	22	23	24	25	26	27	28	29	30
31	32	33	34	35	36	37	38	39	40
41	42	43	44	45	46	47	48	49	50
51	52	53	54	55	56	57	58	59	60
61	62	63	64	65	66	67	68	69	70
71	72	73	74	75	76	77	78	79	80
81	82	83	84	85	86	87	88	89	90
91	92	93	94	95	96	97	98	99	100

"That's a lot of multiples," Chico observed.

"Yeah, fifty of them," Martin added, now sure about this.

I continued, "Krystal marked a dot in the lower left corner of each multiple of three." I carefully laid Krystal's transparency on top of Hayley's. "What do you notice?"

1–100 Chart

1	2	3	4	5	6	7	8	9	10
11	12	13	14	15	16	17	18	19	20
21	22	23	24	25	26	27	28	29	30
31	32	33	34	35	36	37	38	39	40
41	42	43	44	45	46	47	48	49	50
51	52	53	54	55	56	57	58	59	60
61	62	63	64	65	66	67	68	69	70
71	72	73	74	75	76	77	78	79	80
81	82	83	84	85	86	87	88	89	90
91	92	93	94	95	96	97	98	99	100

"Some squares have no dots, some have one dot, and some have two dots, like six and eighteen," Roxanne shared.

"The ones with two dots are multiples of both two and three," Max remarked.

Jared said, "Every six squares has two dots." He came up and counted to show what he meant.

"The squares with two dots go in a diagonal," Sierra said. "Twelve, twenty-four, thirty-six go in a diagonal." She came up and showed the pattern that she noticed.

"Look how many more multiples of two there are than three," Joelle said.

There were no more comments, so I carefully laid the transparency with the multiples of four on top of the first two transparencies.

1–100 Chart

1	2	3	4	5	6	7	8	9	10
11	12	13	14	15	16	17	18	19	20
21	22	23	24	25	26	27	28	29	30
31	32	33	34	35	36	37	38	39	40
41	42	43	44	45	46	47	48	49	50
51	52	53	54	55	56	57	58	59	60
61	62	63	64	65	66	67	68	69	70
71	72	73	74	75	76	77	78	79	80
81	82	83	84	85	86	87	88	89	90
91	92	93	94	95	96	97	98	99	100

Finally, I added the transparency marked with the multiples of six.

1–100 Chart

1	2	3	4	5	6	7	8	9	10
11	12	13	14	15	16	17	18	19	20
21	22	23	24	25	26	27	28	29	30
31	32	33	34	35	36	37	38	39	40
41	42	43	44	45	46	47	48	49	50
51	52	53	54	55	56	57	58	59	60
61	62	63	64	65	66	67	68	69	70
71	72	73	74	75	76	77	78	79	80
81	82	83	84	85	86	87	88	89	90
91	92	93	94	95	96	97	98	99	100

(Multiples of six circled: 6, 12, 18, 24, 30, 36, 42, 48, 54, 60, 66, 72, 78, 84, 90, 96)

"There aren't very many squares that have three dots," Pilar said. "It seems like the more multiples there are, the less squares there are that have all the dots." Several students nodded.

I laid the transparency marked with the multiples of five on top of the others.

1–100 Chart

1	2	3	4	5	6	7	8	9	10
11	12	13	14	15	16	17	18	19	20
21	22	23	24	25	26	27	28	29	30
31	32	33	34	35	36	37	38	39	40
41	42	43	44	45	46	47	48	49	50
51	52	53	54	55	56	57	58	59	60
61	62	63	64	65	66	67	68	69	70
71	72	73	74	75	76	77	78	79	80
81	82	83	84	85	86	87	88	89	90
91	92	93	94	95	96	97	98	99	100

"Oh, wow!" Krystal said. "Only one number has all the marks, and that's sixty." Several other students commented with "That's cool!" and "Oh, wow!"

"I guess we figured out in two ways which squadrons could march in two lines, three lines, four lines, five lines, and six lines," Clay said. "One way was we figured out sixty using numbers on the board, then we figured out sixty again by using hundreds charts. I think it's cool we got the same answer in different ways like that!" I ended the lesson with Clay's comment.

EXTENSIONS

1. Have students explore which squadrons from one hundred to two hundred could march in 2, 3, 4, 5, and 6 equal lines with no extras.

2. Choose a month, March, for example. Tell students the queen has decided that since March is the third month of the year, she'd like the bugs to march in three lines. Which squadrons can do this with no remainders? Then tell them the queen has changed her mind and decided that in March a remainder of one would be OK, because that bug could be the drum major. What squadrons would work for this situation? You can pose these problems using other months; for example, in April, the bugs would march in four lines, in May, five lines, and so on.

3. Have students use the lists of multiples to play the *Division Game* (see Chapter 14).

Questions and Discussion

▲▲▲

▲ *What's your purpose for recording students' thinking on the board?*

This serves several purposes. When I record a student's thinking in this way, I'm valuing that child's efforts. This is an important form of positive recognition. Also, some learners are more visual and are supported when they can see ideas put into written form. In addition, a written record is useful as a reference of what's been said thus far in a discussion and can help students clarify their thinking when they do their own written work. And, at the end of class, I have a written record of what went on that is useful for me when I reflect on the lesson.

▲ *In the beginning, this lesson seems simple for my students. Why is it worthwhile for them to do it?*

While this lesson may seem simple in the beginning, an easy beginning gives students an access point to more complex ideas about division that are presented later in the lesson. Providing students with success at the beginning of a lesson builds confidence and helps prepare them to apply what they already know to problems that involve more complex ideas.

▲ *It seems like the students were using multiples, multiplication, and addition to solve problems in this lesson. How did that help them with division?*

Throughout the lesson, students made use of their knowledge of multiples, multiplication, and addition. Students who are fluent with using and recognizing multiples have an important foundation upon which to build their knowledge of division. When students use prior knowledge in this way, they are making important connections among ideas, thus deepening their own understanding. It's also important to remember that the long division algorithm is dependent on students' ability to use their knowledge of multiples and multiplication efficiently and accurately.

CHAPTER ELEVEN
GRAPE LICORICE

Overview

Purple yarn used to represent grape licorice provides the context for this lesson in which students think about equally dividing a 36-inch piece of grape licorice among 1 to 10 people. As a class, students figure how much licorice each person gets if 1, 2, 4, and 5 people share a 36-inch piece of licorice. Then, working in pairs, students figure the amount each would get if they divided the licorice among 3, 6, 7, 8, 9, and 10 people. The students record the information on a chart and, in a class discussion, share the patterns they notice.

Materials

▲ yarn
▲ optional: yardsticks, 1 for every three to four students

Time

▲ one class period, plus additional time for the extension

Teaching Directions

1. Show students a length of yarn that is longer than 36 inches. (Purple yarn was used for this lesson, but any color will do.) Explain that the yarn represents licorice.

2. With the assistance of a student, use a yardstick to measure and cut off a 36-inch piece of the yarn.

3. Ask students how many inches of licorice you'd get if you ate the entire piece. On the board, draw a two-column chart, sometimes called a T-chart, label the columns, and record as follows:

# of People	# of Inches
1	36

4. Ask students how many inches of licorice each person would get if you and one student in the class shared the licorice equally. As students share and explain their answers, record their thinking on the board. Verify that each of the two people would get 18 inches by folding the yarn in half and measuring. Add the information for two people sharing to the chart.

5. Repeat Step 4 to determine how many inches of licorice each person would get if four people shared.

# of People	# of Inches
1	36
2	18
4	9

6. Repeat Step 4 to determine how many inches of licorice each person would get if five people shared. This time, with the students, discuss how to represent the answer in two ways, with the remainder as a whole number or as a fraction—7 R1 or $7\frac{1}{5}$. Since folding the yarn into five equal lengths is difficult, have a student hold one end of the yarn and measure 7 inches five times for an approximate check of the answer.

7. Ask students to work in pairs to figure the amount of licorice each person would get if 3, 6, 7, 8, 9, and 10 people shared 36 inches of licorice.

8. As students work, circulate through the class, observing and assisting as needed.

9. As a class, complete the chart. Then lead a discussion about patterns students notice on the chart.

Teaching Notes

The Lesson presented in this chapter is based on an idea suggested by Rick Kharas, a teacher in Syracuse, New York. Because Rick used yellow yarn rather than purple, he called his lesson *Lemon Licorice*.

This lesson provides students computational practice with division, reinforces that division requires equal groups, and strengthens their understanding of the remainder—what it is and how to represent it. For some classes, it's appropriate for the students to represent the remainder only as a whole number, for example, R1, while in other classes, students are able to and interested in also representing the remainder as a fraction. Many of the students in the following vignette were interested in thinking about remainders as fractions, and this is included in the discussion. A few students in the class were not yet ready for this idea, and I encouraged them to represent the remainder as a whole number.

While I used a 36-inch piece of yarn as a model in the beginning of the lesson, most of the students didn't need their own piece of yarn to figure how much each person would get if 3, 6, 7, 8, 9, and 10 people shared. However, I made yarn available. Some students found that the yarn was helpful in solving some problems, such as sharing 36 inches of licorice among 8 people, but not helpful for other problems, such as sharing 36 inches among seven people. You'll need to decide if it makes sense for your students to have 36-inch pieces of yarn to use. If it's appropriate for your students to have the pieces of yarn, one piece per pair works well. It's helpful to have several yardsticks and balls of yarn available so several pairs of students can measure and cut their yarn at the same time. Or, if you'd rather not take the time to have your students measure, precut 36-inch lengths for them.

For the extension, however, it's necessary for students to have their own piece of yarn. They choose their own length of yarn to cut and then measure it. As explained earlier, it's a good idea to have several yardsticks and balls of yarn available.

The Lesson

▲▲▲

I held up a brown paper bag for the children to see. As the students watched, I slowly began to pull a strand of purple yarn from the bag. I said to the class, "Inside is a very long piece of purple licorice!" The students giggled as I continued to pull the yarn from the bag. "I tasted one small bite and it tastes like grape."

"It looks like it would taste fuzzy!" Alice said.

"What if it were eggplant flavored?" Pesach commented. The class groaned.

I continued, "I'm going to cut off a piece of this licorice, or yarn, that's thirty-six inches long." With Juan's assistance, I used a yardstick to measure and cut a 36-inch piece of yarn.

I held up the length of yarn I had just cut and said, "Yesterday, I was really hungry and I don't think I would have shared my licorice. How much would I have eaten if I ate the whole piece?"

"Thirty-six inches," the students responded together. I drew on the board a two-column chart, sometimes called a T-chart, labeled the columns *# of People* and *# of Inches,* and recorded the information.

# of People	# of Inches
1	36

I explained, "I wrote a one to indicate that I was the only person who ate the licorice. And the thirty-six tells how many inches I ate."

I continued, "Suppose I'm not as hungry today and I want to share my thirty-six inches of licorice with one other person, Kiana. How much would Kiana and I each get if we shared equally?" I paused to give all students a chance to think about my question. I called on Benito.

Benito said, "You could give Kiana one inch and you eat the rest!" Benito and the others laughed.

Kiana gave Benito a look and then said, "She said we would share equally!"

"OK," Benito said. "Then you would each get eighteen inches."

I asked, "Did someone get a different answer?" No one did. "Who would like to explain why eighteen inches makes sense?"

Alice explained, "Eighteen plus eighteen equals thirty-six and thirty-six is how much you have to share."

I recorded on the board:

Alice $18 + 18 = 36$

Natalia added, "Instead of adding, you could multiply eighteen by two."

I recorded Natalia's idea on the board beneath Alice's:

Natalia $18 \times 2 = 36$

"I know another way still," Wendi said. "You could just divide thirty-six by two, which is like taking half of thirty-six."

I added Wendi's idea to the list:

Wendi $36 \div 2 = 18$

         $\frac{1}{2}$ *of* $36 = 18$

"These are all excellent suggestions," I said. "Two people would eat eighteen inches each." I wrote *2* and *18* on the T-chart.

# of People	# of Inches
1	36
2	18

"I'm going to check to see if what I added to the chart makes sense," I said. "To check, I'm going to fold the yarn in half, one half for Kiana, and one half for me. If I wanted to cut it at the fold, I would have two equal pieces, but I'm not going to cut it. I'll measure it from the end to the fold." I folded the yarn in half and, to the delight of the students, the folded yarn measured 18 inches long.

I then said, "Suppose I decided I didn't want any licorice. Instead I wanted to share all thirty-six inches among Kiana, Marco, Sara, and Pesach. How many people would be sharing my licorice now?"

"Four," the class responded.

"How much would each get if the four people shared it equally?" I asked. "Think about it quietly for just a moment." After a moment I said, "Talk it over with your neighbor." After a few more moments, I asked for the students' attention. "Show me with your fingers how much each person would get." The students each showed nine fingers. "I see you all have nine fingers up. Who would like to explain why nine makes sense?"

Abbie said, "I knew that thirty-six divided by four is nine. I can check by multiplying nine times four and it should equal thirty-six."

I recorded Abbie's thinking on the board:

Abbie $36 \div 4 = 9$

$9 \times 4 = 36$

I asked the students, "Who thought of the problem the way Abbie did?" Several raised their hands. "Who had a different idea?" I called on Kaleb.

Kaleb shared, "My idea is sort of like Abbie's. I know that nine times four equals thirty-six. Nine tells the number of inches each person gets and four tells how many people are sharing the thirty-six inches."

I pointed to where I had written $9 \times 4 = 36$ and said, "So, you're telling us what the nine, and the four, and the thirty-six mean when we're thinking about sharing the licorice." Kaleb nodded.

"How many thought of the problem like Kaleb?" I asked. About half the students raised their hands. "Who thought of it differently?"

Jewell shared next. "I looked at the chart. Two people each got eighteen inches. Four people is twice as many as two, so I think each person would get half as much. Half of eighteen is nine. You could prove it. If you folded the yarn into half again, you would have four equal pieces and it's like each of the first halves gets put in half again. Half of eighteen is nine." If Jewell hadn't suggested folding the yarn a second time to check her thinking, I would have done so.

I held the yarn up so that the students could see it. I folded it in half once, and then in half a second time. I asked Jewell, "Is this what you mean?" She nodded.

Juan said, "Oh yeah! I can see how each half got folded in half again. I didn't think of that before."

"Let's measure and find out," Kalani said. I did as Kalani suggested and verified that the folded length was 9 inches long. "How many people thought of it Jewell's way?" I asked. A few students raised their hands.

Juan had an idea to share. He said, "I wasn't exactly sure at first. I knew eight times four equals thirty-two and that's too small. So I tried nine times four and that equals thirty-six."

I recorded Juan's idea with the rest:

Juan $8 \times 4 = 32$ (too small)

$9 \times 4 = 36$

A few students indicated they solved the problem like Juan.

Tim had a different idea. He explained, "I knew if two people shared, they'd each get eighteen inches. Four people is twice as many, so each person gets half as much. I also know that eighteen is equal to ten plus eight. Ten divided by two equals five. Eight divided by two equals four. Add five and four, and it's nine."

I recorded Tim's idea:

Tim $18 = 10 + 8$

$10 \div 2 = 5$

$8 \div 2 = 4$

$5 + 4 = 9$

No one had any other ideas, so I added the information to the T-chart, leaving space between the 2 and 4 and between the 18 and 9 to fill in the information about sharing the licorice among three people.

# of People	# of Inches
1	36
2	18
4	9

Next I asked, "What if I wanted to share my licorice among five people? How much would each person get?"

"I think there's going to be a remainder," Alycia commented.

"I think each person will get less than with four," Natalia said.

"I don't think we can just divide the amount everyone gets in half this time," Benito added.

"What's the problem we're trying to solve?" I asked.

"Thirty-six divided by five," the students chorused. I nodded and wrote on the board: $36 \div 5 =$.

I said, "Talk it over with your table group. How much will each person get if five people share the licorice equally?" The students were immediately engaged in lively discussions with their table groups. I had to remind a few groups to be sure that every person had the opportunity to share his or her ideas. After several minutes, I asked for the students' attention. Hands waved in the air eagerly.

"Is there a remainder?" I asked.

"Yes," the students replied unanimously.

"Use a whisper voice to tell me how much each person gets," I said.

"Seven remainder one," most students said.

A few said, "Seven and one-fifth." I wrote both answers on the board, explaining I'd heard students say both:

7 R1

$7\frac{1}{5}$

Kiana's hand was up immediately. She explained, "I said seven and one-fifth, but I think it could also be seven with one inch left over. I took the one inch and figured that it could be shared with five people and that would mean each person would get one-seventh. . . ." Kiana paused a moment, then corrected herself. "No, one-fifth because they would each get one out of five equal pieces." Several students nodded their agreement. A few looked puzzled.

I held up the yarn about 1 inch from the end so the students could see. I said, "Kiana says each person gets seven

inches. Seven inches for five people would be thirty-five inches, which leaves this one inch." I indicated the 1 inch of yarn I was holding. "Then Kiana said that we could divide the one inch into five equal pieces and give one-fifth of an inch to each person."

"That's small," Jackson said.

"We should just give the extra inch to you," Nalani suggested.

"Are these answers equivalent?" I asked, pointing to where I'd written 7 R1 and $7\frac{1}{5}$.

"What's equivalent?" Pesach asked.

"The same amount, like equal amounts," Natalia explained. I nodded my agreement with Natalia's explanation.

"If you think they're equivalent, put your thumb up; if you think they aren't equivalent, put your thumb down; and if you aren't sure, put your thumb sideways." All but a few students put their thumbs up.

Alycia commented, "With seven remainder one, there's one inch left, and we don't really know what happens to it. With seven and one-fifth, we know each of the five people got a part of the leftover inch."

"How could we use the yarn to verify each person gets seven inches with one inch left?" I asked.

Isiah commented, "That would be hard because folding the yarn into five equal parts would be hard. You can't just fold it in half one or two times like when we shared with two and four people." Most students nodded their agreement.

I modeled for the students a way to measure. Doing so gave me the opportunity to remind students that measurement is never exact. I asked for a volunteer to help me measure. I chose Jewell and asked her to hold one end of the yarn. I placed a 12-inch ruler at the end she was holding and held the yarn horizontally, pinching it at 7 inches. "That's one share," I said. I moved the end of the ruler to the spot I was pinching and measured another 7 inches. "That's two shares," I said. I continued in this manner for five shares.

When I finished, I said, "This shows that five people can each have seven inches. I can't tell this way that there is exactly one inch left. It's hard to measure exactly, but I'm convinced our answer is right."

To summarize, I said as I pointed to 7 R1 and $7\frac{1}{5}$, "These are two correct ways of writing the answer and they are equivalent. You would be right either way." The students nodded. I added the information for five people sharing to the chart.

# of People	# of Inches
1	36
2	18
4	9
5	7 R1 or $7\frac{1}{5}$

INTRODUCING THE INVESTIGATION

I pointed to the chart and said to the students, "Together, we figured out how many inches of licorice one person, two people, four people, and five people would get if they shared equally a thirty-six-inch piece." I filled in the rest of the numbers to 10 on the left side of the chart. "Your job now is to work with your partner to complete the chart. You'll need to figure out how many inches of licorice each of three people get, then six people, seven people, and so on up to ten people. Even though you're working with your partner, each of you will need to make your own recording sheet." I wrote the following directions on the board as a reminder:

1. *Work with your partner.*
2. *Each person makes a recording sheet.*
3. *Copy and complete the chart on the board. Figure out how many inches of licorice each of 3, 6, 7, 8, 9, and 10 people get.*

# of People	# of Inches
1	36
2	18
3	
4	9
5	7 R1 or $7\frac{1}{5}$
6	
7	
8	
9	
10	

OBSERVING THE STUDENTS

I circulated through the class as the students eagerly got to work. "This will be fun!" Natalia said as she and her partner, Nalani, began. The discussions were animated and students used different methods to solve the problems. I checked on Marco, who sometimes was not clear on directions. He had copied the chart but wasn't sure if there was a particular method he had to use to solve the problems. I explained to him that he and his partner could use any strategies that made sense to them and that they could explain.

"Could you sit and watch a minute to see if I do it right?" Marco asked. I nodded and sat down. He tentatively started to write on his paper $3\overline{)36}$, then he paused and looked to me for approval. I nodded and Marco said, "There are ten threes in thirty-six; I just write it here." He continued to talk aloud as he worked the problem, giving me a rare opportunity to check

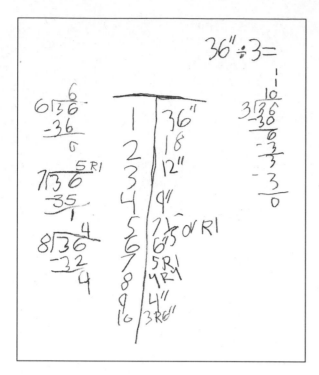

$36'' \div 3 =$

▲▲▲▲▲**Figure 11–1** *Marco successfully completed the task, showing good understanding.*

his understanding, which was solid. (See Figure 11–1.)

I moved on after reassuring Marco I'd be back to check on his progress shortly. When I returned a short while later, he and his partner were doing fine.

I noticed Charlie was making little progress and his partner was frustrated. I asked Charlie to explain the task and what he'd done so far. He accurately explained the task but was uncertain about how to figure the amounts of licorice each person would get. His knowledge of the basic multiplication and division facts was weak and not much help to him for this experience. To give him a concrete way into the investigation, I gave him a 36-inch piece of yarn and a yardstick. I asked him to measure the yarn. He did so, stating that it was 36 inches long. I asked, "If you ate this whole piece of licorice, how many inches would you eat?"

Charlie responded, "All of it."

"How many inches is all of it?" I asked.

"Thirty-six inches," Charlie responded. "Should I write it on the chart?" I nodded.

"How could you use the yarn to show how much two people would get?" I asked.

Without saying anything and with some hesitation and help from his partner, Charlie carefully folded the yarn into two equal parts, measured it, and correctly recorded on his chart. I had found that for Charlie, it was sometimes helpful to repeat previous demonstrations and explanations one-on-one. I then asked Charlie and his partner to find the amounts for each person if four people shared the 36-inch piece of licorice and then if eight people shared it. I chose those numbers because he could use the yarn as a tool, folding it into fourths and eighths and measuring.

I asked Charlie, "Could you use addition to verify each of two people would get eighteen inches of licorice?"

Charlie looked pensive. I waited, watching his face for signs of frustration. After a few moments, he said, "Each person got eighteen inches. Eighteen plus eighteen equals thirty-six, I think." He paused, put one finger on the yardstick at 18 inches, and counted from 18 until he reached 36. He smiled and said, "I counted from eighteen to thirty-six and it's eighteen, so eighteen and eighteen is thirty-six."

I pointed to his recording sheet and asked him to record the addition sentence next to where he recorded 2 and 18 on his chart.

"How many inches should all four pieces of licorice add up to when four people share?" I asked.

"Maybe thirty?" Charlie replied.

"How many inches did both pieces equal when two people shared?" I asked.

"Oh, I get it, it should be thirty-six because that's how much we started with," Charlie said.

"If eight people shared thirty-six inches of licorice, how many inches should all their pieces add up to?" I pushed.

"Thirty-six," Charlie responded with confidence. "If you add up all the pieces, it should be the same as what you started with." I reminded Charlie to find out how much each person would get if four people shared and then if eight people shared, and then I moved on to check on other students.

Benito was working intently on his paper. I noticed that he had made an error in his use of fractions. For seven people, he had written each person would get $5\frac{1}{5}$ inches of licorice, or 5 R1 inches.

I said to Benito, "Tell me how you figured each of seven people would get five and one-fifth inches of licorice."

Benito explained, "Seven times five is thirty-five, so I know seven people could each have five inches. I have thirty-six inches of licorice, and I divided up thirty-five of the inches, so thirty-six minus thirty-five equals one inch left. So that means I have to divide the last inch into five parts."

"Why do you need to divide it into five parts?" I asked. Benito paused and looked confused.

"How many people are sharing the licorice?" I asked.

"Seven," Benito responded quickly. "Oh, I think I see now; I have to divide the licorice into seven parts, one part for each person. I got confused. Each person would get five inches and one out of seven parts of the leftover inch." I nodded my agreement.

Alycia was very proud of her work. She said, "I know these are division problems. And I did the first two as division, but I know my multiplication tables really well and so I used them to figure out the answers."

"Why does your idea work?" I asked.

"Well, multiplication and division are linked," Alycia said and then paused for a few moments to collect her thoughts. "They're opposites in a way. But the

difference is what you know and what you're trying to figure out. In multiplication, you're trying to figure out how many altogether. In division, you already know that. That's the dividend. In multiplication, you know how many groups and how many in each group, but you have to figure one of those things out when you do division. So if I knew how many people and how much licorice altogether, I could just figure out a number to multiply by the number of people that equals the amount of licorice." Alycia gave a huge sigh after her explanation. (See Figure 11–2.)

Tad was pleased with his use of fractions to represent the remainders. He explained to me how he figured out ten people would each get $3\frac{6}{10}$ inches of licorice. Tad said, "I looked at how much five people got. They got seven and one-fifth inches. Ten is five times two, so I knew that ten people would get half as

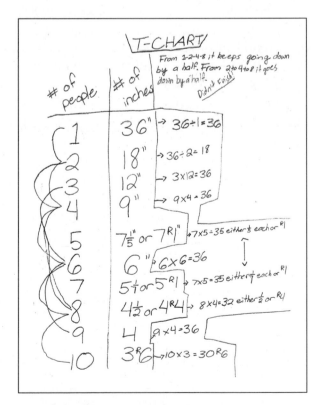

▲▲▲▲▲▲**Figure 11–2** *Alycia used both multiplication and division.*

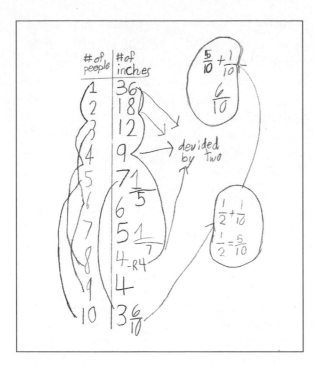

▲▲▲▲▲▲**Figure 11–3** *Tad showed how he figured $\frac{1}{2} + \frac{1}{10}$ was equal to $\frac{6}{10}$.*

# of People	# of Inches
1	36
2	18
3	12
4	9
5	7 R1 or $7\frac{1}{5}$
6	6
7	5 R1 or $5\frac{1}{7}$
8	4 R4
9	4
10	3 R6

much as five. Half of seven is three and a half. Half of one-fifth is one-tenth, I think. One-half is the same as five-tenths. So one-tenth and five-tenths is six-tenths. I wrote it up here." He indicated the upper right corner of his paper. (See Figure 11–3.)

I continued to look over students' shoulders, checking their work and asking and answering questions as needed. Some students finished ahead of the others. I suggested they could either figure out how many inches each person would get if 11, 12, 13, 14, and 15 people shared or search their charts for patterns.

Bart and Tim decided to extend the number of people sharing to fifteen. Initially, the boys used both fractions and whole number remainders to represent leftovers. As they continued to higher numbers, they stopped using fractional remainders. (See Figure 11–4.)

I gave the students a two-minute warning. At the end of two minutes, I asked for their attention. Together, we completed the chart on the board.

Then I asked the students to quietly search the chart for patterns. After a few moments of quiet searching, I asked them to talk over patterns they noticed with their table groups and write about patterns that made sense to them. When every group had recorded some patterns, I asked for the students' attention.

A CLASS DISCUSSION

"What patterns did you notice?" I asked to begin a discussion. Most students had their hands up. I called on Tad.

"I noticed that when numbers double on the Number of People side of the chart, they go in half on the Number of Inches side," Tad shared.

"Can you give us an example?" I asked.

"Like one, two, four, and eight on the Number of People side is doubling," Tad said. "On the Number of Inches side, it goes thirty-six, eighteen, nine, and four and one-half. That's halving."

"Then there's five and ten," Alycia said.

"Oh, what about three and six?" Natalia asked. "What Tad said seems to work for three and six, too." Several other students nodded.

Nalani said, "I noticed that on the Number of People side of the chart, the

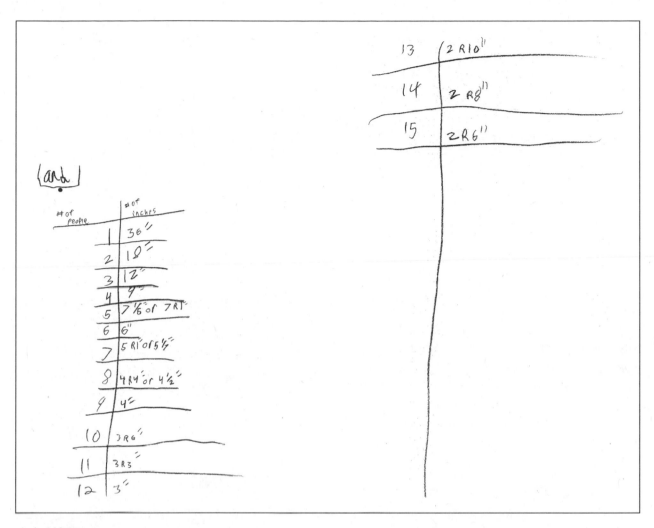

▲▲▲▲▲▲Figure 11–4 *Bart and Tim figured how much each would get if 11, 12, 13, 14, and 15 people shared equally 36 inches of licorice.*

numbers get bigger. The opposite happens on the Number of Inches side."

Kalani observed, "I think what Nalani said happens because the number of people increased but the amount of licorice stayed the same, so the more people there are, the less each person gets."

Brianna shared, "I noticed that five people and seven people switch around."

"Explain more about your thinking," I encouraged Brianna.

"Five people get seven inches and there's one inch left over, and seven people get five inches with one inch left over," Brianna explained. "The five and the seven switched places on the chart."

The students were quiet for a few moments. Tim raised his hand. He said, "This isn't a pattern, but I think there's another answer for ten people."

"Tell us more," I said.

"I think another answer could be three inches plus one-half inch and one-tenth inch," Tim said. "Or it could also be three and one-half inches remainder one."

"Why does that make sense to you?" I asked Tim.

"Three times ten equals thirty," Tim said. "That means each person gets three inches. But there are still six inches left. If each person got one-half inch, that would be five inches. Each person gets three and one-half inches, and that's thirty-five inches. One inch is left. You could divide the last inch into ten very tiny pieces and give each person one very tiny piece. That would be three and one-half inches plus one-tenth of an inch."

I recorded Tim's thinking on the board:

$3 \times 10 = 30$

$\frac{1}{2} \times 10 = 5$

$30 + 5 = 35$ (inches used)

$3 + \frac{1}{2} = 3\frac{1}{2}$ (inches per person)

$1 \div 10 = \frac{1}{10}$

$\frac{1}{10} \times 10 = 1$

$35 + 1 = 36$ (inches used)

$3\frac{1}{2} + \frac{1}{10}$ (inches per person)

Jewell shared next. She said, "This isn't on my paper, but Tim made me think of it. I think another way of writing three and one-half plus one-tenth could be three and six-tenths. I know that five-tenths is equivalent to one-half. So I could change the one-half into five-tenths and then add it to the one-tenth, and it would be six-tenths. Add six-tenths to three, and it's three and six-tenths."

I recorded Jewell's thinking on the board:

$3\frac{1}{2} + \frac{1}{10} = 3\frac{6}{10}$

$\frac{5}{10} = \frac{1}{2}$

$\frac{5}{10} + \frac{1}{10} = \frac{6}{10}$

$3 + \frac{6}{10} = 3\frac{6}{10}$

"That made me think of something else," Tad said. "I think you can divide both numbers in the fraction by two.

Three and six-tenths equals three and three-fifths because six divided by two equals three and ten divided by two equals five."

I recorded Tad's idea along with the others:

$3\frac{6}{10} = 3\frac{3}{5}$

$6 \div 2 = 3$

$10 \div 2 = 5$

$\frac{6}{10} = \frac{3}{5}$

$3\frac{6}{10} = 3\frac{3}{5}$

I said, "As it turns out, all these answers are equivalent ways to represent how much each person would get if ten people shared thirty-six inches of licorice equally." I decided to end the conversation there. Most of the students had had little experience with fractions and some students were starting to get restless. I knew that there would be other times to further explore these ideas about fractions.

EXTENSION

Have students repeat this experience, but this time, they can cut their own yarn using a length of their own choosing other than 36 inches. First they should measure the length of their yarn, then they should share the yarn equally among one to ten people, recording the results on a chart. Finally, students should write about patterns they notice in the chart.

Questions and Discussion

▲ *How can I increase the level of difficulty for my students?*

Increasing either the number of people sharing the licorice or the length of the licorice can increase the level of difficulty. To increase the starting length, measure in centimeters rather than inches. For experience with larger divisors, have the students investigate how much each person would get if up to twenty people shared the licorice equally.

▲ *I don't have access to meter sticks or yardsticks. What are some other ways students could measure?*

Having students create their own paper yardsticks is a worthwhile activity and provides an inexpensive alternative. Sentence strips are useful; most sentence strips are 24 inches long, and by taping together one and one-half sentence strips, students can create a paper yardstick. After taping the strips together, have students mark off and number the inches from 1 to 36. You may want to have students mark off and label the half inches as well. Students can store their yardsticks in their desks by folding them.

CHAPTER TWELVE
THE YARN LESSON

Overview

A length of yarn measuring 656 inches provides a context in this lesson for students to practice computation and measurement skills. To begin, student volunteers measure the yarn in inches using a 60-inch measuring tape. Next, students solve the problem of figuring the length of the yarn in feet. They verify their paper-and-pencil results by measuring the yarn with 12-inch rulers. Finally, students figure the length of the yarn in yards and, as before, verify their paper-and-pencil results by using a yardstick.

Materials

▲ measuring tape, 60 inches long
▲ yarn, 1 piece measuring about 656 inches
▲ 10 paper clips
▲ 5 12-inch rulers
▲ yardstick

Time

▲ two class periods

Teaching Directions

1. Begin by showing students a piece of yarn that measures 656 inches long. Do not tell them the length. Rather, ask for three student volunteers to measure the length of the yarn with the 60-inch measuring tape.

2. Show the volunteers how to measure. Have one student hold one end of the yarn and one end of the measuring tape together while a second student

138

measures one section of yarn using the measuring tape, marking the yarn with a paper clip at 60 inches.

Have the third student keep track of the number of measuring tape lengths with tally marks on the board.

3. After the volunteers have measured the yarn, ask the class to figure the length of the yarn in inches based on the tally marks. In a class discussion, have students share their methods for figuring the total inches. Record their methods on the board.

4. Next, pose the following problem: *Figure the number of feet in the length of yarn.* Remind students that 12 inches equal 1 foot. **Note:** If you haven't yet introduced a procedure for division, you may do so here. See the "Teaching Notes" section for more information.

5. In a class discussion, have students share how they figured the number of feet in the length of yarn.

6. To verify the answer, have one student hold the beginning of the yarn to the floor while a second student gently straightens the yarn from the beginning to the first paper clip, then holds it to the floor. Use five 12-inch rulers laid end-to-end to verify that there are about 5 feet in the first section.

7. Using the information that there are 5 feet in a 60-inch section, have the students figure the length of the yarn in feet for all but the last section. Ask three students to use the rulers to measure the last section to verify that it is 4 feet 8 inches long. Discuss the total length of the yarn in feet.

8. Pose another problem: *Figure the number of yards in the length of yarn.* Have students in pairs discuss strategies for solving this problem. Have volunteers share their ideas.

9. Have students solve the problem and figure the number of yards in the length of yarn. They may use the strategies shared in Step 8 or any other ideas that make sense.

10. In a class discussion, have students share how they figured the number of yards in the length of yarn.

11. To verify the answer, have volunteers measure the yarn with a yardstick.

Teaching Notes

Students in the following vignette had previously experienced the lesson in Chapter 4, "An Introduction to Division Computation: If You Hopped Like a Frog" and were familiar with the alternative algorithms presented in that lesson. If your students haven't had experience with the alternative algorithms presented in that lesson, you can introduce the algorithms in Step 4 of this lesson. To prepare, read the "Teaching Notes" section of Chapter 4 prior to teaching this lesson.

Because of the stretchy nature of yarn, it will most likely become apparent to students during the lesson that measurement is not exact. Even when the material being measured doesn't stretch, measurement is never exact. This is an important idea for students to understand. Time spent during the lesson to explore and discuss the approximate nature of measurement is time well spent.

During the lesson, students begin with the number of inches in the length of the yarn, then many use division to figure the number of feet and then divide once again to figure the number of yards. The problems presented in this chapter are examples of the grouping model of division. For example, students find the number of groups of 12 inches, or feet, in 656 inches. As students solve the problems using division, they reinforce their computation skills and practice using measurement equivalencies such as 12 inches equal 1 foot. However, not all students use division. A few may use multiplication or some other means to figure their answers. An important aspect of this lesson is that no matter how students solve the problems, they have the opportunity to discuss their strategies and use measurement to verify their paper-and-pencil results.

The Lesson

▲▲▲

I gathered the students on the rug. As they settled, I showed them a pile of red yarn I'd brought to class. I explained, "This pile of yarn is really one very long piece. I started to measure the yarn before class but ran out of time. I was using this measuring tape to measure it." I held up a measuring tape that was 60 inches long. (Actually, I had measured the yarn.)

"Hey, the measuring tape is almost as long as you," commented Kaleb, a student who often tried to connect his learning to his world.

I continued, "Before we can start the lesson today, I need some volunteers to help me finish measuring the yarn." The students were eager to help. I called on Neil, Celena, and Elise. Neil matched one end of the yarn with one end of the measuring tape and held them together while Celena carefully measured a length of yarn equal to the measuring tape, pulling gently on the yarn so it was straight but not stretched. Elise's job would be to record tally marks on the board to keep track of

the number of measuring tape lengths it took to measure the yarn.

I placed a paper clip on the yarn with an edge against the end of the measuring tape so that the paper clip actually overlapped the end of the measuring tape.

Placing the paper clips helped us measure fairly accurately while marking off sections of the yarn in a way that would be useful later in the lesson. We repeated this process until we had measured the entire length of yarn. When we were finished, Elise had marked ten tallies and there was a 56-inch length remaining.

I asked, "What does each tally mark represent?"

Cody explained, "Each mark is one length of yarn that's equal to the measuring tape. The measuring tape is sixty inches, so each tally means sixty inches of yarn."

I said, "There are ten tally marks. The last, or eleventh, section of yarn was only fifty-six inches long." I wrote on the board:

10 lengths of 60 inches

1 length of 56 inches

"How long is the yarn?" I asked.

The students thought quietly for a moment, then hands began to go up. When more than half the students had their hands up, I called on Nariko.

Nariko explained, "The piece of yarn is six hundred fifty-six inches long. I know because ten times sixty is six hundred, and then add fifty-six, and it's six hundred fifty-six altogether."

I recorded Nariko's thinking on the board:

10 × 60 = 600

600 + 56 = 656

"That's what I got," Katie commented. Several others also indicated their agreement with Nariko's thinking.

Kaleb, again linking learning with his world, related our measurement to my height: "That's long," he said. "That's a little less than eleven of you!" I nodded my agreement.

To introduce the problem, I said, "We've carefully measured the yarn and it's about six hundred fifty-six inches long. How many feet long is it? Before you start to figure that out, it's important for everyone to know how long a foot is. Who knows?"

Jina replied, "There are twelve inches in a foot."

I recorded this on the board as a reference for the students, writing the relationship in three different ways:

12 inches = 1 foot

12 in. = 1 ft.

12" = 1'

I explained, "The quotation mark symbol is an abbreviation for writing inches, and the apostrophe is an abbreviation for writing foot." I then gave directions: "You may work with your partner or by yourself to figure how many feet long the yarn is. If you've figured out an answer and others are still working, try to solve the problem another way as a check. When you're finished, we'll check by measuring the yarn using a twelve-inch ruler." The students reached for paper and pencils and got to work. As they worked, I circulated through the class, noting the methods the students used to solve the problem.

Justin used what he knew about measurement and multiplication to solve the problem. He explained what he'd written on his paper. "There are twelve inches in a foot. I already know five times twelve equals sixty, so five groups of twelve inches equals sixty inches. If you multiply sixty by ten, you get six hundred. If you multiply five by ten you get fifty. So six hundred inches is equal to fifty feet. Twelve times four equals forty-eight, so that's four more feet. Fifty plus four equals fifty-four. Fifty-six minus forty-eight is eight inches left over. The yarn is fifty-four feet with eight inches left." (See Figure 12–1.)

Kaylee came to me with her paper. "I can't figure out why my answer isn't the same as my table group's. I got forty-four remainder eight and they got fifty-four remainder eight."

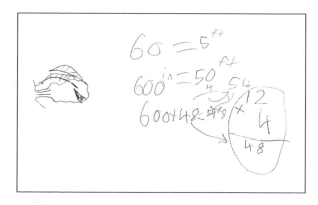

▲▲▲▲▲▲Figure 12–1 *Justin used what he knew about measurement and multiplication to solve the problem.*

I looked at Kaylee's paper and quickly found her error. Pointing to one of the partial quotients of 10 I said, "Tell me about this ten and how you used it to help you solve this problem."

Kaylee explained, "I'm trying to figure out how many feet, or twelves. The ten means there are ten groups of twelve, or ten feet. Ten times twelve is one hundred twenty. The one hundred twenty is down here, and it's what I subtracted from the amount of inches I started with." It was clear that Kaylee understood the problem, the meaning of the numbers, and what she was doing.

I asked, "How many times did you subtract ten groups of twelve, or one hundred twenty?"

"Four," Kaylee quickly responded.

"I see four tens in the partial quotients, but I see something different when I look at how many one hundred twenties you actually subtracted."

Kaylee studied her paper and carefully counted how many times she'd subtracted 120. Then she carefully counted how many 10s she'd written. "Oh my gosh! I forgot to write down one of the tens. I subtracted one hundred twenty five times and only wrote down four tens. I see now." Kaylee got another sheet of paper and reworked the problem correctly, using a slightly shorter method this time. (See Figures 12–2 and 12–3.)

Kelli, who was sitting nearby, said, "My way is sort of like Kaylee's and sort of different."

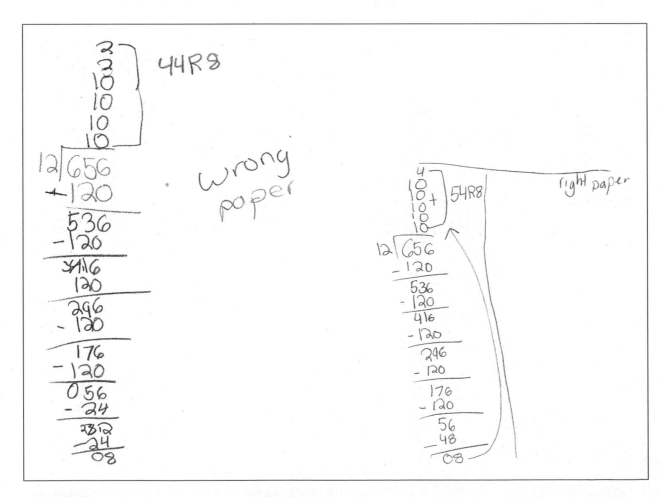

▲▲▲▲▲▲Figures 12–2 and 12–3 *Kaylee found her error and reworked the problem successfully.*

"Tell me more," I said.

Kelli explained, "Well, I used multiplying by tens and multiples of ten like she did, but then I did it a shorter way. I just did fifty times twelve and subtracted six hundred all at once. I know five times twelve is sixty, so fifty times twelve is six hundred." (See Figure 12–4.)

Terrell solved the problem using the short division algorithm. To check the accuracy of his quotient, he used multiplication and the distributive property. He thought of 54 as 50 + 4 and 12 as 10 + 2. His thinking, while shown differently on his paper, was based on the distributive property: [(50 + 4) (10 + 2)] + 8. (See Figure 12–5.)

Tomas and Annie used approaches similar to those Kelli and Kaylee used, but they took advantage of multiples of ten in their partial products. (See Figures 12–6 and 12–7.)

I looked around the room quickly and noted that most of the students had solved the problem using at least one method. I gave a one-minute warning. After a minute, I asked for the students' attention.

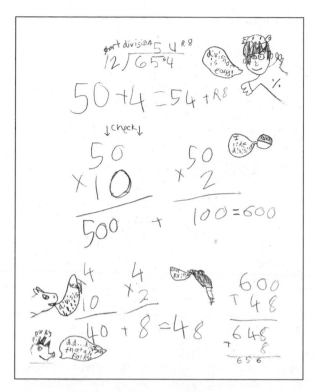

▲▲▲▲▲▲Figure 12–5 *Terrell used multiplication and the distributive property in his second solution.*

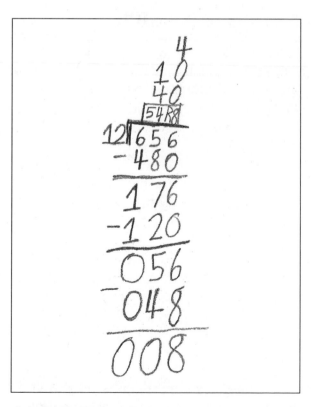

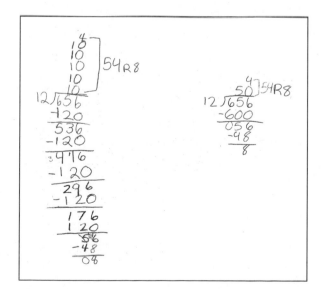

▲▲▲▲▲▲Figure 12–4 *Kelli's second solution showed an increase in her efficiency.*

▲▲▲▲▲▲Figure 12–6 *Tomas's solution took advantage of multiples of ten in his partial product.*

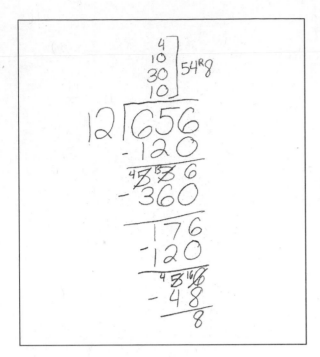

▲▲▲▲▲**Figure 12–7** *Annie's solution also took advantage of multiples of ten in her partial product.*

A CLASS DISCUSSION

When the students were settled, I said, "Raise your hand if you'd like to share you answer." All hands were up. "Tell me your answer in a whisper voice."

"Fifty-four remainder eight," the students chorused.

"Who can explain what fifty-four remainder eight means in relation to the problem we were trying to solve about feet and inches?" I asked. I called on Rachel.

Rachel answered, "We were trying to figure out how many feet were in the yarn and we got fifty-four feet with remainder eight."

"So the fifty-four tells us how many feet long the yarn is?" I asked. Rachel nodded.

"What does the remainder eight tell us?" I could see from the reactions that some students weren't sure how to interpret the remainder in terms of the problem. I waited a moment more to see if more students would raise their hands. Two more did, but at least half of the class didn't volunteer. Rather than call on someone to respond, I wanted to give everyone a chance to think more about my question, so I directed the students to talk in pairs. "Talk with your partner about what the remainder eight tells us. First one of you talks for thirty seconds while the other listens, then when I give the signal, the first talker gets to listen and the first listener gets to talk." As students shared their ideas, I listened in. After thirty seconds, I reminded the students to change roles. After another thirty seconds, I called the class to attention. This time more hands were raised. I called on Elise.

"The remainder eight means that there wasn't enough yarn to make a whole other foot," Elise explained.

"Does anyone have another way to explain?" I asked.

"There were only eight inches left, and you need twelve for a whole other foot," Neil explained.

No one else volunteered. While it took time away from my primary goal of giving the students practice computing, I think that referring back to the context of a problem is important and a valuable use of instructional time. As much as possible, students need to see computation as a tool for solving problems, not as an end in itself. Also, the conversation gave me a chance to reinforce for the class how to record an answer of 54 feet and 8 inches. I wrote on the board:

54 R8

"So this is the answer to six hundred fifty-six divided by twelve," I said. The students nodded.

"And it means fifty-four feet with eight inches left over," I said. Again the students nodded. "Here are other ways to write the answer," I said. I wrote three variations on the board, again to reinforce the abbreviations for feet and inches as well as alternative representations of the answer:

54 feet, 8 inches

54 ft. 8 in.

54'8"

"How did you figure the answer?" I then asked, referring to the computation they did. Again hands were up, as students were eager to share their thinking. I called on Conrad.

Conrad explained, "I used multiplying by ten and multiples of ten mostly. If two times twelve is twenty-four, then twenty times twelve equals two hundred forty." As Conrad continued to explain his thinking, I recorded on the board, reporting the answer in feet and inches:

$$
\begin{array}{r}
4 \\
10 \\
20 \\
20 \\
\hline
12\overline{)656} \\
-240 \\
\hline
416 \\
-240 \\
\hline
176 \\
-120 \\
\hline
56 \\
-48 \\
\hline
8
\end{array} \quad 54'\ R8"
$$

"How many solved the problem as Conrad did?" I asked the students. A few hands went up.

Tomas shared next. "My way is a lot like Conrad's except instead of multiplying twenty times twelve twice, I multiplied forty times twelve. I knew four times twelve equals forty-eight, so forty times twelve equals four hundred eighty. The rest was just like what Conrad did."

I recorded on the board Tomas's thinking:

$$
\begin{array}{r}
4 \\
10 \\
40 \\
\hline
12\overline{)656} \\
-480 \\
\hline
176 \\
-120 \\
\hline
56 \\
-48 \\
\hline
8
\end{array} \quad 54'\ R8"
$$

Several students indicated they solved the problem the same way as Tomas.

Celena shared next. "Tomas and I started out the same way. Forty times twelve equals four hundred eighty. But then I did fourteen times twelve. There were one hundred seventy-six left after I subtracted the four hundred eighty. I knew twelve times twelve equals one hundred forty-four. In my head I added twelve more to one hundred forty-four, which is like adding ten and two more, which equals one hundred fifty-six. Then I added twelve more and that equals one hundred sixty-eight. That's fourteen more groups of twelve. Then there were eight left." I wrote on the board Celena's method, this time using different abbreviations for feet and inches:

$$
\begin{array}{r}
14 \\
40 \\
\hline
12\overline{)656} \\
-480 \\
\hline
176 \\
-168 \\
\hline
8
\end{array} \quad 54\ ft.\ 8\ in.
$$

14 × 12 = ?
12 × 12 = 144
144 + 12 = 156
156 + 12 = 168
14 × 12 = 168

Katie shared, "Instead of writing the numbers above the dividend as Conrad and Tomas did, I wrote them going down the side. I subtracted out ten groups of twelve, or one hundred twenty, five times. Then I subtracted out two groups of twelve, or twenty-four, twice. Altogether that's fifty-four groups of twelve with eight inches left over." I recorded Katie's thinking on the board as follows:

$$
\begin{array}{r}
54 \text{ ft. R8 in.} \\
12\overline{)656} \\
-120 \quad | \ 10 \\
\hline
536 \\
-120 \quad | \ 10 \\
\hline
416 \\
-120 \quad | \ 10 \\
\hline
296 \\
-120 \quad | \ 10 \\
\hline
176 \\
-120 \quad | \ 10 \\
\hline
56 \\
-24 \quad | \ 2 \\
\hline
32 \\
-24 \quad | \ 2 \\
\hline
8 \quad |
\end{array}
$$

Joby had one last idea to share. "I thought in my head, 'Ten times twelve equals one hundred twenty.' Then I thought, 'One hundred times twelve equals twelve hundred.' Half of twelve hundred is six hundred, which is close to six hundred fifty-six. Then I knew that fifty times twelve equals six hundred. Four more groups of twelve equal forty-eight. So far, that's fifty-four groups of twelve. That leaves eight. There are fifty-four feet with eight inches left over."

I recorded Joby's idea on the board:

$10 \times 12 = 120$

$100 \times 12 = 1,200$

$\frac{1}{2}$ of $1,200 = 600$

$50 \times 12 = 600$

$4 \times 12 = 48$

$50 + 4 = 54$

$656 - 648 = 8$

$54'8"$

I asked the students, "Did anyone get a different answer?" No one raised a hand. This didn't surprise me. As the students worked, I had looked over their shoulders, asking them questions to guide them when I noted errors in their computations.

VERIFYING THE ANSWER

Often, large numbers are abstract to students. The measurement aspect of this lesson provided an ideal opportunity for students to verify their answers concretely by carefully measuring the number of feet in the yarn. I asked the students to come to the floor. With the help of several students, I laid the yarn out on the floor along the outer edges of the room. This process intrigued the others, and as we worked, they discussed how far around the room the yarn would go.

I said to the class, "I left the paper clips that we used earlier to help us figure the length of the yarn in inches attached. How many inches is it from the beginning of the yarn to the first paper clip?"

"Sixty inches," the students chorused.

I said, "That's true in all cases except for the length from the last clip to the end of the yarn. How long was that?"

"Fifty-six inches," the students replied in unison.

"Do you think your measurements will match your answers exactly?" I asked. I asked this question to bring to the students' attention that measurement is not exact, particularly when using a material like yarn that has a bit of stretch to it.

Rachel said, "I think it will be close, but because the yarn can stretch, it may not be exact." Several other students nodded their agreement.

Neil added, "Even if the yarn weren't stretchy, it's hard to measure exactly, especially if you have to move the ruler."

"The sections we marked with paper clips can help," I said. I demonstrated what

I meant by asking Nariko to put her finger on the beginning of the yarn and hold it to the floor while I pulled gently to straighten the yarn to the first paper clip without stretching it. I asked Ali to hold the paper clip to the floor. Then I took five rulers, first laying one ruler on the floor along the yarn with an edge at Nariko's finger, then laying a second ruler at its end and continuing that way to Ali's finger, demonstrating that there were 5 feet in the section of yarn.

Justin said enthusiastically, "It turned out to be almost exactly five feet. That's what I thought it would be!"

"Why did you think it would be five feet?" I asked.

"Because there's twelve inches in a foot and five groups of twelve is like five times twelve, and that's sixty," Justin explained.

Samara said, "Instead of multiplication, you can think about it with division. I wondered, 'How many twelves in sixty?' Then I thought, 'Twelve times what equals sixty?' Well, it's twelve times five. Wait a minute, I guess I did think of it as multiplication, too!"

"How many sections did we measure with paper clips?" I asked.

"Ten. That's fifty feet," Kaylee answered.

"And we still have fifty-six inches left," Kelli said.

Tomas, Terrell, and Annie came up and measured the last section of yarn to show that it was 4'8" long.

"That's right!" Samara said. "It's fifty-four feet with eight extra inches."

A SECOND PROBLEM

I said, "I have another problem for you. A yard is thirty-six inches, or three feet, long." I showed the class a yardstick and wrote on the board:

1 yd. = 36 in. = 3 ft.

I continued, "How many yards long is the yarn? How could you figure this out? Talk with your partner. First one of you talks for thirty seconds while the other listens. When I give you the signal, switch so the first talker gets to listen and the first listener gets to talk." I gave the students the signal to begin. At the end of thirty seconds, I reminded them to switch roles, and at the end of the second thirty seconds, I asked for their attention.

Binh shared first. "There are thirty-six inches in a yard, so I think you could solve the problem by dividing thirty-six into six hundred fifty-six."

I wrote on the board, recording Binh's idea symbolically in two ways:

656 ÷ 36 = ?   *36)656*

Jina said, "You could use multiplication to figure out how many thirty-sixes it will take to get to six hundred fifty-six. For example, you could multiply thirty-six by ten and that's three hundred sixty."

I added Jina's idea to the board.

? × 36 = 656

Neil suggested, "If there are three feet in a yard, maybe you could figure out how many yards in fifty-four feet eight inches by dividing it by three." I added Neil's suggestion to the list.

54'8" ÷ 3 =

The students were quiet. I said, "Your next task is figure out how many yards long our yarn is." The students reached for paper and pencils as they talked quietly among themselves about approaches they planned to use. As before, I circulated through the class, reading over shoulders and asking and answering questions as needed. Most students used approaches similar to the ones they used to solve the first problem. When students finished early, I asked them to solve the problem a second way, explaining to them that the second way would provide a good check on their first way. When all students had solved the problem in at least one way, I asked for their attention.

A SECOND DISCUSSION

I asked, "How many yards long is our yarn?" Hands danced in the air.

Katie said, "Eighteen yards with eight inches left over."

Rachel added, "Katie and I worked together and we were both surprised that the remainder of eight inches was the same for both problems."

Joby shared, "We thought that was strange, too; then we realized that there weren't any leftover feet. Fifty-four feet is exactly eighteen yards. Then it made sense that eight inches were left over both times."

The point Rachel made about the remainder of eight being the same for both problems was a good one. I was pleased she brought it up and would have done so during the discussion if she or some other student hadn't.

I said, "Rachel, Katie, and Joby made a good observation about the remainders in both problems being the same. I agree with Joby's thinking about why this happened." Next, I asked, "How many got the answer of eighteen yards with eight inches left over?" Most students raised their hands. "Who would like to explain how you got your answer?" Hands were up quickly. I called on Ali.

Ali explained, "I divided three into fifty-four feet eight inches because there are three feet in one yard. Ten threes is thirty. I subtracted thirty from fifty-four and it was twenty-four. I knew three times eight equals twenty-four. Ten plus eight equals eighteen. And there are no yards in eight inches, so it's eighteen yards eight inches."
I recorded Ali's idea:

$$
\begin{array}{r}
8 \\
10 \\
\hline
3\overline{)54\text{ ft 8 in}} \\
-30 \\
\hline
24 \\
-24 \\
\hline
0
\end{array}
\quad 18\text{ yd. 8 in.}
$$

Justin shared next. "Each section of yarn is sixty inches long. That's five feet, and five feet is the same as one yard and two feet. There are ten sections. That's one yard ten times, which is ten yards, and then two feet ten times, which is twenty feet. Since there are three feet in a yard, twenty feet is six more yards with two feet left over. So far that's ten plus six, which is sixteen yards. There are two feet left over plus the last section, which is one yard, one foot, and eight inches. If I add one yard to the sixteen yards, then it's seventeen yards. Then I add one foot to the two feet left over from before, and that's another yard, which is eighteen yards. Then there are the eight inches that are left. There are eighteen yards and eight inches in the yarn."

I recorded on the board as Justin explained:

1 section = 60 in. = 5 ft.

5 ft. = 1 yd. 2 ft.

10 × 1 yd. = 10 yd.

10 × 2 ft. = 20 ft.

20 ft. = 6 yd. 2 ft.

10 yd. + 6 yd. = 16 yd.

56 in. = 1 yd. 1 ft. 8 in.

16 yd. + 1 yd. = 17 yd.

2 ft. + 1 ft. = 3 ft. = 1 yd.

17 yd. + 1 yd. = 18 yd.

18 yd. 8 in.

Shawn shared another approach. "I divided six hundred fifty-six by thirty-six because there are thirty-six inches in a yard. First I multiplied thirty-six by ten.

That's three hundred sixty. I subtracted the three hundred sixty I used from six hundred fifty-six. That left two hundred ninety-six. That's not enough for ten more groups of thirty-six. In my head, I know that two times thirty-six is seventy-two, so if I double seventy-two, that's one hundred forty-four. If I double that, it's two hundred eighty-eight, which is close. So eight times thirty-six is two hundred eighty-eight. That leaves eight left. It comes out to eighteen yards with a remainder of eight." I recorded Shawn's thinking:

$$
\left.\begin{array}{r} 2 \\ 2 \\ 2 \\ 2 \\ 10 \end{array}\right] \text{18 yd. 8 in.}
$$

$$
\begin{array}{r}
36\overline{)656} \\
-360 \\
\hline
296 \\
-72 \\
\hline
224 \\
-72 \\
\hline
152 \\
-72 \\
\hline
80 \\
-72 \\
\hline
8
\end{array}
$$

$$
\left.\begin{array}{r} 8 \\ 10 \end{array}\right] \text{18 yd. 8 in.}
$$

$$
\begin{array}{r}
36\overline{)656} \\
-360 \\
\hline
296 \\
-288 \\
\hline
8
\end{array}
$$

$$2 \times 36 = 72$$
$$4 \times 36 = 144$$
$$8 \times 36 = 288$$

Annie shared next. "My way started out like Shawn's, but I couldn't figure out eight like he did. Instead I just multiplied thirty-six times two four times. I got the same answer as everyone else." I recorded Annie's thinking:

No one had other ideas to share. As we did before, we measured to verify our results, this time using a yardstick. As before, the students were able to verify their paper-and-pencil results by measuring. **Note:** If you have a meter stick rather than a yardstick, remind the students not use the full length of the meter stick, which is about 39 inches. Model for them how to measure 36 inches, have a student place a finger on the yarn at 36 inches, then continue measuring.

As I ended the math lesson, Kaleb commented, "I liked measuring and discovering my measuring answer was the same as the answer on my paper." Several others showed their agreement.

Questions and Discussion

▲▲

▲ *The students seemed to enjoy measuring the yarn to verify their results, but it seems like it took a lot of valuable instructional time. Wouldn't it be better to use the time to have students solve more problems?*

Verifying results is a valuable, valid use of instructional time. In this case, students are applying and practicing measurement skills to verify their computation while learning that validation of answers doesn't have to come from the teacher or an answer key. They learn that they have tools to determine if their thinking and solutions make sense or need revision. Practicing solving problems for the sake of solving problems without regard for the reasonableness of answers is not time well spent for students.

▲ *I don't have access to tape measures and yardsticks. What are some alternatives?*

Measuring tapes are generally 60 inches long and can be purchased inexpensively. If this is not an option, then tape sentence strips end-to-end. Typically, sentence strips are 24 inches long. You can tape together $2\frac{1}{2}$ sentence strips end-to-end to make 60 inches, the length of a measuring tape. You can tape $1\frac{1}{2}$ strips together to make 36 inches, the length of a yardstick. Cut a sentence strip in half to get a 12-inch ruler. Mark off 1-inch sections along one edge of the sentence strips for more precise measurement. These measuring tools can be stored easily by folding them to an appropriate length.

▲ *Why didn't you require all students to solve the problems using division only?*

In the vignette, most students used division to solve the problems. Of those who did not use division, some liked exploring nonroutine solutions, and a few weren't yet comfortable using division. What is important is that each student makes sense of the problem and uses a method to solve it that produces a reasonable, accurate answer. Using division to solve a problem is not an end in itself; rather, it is a tool to use when appropriate.

CHAPTER THIRTEEN
BEANS AND SCOOPS

Overview

This lesson uses jars, beans, and a coffee scoop for a measurement experience that provides a context to help students learn to divide with two-digit divisors. The lesson also reinforces the connection between multiplication and division, provides practice with multiplying, engages students in analyzing statistical data and in proportional reasoning, and gives students practice computing mentally.

Materials

▲ 10-ounce jar
▲ 32-ounce jar
▲ 1-ounce ($\frac{1}{8}$ cup) coffee scoop
▲ large lima beans, enough to fill the 32-ounce jar
▲ kidney beans, enough to fill the 10-ounce jar
▲ 2 1-gallon plastic zip-top bags (1 for lima beans, 1 for kidney beans)

Time

▲ three class periods

Teaching Directions

1. Before teaching the lesson, put the kidney and lima beans each in their own zip-top plastic bag. Also, find out how many scoops of beans fill each jar (to the very top), how many lima beans each jar holds, and how many kidney beans the smaller jar holds. (Read the "Teaching Notes" section for more details about this.)

2. Show the class the small jar, the scoop, and the bag of kidney beans. Ask: "How many scoops of beans do you think will fill the jar?" Give all who would like to guess the chance to do so. Then fill the jar with three scoops of beans and give students a chance to readjust their estimates.

3. Continue filling the jar to determine the number of scoops it holds. (In the lesson described, twelve scoops filled the jar.)

4. Ask: "How could we figure out how many beans fill the jar without counting all of them?" Typically, a student will suggest counting the beans in one scoop and multiplying by the number of scoops. If no one suggests this, make the suggestion and have students talk about why this method would work.

5. Then tell the students that you've already counted how many beans fill the jar. Write the number on the board. (In the lesson described, 470 kidney beans filled the 10-ounce jar.) Talk with the students about why dividing 470 by 12 or thinking "What times 12 gives 470?" would tell approximately how many beans fill the scoop. Discuss the connection between multiplication and division.

6. Ask each student to turn to a neighbor and figure out, together in their heads, the answer to 470 divided by 12. Then lead a class discussion about their thinking and record their ideas on the board.

7. Present a paper-and-pencil algorithm for doing the division. (**Note:** Use the algorithm introduced in Chapter 4, "An Introduction to Division Computation: If You Hopped Like a Frog." See the "Teaching Notes" section of this chapter for information about the format used in this lesson.)

8. Verify the answer by giving several students a scoop of kidney beans to count. Most likely, the counts will differ. Remind the students that measurement is never exact.

9. Pour the kidney beans back into the bag and show the class the bag of lima beans. Ask: "If I fill the jar with scoops of lima beans, how many scoops do you think it will take to fill the jar?" After students have shared their ideas, scoop lima beans to verify that it still takes twelve scoops to fill the jar.

10. Ask: "About how many lima beans do you think will fill the scoop?"

11. After students have given estimates, tell them that you've already counted how many beans fill the jar. Write the number on the board. (In the lesson described, 212 lima beans filled the 10-ounce jar.) Talk with the students about why dividing 212 by 12 would tell approximately how many lima beans fill the scoop.

12. Ask each student to turn to a neighbor and figure out, together in their heads, the answer to 212 divided by 12. Then lead a class discussion about their thinking and record their ideas on the board.

13. Begin Day 2 by modeling the paper-and-pencil algorithm for solving 212 ÷ 12.

14. Give a scoop of lima beans to every two or three students to count. List on the board the number of beans in each. Then order the numbers from smallest to largest and discuss what is a reasonable number to use to describe the number of lima beans that fill the scoop.

15. Show the students the large jar filled with lima beans and write a problem on the board for the students to solve on their own. Circulate as they work. At the end of the period, collect their papers.

> *A scoop of lima beans holds about 18 beans.*
>
> *The jar has 676 beans it.* (Use the number you got when you counted.)
>
> *About how many scoops of lima beans fill the jar?*

16. On Day 3, return their papers and have them share what they did with their partners.

17. On subsequent days, give the students additional practice.

Teaching Notes

To prepare for the lesson, I collected a 10-ounce jar, a 32-ounce jar, a 1-ounce coffee scoop (a square, stainless steel scoop with "$\frac{1}{8}$ cup" imprinted on it), a bag of large lima beans, and a bag of kidney beans. I filled the smaller jar with lima beans so that the beans were level at the very top of the jar, then dumped them out on my desk and counted them. This was laborious to do but was important to my planning. Also, even though the jar was a 10-ounce jar, I knew that filling it to the very top resulted in filling it with about 12 ounces of beans, since the 10-ounce capacity of the jar refers to its capacity to just below its lip. I did the same with the larger jar, filling it with lima beans and then counting them. And finally I filled the smaller jar with kidney beans and counted them. Here is what I found out:

▲ The small jar held 212 lima beans.

▲ The large jar held 676 lima beans.

▲ The small jar held 470 kidney beans.

When you prepare for the lesson, your numbers may vary. Use the counts that you come up with.

Next I filled the small jar with scoops of beans, tapping gently to settle the beans when the jar was about half filled and just before it was completely filled. I repeated this for the large jar. When filling each jar, the last scoop resulted in a few beans protruding above the top of the jar. That's why I included "almost" in the following information.

▲ The large jar held almost 38 scoops.

▲ The small jar held almost 12 scoops.

To check the information I had gathered, I thought about the sizes of the jars. The capacity of the larger jar is just over three times the capacity of the smaller jar. To be more accurate, it's 3.2 times larger. With the lima beans, $212 \times 3.2 = 678.4$, so 676 was a reasonable count. Also, 12×3.2 equals 38.4, so the number of scoops for each jar was reasonable, too.

Using jars, beans, and a scoop for this lesson is important for several reasons. One reason is to provide the students with a concrete reference for verifying their thinking. Too often when thinking about numbers, especially large numbers, students only think about quantities abstractly. Also, too often when students are computing with large numbers, especially when using the standard division algorithm, they focus only on the steps of the procedure without also paying attention to making sense of the numbers, and therefore, they get lost.

Another reason for using jars, beans, and a scoop is to provide a context that allows not only for reasoning with large numbers but also for engaging the students with ideas about measurement, statistics, and proportional reasoning. The breadth of the mathematics curriculum is demanding, and the school year seems short for accomplishing all that is needed. While a lesson has a primary purpose, it's valuable to incorporate into a lesson as broad a range of mathematical ideas as possible. Asking whether the small jar will hold the same number of scoops of lima beans as kidney beans gives students experience with the idea of volume. (And scooping the beans is essential to verify or challenge their ideas.) Showing the students that the coffee scoop is labeled "$\frac{1}{8}$ cup," which is the same as 1 ounce, introduces or reinforces these standard measures. Giving several students each a scoop of beans to count, and then listing their different counts, helps reinforce for students that measurement is never exact. Analyzing the different counts to decide which number is best to use to describe the number of beans in a scoop calls for a statistical analysis that supports the development of understanding about averages. Comparing the numbers of beans and scoops in the smaller and larger jars, as I did earlier to verify my own counting, engages students in proportional reasoning.

A third reason for using beans and scoops is because it helps motivate the students to engage with the mathematics of the lesson. Scooping beans engages the students' curiosity and stimulates their imaginations. It takes mathematics off the pages of textbooks and presents ideas in a fresh way, which helps enlist the students' interest. The actual scooping and counting not only interests the students but shifts the source of verification of the students' thinking from the teacher or an answer book to the physical materials, and this is empowering for them. Although doing all of this counting of beans and scoops was laborious, I felt it was necessary.

The alternative algorithm for long division introduced in Chapter 4, "An Introduction to Division Computation," was new enough to this class that I took the opportunity to make a careful, step-by-step presentation of it for the first two problems presented—$470 \div 12$ and $212 \div 12$. However, if your students are more proficient with the alternative algorithm, you might want to have a student demonstrate it on the board or have the students use the paper-and-pencil alternative algorithm to solve all three problems—$470 \div 12$, $212 \div 12$, and $676 \div 18$.

You'll notice that the format for recording partial quotients in this lesson reflects one of the ways used in Chapter 4, "An Introduction to Division Computation," and Chapter 12, "The Yarn Lesson." The second alternative below was preferred by the regular teacher of this particular class.

$$
\begin{array}{r}
9 \\
20 \\
10 \\
\hline
12\overline{)470} \\
-120 \\
\hline
350 \\
-240 \\
\hline
110 \\
-108 \\
\hline
2
\end{array}
\quad 39\ R2
\qquad\qquad
39\ R2
\begin{array}{l}
12\overline{)470} \\
-120 \quad 10 \\
350 \\
-240 \quad 20 \\
110 \\
-108 \quad 9 \\
2
\end{array}
$$

Students do not have difficulty understanding either of these ways to record the partial quotients. In this lesson, you'll see examples of student work with the second format for 676 ÷ 18.

The Lesson

▲▲

DAY 1

I began the lesson by showing the students the small jar, the scoop, and the bag of kidney beans. "How many scoops of beans do you think will fill the jar?" I asked. I gave every student who was interested in guessing a chance to do so. Their guesses ranged from seven to fourteen.

I then put three scoops of beans in the jar and gave the students the opportunity to change their estimates. The range of their estimates narrowed; the smallest estimate was now nine and the largest was thirteen.

I continued filling the jar. "I'm going to fill the jar to the very top," I told the students. After eleven scoops, the jar was nearly full. I put in a twelfth scoop, and even though a few beans bulged over the top, the students were satisfied that twelve scoops of beans filled the jar.

"So now we know that it takes just about twelve scoops of kidney beans to fill the jar," I said. "But that doesn't tell us how many beans there are in the jar. Do you have any ideas about how we could find that out without counting all of the beans?"

Holly answered, "If we knew how many beans were in a scoop, we could just multiply," she said.

"What would you multiply?" I asked.

"You'd multiply twelve times the number of beans in a scoop," she said. I wrote on the board:

12 scoops × number of beans in a scoop = total number of beans

"Is this what you mean?" I asked Holly. She agreed, and so did others.

I then said, "Well, I actually already counted the total number of beans in the jar. There are four hundred seventy." On the board, I replaced "total number of beans" with *470 beans*.

12 scoops × number of beans in a scoop = 470 beans

Then I shortened the sentence, explaining to the students, "I'm making this sentence shorter by replacing 'number of beans in a scoop' with the abbreviation of *n*."

12 × n = 470

"So we know the number of scoops it takes to fill the jar and the total number of beans," I said, pointing to the two numbers in the equation as I referred to them. I then pointed to the *n* and asked, "Who can tell me what this *n* stands for?"

"It's the number of scoops," Pierre responded.

Hands flew up to disagree, but Pierre quickly corrected his answer. "I mean it's the number of beans in a scoop," he said.

"How could you use what we know so far to figure out the number of beans in a scoop?" I asked.

"You can divide," Anita said.

"Raise a hand if you agree that you could divide," I said. Almost all hands were up.

"What would you divide by what?" I asked. Rather than call on one student to respond, I asked them to talk with their partners about my question. The room got noisy for a moment and then began to quiet down as children raised their hands to report. I called on Billy.

"You divide four hundred seventy by twelve," he said. I recorded on the board so that the division equation was underneath the multiplication equation:

$12 \times n = 470$

$470 \div 12$

"And what will the answer to four hundred seventy divided by twelve tell us?" I asked.

Jo responded, "The number of beans in a scoop." I completed the equation:

$12 \times n = 470$

$470 \div 12 = n$

I then raised a question to have the students think about how these two equations related to each other. "The first equation says that twelve times n equals four hundred seventy, and the second says that four hundred seventy divided by twelve equals n. Both use the same three numbers—twelve, four hundred seventy, and whatever number n is. But how can we use numbers to write a multiplication sentence and then use the same numbers to write a division sentence?"

Jorge explained, "It's like they're opposites. You use the same numbers, but one is multiplying and one is dividing."

"Can you give an example to explain what you mean?" I asked.

"OK," Jorge said. "You can go seven times four and you get twenty-eight. But then you can go twenty-eight divided by the seven, and you get four." I recorded on the board:

$7 \times 4 = 28$

$28 \div 7 = 4$

Kara added, "If you didn't know how much was twenty-eight divided by four, you could figure out how many fours made twenty-eight, and you'd get the answer. So they're kind of the same."

The Students Solve the Problem

"So if we're trying to figure out the number of kidney beans there are in a scoop, if we knew what times twelve gave four hundred seventy, or how much was four hundred seventy divided by twelve, then we'd know?" I asked. Kara and others nodded in agreement.

"Please turn to your neighbor and talk about how you might figure out, in your heads, the answer to four hundred seventy divided by twelve," I directed. Having the students talk in pairs would give more of them a chance to try out their thinking. After a few moments, I called the class back to attention. More than half the students had their hands raised. I called on Carmen.

She said, "Twelve times four is forty-eight, so twelve times forty is four hundred eighty, and that's too big. So if you take off twelve from the four hundred eighty, then you have twelve times thirty-nine. Four hundred eighty minus twelve is four hundred sixty-eight, and that's really close." I wrote on the board as Carmen explained:

$12 \times 4 = 48$

$12 \times 40 = 480$

$12 \times 39 = 480 - 12$

$480 - 12 = 468$

"So how many beans do you think are in a scoop?" I asked Carmen.

"Maybe thirty-nine or maybe forty," she said. "They wouldn't all be the same."

Next I called on Anita. She said, "I did it by dividing, but I wrote it the other way, you know, with the line like this." She gestured in the air and I wrote the problem as if it were set up for long division. Anita was proficient using the standard algorithm, as were some of the other students in the class. Following Anita's directions, I recorded:

$$
\begin{array}{r}
39 \text{ R2} \\
12\overline{)470} \\
-36 \\
\hline
110 \\
-108 \\
\hline
2
\end{array}
$$

"What does the remainder of two mean?" I asked Anita.

She answered, "There are two extra beans, so two of the scoops will have forty beans and the rest will have thirty-nine beans."

I then used this problem to model for the class an alternative to the procedure that Anita showed. I had introduced this to the students before, but I felt that they would benefit from a review. I wrote the problem on the board, drawing a vertical line on the right side of 470, starting at the right of the division bar:

$$12\overline{)470}$$

I said, "Watch and listen as I explain another way to do the division. We're trying to figure out how many beans fill one scoop if four hundred seventy beans fill twelve scoops." Next to the problem on the board, I drew twelve scoops.

I explained, "I know that we really don't have twelve scoops. I only have one scoop, but I scooped beans twelve times to fill the jar. So each scoop I drew represents one time that I used the scoop. Now our job is to figure out about how many beans fill the scoop. I'll start with a friendly number. Suppose ten beans filled a scoop."

"That's not enough," Simon said. "That would only use up one hundred twenty beans, and there are four hundred seventy."

"You're right, Simon," I responded, "but it's a start." I recorded 10 to the right of the vertical line in the problem.

I then said, "If I took out twelve scoops with ten beans in each, as Simon said, that would use up one hundred twenty beans, and there would be three hundred fifty beans left." I showed how to record this and I also wrote 10 in each scoop I had drawn.

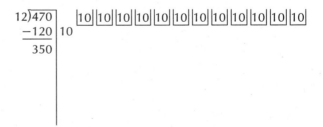

I continued, "So with three hundred fifty beans left, I have enough to take out twelve scoops with twenty beans in each.

That would use up two hundred forty
more beans." I stopped to record:

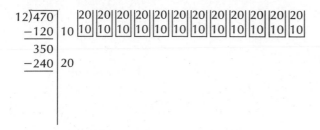

```
12)470    |20||20||20||20||20||20||20||20||20||20||20||20|
-120  10  |10||10||10||10||10||10||10||10||10||10||10||10|
 350
-240  20
```

"Now you have one hundred ten beans
left," Dan said. I agreed and recorded:

```
12)470    |20||20||20||20||20||20||20||20||20||20||20||20|
-120  10  |10||10||10||10||10||10||10||10||10||10||10||10|
 350
-240  20
 110
```

I said, "So far, I figured out that if a
scoop held thirty beans, there would be
one hundred ten beans left to fill the jar."
I pointed first to the 10 and 20 recorded to
the right of the line, and then to the 110.
"There aren't enough beans to put ten
more beans in each scoop. Who can explain why?"

Monique said, "You need one hundred
twenty beans for ten scoops, but you only
have one hundred ten."

"You can put in nine more," Hiroshi
suggested.

"If I scooped nine beans twelve times,
how many beans would that use?" I asked.
I waited a moment for hands to go up,
then I called on Gloria.

"One hundred eight," she said. I
recorded:

```
12)470    |9||9||9||9||9||9||9||9||9||9||9||9|
-120  10  |20||20||20||20||20||20||20||20||20||20||20||20|
 350      |10||10||10||10||10||10||10||10||10||10||10||10|
-240  20
 110
-108  9
   2
```

"So what do we know now?" I asked.

Christian said, "Each scoop has twenty-
nine beans in it." Many students com-
plained about Christian's idea. "Wait,
wait," he said, "I mean each scoop has
thirty-nine beans in it." The others now
agreed.

"And there are two extra beans," Holly
said.

"So two of the scoops have forty
beans," Jorge added.

I confirmed, "Yes, ten plus twenty is
thirty, plus nine more is thirty-nine. And
there are two beans left over." I modeled
how to record the answer:

```
          39 R2
12)470
-120    10
 350
-240    20
 110
-108     9
   2
```

Verifying the Answer

"Let's actually scoop some beans and see
how many beans there are in a scoop," I
said. "But first I want to know if you'll
be mathematically disappointed if the
scoops don't come out to be thirty-nine
or forty."

"They should be close if they're not exact," Jorge said.

"Maybe there's a broken bean," Sherea
said.

"I'd be disappointed," Billy said
dramatically.

I scooped three scoops of kidney beans
and gave them to different students to
count. The counts were thirty-eight, thirty-
nine, and forty-one. I collected the beans
and said, "It's important to remember that
measurement is never exact. Even though
I try to scoop the beans carefully, I can't
be exact."

Scooping Lima Beans

"Now I have a different question to ask you," I said. I poured the kidney beans back into the baggie and showed the class a baggie of lima beans. "If I fill the jar this time with scoops of lima beans, how many scoops do you think it will take to fill the jar?"

This question didn't relate to the multiplication and division problems I had planned for the students, but it served to stimulate them to think about the idea of volume. The jar was a 10-ounce jar, but filling it to the very top increased its capacity to almost 12 ounces, which is why it took twelve 1-ounce scoops to fill it with kidney beans. It would also take twelve 1-ounce scoops of lima beans to fill the jar to the very top. Similarly, it would take twelve scoops of any size beans, or rice, or water, or any other material.

However, the students in this class responded to my question in the same way that many children (and adults) do. Davey, for example, said, "It would be full with five scoops."

Christian differed. "I think it will take about seven."

Sally said, "Maybe ten, but not as many as twelve."

Jorge, however, said, "I think it's a trick question. A scoop is a scoop, so it should take the same."

Anne said, "I agree with Jorge, but it could take one or two scoops less."

Jonah said, "It's like that problem of Which weighs more—a pound of gold or a pound of feathers?" The conversation was lively. I resolved the problem by scooping lima beans to fill the jar, verifying that twelve scoops filled the jar. Then I poured the beans back into the baggie.

"Who can explain why it took the same number of scoops of lima beans as kidney beans?" I asked.

Pierre said, "First I thought that the smaller beans would pack better and be closer together. But now I think that the spaces in between the lima beans in the scoop are also in between the lima beans when they are in the jar."

Jorge said, "A scoop is a scoop."

While it seemed that all of the students had been convinced that it took the same number of scoops to fill the jar with lima beans as it had with kidney beans, some confusion became evident when I asked another question. "What if I filled the jar with scoops of rice?" I asked. "How many scoops do you think it would take?"

Conversation broke out again. Asking this question pointed out the fragility of some of the students' thinking. Some of the students who had seemed very convinced about the two different beans were now unsure.

I asked for the students' attention. "I'm not going to scoop rice now," I said. "I'd like you to think about this for a day or so, and then we'll try it."

I settled the students and held up the emptied jar, the scoop, and the bag of lima beans. "What do we know so far about the jar, the scoop, and the lima beans?" I asked.

Kara said, "It takes twelve scoops of lima beans to fill the jar." I wrote on the board:

12 scoops of lima beans fill the jar.

The class was silent for a moment. Then Jonah raised a hand.

"There aren't as many lima beans in the jar as with the other beans," Jonah said.

"The lima beans are much bigger," Jo added. I recorded on the board:

Fewer than 470 lima beans fill the jar.

"And not as many will be in a scoop," Billy added. I recorded:

Fewer than 39 lima beans fill a scoop.

A Different Problem

"About how many lima beans do you think will fill the scoop?" I asked. "Think about the size of a lima bean compared with the size of a kidney bean." I made the beans available so that students could take one of each to compare. In this way, the students had the option of using the comparative sizes of the beans to make their estimates. Some students were able to reason proportionally, and others merely guessed. The estimates ranged from ten to twenty-five.

"Can't we figure out the number of lima beans in a scoop the way we did with the kidney beans?" I asked.

"We could if we knew how many beans filled in the jar," Anita said.

"I counted them," I said. "I filled the jar with lima beans, dumped them out on my desk, and counted two hundred twelve beans." I wrote on the board:

212 lima beans fill the jar.

Then I said, "If we're trying to figure out the number of beans in a scoop, the value of *n* for lima beans, let's write both a division and a multiplication sentence that will tell us how to do this."

Pierre reported, "You can do two hundred twelve divided by twelve."

As I recorded on the board, I said, "So we could think: 'Two hundred twelve beans divided into twelve scoops gives us the number of beans in a scoop.'"

212 ÷ 12 = n

Sally then said, "Or you could think, 'What number times twelve is two hundred twelve?'"

I said as I recorded, "So twelve scoops times the number of beans in a scoop should give us two hundred twelve beans altogether."

12 × n = 212

I then said, "Right now, I'd like you to talk with your partner and together figure out in your heads about how many beans are in a scoop of lima beans. You can think about what the answer is to two hundred twelve divided by twelve. Or you can think about 'Twelve times what number gives two hundred twelve?' Then we'll

talk about the different ways you thought about solving the problem." I gave the students a few minutes to talk together. When I sensed that the conversations were slowing down, I asked for their attention.

Solving 212 ÷ 12

Kara reported first. "We knew that twelve times twelve is one hundred forty-four. So that told us there had to be more than twelve beans in a scoop. So we just tried six more beans, and six twelves is seventy-two. And if you add seventy-two to one hundred forty-four, you get two hundred sixteen, which is pretty close." I recorded on the board:

12 × 12 = 144

12 × 6 = 72

144 + 72 = 216

"How did you add one hundred forty-four and seventy-two in your heads?" I asked.

"We counted by tens," Kara's partner, Anne, explained. "From one hundred forty-four we went one hundred fifty-four, sixty-four, seventy-four, eighty-four, ninety-four, then two hundred four, then two hundred fourteen, and two more makes two hundred sixteen." Anne used her fingers to keep track of the tens she was adding.

"So how many lima beans do you think there are in a scoop?" I asked the girls.

They were silent for a moment, and then Kara said, "Oh, I know, it's twelve plus six. That's eighteen. But that's a little too much. Some scoops will have only seventeen." I added to what I had recorded:

17 or 18 lima beans fill a scoop.

"Did anyone solve the problem the same way that Kara and Anne did?" I asked. Some hands went up.

"But we got two hundred fourteen," Hiroshi said. "We forgot to add on the extra two."

"Did anyone think about the problem as a division problem?" I asked. Hands went up and I called on Holly. She said, "First we thought: 'How many times does twelve go into two hundred twelve?' We knew that twelve goes into twelve one time, so we then had to figure out how many times twelve went into two hundred." I interrupted Holly to recap what she said. As I did so, I recorded on the board:

$212 \div 12 = n$

$212 = 200 + 12$

$12 \div 12 = 1$

$200 \div 12 = ?$

I said, "So you were trying to figure out how much was two hundred twelve divided by twelve. You knew that two hundred twelve was two hundred plus twelve. And you know that twelve divided by twelve is one. So now you had to figure out how much was two hundred divided by twelve. How did you do that?"

Holly's partner, Jo, explained, "We thought about one hundred. Twelve times eight is ninety-six, and that's the closest you can get to one hundred because there's four left over. So two hundred divided by twelve is eight plus eight more, and then there's eight left over." I recorded:

$100 \div 12 = 8 \ R4$

$200 \div 12 = 16 \ R8$

"Now what?" I asked.

Holly said, "So it's sixteen, plus the extra one, makes seventeen, with eight beans extra. And we agree that that's almost one more bean in a scoop, so it could be eighteen." I recorded:

$16 + 1 = 17$

There are 8 extra beans.

It could be 18 beans in a scoop.

By now it was time to end math class for the day. I said to the students,

"Tomorrow we'll count some scoops of lima beans and see how our counts compare with your answers. Then I'll give you a problem to try on your own."

DAY 2

Before counting the number of lima beans in a scoop, I began class by using the same method that I had shown the day before for dividing 470 by 12 to divide 212 by 12 and figure out about how many beans were in a scoop. I wrote the problem on the board. This time, I didn't draw the twelve scoops as I had done the day before.

$$12\overline{)212}$$

"See if you can follow what I do and how I'm thinking," I said. "We know that there are two hundred twelve beans in the jar, and that it takes twelve scoops to make the two hundred twelve beans. The problem is to figure out about how many beans fill a scoop. Do you think at least ten beans can fit in a scoop?"

Several students nodded. "Talk with your partner about how you can be sure that each scoop has at least ten beans." Conversation broke out. I waited a few minutes and then called the class to attention. I called on Anne.

"If there were ten beans in every scoop, that would take care of one hundred twenty beans, and there are still more left," she explained.

I nodded and asked, "Does anyone have another way to explain?"

Pierre said, "I know that ten times twelve is one hundred twenty because you just add on a zero to times by ten. And like Anne said, there are more beans than that." I then recorded:

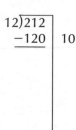

```
  12)212
    -120 | 10
```

I continued, "I'll subtract to see how many beans are left to divide among the twelve scoops." I did the subtraction and recorded.

```
  12)212
    -120 | 10
     ----
      92
```

"So we have ninety-two beans left," I said. "Can I fit ten more beans in each scoop? Talk with your partner about that." After a moment, I interrupted the class and called on Jorge.

He said, "There aren't enough beans left to put ten more in each scoop. You need one hundred twenty for that, and you don't even have one hundred."

"How about if I put half as many beans in each scoop?" I asked. "Can I put five beans in each scoop? Share your thinking about this with your partner."

It seemed obvious to the students that each scoop could hold five more beans. Sally explained why that would use up sixty beans. "Half of one hundred twenty is sixty. I know that because half of twelve is six, so half of one hundred twenty is sixty."

Jonah explained it differently. "Ten times five is fifty, and two more fives is ten, so it's sixty altogether." I recorded, showing that thirty-two beans still remained:

```
  12)212
    -120 | 10
     ----
      92
     -60 | 5
     ----
      32
```

I said, "We've taken care of all but thirty-two beans. What do you think I can do next?" Again, I asked students to talk with their partners. When I called them to attention, more than two-thirds had their hands raised.

Monique said, "You can put two more beans in each scoop. That's the best you can do."

"Why do you say that?" I asked her.

Monique explained, "Because that would use up twenty-four more beans, and three in each scoop would use up thirty-six beans, and you only have thirty-two beans left." I recorded:

```
  12)212
    -120 | 10
     ----
      92
     -60 | 5
     ----
      32
     -24 | 2
```

"If we put two more beans in each scoop, how many extra beans will we have left?" I asked. Students talked for a moment and then hands went up. I asked the class to give the answer to my question in a whisper voice. Then I recorded:

```
  12)212
    -120 | 10
     ----
      92
     -60 | 5
     ----
      32
     -24 | 2
     ----
       8
```

"What's the answer to the problem?" I asked.

"Seventeen remainder eight," Francis said. I recorded the answer.

$$\begin{array}{r} 17 \text{ R}8 \\ 12\overline{)212} \\ -120 \quad | \quad 10 \\ \overline{92} \\ -60 \quad | \quad 5 \\ \overline{32} \\ -24 \quad | \quad 2 \\ \overline{8} \end{array}$$

"What does the remainder eight tell us?" I asked.

Carolyn said, "You could put another bean in eight more scoops, but not in all twelve of them."

"If I give you a scoop of lima beans to count, about how many lima beans do you think will be in the scoop?" I asked. Students had several answers.

"Maybe seventeen, maybe eighteen," Sherea said.

"Seventeen in some and eighteen in some," Anita added.

"It could be more or less," Jorge said. "You can't be sure with the beans."

Counting Scoops of Lima Beans

"Let's find out," I said. "Let's count some scoops of lima beans and see what we learn." I placed a scoop of lima beans in front of every two or three students. After the students counted, I had each group report and I listed the numbers as they did so:

19

20

17

16

18

18

19

21

18

17

"They're all different," Enrique said.

"No, there are two of some of them," Carolyn added.

"They're pretty close," Francis said.

I then said, "It doesn't surprise me that the numbers are different. I know that measuring is never exact. Even though I tried to make scoops the same, as I did with the kidney beans, I knew that there would be differences. But we can analyze these numbers and come up with one that we agree is the typical number of lima beans in a scoop. To do this, it helps to look at the numbers in order." With the students' help, I reordered the numbers from smallest to largest.

16

17

17

18

18

18

19

19

20

21

"What number should we use for a typical scoop of lima beans? Does what we figured out make sense?" I asked.

Christian said, "I think eighteen is right because it's in the middle."

"What do you mean by it being in the middle?" I asked.

"Well, it's two away from sixteen and three away from twenty-one, so it's sort of in the middle," he explained.

"That's one way to think about it," I said. "We can also look at which number is in the middle of our list." I used fingers to point to the numbers in the list, starting at the top and the bottom simultaneously, to show that the middle of the list was between two of the 18s. "This is one way that statisticians think about deciding on a typical number from a list in order. The number in the middle is called the median.

When there isn't a number in the middle, but a space as on our list, then the median is in between the two numbers closest to the middle. And since both those numbers are eighteen, eighteen is the median." I wrote *median* on the board next to the two 18s in the middle of the list.

When I do this activity, I also like to introduce the students to the idea of *mode*, the number that occurs more often than any other. For our data, 18 was also the mode.

"Isn't there a way to average the numbers?" Monique asked. "Don't you add them all up and divide?" Students often learn this technique without really understanding what it means or why it works. I decided not to take the time to discuss this but asked Monique to use a calculator to add and divide.

"It's eighteen point three three three three, like that," she reported. "So eighteen seems good."

"We were right!" Davey said.

Another Problem

I then showed the class the large jar filled with lima beans. As the students watched, I wrote on the board:

A scoop of lima beans holds about 18 beans.

The jar has 676 beans in it.

About how many scoops of lima beans fill the jar?

"Who would like to read this problem aloud?" I asked. I called on Carolyn to do so.

"The answer has to be much bigger than twelve," Simon offered.

"Why do you think that?" I asked.

"Because the jar is really big," he said.

"The jar looks two times as big, maybe three times," Jorge added.

"About how many scoops did the small jar hold?" I asked.

"Twelve," the students responded in unison.

"So this has to have maybe twenty-five, maybe thirty, maybe more," Francis said.

"It's always good to have an estimate in mind before solving a problem," I said. "Then you have a way to check if the answer you figure out is reasonable. To figure out the answer, you can think of solving a division problem or a multiplication problem. Who has an idea about what division or multiplication problem you need to solve?"

Hiroshi suggested a division problem. "You go eighteen divided by six hundred seventy-six," he said. This reversal is a common error. I wrote on the board:

$18 \div 676$

"No, no, that's not what I meant," Hiroshi said and then corrected himself. "I meant six hundred seventy-six divided by eighteen." I wrote:

$676 \div 18 = n$

"What does the n in my equation stand for?" I asked.

"It's the number of scoops," Anita said, and then added, "If you divide six hundred seventy-six by eighteen, you get the number of scoops."

Holly then said, "You could write the problem the other way, with the line." I recorded on the board:

$$18\overline{)676}$$

"Can you explain what the numbers mean?" I asked, again linking the numbers to the problem.

"Six hundred seventy-six is the amount of beans and eighteen is the number of beans in one scoop," Holly responded.

Sherea then suggested how to represent the problem with multiplication. "You go blank times eighteen equals six hundred seventy-six," she said. I recorded Sherea's idea, writing n to represent the blank:

$n \times 18 = 676$

"Is it OK to use n for the blank?" I asked. Sherea nodded.

I then said, "Instead of talking about this problem as a class, I'd like you each to solve it on a sheet of paper. We can check your answers later by emptying the jar and counting the scoops it takes to re-fill it, but right now I'd like you to solve the problem in at least two different ways so that you're sure about your answer."

"Can we work together?" Simon wanted to know.

"It's fine for you to talk with the others at your table," I said. "But I'd like each of you to complete your own paper."

"Can we do it the way you showed?" Pierre asked.

"You can do it any way you'd like, as long as it makes sense to you," I replied.

Observing the Students

As typically happens when students face a problem on their own, some confusion broke out. In a class discussion, it often seems as if everyone understands what we're doing. But having students solve a problem by themselves reveals who under-stands and who doesn't.

Enrique motioned me over and said, "I can't remember how to start. Do I do eighteen into sixty-seven or eighteen into six hundred seventy-six?" Enrique was thinking of the standard algorithm of di-vide, multiply, subtract, and bring down. Rather than answer Enrique's question and focus him on the standard algorithm, I de-cided to try to move Enrique toward solv-ing the problem in another way, relying on what he knew about multiplying.

I said, "It seems that you're not comfort-able solving the problem by dividing. How could you think about multiplication to solve the problem?" Enrique looked at me

blankly, so I directed his attention to the board where I had written $n \times 18 = 676$.

After looking at the board for a mo-ment, Enrique said, "Oh yeah, I guess I could use multiplication," and he recorded a multiplication equation on his paper, using s for the number of scoops and reversing the order of the factors: $18 \times s = 676$. To make sure Enrique really understood what he had written, I asked, "What does the s mean?"

Enrique answered easily, "That's the number of scoops that will fill the big jar. Oh, I think I can use eighteen and keep multiplying it by numbers until I get to six hundred seventy-six." He began writing on his paper:

$18 \times 10 = 180$

$18 \times 20 = 360$

Since Enrique appeared to have a way to progress, I circulated around the table and next looked over Sherea's shoulder. She had been stuck but had overheard my conversation with Enrique and was now writing multiplication sentences similar to Enrique's.

Davey had used multiplication and trial and error to figure that 18 times 37 is 666. "That's only ten beans away from another scoop," he told me. "But nine beans make half of a scoop, so I think the answer is thirty-seven and a half scoops plus one extra bean."

"Can you explain your idea in writing?" I asked.

Davey nodded. I left him to write. On his paper, underneath where he had multi-plied 37×18 to get 666, Davey wrote $18 \times \frac{1}{2} = 9$ and added 9 to 666 to get 675. Then he wrote:

When you were hear I wrote $18 \times 37 =$ _____ and now I wrote $18 \times \frac{1}{2} = 9$. So I added 9 to 666 and it = 675 and it would only be one from the anser so that's the closest you cn get that's my answer. 18 is a whole scoop and 9 is a hafe of a scoop so if you add a hafe of a scoop it would be one away.

Beans and Scoops   165

I went back to check on Enrique and Sherea and found that they had both gotten quite far. Both had figured out that 40 was too many scoops because 18 × 40 = 720. Enrique had tried multiplying 39 × 18 and got 702, which was still too big. He wrote: *I think it takes 36 or 37.* Sherea, however, had multiplied 18 × 38 to get 684. Then she tried 18 × 37 to get 666, and checked this by multiplying 37 × 18. She wrote: *I think there will be about 37 or 38 scoops in the jar.* (See Figure 13–1.)

Anita solved the problem by dividing and did so two different ways, first using the standard algorithm and then using the subtraction method. She wrote: *I think there are 37 scoops of lima beans with the remainder of 10 beans in a scoop.* (See Figure 13–2.)

Anita was one of the students who could use the standard long division algorithm. Several other students who had tried using the standard algorithm either got stuck or confused, or made an error when they had to divide 18 into 676. I was struck by the fact that students who ran into difficulty with the standard long division algorithm had no tools for finishing the problem another way.

This reminded me that reasoning doesn't necessarily help with the standard algorithm, and students don't have a way out when they run into a problem. Some students who seemed to totally understand the lesson up to this point were unable to arrive at an answer because they couldn't successfully use the algorithm. On the other hand, when students thought about the problem in a different way, drawing on

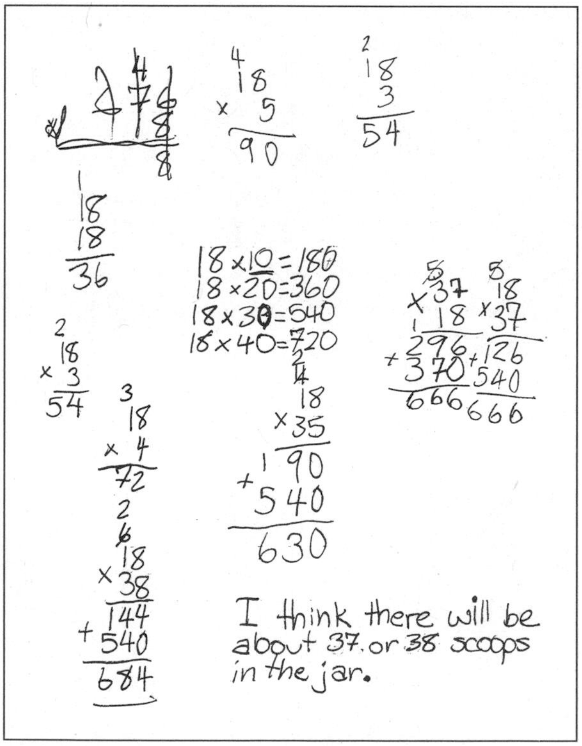

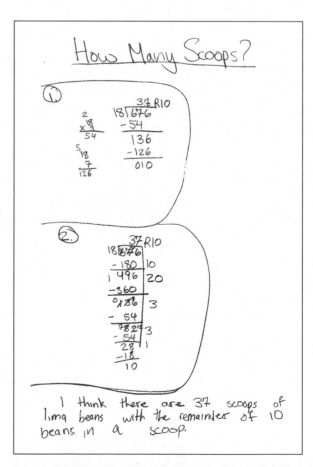

▲▲▲▲▲▲**Figure 13–1** *Sherea solved the problem of 676 ÷ 18 by doing successive multiplications. It's interesting to note that she checked 37 × 18 by then multiplying 18 × 37, an indication of her lack of confidence.*

▲▲▲▲▲▲**Figure 13–2** *Anita's paper shows her ability to use the standard algorithm— divide, multiply, subtract, bring down—as well as the alternative algorithm.*

their number sense and not focusing on the procedure of standard long division, as did Enrique and Sherea, even students who struggled some in math were able to think through the problem and arrive at a reasonable solution.

At the end of class, I collected all of the students' papers, whether or not they had finished.

DAY 3

I explained to the students that I was going to return their papers. "Share what you've done with your partner," I said. "Then, those of you who haven't yet finished should complete your papers. And those of you who already showed two

ways should see if you can figure out another way to solve the problem." Having the students talk among themselves gives all of them a chance to explain their work and learn from one another. As I had done the day before, I circulated, listening and offering help.

Most of the students were able to use the division method I had shown the day before. Sherea was particularly delighted with her success. (See Figure 13–3.)

Simon spent most of his time finishing his explanation that he had begun the day before. (See Figure 13–4.)

This lesson was one of many in which the students would have the chance to practice solving division problems. Over time, and with practice, the students became proficient with this alternative algorithm. Figure 13–5 shows how Monique used the algorithm to solve this problem.

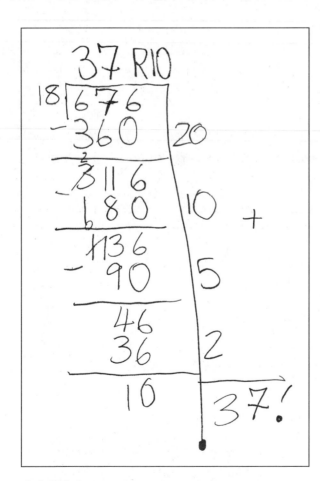

▲▲▲▲▲▲Figure 13–3 *Sherea was pleased to have learned how to use the alternative algorithm for long division.*

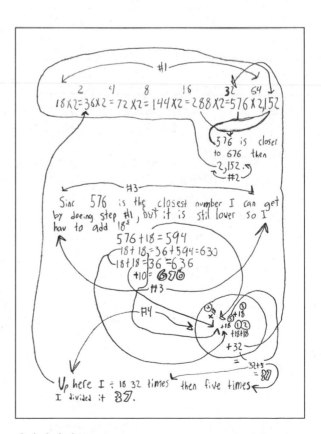

▲▲▲▲▲▲Figure 13–4 *Simon worked hard on the first day to explain his logic for figuring out the answer to 676 ÷ 18.*

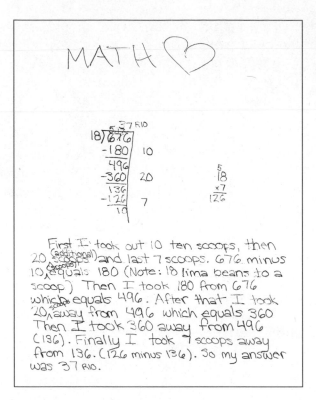

▲▲▲▲▲▲**Figure 13–5** *Monique related her numerical recording to the beans and scoops.*

Questions and Discussion

▲▲▲

▲ *Since you want students to have several strategies for solving division problems, why not also teach them the standard algorithm?*

Yes, I do want students to have several strategies available to them for solving any problem. But it's important that they understand the logic behind the strategies that they use and keep their focus on the meaning of the numbers. When students use the method of dividing, multiplying, subtracting, and bringing down, they seem to focus on the digits in the dividend, not on the meaning of the number, and they tend to follow the steps without paying attention to the problem at hand. Therefore, careless errors are common and typically go unnoticed by students. I do not think it's necessary or productive to teach that method.

▲ *When Enrique was having difficulty, why did you focus him on multiplying? Why didn't you focus him on the alternative algorithm you had just taught?*

Enrique was a student who learned slowly and lacked confidence. To help him, I wanted to build on what he knew and, therefore, I steered him toward using his knowledge of multiplication to solve the division problem. I felt that this would not only help him be successful but also strengthen for him the important connection between multiplication and division. A decision like this one is representative of the many professional decisions we have to make during the course of classroom lessons.

CHAPTER FOURTEEN
THE DIVISION GAME

Overview

The *Division Game* helps students relate multiples to division and gives them experience with the terminology of *multiple, factor, divisor, divisible,* and *common multiple.* The game reinforces and extends the concepts in the lesson *A Remainder of One.* Students play the game in groups of five and use the lists that they generated in *A Remainder of One* of multiples up to 100 for the numbers 2, 3, 4, 5, and 6. While the game has a winner, students work cooperatively with one another to play.

Materials

▲ 3-by-5-inch index cards cut in half, 144 half cards per group of five students (you may choose to provide more in case students make errors on some of the cards)

▲ 3-by-5-inch index cards of a second color, 10 per group of five students, labeled with pairs of numbers as follows: 2, 3; 2, 4; 2, 5; 2, 6; 3, 4; 3, 5; 3, 6; 4, 5; 4, 6; 5, 6.

▲ quart-size zip-top baggies, 1 per group of five students, to hold the 144 half cards and 10 cards with number pairs described above

▲ optional: rules for the *Division Game* to distribute to students (see Blackline Masters)

Time

▲ two class periods

Teaching Directions

1. Show students a zip-top baggie with 144 blank cards (3-by-5-inch index cards cut in half). (I put 150 cards in each baggie to provide extras in case students make mistakes when they write on the cards.) The baggie should also contain 10 index cards of a second color that are numbered as described in the "Materials" section.

2. Explain to students that working with their group of five, they'll use their lists of multiples to write numbers on the blank cards, which will be called multiple cards. They should write each multiple from each list on a card. You may want to give them a procedure for doing this, such as having each student make the cards for a different multiple.

3. With a group of five students, model the *Division Game* using the following rules:

The Division Game

You need:
  a group of five
  1 set of 144 cards with multiples
  1 set of 10 cards with factor pairs
  lists of multiples from 1 to 100 for 2, 3, 4, 5, and 6

Rules

The object of the game is to be the first player to have five cards with multiples of both the numbers on your factor card.

1. Mix and place the ten cards with factor pairs facedown. Then each player takes a factor card and places it faceup in front of him or her.

2. Mix the cards with the multiples. One player deals each player in the group five multiple cards, and players place their multiple cards faceup in front of them. Place the remaining multiple cards facedown in a pile and turn the top multiple card faceup to begin a discard pile.

3. On your turn, you may take the top multiple card from the deck or you may draw the top card from the discard pile. Then you must discard one multiple card, always keeping five cards in your hand. Remember, you want to keep cards that are multiples of both numbers on your factor card. You may refer to the lists of multiples to help you decide if a multiple card is one you want to keep or discard.

4. Players take turns repeating Step 3 until one player has five cards that are multiples of both of the numbers on his or her factor card.

5. The winning player must tell a division sentence to explain how each number on the multiple cards is divisible by both of the factor numbers.

---

4. When students understand how to play the *Division Game*, have them play in groups of five.

5. When a student asks whether it's OK to have two or more multiple cards with the same number in his or her hand, interrupt the class to explain this is OK.

6. Lead a class discussion for students to share what they learned, what they noticed, and what they discovered.

Teaching Notes

The lesson *A Remainder of One* (see Chapter 10) is a prerequisite for this lesson. In *A Remainder of One*, students create lists of the multiples up to 100 for the numbers 2, 3, 4, 5, and 6. There are a total of 144 multiples on the five lists, and students transfer these numbers to cards to use for playing the *Division Game*. Students also use the lists as a reference for making decisions as they play. Both the *Division Game* and *A Remainder of One* help students relate multiples to division and give them experience with the terminology of *multiple, factor, divisor, divisible,* and *common multiple*.

To play the *Division Game,* each player has a factor card with a pair of factors on it and tries to get five multiple cards with numbers that are multiples of both of the numbers on their factor card. There are 10 factor cards with the following pairs of numbers on them: 2, 3; 2, 4; 2, 5; 2, 6; 3, 4; 3, 5; 3, 6; 4, 5; 4, 6; 5, 6. This is not a fair game because of the 144 multiple cards, some work for more factor cards than others. To understand why, it is useful to think about the probabilities. It helps to begin with the number of multiples on each list:

Multiples of 2	50
Multiples of 3	33
Multiples of 4	25
Multiples of 5	20
Multiples of 6	16

These numbers add to 144, the number of multiple cards used in the *Division Game*. If your factor card had the numbers 5 and 6 on it, fewer of those multiple cards would be useful than if your factor card had, for example, the numbers 5 and 2 on it, since there are more multiples of two than there are of six. This becomes evident to students after they've had some experience playing the game.

When asked which factor card gives the best chance for collecting a hand of winning multiple cards, students typically choose the factor card with the numbers 2 and 3. They typically explain that this is so because two and three have more multiples than the other numbers—eighty-three multiples combined. However, this doesn't take into account the entire situation.

If we think about just the multiples of 3, more than 33 cards of the 144 cards are multiples of 3. All of the multiples of 6 are also multiples of 3, so that's another 16 cards. From the multiples of 4 cards, 8 are also multiples of 3—12, 24, 36, 48, 60, 72, 84, and 96. From the multiples of 5 cards, 6 are also multiples of 3—15, 30, 45, 60, 75, and 90. And from the multiples of 2 cards, 16 are also multiples of 3—6, 12, 18, 24, 30, 36, 42, 48, 54, 60, 66, 72, 78, 84, 90, and 96. Altogether, 79 of the 144 cards are multiples of 3!

We can use this information to figure out the total number of cards that are multiples of *both* 2 and 3 by keeping in mind that multiples of 2 have to be even. So the multiples that work for both 2 and 3 include the even-numbered cards from the 79 that work for 3 alone. These include 16 from the 2s list, the 16 even numbers from the 3s list, the 8 that work for both from the 4s list since they're all even, the 3 even multiples on the 5s list—30, 60, and 90, and all 16 from the 6s list since they're also all even. Add these: 16 + 16 + 8 + 3 + 16 = 59. So, 59 of the 144 cards are multiples of both 2 and 3, or we could say that $\frac{59}{144}$ of the cards work for the factor card with 2 and 3 on it.

If we do the same analysis for the factor card with 2 and 4 on it, we find that more than 59 cards work. Every other number on the 2s list is a multiple of both 2 and 4, so 25 of those cards are multiples of 4. Eight of the multiples of 3 cards are multiples of 2 and 4—12, 24, 36, 48, 60, 72, 84, and 96. All 25 numbers from the multiples of 4 list are also multiples of 2. From the multiples of 5 cards, 5 are multiples of 2 and 4—20, 40, 60, 80, and 100. And from the multiples of 6 cards, 8 are multiples of 2 and 4—12, 24, 36, 48, 60, 72, 84, and 96. Add these: 25 + 8 + 25 + 5 + 8 = 71. So 71 of the 144 cards are multiples of both 2 and 4, or we could say that $\frac{71}{144}$ of the cards work for the factor card with 2 and 4 on it.

The following chart shows the number of cards out of 144 that have common multiples for each pair of factors:

Factors	Common Multiples
2, 3	$\frac{59}{144}$
2, 4	$\frac{71}{144}$
2, 5	$\frac{31}{144}$
2, 6	$\frac{59}{144}$
3, 4	$\frac{33}{144}$
3, 5	$\frac{19}{144}$
3, 6	$\frac{59}{144}$
4, 5	$\frac{17}{144}$
4, 6	$\frac{33}{144}$
5, 6	$\frac{13}{144}$

While this analysis can provide students with a valuable mathematical experience in the area of data analysis and probability, it may be too complex for your students. However, even realizing that the game is not fair gives students experience with an important and basic concept of probability. And, for a challenge, some students might be interested in exploring how to make the *Division Game* a fair game.

The Lesson

▲▲

DAY 1

I asked the students to sit on the rug with their group from *A Remainder of One*. When the students were settled, I held up a plastic baggie containing 150 blank white 3-by-5-inch index cards. (While 144 blank white cards are required, I provide the extra 6 in case of errors.) Also in the baggie were 10

3-by-5-inch blue index cards, each marked with a pair of numbers from 2 to 6 and held together with a rubber band. (See "Materials" section for directions on how to label the blue cards.)

I said, "In a few moments, I'll give each group a baggie like this one. Leave the blue cards in the baggie and take out the white cards. You're going to record the multiples from your lists on the white cards." As I continued to give oral directions, I also demonstrated exactly what I wanted the students to do. "To do this, take one white card, write one multiple on it, set it aside, take another white card and write the next multiple on it, and so on until you've written each multiple from your list on a white card." I paused a moment, then asked, "How do you suppose I knew how many cards to put in your bag?" The students sat still with blank looks. Pilar raised her hand and then changed her mind. Sierra raised her hand slowly.

Sierra explained, "I think you can figure it out by looking at the lists of multiples. There are fifty multiples of two on our lists, so that's fifty cards for the twos. There are twenty-five multiples of four, so that's twenty-five cards for the fours, then twenty for the fives, thirty-three for the multiples of three, and there are sixteen multiples of six."

I said, "To figure the number of cards for each bag, I added up the number of multiples just as Sierra suggested: Fifty plus thirty-three plus twenty-five plus twenty plus sixteen. It comes out to be a little less than one hundred fifty—one hundred forty-four, to be exact. There are one hundred fifty cards in each bag, so there will be some extras in case you make an error and need a new card. Remember to write one multiple on each card."

Kaleb had one last idea to share. He said, "Hey, there's a pattern! The twos list has fifty multiples and needs fifty cards. The fours list, which is two doubled, has only twenty-five multiples. Four doubles, but the number of multiples halved." Several students nodded their agreement with Kaleb's thinking.

There were no further comments and no questions. The students got to work. Those who finished first helped their group members. In about ten minutes, each group had a set of multiple cards.

Introducing the *Division Game*

I asked Max's group if they were willing to play a game with me to model the game for the rest of the students. They agreed. I then said to the rest of the class, "Max's group has agreed to play a new game with me. I'd like the rest of you to observe carefully so you'll know how to play the game with your group." The others gathered around Max's group.

I gave directions. "This game is called the *Division Game*. To play, your group needs the white cards you made with the multiples on them, your papers with the multiples listed, and the blue cards that should still be inside your baggie." I removed the blue cards from Max's group's baggie and showed them to the students, explaining, "There's a different pair of numbers on each blue card. The numbers I used to make the pairs are two, three, four, five, and six, the same numbers we've been using to think about the numbers of lines in which the squadrons can march in *A Remainder of One*. You'll use these numbers as factors, so we'll call these blue cards the factor cards. Before the game begins, mix the blue cards and place them facedown. Then each group member takes one." I mixed the blue factor cards, placed them facedown, took one, and waited for the other members of Max's group to do the same. I set the remaining blue factor cards aside.

I next explained, "When you've drawn your factor card, place it faceup in front of you so everyone in your group can see it." I turned my factor card faceup and the others did the same.

I continued, "Next, someone in the group mixes the white multiple cards and deals five to each member of the group." I quickly mixed the cards and dealt five white multiple cards to each student in the group and to myself. I then placed the remaining white multiple cards facedown where all players could reach them and turned the top white multiple card faceup to begin a discard pile. "Everyone should place his or her multiple cards faceup above your factor card so we can see what each other has. I have four, forty-two, one hundred, fifty-two, and seventy-two."

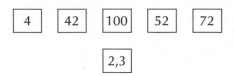

The others also arranged their cards faceup in a row in front of them.

"My blue factor card has a two and a three on it, and that tells me I want to have five multiple cards with numbers that are divisible by both two and three." I pointed to my first multiple card and asked, "Is four divisible by two and three?"

"It's a multiple of two," Chico said.

"I agree four is a multiple of two," I replied. "But I'm looking for cards with numbers that are a multiple of *both* two and three. Is four divisible by three?" Chico shook his head. I purposely interchanged the terminology of *multiple* and *divisible* to reinforce the relationship between them.

"Four isn't a good card for me because it's not divisible by two and three, so I'll try to replace it," I summarized. "Is the number on any of my cards a multiple of both two and three?"

Jared said, "Forty-two is a multiple of both two and three." Many students nodded their agreement.

"How do you know?" I asked Jared. "How much is forty-two divided by two and how much is it divided by three?"

Jared answered the first question easily. "Forty-two divided by two is twenty-one and there's no remainder." He paused to think and then said, "Forty-two divided by three is fourteen, and there's no remainder."

Because not all of the students were as fluent with dividing as Jared, I said, "Please check your multiple lists to be sure that forty-two is on the lists for both two and three." As the students checked their lists, I wrote on the board:

$42 \div 2 = 21$

$42 \div 3 = 14$

I called the class to attention and the students confirmed that 42 was on both lists.

"And it's not on the others," Roxanne said. "I checked." I gave a moment for the students to verify her idea.

I turned to Jared. "How did you come up with the answers of twenty-one and fourteen?" I asked, pointing to the equations I had written on the board.

Jared said, "Twenty-one was easy. Forty divided by two is twenty, so forty-two divided by two is twenty-one. For three, I knew that three goes into forty-five fifteen times, and forty-two is three less than forty-five."

While some could follow Jared's reasoning, or figure out the answers on their own, I knew others couldn't. I gave them another way to figure, using their multiple lists. I began, "If you start at the top with the two, and count the numbers on the twos list, we can check how many multiples of two there are up to one hundred."

"There are fifty," Sierra said, as she had before.

"Yes," I agreed, "but if you count down to forty-two, you'll find that it's the twenty-first multiple on the list." The students counted to verify this.

"It takes twenty-one twos to make forty-two. Now count down on the threes list to forty-two to see how many threes it takes." They counted and verified that forty-two divided by three is fourteen.

Returning to the game, I said, "So, I want to keep the card with forty-two on it.

Do I have any other cards with numbers that are divisible by both two and three?" Carson suggested 72. I asked the students to verify that 72 is a multiple of 2 and 3 and to figure out the answers to 72 ÷ 2 and 72 ÷ 3.

I continued, "To win the game, I must be the first to have five cards with numbers that are divisible by both two and three. Any questions so far?" There were none.

I said, "I'll go first to show how to take your turn. Either I can take the top card from the pile that's facedown, or I can take the top card from the discard pile. The discard pile has a thirty-two on the top. Thirty-two is divisible by two, but not by three. That's not going to help me. I'll take the top card from the pile that's facedown." I turned over the top card and continued, "I got a twenty-four. Should I keep it and discard one of the other cards, or should I discard the twenty-four?" Most students agreed that I should keep the 24. "Why does it make sense to keep the twenty-four?" I probed.

Chico explained, "It's an even number, so I know it's divisible by two. And if I count by eights—eight, sixteen, twenty-four—there are three eights, so twenty-four is divisible by three."

Shelly added, "You could figure it out by multiplication, too. Two times twelve is twenty-four and so is three times eight."

"If I don't discard the twenty-four, then what card should I get rid of?" I asked. Hands shot up. I called on Kaleb.

"I think you should get rid of the hundred," Kaleb said. "It's divisible by two. Two times fifty equals one hundred, so that means it's divisible by both two and fifty. But one hundred isn't divisible by three. The closest you can get to one hundred if you count by threes is ninety-nine. It won't work, so you should discard it."

Krystal explained why I should discard either the 52 or the 4. She said, "Four is

divisible by two. Two, four. But four is only one bigger than three. That means if you divide four by three, you'll get one remainder one. It won't work. And with fifty-two, it's divisible by two because it's an even number, but I don't think it's divisible by three. I knew forty-two was divisible by three from earlier, so I started counting by threes beginning with forty-two. Forty-two, forty-five, forty-eight, fifty-one. I didn't land on fifty-two, so I don't think fifty-two is divisible by three."

Natalie said, "Krystal's idea gave me an idea. I think another way to prove fifty-two isn't divisible by three is to start with forty-two, which is divisible by three. The difference between forty-two and fifty-two is ten. Three can't go into ten evenly, so I don't think it can go into fifty-two, which is ten bigger than forty-two."

I said to the class, "You shared good reasons that your advice to keep the twenty-four makes sense and explained how you know the others aren't divisible by both two and three. I'll take your advice. I'll keep the twenty-four and discard the hundred." I placed the 100 card on top of the discard pile. "It's Max's turn. What pair of numbers does Max have on his blue factor card?" I asked.

"Five and six," chorused the class.

"Is one hundred a card that will help him?" I asked.

"No!" the students replied.

Max commented, "I don't have any cards that work yet. I hope I get a thirty because I think that would work." Max drew a card with 40 on it and placed it on the discard pile.

Shelly was next. "Forty works for me!" she said. Her blue card had the numbers 2 and 4 on it. She took the card and discarded a 5.

The students were following the game easily at this point and were eager to get started playing with their groups. As a reminder, I said, "To win, all five of the numbers on your white cards must be multiples of both numbers on your blue factor card." There were no questions at this time. However, there was one additional rule I decided not to address until it came up as students played. There are duplicates of some numbers on the multiple cards. For example, there are five 60s in the deck because 60 is a multiple of 2, 3, 4, 5, and 6. As students play, someone will eventually ask, "Is it OK to have two or more of the same number in your hand?" The answer to this question is yes, it's OK to have two or more of the same number. I save discussion of this point until it comes up and students have had a chance to become familiar with playing the game.

Observing the Students

It took only a few minutes before all the students were engaged in playing the game. Their eagerness to play motivated them to make quick decisions about who would deal the cards and who would go first. As the students played, I noticed teamwork in action as entire groups studied the lists of multiples to help each member decide which cards to hold and which to discard.

Roxanne called me over to her group. "I just want to be sure. I think I won. My blue card is two and three. The cards in my hand are eighteen, seventy-two, thirty-six, forty-two, and eighteen."

"Why do you think you won?" I asked.

"Because me and my group checked on the lists and all my numbers are on the two list and also on the three list," Roxanne explained.

"Can you verify you won by doing the division?" I pushed.

Roxanne explained, "Well, eighteen divided by two equals nine. Two groups of nine equals eighteen. Eighteen divided by three equals six and six times three equals

eighteen. That works. I have two eighteens, so I know those two cards work. I already know forty-two works from the class discussion. Forty-two divided by two equals twenty-one and forty-two divided by three equals fourteen. Thirty-six is easy. It's an even number, so it's divisible by two. And thirty-six divided by three is twelve. Twelve times three equals thirty-six. That leaves seventy-two. I know two works because it's even. Half of seventy is thirty-five, so half of seventy-two equals thirty-six. Seventy-two is hard for three. I had to look on the threes list of multiples to find it."

"How could you use the list to figure out how many threes in seventy-two?" I asked Roxanne.

She paused a moment. Autumn, another member of the group, leaned over and said, "I think you can count how many threes on the list until you get to seventy-two." Together, Autumn and Roxanne counted twenty-four multiples of three.

Elonzo said, "I know another way. There are twenty-five threes in seventy-five. If you subtract one group of three from seventy-five, you get seventy-two. That's one less group of threes, so twenty-four threes."

"I think you've won," I said to Roxanne. She smiled.

DAY 2

I started by giving the students additional time to play the game. Autumn called me over. She explained, "I think some pairs of numbers are easier to get than others, but I'm not exactly sure."

"What makes you say that, Autumn?" I probed.

"I think Elonzo, who has five and six on his blue factor card, doesn't have as good a chance of winning as someone with a two and three on their factor card," Autumn explained. "The list of multiples of five and the list of six aren't as long as the twos and threes. It just doesn't seem quite fair to me." I was impressed that Autumn had noticed this and planned to raise the question of fairness later during a class discussion about the game.

I said, "You've raised an interesting point, Autumn. I think you and your group should play again. Each of you take a new blue factor card and see if you still feel the same way when you finish another game. Also, I'd like you and your group to share what you find out about this when we have our class discussion." The group nodded and prepared to play another game.

Natalie came to me and said, "We have a question. My pair of numbers is two and four. I have a sixty, which is divisible by two because it's even, and by four—there are four fifteens in sixty. Then I drew another sixty. Can I have two sixties or should I put the second sixty back and draw again?"

"Let's go talk with your group and see what they think about it," I suggested. When we got to Natalie's group, I said, "Natalie has asked me if it's OK to have two sixties in her hand. Before I tell you the rule about that, I'm interested in what you think about having two of the same number in your hand." I asked the students about their thinking before clarifying the rule because I was interested in their observations and intuitive feelings about the numbers and their multiples and how they influenced the game.

Hayley said, "It should be like drawing any other card. If sixty is a good number for her, she should be able to keep it. If it's a bad number, she would just get rid of it like any other bad number."

Chico shrugged and explained he wasn't sure.

Katie agreed with Hayley and commented she didn't think the game was fair because some pairs of numbers on the blue factor cards had more ways to win than others. Like for Autumn, her experience studying the lists of multiples as she played the game led to her awareness of this idea.

I told the group the rule. "It's OK to have more than one card with the same number," I said.

Ashton was the next winner. He explained, "I won because my group helped me. We all helped each other, actually." His group decided to continue playing until there was a second-place winner.

Krystal and her group were having an intense discussion about the issue of having more than one card with the same number in one's hand. This time, I decided to interrupt the entire class and address this point. I asked for the students' attention.

I said, "There's a question about the game I need to answer. The question is: Should a player be allowed to have two white multiple cards with the same number, or perhaps three or four or five white cards with the same number? The answer is: It's OK to have two or more white multiple cards with the same number."

There were no comments and the students returned to their games. I circulated and observed for another five minutes, then gave the students a one-minute warning to finish their games. At the end of one minute, I asked for their attention.

I said, "Please collect the cards into two piles, put them in your baggie, and return the baggie to me. Bring your list of multiples and come sit on the floor with your group." It took only a couple of minutes for the students to do as I asked. As they got settled, I reminded them to put their papers on the floor in front of them. I find this keeps the students from rattling their papers and creating a distraction yet allows them visual access to their work.

A Class Discussion

To begin the discussion, I asked the students, "What did you think about the game?" Several replied they liked it and that it was fun.

"What did you notice, learn, or discover?" I asked.

Malina said, "I think I learned more about numbers and what other numbers they're divisible by." Several students nodded their agreement.

Diego said, "Some numbers are easier than others."

"Explain some more about that," I encouraged Diego.

Diego explained, "Well, it seems easier to find multiple cards for some blue cards and not so easy for others. And another thing: Some numbers are harder to divide. Like I thought ninety-seven divided by three was hard to figure out. But not twenty divided by five."

Natalie said, "Some factors are easier to figure out, like Diego said. Like all even numbers are divisible by two and all numbers with a five or a zero in the ones place are divisible by five. But sometimes I thought the threes were hard."

Autumn said, "I don't think this game is very fair!"

Katie said, "I agree. I think the best white card to get is sixty because it's a multiple of all the numbers on the blue cards."

"How could you show that?" I asked.

"By looking on the lists," Katie said.

I said to the rest of the class, "Please check your lists and see if sixty is on all of them." The students confirmed 60 appeared on all lists.

"I think Autumn and Katie are right," Kaleb said. "I think that because the lists are different lengths. There aren't very

many multiples on the sixes list, but there are lots on the twos."

"Hey, he's right! I hadn't noticed that," Clay said.

"What does the length of the list have to do with whether or not the game is fair?" I asked. I gave the students a few moments to think quietly, then asked them to share their ideas with their neighbors. After a few minutes, I asked for their attention.

Elonzo shared, "I think how many are on each list matters because each number represents one card. In the beginning, we used all the numbers on all the lists to make the multiple cards. Some numbers have more cards, like six, because they're on more lists." Elonzo checked his lists and continued. "Six is on the twos list, the threes list, and the sixes list. But five is only on the fives list." The students checked their lists and verified Elonzo's reasoning.

Jared said, "If a list of multiples has fewer numbers, then there are fewer cards. So the sixes don't have as many cards, so there's less chance of getting a card that's a multiple of six."

"And there are more numbers on the twos list, so there are more multiple cards that are divisible by two," Hayley said.

Sierra said, "So that means that you want the two numbers with the longest lists of multiples on your blue factor card."

"What factor card would you want?" I asked the students. Hands shot into the air. "Tell me in a whisper voice."

"Two and three," they chorused. Even though this card is a good choice, I knew there were actually more multiple cards for the factor pair 2 and 4. However, I decided to wait for another day to explore this.

"What numbers don't you want?" I probed.

"Five and six," the students agreed.

There were no more comments, so I ended the discussion.

Questions and Discussion

▲▲

▲ *Why does it make sense to spend class time playing a game like this?*

Games offer reinforcement and worthwhile practice of skills previously learned. In this case, the *Division Game* is a direct application of concepts developed in the lesson *A Remainder of One*. Students apply what they learned about factors, multiples, common multiples, and divisibility in a game that is repeatable throughout the year.

▲ *Would the game be good to play after the students have learned more about the divisibility rules, especially about the rule for divisibility by three?*

Yes, the game would be fine used this way, or even without the lists of multiples for reference for more of a challenge. But I still recommend starting as described here, giving all the students the maximum support for playing.

CHAPTER FIFTEEN
THE FACTOR GAME

Overview

The *Factor Game* gives students practice with basic division facts and increases their fluency, understanding of, and familiarity with the relationship between numbers and their factors. The game also gives students experience with the concept of proper factors—those factors that are smaller than the number itself. After the teacher introduces and models the game for the class, students play in pairs. After a discussion, they play again, adjusting the challenge of the game by increasing the range of the numbers used.

Materials

▲ recording sheets, at least 1 per pair of students (see Blackline Masters)
▲ optional: overhead transparency of recording sheet (see Blackline Masters)
▲ rules for the *Factor Game,* 1 per pair of students (see Blackline Masters)

Time

▲ one class period to introduce the game, followed by additional class time for playing and for extensions

Teaching Directions

1. Write the numbers from *1* to *15* on the board.

2. Review with students the meaning of *factor.*

3. Tell students that you are going to teach them how to play the *Factor Game.* Tell them that the object is to get more points than your partner. Explain the two ways points are scored in each round:

1. Select a number from the list that isn't yet crossed out and record it as your score for the round.

2. Find all the proper factors of the number your opponent selected that aren't yet crossed out, and the sum of those factors is your score for the round.

4. Project an overhead transparency of a score sheet (see Blackline Masters) or draw a sample on the board. Write the numbers from *1* to *15* at the top of the sheet.

number list				number list			
1 2 3 4 5 6 7 8 9 10 11 12 13 14 15				1 2 3 4 5 6 7 8 9 10 11 12 13 14 15			
proof	score	score	proof	proof	score	score	proof

_____ had _____ points.

_____ had _____ points.

_____ wins by _____ points.

_____ had _____ points.

_____ had _____ points.

_____ wins by _____ points.

5. Distribute a copy of the *Factor Game* rules to each pair of students (see Blackline Masters). Play two games with the class using the transparency as a guide to model how to play and how to record.

6. Have the students play the *Factor Game* in pairs. In the event there is an odd number of students, you can play with the extra student or have one group of three and the players take turns playing each other.

7. Lead a class discussion for students to talk about what they thought about the game and what they discovered.

8. Have students play again, increasing the range of the numbers used.

Teaching Notes

There are two ways students can write a division sentence to prove a factor is theirs. For example, suppose Player 1 chooses twelve. Player 2 could prove that three is a factor of twelve by writing *12 ÷ 4 = 3* or *12 ÷ 3 = 4*. In the first situation the student thinks, "Twelve divided by what number equals three?" In the second situation the student thinks, "Twelve divided by three equals what number?" The first idea is represented symbolically as 12 ÷ □ = 3; the second is represented as 12 ÷ 3 = □. I've taught the lesson using both interpretations. Most students enjoy the first way and the added challenge of figuring out the missing divisor, as I used in the vignette. Whichever way you choose, it's important to model and use only one way of writing division sentences to avoid confusion and provide consistency for your students.

For younger, less experienced learners, use the numbers from one to fifteen. For a more challenging experience, students can increase the range to include larger numbers, for example from one to twenty or twenty-five.

The Lesson

▲▲

I began the lesson by writing the numbers from *1* to *15* on the board. As I did so, the students talked quietly among themselves about what they thought my purpose was. By the time I had finished writing the numbers, the students were quiet, ready to find out what we were going to do.

1 2 3 4 5 6 7 8 9
10 11 12 13 14 15

I said, "Today I'm going to teach you how to play a game, and then you'll have the opportunity to play it with a partner. The game uses the numbers I've written on the board. It's called the *Factor Game* because it involves factors." I wrote the word *factor* on the board and then continued. "Who would like to remind us what a factor is?"

Brody volunteered, "You multiply factors to get products in multiplication."

Wendi added, "I think if a number is a factor of a number, it goes into it evenly with no remainder."

"I get confused with factor and multiple," Natalia commented. "Is it true that twenty-five is a multiple of five and five is a factor of twenty-five?" I nodded. It's not uncommon for students to confuse factors and multiples. There were no other comments.

I continued, "Brody, Wendi, and Natalia are all correct. You multiply factors to get

a product; if a number is a factor of another number, it can be divided into that number with no remainder; and Natalia gave a good example when she explained that five is a factor of twenty-five.

"The object of the *Factor Game* is to get more points than your partner. You get points in two ways. When it's your turn, you get to select a number that hasn't been used from the list of numbers from one to fifteen, cross it out, and then you get that number of points. For example, if I choose and cross out twelve, then I get twelve points. But, there's a second way to get points. When it's your partner's turn to select a number, you get the sum of all the proper factors of your partner's number that haven't already been crossed out. Proper factors are the factors of a number that are less than the number itself. For example, if I choose twelve, its proper factors are one, two, three, four, and six. My partner would get the sum of all these factors that hadn't yet been crossed out. My partner could get sixteen points."

"Choosing twelve would be a bad move," Cruz said, giggling. "Your partner would be beating you by four points and it's your turn! You'd have twelve and your partner would have sixteen."

I nodded my agreement with Cruz. "What would be a good number to select?" I asked Cruz and the other students. I paused until about half of the students had their hands raised. I called on Jewell.

Jewell said, "I think maybe a prime number. If you choose a prime number, all your partner will get is one."

"Would fifteen be a good choice?" I asked. "If you think fifteen is a good choice, put your thumb up; if you think it's a bad choice, put your thumb down; if you're not sure, put your thumb sideways." Most students put their thumbs down.

I continued, "Most of you put your thumb down, meaning there's a better choice than fifteen. Why is there a better choice than fifteen?"

Pesach explained, "Fifteen isn't prime, so your partner would get a lot of factors."

This was the second mention of prime, and I asked, writing *prime* on the board, "What does prime mean?"

Wendi said, "It means just the number itself and one can go into it evenly with no remainder. Fifteen's not prime because three and five can go into it with no remainders." Several students nodded.

Tim added, "Your partner could add up one, three, and five, and get . . . let's see . . . nine points. That's better than sixteen but still not so good."

Benito said, "I know a better choice than fifteen. You should take thirteen. It's the largest prime number on the list." Some students nodded their agreement with Benito while several still looked perplexed. I chose not to discuss Benito's idea but instead moved forward with the game to give students the chance to think about and experience Benito's observation.

"We're going to play a game together so you'll better understand the rules," I said. "It's going to be me against all of you." The class was excited about this. "When it's your turn you'll talk over your choices with your table group. The table group I call on will choose the number for all of you. To keep track of the game, we'll use a score sheet that looks like this."

I projected an overhead transparency of the score sheet (see Blackline Masters). (You can also draw the score sheet on the board.) I continued to explain, "First write your names." To model this direction, I wrote *Mrs. Wickett* above the left column and *Class* above the right column.

"Then write the numbers from one to fifteen at the top of the sheet," I said, quickly doing so.

| 1 | 2 | 3 | 4 | 5 | 6 | 7 | 8 | 9 |
| 10 | 11 | 12 | 13 | 14 | 15 |

Mrs. Wickett		Class	
proof	score	score	proof

"I'm going to go first," I said and paused a moment. "I think I'll choose the number fifteen. It's the biggest number on the list." The strategy of beginning with the highest prime number as suggested by Benito, Jewell, and others is an excellent strategy, but one that only some students understood. I chose fifteen to model for the students what happens when the number chosen has several factors. I also chose fifteen because it provided the opportunity to show students how to record. The reaction from the students varied. Some were pleased with my choice while others moaned and groaned. "I get fifteen and you get the proper factors of fifteen. Remember, the proper factors are the factors that are less than fifteen," I explained as I crossed 15 off the list of numbers to show it was used and recorded my score as follows:

	1	2	3	4	5	6	7	8	9
		10	11	12	13	14	~~15~~		

Mrs. Wickett		Class	
proof	score	score	proof
	15		

"What score do you get? Remember, you get the sum of the proper factors of fifteen." After allowing the students a few moments to discuss this with their table groups, I asked for their attention. I said, "Tommy, what's one factor of fifteen?"

"Five," Tommy responded. The other students nodded to show their agreement with Tommy.

"I agree that five is a factor of fifteen," I said. "Using division, how could you prove it?" The students thought a moment, then hands began to go up.

Wendi said, "It's like you have to figure out 'Fifteen divided by what number gives five with no remainder?'" I wrote Wendi's idea on the board as follows:

$15 \div \square = 5$

"What number could we put in the box to make the equation true?" I asked. Hands flew into the air. "Show me using your fingers." Immediately students held up three fingers each. "To show the class gets five, I'll write the division sentence to prove that five is a factor of fifteen."

I quickly recorded the division sentence on the class's side of the score sheet and crossed 5 off the list of numbers.

	1	2	3	4	5	6	7	8	9
		10	11	12	13	14	~~15~~		

Mrs. Wickett		Class	
proof	score	score	proof
	15		
		5	$15 \div 3 = 5$

Sara said, "There's another factor of fifteen. Don't we get that one, too?"

"What other number is a factor of fifteen?" I asked Sara.

Sara explained, "Actually, there are two more numbers, one and three."

"Can you prove that one and three are factors of fifteen so the class can have them for its score?" I asked.

Brody said, "We can prove it with division. For three we have to figure out what to divide fifteen by to get three. It's five." A few students cheered for Brody.

I asked Brody to come to the overhead and record his division sentence on the class's side of the score sheet. He recorded on the score sheet: $15 \div 5 = 3$.

Tim said, "I know what to do to prove that we get one for our score. I have to figure out, 'Fifteen divided by what number equals one?' It's fifteen, so I write, 'Fifteen divided by fifteen equals one.'" Tim came to the overhead and wrote his division sentence on the class's side of the score sheet: $15 \div 15 = 1$. I reminded Tim to cross off the 3 and the 1 to show they'd been used.

"Are there any other factors of fifteen that are smaller than fifteen itself?" I asked. The students shook their heads. I said, "The next step is to add up your points." I paused a moment as students figured the total points. Then I said, "Use your fingers to show how many points the class gets." The students held up nine fingers each. "The class has nine points; I have fifteen points," I said as I wrote the class's total on the score sheet.

X̶ 2 X̶ 4 X̶ 6 7 8 9
10 11 12 13 14 X̶5̶

Mrs. Wickett		Class	
proof	score	score	proof
	15		
		5	15 ÷ 3 = 5
		3	15 ÷ 5 = 3
		1	15 ÷ 15 = 1
		9	

"Because we used the fifteen, the one, the three, and the five, they are crossed off the list. We can use a number only once during a game. It's the class's turn to choose a number now, but first there's an important rule you need to know before choosing which number you'd like. Whenever you choose a number, there must be at least one factor of that number that hasn't yet been used. For example, could I choose three?"

"No," the class chorused.

Brody explained, "The only other factor of three besides three is one, and one is already used." I nodded.

I said, "Talk with your table group and decide which number would be a good choice for the class. I'll call on one group to choose a number for the class's turn." The class quickly came alive with conversations about which number to choose. Initially Brody's table thought thirteen would be a great choice until Benito pointed out that the only factor of thirteen besides thirteen is one, and it had been used. Jewell's table discussed eight as a possibility. Jodi pointed out that if the class chose eight, I'd get two and four for a total of six points. The group agreed that wasn't a good choice. After a couple of minutes, I asked for the students' attention. Hands were dancing, as students were eager to choose their number. I called on Nalani's table.

The group said in unison, "Ten!"

"Why did you choose ten?" I asked.

Brianna explained, "We get ten and there's only one factor of ten that hasn't been used and that's two. We get ten and you get two." I asked Brianna to come to the overhead, record 10 on the score sheet, and cross it off the list.

I said, "I have to prove that two works. I have to figure out 'Ten divided by what number equals two?' I know that ten divided by five equals two. I'll write that on my side of the score sheet." I wrote 10 ÷ 5 = 2 and then said, "I'm going to cross off the two because I used it. My score is seventeen and yours is nineteen. I'm behind, but it's my turn to choose a number."

X̶ X̶ X̶ 4 X̶ 6 7 8 9
X̶0̶ 11 12 13 14 X̶5̶

Mrs. Wickett		Class	
proof	score	score	proof
	15		
		5	15 ÷ 3 = 5
		3	15 ÷ 5 = 3
		1	15 ÷ 15 = 1
		9	
10 ÷ 5 = 2	2	10	
	17	19	

I studied my choices for a few moments. "Can I choose four?"

The class chorused, "No."

Tommy said, "Four won't work because the factors you'd get are one and two, and they're already crossed off."

"What about six?" I asked.

"No," the class again chorused.

Alycia said, "Six doesn't work because the factors are one, two, and three, and they're already used."

"What about seven?" I asked.

"Won't work," Abbie said. "It's prime and one is already used."

"Well, what will work?" I asked.

"Try fourteen," Cruz said.

"Ahh! Fourteen," I replied. "I get fourteen." I recorded *14* on the recording sheet and crossed it off the list. "Talk with your table group about what you get." In only seconds, the students had their hands up. I called on Tim's group.

Tim said, "We get seven. To prove it, fourteen divided by two is seven." Tim came to the overhead and wrote the division sentence: *14 ÷ 2 = 7*. I reminded him to cross off the 7.

"Are there any other factors of fourteen that haven't been used?" I asked. There were none. Tim found the total for the class while I found my total.

X̶ X̶ X̶ 4 X̶ 6 X̶ 8 9
X̶ 11 12 13 X̶ X̶

	Mrs. Wickett		Class	
	proof	score	score	proof
		15		
			5	15 ÷ 3 = 5
			3	15 ÷ 5 = 3
			1	15 ÷ 15 = 1
			9	
10 ÷ 5 = 2		2	10	
		17	19	
		14	7	14 ÷ 2 = 7
		31	26	

"It's the class's turn. Talk with your table group about which number you'd like to choose." After a few moments, hands started to go up. I called on Wendi's table.

Wendi said, "We think twelve is the best choice." Her table group gave her a thumbs-up. I asked Wendi to come to the overhead, record the class's score, and cross off the 12.

I said, "I think the only proper factors of twelve left are six and four. I get six and four. To prove it, I know that twelve divided by two is six and twelve divided by three is four." I wrote *12 ÷ 2 = 6* and *12 ÷ 3 = 4* on the score sheet and crossed off the 6 and 4. Wendi added the class's score and I added mine.

X̶ X̶ X̶ X̶ X̶ X̶ X̶ 8 9
X̶ 11 X̶ 13 X̶ X̶

	Mrs. Wickett		Class	
	proof	score	score	proof
		15		
			5	15 ÷ 3 = 5
			3	15 ÷ 5 = 3
			1	15 ÷ 15 = 1
			9	
10 ÷ 5 = 2		2	10	
		17	19	
		14	7	14 ÷ 2 = 7
		31	26	
12 ÷ 2 = 6		6	12	
12 ÷ 3 = 4		4	38	
		41		

"It's my turn to choose a number," I said. After pausing a moment to study the list, I asked, "Hum, are there any numbers I can choose?"

Benito responded, "Only eight, nine, eleven, and thirteen are left. None of those numbers have any factors left."

Alycia added, "The proper factors of eight are one, two and four. They're all crossed off the list. The proper factors of nine are one and three. They're crossed off too. The only proper factor of eleven is one. It's been used. It's the same thing with thirteen, the only proper factor is one and it's crossed off."

Jackson said, "It looks like you won by three points." I completed the score sheet.

X̶ X̶ X̶ X̶ X̶ X̶ X̶ 8 9
X̶0̶ 11 X̶2̶ 13 X̶4̶ X̶5̶

Mrs. Wickett		Class	
proof	score	score	proof
	15		
		5	15 ÷ 3 = 5
		3	15 ÷ 5 = 3
		1	15 ÷ 15 = 1
		9	
10 ÷ 5 = 2	2	10	
	17	19	
	14	7	14 ÷ 2 = 7
	31	26	
12 ÷ 2 = 6	6	12	
12 ÷ 3 = 4	4	38	
	41		

Mrs. Wickett has <u>41</u> points.

The class has <u>38</u> points.

Mrs. Wickett wins by <u>3</u> points.

I've learned that playing just one time isn't sufficient for all students to learn how to record correctly, so I played a second game to model again what they were to do. Jewell volunteered to play against me and chose to go first. She selected thirteen. We played the game, encouraging assistance and suggestions from the rest of the class whenever possible, and to the delight of the class, Jewell won. As we played, I reinforced for the students the importance of crossing out the numbers as they used them and recording division sentences to prove that numbers were factors of the chosen number.

After Jewell and I finished our game, I gave the following instructions to the students: "In just a moment, you'll have the opportunity to play the game with a partner. Your partner will be the person sitting beside you. Instead of using the numbers one to fifteen, if you'd like, you and your partner may use the numbers from one to twenty. Remember, you must use a division sentence to prove that each number you score is a factor of the selected number. You need just one recording sheet for your game, which I'll bring to you in just a moment. You'll notice you can play two games on one sheet. Are there any questions?" There were none. I passed out the recording sheets and, as I did so, I made certain each student had a partner.

OBSERVING THE STUDENTS

As I circulated through the class, I noticed that Natalia and Pesach were having difficulty. The rest of the students were engaged in the activity, so I sat down to work with them. Pesach went first and chose six. Natalia was having difficulty figuring out how to record the division sentences to show that one, two, and three were all factors of six.

I said, "Which number would you like to start with?"

Natalia responded, "One."

I asked, "Six divided by what number equals one?" To give Natalia, a second language learner, a visual clue, I wrote on the score sheet: *6 ÷ _____ = 1.*

Natalia thought for a moment, then responded, "Six divided by six is one. Is that what I write on my paper?" I nodded. She smiled and quickly recorded the division sentence.

"Are there any other factors of six that haven't been used yet?" I asked.

"Two," Natalia said. "Should I write, 'Six divided by blank equals two'?" I nodded. "I know what goes in the blank. It's three. There's another factor. It's three. The division sentence is six divided by three." Natalia paused, then corrected herself, "Six divided by two is three." She recorded the equation and then asked if she should add her score. I nodded. Then she crossed off the numbers 1, 2, 3, and 6 to show they had been used.

"It's your turn to select a number," I said. "Remember there has to be at least one unused factor of the number you choose." Natalia looked uncertain as she studied the list of numbers.

"I choose ten," Natalia said as she wrote 10 on the score sheet and crossed off the 10. "I have sixteen now."

Pesach looked bewildered. He said, "Five is a factor of ten, and it hasn't been used. But two has been used. How do I get the five without using the two?" At first I didn't understand Pesach's confusion, but after some thought, I figured out what was troubling him.

"I think I understand," I said. "You can use the two as a divisor, you just can't count it as a factor and include it in your score since it was already used."

Pesach's face lit up. "I get it now. I write on the paper, 'Ten divided by two is five.' I add five to the six I already had and now I have eleven. I was so confused, but I get it now." Pesach quickly wrote the division sentence and his total score on the score sheet, then asked, "Do I choose a number now?" I nodded. I watched a few more minutes as Natalia and Pesach played and then moved on to observe other children. (See Figure 15–1.)

I noticed that several students weren't recording their division sentences. I reminded them that it was necessary to write a division sentence to prove that a number was a factor.

Jewell and Kaneisha played several games using the numbers one to sixteen. As I looked at their work, I noticed they recorded accurately. (See Figure 15–2.) The girls asked if they could play another game

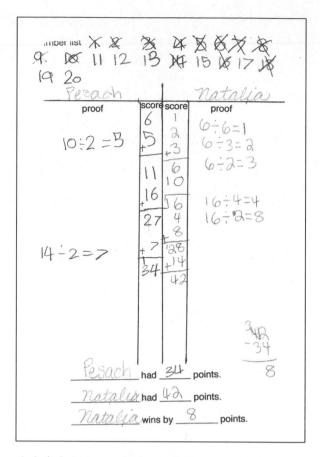

▲▲▲▲▲▲Figure 15–1 *Pesach and Natalia's completed game.*

and use the numbers from one to twenty-five. I nodded and they got to work quickly.

When I noticed that most pairs had played at least one game and were involved in playing a second game, I gave a three-minute warning, hoping that would give everyone a chance to reach a stopping point. At the end of three minutes, I asked for the students' attention. Figure 15–3 shows one more pair's completed game.

A CLASS DISCUSSION

"What did you think of the game?" I asked to begin the discussion.

"I liked it, but I had to think hard about writing a division sentence for the factors," Sara shared.

"I liked it because I won a lot!" Joaquin explained.

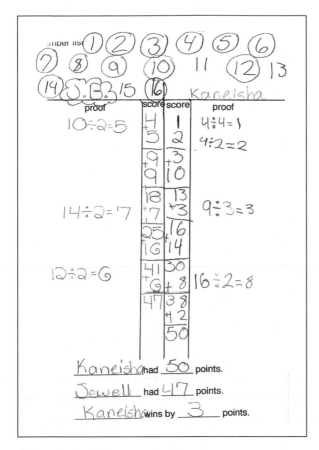

▲▲▲▲▲▲**Figure 15–2** *Jewell and Kaneisha played to 16 rather than 15.*

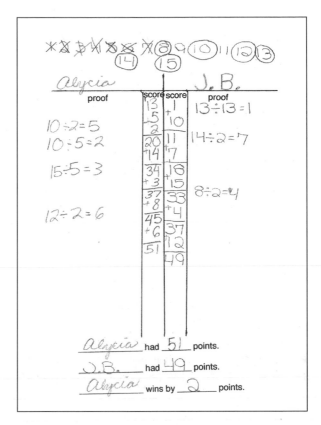

▲▲▲▲▲▲**Figure 15–3** *Alycia started with 13, the largest prime number listed.*

"Sometimes there were numbers we couldn't use," Cruz said.

"What kind of numbers couldn't you use?" I asked.

"They were mostly prime numbers, but not all of them," Cruz said.

"Why do you think that is?" I probed. Cruz shrugged, but Alycia had an idea.

Alycia said, "Jay and I discovered that if you're first, you want to choose the largest prime number."

"Why do you think that's so?" I asked.

Alycia explained, "With a prime number, the only factor besides itself is one. The first number chosen uses the one no matter if it's a prime number or not. So if you take the biggest prime number, the most points your partner can get on that turn is one."

Wendi added to Alycia's thinking, "The only other way to get a prime number is to get it as a factor. For example, if the one is gone, you could still get the five if your partner takes ten because five is a factor of ten."

Sara said, "Nalani and I found out you have to be really careful when you choose a number or your partner could get more points from the factors than you get for the number you choose; like with twelve, your partner could get sixteen points. But, that seems to only happen early in the game."

Benito said, "At the end of the game, the only numbers I could choose were sixteen and fourteen. I noticed that either way, my partner would get half the points I did. I thought that was interesting."

"That happened to Jodi and me," Jackson commented.

Natalia raised her hand shyly and said, "I liked the game because I got to practice division, but I also had to think hard about what the numbers mean in the problem.

The Factor Game   189

Sometimes my mind got twisted, but then I got it straight again."

EXTENSIONS

1. To increase the difficulty of the game, increase the range of the numbers students use to play the game. For example, in the vignette, Jewell and Kaneisha asked to use the numbers from one to twenty-five, making their game more challenging. On another day, Nalani and Natalia played with the numbers from one to twenty. (See Figure 15–4.)

2. Lead a discussion about how numbers compare with the sum of their proper factors. Remind students that proper factors are the factors of a number that are less than the number itself. Write on the board:

> 6
>
> 10
>
> 12

Ask the students to identify the proper factors of each. Then have them figure the sums and record:

> 6:   1 + 2 + 3 = 6
>
> 10:   1 + 2 + 5 = 8
>
> 12:   1 + 2 + 3 + 4 + 6 = 16

Compare the sums with the numbers. Tell the students: "A number is abundant if the sum of its proper factors is greater than it is. A number is deficient if the sum of its

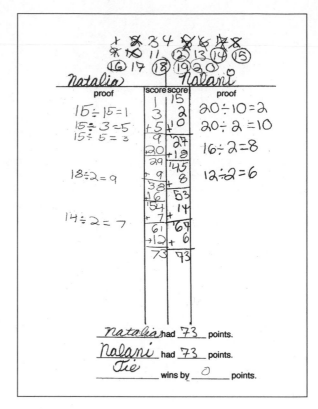

▲▲▲▲▲▲**Figure 15–4** *Natalia and Nalani played using the numbers from 1 to 20. Natalia made an error, missing 4 as a factor of 20.*

proper factors is less than it is. And if the sum of the proper factors is equal to the number, then the number is called perfect."

Have students investigate which numbers from 1 to 30 are perfect, abundant, and deficient. (From 1 to 30, only 6 and 28 are perfect numbers; the next perfect number is 216.) See the chart below for an example.

#	proper factors	sum of proper factors	
1	1	0	deficient
2	1	1	deficient
3	1	1	deficient
4	1, 2	3	deficient
5	1	1	deficient
6	1, 2, 3	6	perfect
7	1	1	deficient
8	1, 2, 4	7	deficient

9	1, 3	4	deficient
10	1, 2, 5	8	deficient
11	1	1	deficient
12	1, 2, 3, 4, 6	16	abundant
13	1	1	deficient
14	1, 2, 7	10	deficient
15	1, 3, 5	9	deficient
16	1, 2, 4, 8	15	deficient
17	1	1	deficient
18	1, 2, 3, 6, 9	21	abundant
19	1	1	deficient
20	1, 2, 4, 5, 10	22	abundant
21	1, 3, 7	11	deficient
22	1, 2, 11	14	deficient
23	1	1	deficient
24	1, 2, 3, 4, 6, 8, 12	36	abundant
25	1, 5	6	deficient
26	1, 2, 13	16	deficient
27	1, 3, 9	13	deficient
28	1, 2, 4, 7, 14	28	perfect
29	1	1	deficient
30	1, 2, 3, 5, 6, 10, 15	42	abundant

6 and 28 are perfect

12, 18, 20, 24, and 30 are abundant

1, 2, 3, 4, 5, 7, 8, 9, 10, 11, 13, 14, 15, 16, 17, 19, 21, 22, 23, 25, 26, 27, and 29 are deficient

Questions and Discussion

▲▲

▲ *What is the value of playing games in math class?*

Games provide a good opportunity for students to practice skills. When students play the *Factor Game,* they practice division and multiplication skills as they gain facility with the relationship between numbers and their factors. Discuss with students the mathematical benefit of games they play. This helps them think about the underlying mathematics. Also, then students can explain to their parents the mathematical value of the games they play in class, which can help parents see that learning is, in fact, taking place and there is a valid educational reason for the game.

▲ *Could this game be used for homework?*

Absolutely. Once the students are comfortable with the game, they can teach it to their parents or older siblings. The experience and insights students gain from playing the game at home can provide a foundation for rich classroom discussion. Also, sharing the game at home gives students the opportunity to share what they are learning in school and provides parents a tool to use to help their children practice skills in a meaningful, enjoyable way.

CHAPTER SIXTEEN
LEFTOVERS WITH 100

Overview

In this lesson, students learn the game *Leftovers with 100* and play it in pairs. The game provides students practice with division and gives them experience thinking about the significance of remainders. To play, students choose a number to use as a divisor and keep their leftovers, or remainders, as their score. At the end of the game, the players add their remainders, or leftovers, and the player with the larger sum wins. As students try to get large remainders with every turn, they focus their attention on the relationships between divisors and dividends.

Materials

▲ rules for *Leftovers with 100,* either 1 to post, 1 per pair of students, or 1 for an overhead transparency to project (see Blackline Masters)

Time

▲ one class period, plus additional time for repeat experiences with playing the game and follow-up discussions

Teaching Directions

1. To model for students how to record the game, write on the board the title and the numbers from *1* to *20*. Also, title a column *Start Number* and write *100:*

Leftovers with 100

1	*2*	*3*	*4*	*5*	*6*	*7*	*8*	*9*	*10*
11	*12*	*13*	*14*	*15*	*16*	*17*	*18*	*19*	*20*

Start Number

100

2. Present the rules for playing *Leftovers with 100.* You may want to duplicate a copy for each pair of students, make an overhead transparency to project, or post a copy for the class to see.

Leftovers with 100

You need:
  a partner

Rules

1. Set up a recording sheet as shown.

> Leftovers with 100
>
> 1 2 3 4 5 6 7 8 9 10
> 11 12 13 14 15 16 17 18 19 20
>
> Start number
> 100

2. Player 1 chooses a divisor from 1 to 20 and divides the start number, 100, by the divisor chosen. Player 2 records the division crosses out the divisor, and circles and labels the remainder with Player 1's initial.

3. Both players subtract the remainder from the start number to get the next start number.

4. Player 2 uses the new start number, chooses a divisor that hasn't yet been crossed out, and divides. (Divisors can be used only once!) Player 1 records the division, crosses out the divisor, and circles and labels the remainder. Both players subtract the remainder from the start number to get the next start number.

5. Players continue taking turns until the start number reaches 0.

6. Players add their remainders. The player with the larger sum wins.

7. Check that the sum of both players' remainders equals one hundred. If not, you've made an error.

Question: Why should the sum of both players' remainders equal one hundred?

---

3. With a student volunteer, model several rounds of play. For each round of this introductory game, ask others in the class about what makes good or bad choices for divisors and why.

4. Give the students the opportunity to ask questions or clarify the rules. Then have students play the game in pairs.

5. As students play the game, monitor the class to make certain that students are recording correctly and accurately. Ask students about what they notice as they play the game.

6. Lead a class discussion about what the students noticed or discovered about the game of *Leftovers with 100*. Useful questions for a discussion include the following:

▲ How did you decide which divisors were good to choose?
▲ What was hard about the game?
▲ The new start number each time is the previous divisor times the answer without the remainder. Why does this make sense?
▲ At the end of a game, why does it make sense for the total of both your remainders together to be hundred?
▲ What would make this game easier? Harder?

Teaching Notes

Prior to playing *Leftovers with 100*, it's helpful for students to have experience with thinking about divisibility rules. The lessons in Chapters 7, 8, and 9, which explore divisibility rules, are useful for this. This background knowledge will help students choose divisors that produce the largest remainders possible. For example, in the vignette, the students knew that 1, 2, 4, 5, 10, and 20 were poor choices for divisors when the dividend, or start number, was 100 because all of these choices would yield a remainder of 0. Seventeen, however, is a good choice for a divisor because dividing 100 by 17 yields a remainder of 15.

The game of *Leftovers with 100* provides an excellent context for students to apply their skills with divisibility rules, to practice computation, to deepen their understanding about the meaning of the different numbers in a division problem, and to improve their number sense and problem-solving skills.

The Lesson

▲▲

"I have a game I'd like to share with you today," I said to begin the lesson.

"This will be fun!" Sean said eagerly.

"Is it a hard game?" Saul asked. Saul was sometimes uncertain and hesitant to accept a challenge.

"I think it's going to be a challenge for you," I replied, "but I think you have the skills to handle it." Saul smiled and nodded. I continued. "The game is called *Leftovers with one Hundred*."

"We played a game called *Leftovers* last year," Korina said.

"Do any of the rest of you remember playing *Leftovers*?" I asked. A few nodded their heads. *Leftovers* is included in *Teaching Arithmetic: Lessons for Introducing Division, Grades 3–4*, by Maryann Wickett, Susan Ohanian, and Marilyn Burns (Math Solutions Publications 2002).

"The game you'll learn about today is similar to *Leftovers*, but there are some differences, too. It will be easy for all of you to learn, whether or not you've played before. To show you how to play the game, I need a volunteer to be my partner." Hands flew into the air and I asked Skylar. While Skylar walked to the front of the room, I wrote on the board:

Leftovers with 100

| 1 | 2 | 3 | 4 | 5 | 6 | 7 | 8 | 9 | 10 |
| 11 | 12 | 13 | 14 | 15 | 16 | 17 | 18 | 19 | 20 |

Start Number

100

I explained as I pointed to what I'd written on the board, "You'll make your recording sheet so it looks something like this. You'll play with a partner and you'll just need one recording sheet for the two of you. Before you play, write the title and the numbers from one to twenty as I did. Then start a column titled 'Start Number' and write 'one hundred' to begin the column. Be sure to write both your names on your recording sheet." I asked Skylar if he was ready and he nodded his head eagerly.

"I'm going to beat you," Skylar teased. The class giggled.

"Perhaps," I said. "We'll see soon enough. Thank you for volunteering to help me show the others how to play. This time I'm going to go first to show what to do. Something important to remember is at the end of the game, both players add their remainders, and the player with the larger sum wins. To begin the game, the first player starts with a start number, or dividend, of one hundred. Because I'm the first player, I start with one hundred and I have to choose a divisor from the numbers listed from one to twenty. Then I'll divide one hundred by the divisor I chose, and Skylar will record on our sheet. What divisor would be a good choice?"

Lucas explained, "If you want to win, then you have to choose a divisor that will give a big remainder." The other students nodded.

"What would be a bad choice?" I asked.

Lupe said, "One would be bad because one goes into all numbers with no remainder."

Elli added, "Since you're starting with one hundred, two would be a bad choice.

One hundred is even and two is a factor of all even numbers."

I said, "If you agree with Elli, put your thumb up; if you disagree, put your thumb down; if you're not sure or confused, put your thumb sideways." Thumbs popped up quickly. "Are there any other numbers that would be poor choices for my first move?"

"Ten would be bad," Alberto said. "Ten times ten equals one hundred, so there wouldn't be any remainder."

Beth said, "Five goes into one hundred equally. If you count by fives, it takes twenty fives to get to one hundred. Also, if you think about money, there are twenty nickels in one dollar."

"I know another thing about fives," Catalina said. "If ten works, then five works because two fives make ten."

Korina added, "Numbers that five can be divided into end in five or zero. One hundred ends in zero, so five will go into it with no remainders."

"What number on the list would make a good choice?" I asked. I paused, as students weren't certain about this. Slowly, hands started to go up. When about half the students had their hands raised, I called on Derek.

"Maybe three," Derek said with uncertainty. "I think with three there would be a remainder of one because if you count by threes, you land on ninety-nine, and that's one away from one hundred."

"What about nineteen?" Zoe wondered aloud. "I think nineteen would have a remainder of five."

"Tell me more about your thinking," I encouraged Zoe.

"Well, I know that five times twenty is one hundred," Zoe explained slowly with thought. "Nineteen is one less than twenty, so I think five groups of nineteen would be ninety-five because five groups of twenty is one hundred. Then one hundred minus ninety-five is five and that five would be left over."

I recorded Zoe's thinking on the board:

$5 \times 20 = 100$

$5 \times 19 = 95$

$100 - 95 = 5$

"Hey, I think Zoe's right about five times nineteen equals ninety-five," Jayne said. "Ninety-five is divisible by five because there's a five in the ones place and nineteen is one group less of five than twenty. It makes sense. That's cool!"

"I like Zoe's idea of using nineteen as the divisor," I said. "Since it's my turn to pick a divisor and divide, Skylar will record on our recording sheet. To record my turn, Skylar, write, 'One hundred divided by nineteen equals five remainder five.' Then circle the remainder and write my initial since it's my turn." Skylar recorded:

Leftovers with 100

1   2   3   4   5   6   7   8   9   10
11 12 13 14 15 16 17 18 19 20

Start Number

100        $100 \div 19 = 5\ R\textcircled{5}\ W$

I continued, "My turn is over. It's Skylar's turn, but before he can have his turn, we have to do two things. First, Skylar has to cross off nineteen from the list of divisors. We only get to use each number listed once in a game." Skylar crossed off the 19. I continued, "Then we have to subtract my remainder of five from my start number of one hundred to create a new start number for Skylar to use." Skylar told me with confidence that his start number was ninety-five. His classmates indicated their agreement with Skylar with thumbs up.

"Since it's Skylar's turn, I record," I said. I wrote *95* under the Start Number column. Skylar looked overwhelmed. I suggested he call on his classmates for advice. He called on Everett.

"Maybe fifteen," Everett said without explanation.

"What's the remainder?" Skylar asked Everett.

After a moment's thought, Everett said, "Well, I'm pretty sure that six fifteens equals ninety. Two fifteens makes thirty. There are three thirties in ninety, so three times two is six. You'd have a remainder of five." Skylar wasn't convinced and called on Kenzie.

"There might be a better choice, but I think this one's pretty good," Kenzie started off. "If you use twenty as the divisor, then I think you can get a remainder of fifteen. Four times twenty is eighty, and ninety-five minus eighty is fifteen."

"Oh yeah!" "That's right!" "Good idea!" were some of the responses from the other students.

Skylar turned to me and told me to write $95 \div 20 = 4\ R15$. He also reminded me to circle the remainder of 15, to put his initial beside the problem, and to cross off 20. I did **as instructed**.

Leftovers with 100

1   2   3   4   5   6   7   8   9   10
11 12 13 14 15 16 17 18 ~~19~~ ~~20~~

Start Number

100             $100 \div 19 = 5\ R\textcircled{5}\ W$

95              $95 \div 20 = 4\ R\textcircled{15}\ S$

"There's one more thing to be done before it's my turn," I said. "Does anyone remember what that is?"

"Oh, I know," Joey said. "You have to subtract the remainder from ninety-five."

"That's exactly what I was thinking," I replied.

Skylar said, "Ninety-five minus fifteen is eighty."

"I agree," I responded. "Since it's my turn, you get to record." Skylar recorded *80* in the Start Number column.

Several students gave me their suggestions eagerly. Sean, with a gleam in his eye, suggested I use one as the divisor. Lucas, like a knight in shining armor, protested. Johanna suggested I use eighteen as the divisor. She explained, "Eighteen gives a remainder, but I don't think it's the biggest. I'm not sure, really. Eighteen goes into eighty four times. Eighteen times four is . . . um, seventy-two, I think."

"How did you figure that?" I asked.

Johanna explained, "Well, ten times four is forty. Then eight times four is thirty-two. So forty and thirty-two make . . . seventy-two."

"I think I'll use your suggestion of eighteen, Johanna," I said. Skylar recorded my turn on the board as follows:

Leftovers with 100

1	2	3	4	5	6	7	8	9	10
11	12	13	14	15	16	17	~~18~~	~~19~~	~~20~~

Start Number

100	$100 \div 19 = 5\ R\circled{5}$ W
95	$95 \div 20 = 4\ R\circled{15}$ S
80	$80 \div 18 = 4\ R\circled{8}$ W

"Skylar is ahead by two," Catalina commented.

"What's Skylar's score so far?" I asked the students.

"Fifteen," the class chorused.

"What's my score?"

"Thirteen," the students responded together.

"How will Skylar and I create a new starting number?" I asked to reinforce this part of the game.

Kylie explained, "You subtract the remainder from the last starting number. Eighty minus eight is seventy-two."

"Hey!" Everett said, coming to life suddenly. "Seventy-two is the same thing as eighteen times four. That's weird." I paused a moment to give the students time to think about Everett's comment.

Kerri added, "Twenty times four is eighty, and that's a start number, too. I think there's a pattern, but I'm not sure." There were no other comments. I decided to move on and bring up this point again when the students had more experience with the game.

"It's Skylar's turn, so I get to record," I said.

Skylar again sought the counsel of his classmates. Several students made suggestions. After giving the suggestions some thought, Skylar decided to use eleven as his divisor.

Skylar said, "My dividend is seventy-two. So seventy-two divided by eleven is six with a remainder of six. Six times eleven is sixty-six. Seventy-two minus sixty-six is six."

I recorded Skylar's turn on the board as follows:

Leftovers with 100

1	2	3	4	5	6	7	8	9	10
~~11~~	12	13	14	15	16	17	~~18~~	~~19~~	~~20~~

Start Number

100	$100 \div 19 = 5\ R\circled{5}$ W
95	$95 \div 20 = 4\ R\circled{15}$ S
80	$80 \div 18 = 4\ R\circled{8}$ W
72	$72 \div 11 = 6\ R\circled{6}$ S

"Sixty-six would be the next starting number," Korina noticed. "Sixty-six equals eleven times six, which is the problem that Skylar used to help him figure out his turn." Several other students nodded their agreement with Korina.

"I agree that sixty-six would be the next starting number," I said to confirm what Korina had shared.

The students seemed to understand how to play and I was interested in giving all of them firsthand experience with the game, so I said, "I think you have the idea of the game. The game ends when the start number is zero, but Skylar and I are going to stop here so the rest of you can play. To figure out who is the winner, add the remainders."

"Skylar has twenty-one," Elli said.

"Do you agree with Elli's total?" I asked Skylar. He nodded.

"You only have thirteen," Kerri said.

"I agree, five plus eight is thirteen," I said. "Skylar wins. Skylar, thanks for being my partner and helping me show the rest of the students how to play." Skylar returned to his seat as I wrote our scores under our recording to model for the students how to record their scores when they played:

Leftovers with 100

1 2 3 4 5 6 7 8 9 10

~~11~~ 12 13 14 15 16 17 ~~18~~ ~~19~~ ~~20~~

Start Number

100	$100 \div 19 = 5 R\textcircled{5}$ W
95	$95 \div 20 = 4 R\textcircled{15}$ S
80	$80 \div 18 = 4 R\textcircled{8}$ W
72	$72 \div 11 = 6 R\textcircled{6}$ S

Skylar 21   Mrs. Wickett 13

I continued, "You look eager to start playing. Do you have questions?"

"Do we play with our regular partners?" Valerie asked. I nodded.

"How do we know who goes first?" Derek asked.

"I'll let you and your partner decide," I responded. "If the two of you can't decide, raise your hand and I'll decide for you. I think you can work this out yourselves, though."

Sterling asked, "Can we use calculators?"

I responded, "I'm not sure how the calculator will help you."

Joey added, "It doesn't tell you the remainder."

"Yes, it does," Beth said. "If you divide nine by two, the calculator will give you four point five, and the point five is the remainder."

"Oh yeah," Joey said.

Everett said, "But if you divide nine by two, you get four remainder one." Now Beth and Joey were confused.

"I don't think I'll use the calculator," Sterling said.

"Don't be hasty," I said. "The problem you'll face is how to figure out the remainder, and then you'll use the remainder to figure out the new start number. Remember, you have to subtract the remainder from the previous start number."

Kenzie then said, "I know. If it's point five, and you're dividing by two, then that's the same as one because point five is half, and half of two is one." Some of the students were following the conversation but weren't sure about Kenzie's idea, and some weren't really listening, so I ended the discussion and let them get started playing.

OBSERVING THE STUDENTS

I left the recording of the game between Skylar and me on the board as a model for the rest of the students. I noticed many students referring to the board as they played, and there were few questions. I circulated through the class, looking over shoulders to check that students were recording and computing accurately.

In a few minutes, Sterling called me over. He had figured out a way to use the calculator. He was doing $100 \div 19$. He did this on the calculator and got 5.2631578. He said to me, "So, I just take the five and don't pay attention to the rest. Then I multiply five times nineteen." He stopped and did this on the calculator. "That gives me ninety-five, so I know that the remainder is five."

Cliff and Saul were eager to share their work. "Look!" Cliff said, "We figured out how to get big remainders. We're already down to forty as our starting number."

Saul added, "Right now, Cliff's winning. He has thirty-six and I have twenty-four, but it's my turn."

Cliff countered, "I think I'll still be ahead. I think the biggest remainder Saul can get is eight. To get a big remainder, I think you have to use a big divisor."

Saul thought about this for a moment. "I think Cliff's right. I think sixteen is my best choice. It's a big divisor, but it still only gives me a remainder of eight. I think I'll keep trying just to make sure."

I left the boys to continue playing their game.

Korina came running to me with a calculator in her hand. "This calculator isn't helping. I put the numbers in and I got a decimal, like Beth said would happen, but how am I supposed to know what that means?"

"That's a good question," I said. Jayne and Kylie, who were sitting nearby and listening, had an idea.

Jayne suggested, "Maybe if the decimal is point five you could figure out what the remainder is. Like if you were dividing something by four and your answer was some number point five, I think the point five would be like a remainder of two."

"How do you know that?" I asked Jayne.

"Well, point five means one-half," Jayne said and then continued with uncertainty. "So I think it means half of the divisor is the remainder. So half of four would be two. Or if the divisor was eight, then the point five would be like a remainder of four. I think it could get weird with odd numbers." I nodded my agreement.

Kylie had another idea about how Korina could use the calculator. Kylie explained, "Well, you could multiply. Like if you're dividing fifteen into eighty and you thought there were five fifteens in eighty, you could multiply five times fifteen and see how close it was to eighty. I think five times fifteen is seventy-five, but I could check to be sure with a calculator." I nodded my agreement with Kylie's suggestion. I wasn't sure either of these suggestions was helpful to Korina, but what Kylie and Jayne shared gave me insight into their understanding.

Sean and Lucas were involved in an intense discussion. As I walked up to the boys, Sean asked me, "Is it possible to have a remainder as big as fifteen?"

"What do you boys think about that?" I asked.

"I don't think it's possible," Sean said, "but Lucas does. I think he's wrong."

I turned to Lucas and asked, "What do you think, Lucas?"

"I think any number can be a remainder," Lucas explained. "What can be a remainder depends on the divisor."

"What was the divisor in the problem you're discussing?" I asked.

"It's nineteen," Lucas said. "I think as long as the remainder is smaller than the divisor, it's OK because there isn't enough for another group."

I replied, "I think if the divisor is nineteen, then it's possible to have a remainder of fifteen."

"Oh, darn!" Sean said. "That was a really smart move, Lucas. Now you're really winning. I have five and Lucas has thirty-eight!" (See Figure 16–1.)

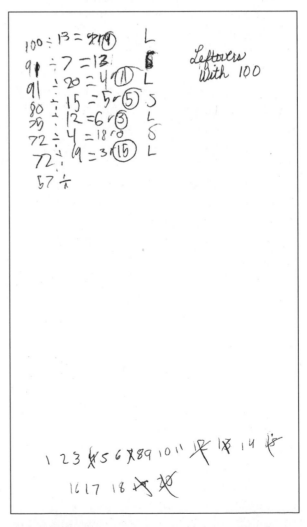

▲▲▲▲▲▲Figure 16–1 *Sean and Lucas's partially completed game.*

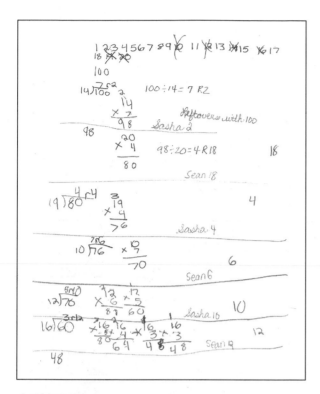

▲▲▲▲▲**Figure 16–2** *Skylar and Sasha changed how they recorded the game but showed their thinking clearly. While Sasha made an error when he multiplied 12 × 6, it didn't affect the next start number.*

I noticed as I continued to circulate that Skylar and Sasha showed how they did the dividing and, after two rounds, changed their way of recording their work. Their paper clearly showed how the boys figured their answers. (See Figure 16–2.)

Elli and Lupe recorded their division using another method. (See Figure 16–3 on page 202.)

Jael and Johanna used a calculator to help them with the game. Johanna explained, "We take the divisor and we multiply the divisor by the number of times we think it goes into the starting number. It's tricky because you want a remainder that's almost as much as the divisor, but when you multiply, you can't get a number bigger than the start number. If you think about what is half of the start number and then go one higher, you'll get the best remainder. For

example, if sixteen is the start number, half of sixteen is eight, so nine is the best divisor to pick."

"What does the start number mean?" I asked.

Jael replied, "It tells how many of something you have when the problem starts. Like there were nine balloons. The nine tells how many balloons there are at the start of the problem."

Johanna added, "The start number is like a dividend, I think."

I replied, "I agree with both of you. The start number is the number in the whole group and is also called the dividend."

Jael volunteered, "The divisor tells how many groups or how many in each group." I nodded.

"We're keeping score like this," Johanna said, pointing to their paper. "We just keep adding the new remainder after each turn so we don't have to add a bunch of numbers at the end." I nodded and moved on. (See Figure 16–4 on page 202.)

Catalina caught an error made by Everett, her partner. He had divided 57 by 6 and gotten an answer of 8 R9. Catalina said, "That can't be right. You can't have a remainder that's bigger than what you're dividing by. If you have a remainder bigger than the divisor, then there's enough for another whole group!" This seemed to be a big discovery for both students.

Both students paused a moment to consider the situation. Finally, Everett said, "I know I have to have a divisor bigger than the remainder. If I double six to make twelve, then the problem is fifty-seven divided by twelve. Twelve is bigger than nine, and because I doubled the divisor, I think the quotient will be half of what it was. Half of eight is four and the remainder will be the same."

Catalina said, "I think that's right. I know four times twelve and it's forty-eight

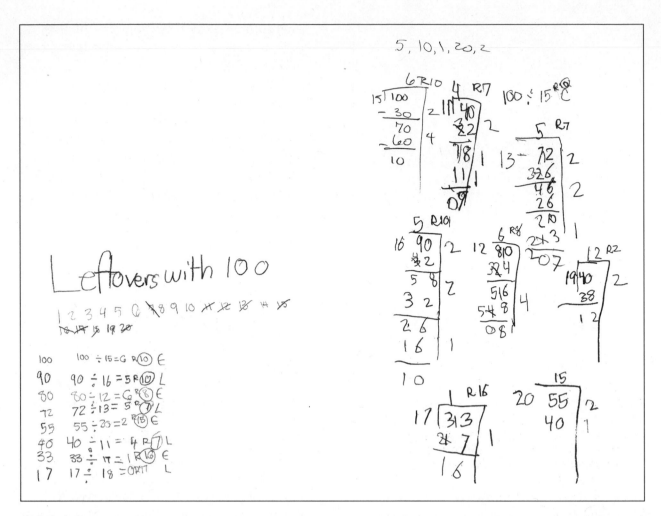

▲▲▲▲▲▲**Figure 16–3** *Lupe made an error when she divided 40 by 11. However, it didn't affect the next start number. Elli used scratch paper to show how she figured her answers.*

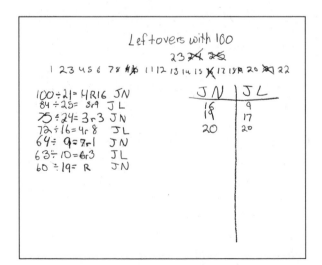

▲▲▲▲▲▲**Figure 16–4** *Jael and Johanna kept a running total and used divisors up to 25 instead of 20.*

and then add the remainder of nine, which is fifty-seven. That's amazing!" I left the two to complete the game. (See Figure 16–5.)

Derek and Alberto played a second game with divisors from one to thirty. They found that the game was a little harder when they chose the larger divisors, but it was much quicker and required fewer rounds. (See Figure 16–6.)

Many of the students were close to finishing their first game. I gave the class a two-minute warning. At the end of two minutes, I asked for the students' attention for a class discussion.

▲▲▲▲▲▲Figure 16–5 *Catalina and Everett's completed game.*

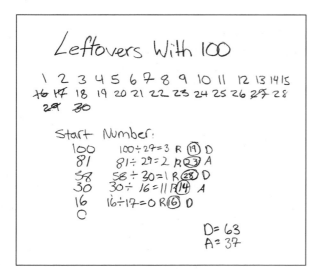

▲▲▲▲▲▲Figure 16–6 *Derek and Alberto played the game with divisors from 1 to 30. They reported the game to be harder but shorter.*

A CLASS DISCUSSION

"What did you think about the game *Leftovers with 100*?" I asked. Hands flew into the air, as students were eager to share.

Elli said, "It was hard, but it was cool. We had to do a lot of math if we really wanted to find the biggest remainder."

Derek added, "My brain hurts. I think I did something like a hundred math problems. But I won!"

Zoe said, "Elli and I discovered something. At the end, you can get a lot of leftovers once the starting number gets below twenty. We got to thirteen as the starting number, and fourteen was left as a divisor, so I took fourteen and got all thirteen because thirteen divided by fourteen is zero with a remainder of thirteen."

Kenzie said, "Beth and I figured that out, too, but not until the starting number was five. Then Beth figured out she could divide five by six and the answer would be zero remainder five, and she got the five."

Beth said, "I have a question. Everett and Derek added up all their leftovers together and it came out to one hundred. When Kenzie and I added ours up, it was only eighty-eight. I don't get it."

I asked Derek and Everett along with the rest of the students, "Why does it make sense that the total of both players' remainders should total one hundred if you finish the game?"

Niki had an idea. "Well, if you start with one hundred, and you keep dividing until you get to zero, then the remainders have to add up to one hundred because the only way to make the starting number go down is to subtract out the remainders."

"Oh yeah!" replied several students.

I said to Beth, "You and Kenzie finished your game, correct?" Beth nodded. "I think it's possible you made an error somewhere and perhaps you and Kenzie should go back and check." Beth and Kenzie moaned.

"Can someone help us?" Beth asked.

Everett and Derek volunteered. The four of them went to the back of the room while the rest of the students continued with the discussion. After a few moments, the four blurted out, "We found it! We found the mistake."

"What happened?" I asked.

Kenzie explained, "When we subtracted twelve from seventy-six, we got fifty-two."

"Fifty-two is the answer to seventy-six minus twenty-four, not twelve," Derek added.

"We found another mistake, too," Beth said. "When we did forty divided by nine, we put the answer thirty-six remainder four, but the answer is really four remainder four. Four times nine is thirty-six and we put that instead." (See Figure 16–7.)

"We noticed something," Kylie said. "We discovered that if you look at the divisors that haven't been used and try to think of a multiple of one of the divisors that's just a little bigger than your dividend or starting number, you can get a big remainder. For example, if your dividend is fifteen and eight is a divisor you could

choose, it would be a good choice because the multiples of eight go eight, sixteen, and sixteen is just one bigger than fifteen, so there should be a big remainder. There would be a remainder of seven for that problem." Several students nodded their agreement.

"We noticed that the new start number is always the same as the whole number part of the previous quotient times the previous divisor," Lucas shared. "If you look up on the board, you can tell. Look where it says eighty divided by eighteen equals four remainder eight. Well, four times eighteen is seventy-two, which is the next start number. In the top problem where it says one hundred divided by nineteen equals five remainder five, five times nineteen is ninety-five, which is the new start number."

There were no additional comments. Cliff had a question. "Can we do this again tomorrow? I think I have some other ways from the discussion that maybe I could use that might help me win." I told Cliff and the others we would play again and ended the lesson for the day.

Over the next several days, I provided time for the students to play and we continued to discuss strategies and patterns. Also, I assigned the game for homework, asking the students to teach someone at home to play and then report back to class what they experienced.

EXTENSIONS

1. For an easier game, use fifty for the first start number and divisors from one to fifteen.

2. For a harder game, use two hundred for the first start number and divisors from five to thirty.

3. Change the goal so that the player with the smaller sum of remainders wins.

▲▲▲▲▲Figure 16–7 *Beth made a common error when recording 40 ÷ 9.*

204   **Lessons for Extending Division**

Questions and Discussion

▲▲▲

▲ *Do you always allow students to make decisions such as who goes first in a game?*

My decision depends on the students and the activity. However, I like to give students as much freedom to make their own decisions as possible. The class in the vignette was able to handle decisions of this nature. When students aren't able to handle making decisions, I sometimes give them guidelines; for example, the person whose birthday comes first in the year goes first, or the person whose name is closer to the end of the alphabet goes first, or the younger person goes first.

▲ *Don't students make a lot of mistakes when they play games?*

My experience has been that students make fewer mistakes when they play games than when they do routine drill-and-practice sheets. Students need to practice their computational skills, and this game provides practice. Fewer mistakes are made because a student's partner is paying close attention and often catches errors. Also, as I circulate through the class, I spot-check the students' work, and when I see a mistake, I call it to the attention of the students immediately. This type of immediate intervention can reduce the chances of students practicing skills incorrectly.

One mistake to watch for is how the students write the quotients. Sometimes they multiply the divisor by the estimated number of times it goes into the start number and write the product as the quotient rather than the estimated number of times the divisor goes into the start number. For example, in Beth and Kenzie's game, Beth was computing $40 \div 9$ and wrote the quotient as 36 R4. She got the thirty-six by multiplying the divisor of nine by four, the number of times she thought nine would go into forty. When she multiplied four times nine to check her thinking, she got thirty-six and mistakenly wrote it as part of the quotient.

CHAPTER SEVENTEEN
DIVISION RIDDLES

Overview

In this chapter, students first work as a whole class using mathematical clues to solve riddles for four division problems: $9 \div 9 = 1$, $12 \div 12 = 1$, $20 \div 19 = 1$ R1, and $101 \div 98 = 1$ R3. The clues give students practice with divisibility rules, division, and multiplication and reinforce the idea that many division problems can have the same quotient. The lesson reinforces ideas about the relationships among the dividend, divisor, and quotient that were explored in Chapters 2, 5, and 6. Next, working as a class, the students create a division riddle by writing clues for a division problem with the quotient of two. Finally, working in pairs, students write division riddles for problems with a quotient of two and later share their riddles in class discussions.

Materials

▲ chart paper

Time

▲ two class periods, plus time on other days for students to share their riddles and additional time for extensions

Teaching Directions

1. Tell the students that you have a division riddle and that you're thinking of a division equation with the quotient of one. Write on the board: *Clue 1: The quotient equals 1.*

2. Ask them for possibilities of equations that would and would not work. Have them explain their reasoning. List their suggestions on the board in columns titled Yes and No.

3. When you feel comfortable that students can identify problems for each list, write on the board: *Clue 2: The divisor is odd.* Ask students which problems on the Yes list can be eliminated or added based on this new information. Have students explain their reasoning.

4. Repeat Step 3 for two more clues:

> *Clue 3: The divisor has 1 digit.*
> *Clue 4: The divisor is greater than 8.*

After Clue 4, students should know the solution: $9 \div 9 = 1$. Point out to the students that these four clues lead to only one possible solution.

5. Repeat Steps 1 through 4 for the following three riddles. After they solve each, have them check the solution they come up with against each of the clues. Reinforce that each clue narrows the possible answers, and the final clue leads to one and only one correct division equation. Also point out that the third riddle is a poor example of a division riddle because the solution is revealed in the second clue.

> *Riddle #2*
> *Clue 1: The quotient = 1.*
> *Clue 2: The dividend is a whole even number.*
> *Clue 3: The divisor is greater than 10 and less than 20.*
> *Clue 4: The divisor is a multiple of 3.*
> *Clue 5: The divisor is less than 15.*
>
> *Riddle #3*
> *Clue 1: The quotient = 1 R1.*
> *Clue 2: The dividend is 2 × 10.*
>
> *Riddle #4*
> *Clue 1: The quotient = 1 R3.*
> *Clue 2: The dividend is odd.*
> *Clue 3: The dividend is a 3-digit number.*
> *Clue 4: The divisor is a 2-digit number.*

6. Copy onto chart paper the four riddles the students solved and post the chart for their reference on Day 2.

7. On Day 2, together with the students, create clues for a division riddle for the quotient of two. Begin by brainstorming and listing on the board division problems with a quotient of two and then selecting one to use as the answer to the riddle. Write it on the board. In the vignette, I used $30 \div 15 = 2$, but you may wish to choose a different division equation from the list your students generate.

8. Next, ask students to talk in pairs about what a first clue might be for the problem. Record on the board: *Clue 1: The quotient = 2.*

9. With the help of the students, write three to six more clues, with the last one eliminating all possibilities but the correct division equation.

10. Tell the students that, working in pairs, they should select a different division equation for the quotient of two and write it on the back of their paper. Their first clue should state: The quotient equals 2. Then they should write three to six additional clues, narrowing the possibilities with each clue, with a final clue that eliminates all other possibilities but the correct solution.

11. As students work, read over their shoulders, offering guidance as needed.

12. Tell students who finish early to write a second division riddle either for another division equation with the quotient of 2 or for a division equation with the quotient of 2 R1.

13. Over the next few days, have pairs present their riddles for others to solve.

Teaching Notes

Solving and writing division riddles gives students an opportunity to reinforce and apply skills they learned in earlier chapters in this book. For example, in Chapter 6, "The Quotient Stays the Same," students explored relationships among dividends and divisors that produced the same quotient. They learned that a quotient of 2 is produced when the divisor is exactly one-half of the dividend, or the dividend is twice the divisor. Also, a quotient of 2 R1 occurs when the dividend is twice the divisor plus one more. In this lesson, students revisit this previous thinking and also apply the divisibility rules they learned in Chapters 7, 8, and 9. They gain computation practice in division and multiplication and reinforce their understanding of the connection between multiplication and division.

In the vignette, on the first day, I presented four riddles to the class. The first two had the same quotient, which I did purposely to give the students an easy entry into thinking about interpreting clues. For the third riddle, I used only two clues, to model a riddle that was neither interesting nor challenging enough, preparing the students for writing their own riddles. The fourth riddle was a model of what I expected them to write. Following are the clues for the four introductory riddles. For each riddle, I presented the clues one by one, allowing the students to describe after each clue what they then knew.

> *Riddle #1*
>
> *Clue 1: The quotient equals 1.*
>
> *Clue 2: The divisor is odd.*
>
> *Clue 3: The divisor has 1 digit.*
>
> *Clue 4: The divisor is greater than 8.*

Riddle #2

Clue 1: The quotient = 1.

Clue 2: The dividend is a whole even number.

Clue 3: The divisor is greater than 10 and less than 20.

Clue 4: The divisor is a multiple of 3.

Clue 5: The divisor is less than 15.

Riddle #3

Clue 1: The quotient = 1 R1.

Clue 2: The dividend is 2 × 10.

Riddle #4

Clue 1: The quotient = 1 R3.

Clue 2: The dividend is odd.

Clue 3: The dividend is a 3-digit number.

Clue 4: The divisor is a 2-digit number.

The Lesson

▲▲

DAY 1

To begin the lesson, I gathered the students on the rug and said, "I have a division riddle. I'm thinking of a division equation with a quotient of one. What division equation could I be thinking of?" After a brief moment of thinking, hands began to jump into the air. When most of the students had their hands up, I called on Kaylee.

"It could be five divided by five," Kaylee said.

I said to the class, "If you think my division equation could be five divided by five, put your thumb up; if you don't agree, put your thumb down; and if you're not sure, put your thumb sideways." The students indicated their agreement with Kaylee's suggestion. To help students keep track of the information shared, I wrote on the board:

Clue 1: The quotient equals 1.   *Yes*   *No*

$5 \div 5 = 1$

Jina shared next. "I think you might be thinking of eighteen divided by one."

The students gave Jina a thumbs-down. Jina had a look of confusion on her face, paused a moment, then corrected herself. "Oops! Eighteen divided by one would be eighteen. It should be eighteen divided by eighteen equals one." The others responded with their thumbs up. I added Jina's suggestions to the lists on the board:

Clue 1: The quotient equals 1.   *Yes*   *No*

$5 \div 5 = 1$ $18 \div 1 = 18$

$18 \div 18 = 1$

Elise next suggested $25 \div 25$. She explained, "I'm sure twenty-five divided by twenty-five could be your equation because you can think of the problem as how many groups of twenty-five in twenty-five and the answer to that is one. Or you could think how many would be in each of twenty-five groups, and that would be one, too." All students indicated their agreement with Elise's thinking. I added her idea to the list:

Clue 1: The quotient equals 1.   *Yes*   *No*

$5 \div 5 = 1$ $18 \div 1 = 18$

$18 \div 18 = 1$

$25 \div 25 = 1$

I then asked, "What do you notice about the problems on the Yes list?" All hands were up.

Joby explained, "The dividend and the divisor are the same on the Yes list, and I think that will happen to any division problem with a quotient of one. Like one hundred divided by one hundred is still one, and so is three thousand, four hundred ninety-three divided by three thousand, four hundred ninety-three."

I added Joby's division problems to the list and asked, "What's another example that can't be the equation I'm thinking of?" Again, hands were quickly in the air.

Rachel said, "Two hundred divided by seven won't work. I don't know the answer, but I know it isn't one because the divisor and dividend are different. They'd have to be the same for the quotient to be one."

I said to the students, "If you think Rachel's equation of two hundred divided by seven could be my equation, put a thumb up; if you think it could not be my equation, put your thumb down; and if you're not sure, put a thumb sideways." All thumbs were down. I recorded on the board the information shown in the first box, below.

After spending a few minutes with the class figuring out the answer to Rachel's problem, I continued. It seemed clear to the students that division equations with the same dividend and divisor produced an answer of 1. If I thought that some students didn't understand, I would have discussed other division equations with the class—for example, $88 \div 8$, $15 \div 5$, $36 \div 36$, and so on—asking the students if each produced a quotient of 1 or not and how they knew this, then recording them on the board.

I then gave the students a second clue and wrote it on the board under Clue 1 (see the second box, below).

"Which of the equations on the Yes list can we eliminate based on Clue Two?" I asked the students. Hands flew into the air.

Yolanda responded, "That's easy! You can get rid of the problems with even numbers, like eighteen divided by eighteen."

"I just thought of something," Jina said with a look of surprise on her face. "If the quotient is one and the divisor is even, then the dividend has to be even because the dividend and the divisor are the same number. That seems so simple now, but I just got it."

Terrell said, "Besides eighteen divided by eighteen, you should also cross off one hundred divided by one hundred because one hundred is an even number. The rest

Clue 1: The quotient equals 1.	Yes	No
	$5 \div 5 = 1$	$18 \div 1 = 18$
	$18 \div 18 = 1$	$200 \div 7 = ?$
	$25 \div 25 = 1$	
	$100 \div 100 = 1$	
	$3{,}493 \div 3{,}493 = 1$	

Clue 1: The quotient equals 1. Clue 2: The divisor is odd.	Yes	No
	$5 \div 5 = 1$	$18 \div 1 = 18$
	$18 \div 18 = 1$	$200 \div 7 = 28\ R4$
	$25 \div 25 = 1$	
	$100 \div 100 = 1$	
	$3{,}493 \div 3{,}493 = 1$	

are odd, so one of them could be the equation you're thinking of." The other students nodded (see the first box, below).

I then asked the students, "What do we now know about the dividend and the divisor, and how do we know?"

Justin said, "We know they both have to be odd numbers because the quotient is one and the clue says the divisor is odd, so that means the dividend is odd because they have to be the same number."

Ali mused aloud, "I know we got rid of a lot of possibilities when we found out that even numbers wouldn't work, but that still leaves a lot of numbers that are odd. I think I need another clue."

I replied, "I agree, you do need another clue to narrow down the possibilities even further. Here's Clue Three: The divisor has one digit. What do we now know about

the divisor?" Most hands popped up immediately. I asked the students to turn and talk to their neighbors about what they now knew as I recorded this clue (see the second box, below).

I then called on Elise. She reported, "It has to be one, three, five, seven, or nine. Those are all the odd numbers with one number in it." I wrote these numbers on the board.

"Do you mean that these are all of the odd numbers that have only one digit?" I asked, paraphrasing Elise's statement for clarity. Elise nodded in agreement.

"You have to cross off twenty-five divided by twenty-five and three thousand, four hundred ninety-three divided by three thousand, four hundred ninety-three," Kaleb said. I did this (see the last box below).

Clue 1: The quotient equals 1.	Yes	No
Clue 2: The divisor is odd.	$5 \div 5 = 1$	$18 \div 1 = 18$
	~~$18 \div 18 = 1$~~	$200 \div 7 = 28\ R4$
	$25 \div 25 = 1$	
	~~$100 \div 100 = 1$~~	
	$3,493 \div 3,493 = 1$	

Clue 1: The quotient equals 1.	Yes	No
Clue 2: The divisor is odd.	$5 \div 5 = 1$	$18 \div 1 = 18$
Clue 3: The divisor has 1 digit.	~~$18 \div 18 = 1$~~	$200 \div 7 = 28\ R4$
	$25 \div 25 = 1$	
	~~$100 \div 100 = 1$~~	
	$3,493 \div 3,493 = 1$	

Clue 1: The quotient equals 1.	Yes	No
Clue 2: The divisor is odd.	$5 \div 5 = 1$	$18 \div 1 = 18$
Clue 3: The divisor has 1 digit.	~~$18 \div 18 = 1$~~	$200 \div 7 = 28\ R4$
	~~$25 \div 25 = 1$~~	
	~~$100 \div 100 = 1$~~	
	~~$3,493 \div 3,493 = 1$~~	

"We need another clue," Cody said.

"OK," I replied, "here it is. The divisor is greater than eight." I recorded on the board (see below).

All of the students were eager to share. To give all a chance to respond, I said, "Show me with your fingers what you think is the divisor." The students held up nine fingers each.

I wrote on the board:

$$\_\_ \div 9 = 1 \qquad 9)\overline{}^{\,1} \qquad \frac{\_\_}{9} = 1$$

I continued, "If the quotient is one and the divisor is nine, what do we know about the dividend?"

Cody shared, "The dividend is ten." I was surprised by Cody's answer and reminded I mustn't make assumptions about what my students understand and of the importance incorrect answers play in providing counterexamples.

I completed the problems using Cody's suggestion:

$$10 \div 9 = 1 \qquad 9)\overline{10}^{\,1} \qquad \frac{10}{9} = 1$$

"How can we check that these problems are correct?" I asked Cody.

Cody paused a moment, then explained, "I think I might have made a mistake. I think there really might be a remainder if the dividend is ten and the divisor is nine." I was pleased Cody saw his error and I encouraged him to explain. Cody continued, "You could use sharing ten cookies with nine kids. Each kid would get one cookie

and there'd be one cookie left over. I think the dividend should really be nine, not ten." The others indicated their agreement with Cody. I erased the 10s and replaced them with 9s as Cody suggested.

$$9 \div 9 = 1 \qquad 9)\overline{9}^{\,1} \qquad \frac{9}{9} = 1$$

After a few moments of thought, Nariko said, "I noticed something. All numbers are divisible by themselves and no matter what the number is, the quotient will always be one, even if it's a decimal, like one and twenty-five–hundredths divided by one and twenty-five–hundredths, or a fraction, like five and one-half divided by five and one-half." Although many students followed and agreed with Nariko's thinking, a few were uncertain. I decided to present a second riddle.

A Second Riddle

Using the same procedure I had used before, I wrote the first clue on the board beside the clues for the first riddle. I used the same first clue for this riddle. When learning something new, it's valuable to have something familiar to relate to. Keeping the quotient the same allowed the students to make use of their experience with the first riddle.

Clue 1: The quotient = 1.

"What do we know so far?" I asked.

Neil explained, "The divisor and dividend are the same number because all numbers are divisible by themselves and equal one when they are divided by themselves."

	Yes	No
Clue 1: The quotient equals 1.	$5 \div 5 = 1$	$18 \div 1 = 18$
Clue 2: The divisor is odd.	~~$18 \div 18 = 1$~~	$200 \div 7 = 28\ R4$
Clue 3: The divisor has 1 digit.	~~$25 \div 25 = 1$~~	
Clue 4: The divisor is greater than 8.	~~$100 \div 100 = 1$~~	
	~~$3,493 \div 3,493 = 1$~~	

Rachel said, "I think you really need to give us another clue."

I responded, "Clue Two is: The dividend is an even number." I recorded Clue 2 on the board under the first clue.

Clue 1: The quotient = 1.

Clue 2: The dividend is a whole even number.

Katie said, "If the dividend is an even number, then so is the divisor. That means no odd numbers, fractions, or decimals. That helps, but we still need more clues." There were no other comments.

I said, "Here's Clue Three: The divisor is greater than ten and less than twenty." I paused to write the clue on the board, giving the students time to think. "What numbers won't work?"

Clue 1: The quotient = 1.

Clue 2: The dividend is a whole even number.

Clue 3: The divisor is greater than 10 and less than 20.

Most of the students had their hands up. I called on Binh, who said, "All numbers less than ten won't work."

"Will ten work?" Kaylee asked.

Celena responded, "The clue says the divisor is greater than ten, so I think that means ten won't work." Most students still looked a little uncertain, so I nodded my agreement with Celena to verify her idea.

Elise shared, "The divisor has to be an even number between eleven and up to nineteen."

I asked, "Could the divisor be twenty-four?" The students gave my question a thumbs-down.

"Too big!" they chorused.

"Based on the clues we have so far, what numbers would work?" I asked.

The students responded with fourteen, twelve, sixteen, and eighteen, and I listed these on the board. Then I asked the students if any other numbers were possible according to the clues. The students shook their heads "no."

I continued, "Each clue narrows the possibilities. We have only four possible numbers left. My next clue should reduce the number of possibilities even more. Clue Four is: The divisor is a multiple of three." I wrote this on the board under the other clues:

Clue 1: The quotient = 1.

Clue 2: The dividend is a whole even number.

Clue 3: The divisor is greater than 10 and less than 20.

Clue 4: The divisor is a multiple of 3.

The students talked among themselves with excitement. I settled them and then said, "Show me with your fingers how many numbers are possible now." Each student quickly held up two fingers. It was apparent they all understood what we were doing.

Celena explained, "Twelve is one possibility. I can prove it two ways. First, it's a small number so I can count by threes and I will land on twelve—three, six, nine, twelve. That's one way. The other way is I can add the digits. One plus two equals three. Three is divisible by three, so that means twelve is, too."

Justin shared, "You can prove it by multiplication, too. Just think, 'Three times what number equals twelve?' If there is no number, then twelve isn't a multiple of three, but there is, and it's four, so twelve is divisible by three."

"I think Justin should say 'whole number' instead of just 'number,'" Nariko commented. Several others nodded their heads.

"Is twelve the only one of the four numbers that's divisible by three, or is there another number?" I asked. Most students had their hands up. I asked them to use a whisper voice to tell me the number.

"Eighteen," the students responded.

Kaylee explained, "Add the digits, one plus eight, that equals nine. Nine is divisible by three, so that means eighteen, is too."

"Six times three is eighteen," Kaleb added.

I asked, "Are there any other numbers that could work?"

"No," the students responded together.

Shawn commented, "That means your equation has to be twelve divided by twelve or eighteen divided by eighteen. That's cool—out of all the division problems in the world, we have it narrowed down to just two." No one added anything else.

"Here's the final clue," I said as I added the last clue to the list on the board:

Clue 1: The quotient = 1.

Clue 2: The dividend is a whole even number.

Clue 3: The divisor is greater than 10 and less than 20.

Clue 4: The divisor is a multiple of 3.

Clue 5: The divisor is less than 15.

"It's twelve divided by twelve!" the students said.

Kaleb concluded, "I think this riddle is more proof that Nariko's idea is right that when the dividend and divisor are the same the quotient will always equal one, or when the quotient is one, then the dividend and divisor have to be the same."

The students were eager to do another riddle. I decided to change the quotient to add a bit of a challenge. And, at the same time, I would model a riddle with only two clues, making it neither as interesting nor as challenging as the first two. This would help prepare the students for what I expected when they created their own riddles.

A Third Riddle

I said, "As some of you have noticed, the clues in the riddles we've done so far have narrowed the possible division problems with each new clue, with the last clue leaving only one possibility. This is something you will need to consider later when you have the chance to write your own riddle with a partner. This riddle has a different quotient than the other two you've solved. Here's the first clue." I wrote the clue on the board:

Clue 1: The quotient = 1 R1.

I continued, "Talk with your partner about what kinds of division sentences have a quotient of one remainder one." The room erupted with lively conversations. After giving the students a few moments to discuss their ideas, I called them to order.

Jina said, "I think the dividend will have to be one bigger than the divisor." The others put their thumbs up, indicating their agreement with Jina's idea.

"Who would like to give us an example of Jina's idea?" I asked. Most hands were up.

Cody shared, "I know one that works for sure. It's the first answer I gave for the first riddle. Ten divided by nine works! I know because 'Ten divided by nine equals one remainder one' means that in ten, there is one group of nine with one something left over."

Neil added, "You can check it by multiplying one times nine, which is nine, and then adding the remainder of one to nine to get ten."

I recorded on the board Neil's idea:

$10 \div 9 = 1\ R1$ *multiplication check*
$(1 \times 9) + 1 = 10$

To check for understanding, I posed the following problem to the students: "Would fourteen divided by ten give a quotient of one remainder one? If you think yes, put a thumb up; if you think no, put a thumb down; and if you're not sure, put a thumb sideways." Almost all thumbs were down, indicating that $14 \div 10$ would not equal 1 R1; a few students didn't respond. I didn't worry. I knew that some of them needed more time to think about a question such as I had posed, and they would have time when they worked on their own.

Katie explained, "The answer to fourteen divided by ten is one remainder four.

The problem means you have fourteen and you want to split the fourteen into ten groups. How many would be in each group? There would be one in each group with four left over."

Binh had a different way to explain. He said, "The problem could mean that you have fourteen of something and you want to know how many groups of ten are in the fourteen things you have, like how many dimes are in fourteen pennies? The answer is one dime with four left over."

I then asked, "What's another division problem that has one remainder one as the quotient?"

Joby suggested, "One thousand divided by nine hundred ninety-nine." The students gave his suggestion a thumbs-up. I started Yes and No lists on the board and recorded Joby's suggestion along with Cody's earlier idea and $14 \div 10 = 1\ R4$:

Yes	No
$10 \div 9 = 1\ R1$	$14 \div 10 = 1\ R4$
$1,000 \div 999 = 1\ R1$	

"I know another problem that won't work," Elise said. "Fifteen divided by twelve won't work because the dividend is three more than the divisor, so that means the remainder will be three. Fifteen divided by twelve is one remainder three." A few students seemed to follow Elise's explanation, but most looked puzzled. I recorded her suggestion on the No list and then decided to move on, as I knew there would be other opportunities to see if her idea that the difference between the dividend and divisor equals the remainder always works.

A few more students shared their ideas for division problems with the quotient of 1 R1, and I recorded them on the list of Yes problems. I then gave a second clue. I said, "The second clue is: The dividend equals two times ten." I wrote the second clue under the first, knowing I'd given away the answer. I wanted to establish the criteria for the

students' riddles that they should have at least four clues before you could figure out an answer.

Clue 1: The quotient = 1 R1.

Clue 2: The dividend is 2 × 10.

"That's too easy!" "Hey, you gave it away!" were some of the responses from the students.

Terrell said, "The dividend is twenty because two times ten is twenty. That means the divisor is nineteen. Twenty divided by nineteen equals one remainder one. That was too short and too easy!"

I asked, "What made this riddle so easy?"

Celena explained, "Once we knew the dividend was twenty, then the divisor was easy. You should have given us some other clues in between that would more slowly get rid of the division problems that won't work."

The students were eager to do more. I decided to do one additional riddle before writing a riddle together as a class.

A Fourth Riddle

I wrote the first clue on the board:

Clue 1: The quotient = 1 R3.

I asked the students, "What do we know about the relationship between the dividend and the divisor?"

Katie explained, "The dividend has to be three bigger than the divisor for the quotient to equal one remainder three."

"That's often true, but what about six divided by three?" I asked, posing a counterexample. I wrote on the board:

$6 \div 3 = 1\ R3$

I gave the students a couple of moments of quiet think time. Then I said, "Talk with your neighbor about Katie's idea that the dividend has to be three larger than the divisor to get a quotient of one remainder three, and then discuss the problem I just wrote on the board. First one of you talks for thirty seconds while the other listens. When I give you the signal, the first talker gets to listen and the first listener gets to talk." I gave the students a signal to begin, then at the end of thirty seconds, I reminded them to switch roles. After another thirty seconds, I asked for the students' attention.

Cody shared first. He said, "The problem six divided by three doesn't work because if you had a remainder of three, you'd have enough for another group. The answer to six divided by three should be two, not one remainder three."

Shawn added, "The remainder has to be smaller than the divisor or there's enough for another group."

Nariko said, "I think Katie's idea works for many problems, but not ones with divisors that are three or less than three. Like, I don't think five divided by two equals one remainder three, because in the remainder there's enough for another group of two. The answer for five divided by two should be two remainder one, not one remainder three." The students sat quietly, considering what Nariko had said. I wrote on the board:

$5 \div 2 = 2 \ R1$

Joby added, "Another one that won't work is four divided by one equals one remainder three. The difference between the dividend and the divisor is three, but the real answer to four divided by one isn't one remainder three; the quotient is really four." I wrote on the board:

$4 \div 1 = 1 \ R3$

Katie said, "I think my idea works as long as the divisor is larger than three, like seven divided by four equals one remainder three." I wrote on the board:

$7 \div 4 = 1 \ R3$

There were no other comments, so I wrote another clue on the board:

Clue 1: The quotient = 1 R3.

Clue 2: The dividend is odd.

Kaylee commented, "If the dividend is odd, then the divisor has to be even because an odd number minus an odd number is an even number. You subtract three from the dividend to get the divisor. Three is odd and the dividend is odd. For example, seven minus three equals four, or nine minus three equals six."

I said, "So we know the dividend is odd and the divisor is even. Here's the next clue." I wrote on the board beneath the other clues:

Clue 1: The quotient = 1 R3.

Clue 2: The dividend is odd.

Clue 3: The dividend is a 3-digit number.

I asked, "What do we know now?"

Kaleb explained, "The smallest three-digit odd number is one hundred one and the largest three-digit odd number is nine hundred ninety-nine. So the dividend could be one of those two numbers or any odd number between them."

I wrote the next clue on the board:

Clue 1: The quotient = 1 R3.

Clue 2: The dividend is odd.

Clue 3: The dividend is a 3-digit number.

Clue 4: The divisor is a 2-digit number.

The students talked among themselves. After a few moments, I called them to attention.

Cody shared, "I think your equation is three hundred thirteen divided by twelve equals one remainder three." I wrote the problem on the board so the others could consider it:

$313 \div 12 = 1 \ R3$

Joby's hand shot into the air. "I think I disagree with Cody. I think there are more than twenty twelves in three hundred thirteen. Twenty times twelve is two hundred forty, and three hundred thirteen is larger than two hundred forty."

Cody corrected his guess. "I know! It's thirteen divided by twelve equals one remainder three." I wrote on the board:

$13 \div 12 = 1 \ R3$

I decided to use Cody's second guess as an example of how students should check their possible solutions against each of the clues given. I said, "Let's check Cody's idea against each of the clues. Is the dividend odd?" The students nodded. "Is the divisor even?" Again the students nodded.

Cody interrupted, "My idea doesn't work because the quotient to thirteen divided by twelve isn't one remainder three, it's one remainder one. And the dividend isn't three digits. I need more time to think. You can call on someone else, and I'll raise my hand when I have a different idea."

Using a student's idea as I used Cody's requires knowledge of your students. Cody enjoyed playing with ideas and when he made an error, rather than get upset, he simply tried something else. I use caution in the classroom, however, when putting up students' ideas for scrutiny by the others, as this is not the case with all children.

Celena said, "I think it's one hundred five divided by one hundred two equals one remainder three." I recorded Celena's suggestion on the board:

$105 \div 102 = 1 \ R3$

I said, "Let's check each part of your suggestion against the clues." I paused a moment to give Celena the chance to do this.

"Oops! One hundred two isn't a two-digit number," Celena said.

Cody had his hand up once again. He said, "This time I have it for sure! I checked everything with the clues. Your division equation has to be one hundred one divided by ninety-eight equals one remainder three." I wrote on the board:

$101 \div 98 = 1 \ R3$

Cody explained, "The dividend is an odd three-digit number, the divisor is an even two-digit number, and the quotient is one remainder three. In one hundred one, there is one group of ninety-eight and there are three left over." The students cheered for Cody and his persistence. I ended the lesson for the day on that note. After class, I copied onto chart paper the clues for the four riddles we'd solved so that the students could have them as a reference when writing their own clues.

DAY 2

My plan for today was to write one division riddle together with the class and then have the students work in pairs to write their own division riddles. Next, I planned to have at least one pair of students share a riddle with the class and then have others share their riddles on other days.

To begin, I pointed to the chart paper with the riddles from the previous day and said, "Yesterday, we worked together to solve these riddles. An important thing some of you noticed about the riddles is that each clue reduces the number of possible division equations that could be the solution to the riddle until the final clue, which leaves only one possibility. No one clue is enough by itself. And you can't solve the riddles with only two clues, either. The third riddle was too short and told us almost immediately what the answer was to the riddle. It wasn't a very interesting challenge." The students listened quietly, nodding as I spoke. I continued, "Today, we'll write one division riddle together, then you'll work with a partner to write your own division riddle. Later, you'll have the chance to share your riddles with the rest of the class." The students were eager to get started.

Ali, who always enjoyed going beyond the requirements of an assignment, asked, "Can we do more than one riddle? And can we make it extra hard?"

I responded, "You may do more than one riddle if you and your partner would like to do that. Also, you may make your riddle as hard as you and your partner would like, but you and your partner must be able to solve your riddle and prove that the clues and solution make sense." Ali and the others indicated their understanding by nodding.

I said, "For now, let's concentrate on writing a riddle together. First you decide on the quotient you'd like to use. We know that many different division problems can have the same quotient. The quotient for our riddle will be two."

This information sparked conversations among the students as they discussed division equations with a quotient of two. I let them talk with each other for a few moments, then settled them once again. "First, we need to decide which division equation with a quotient of two we're going to use for the answer. Then we'll figure out clues. What do we know about division equations with a quotient of two?" Hands leaped into the air.

Kaylee explained, "I know that the divisor has to be half the dividend. An example would be eight divided by four equals two. Four, the divisor, is half of eight. That's because there are two fours in eight. Two times four equals eight."

I recorded on the board:

$8 \div 4 = 2$

Terrell suggested, "Twenty-four divided by twelve is two. I know because twelve plus twelve is twenty-four."

Kaleb said, "I know a division problem with bigger numbers that works. One thousand divided by five hundred is two. Two times five is ten, so two times five hundred is one thousand."

Jina made one last suggestion. She said, "Thirty divided by fifteen works. Half of thirty is fifteen, so thirty divided by fifteen is two; two halves make a whole."

I added Terrell's, Kaleb's, and Jina's suggestions to the list:

$8 \div 4 = 2$

$24 \div 12 = 2$

$1,000 \div 500 = 2$

$30 \div 15 = 2$

I pointed to the list and said to the students, "Kaylee said a few moments ago that the divisor had to be half the dividend for the quotient to equal two. Is that true of these division problems? Show me with your thumb." All thumbs were immediately up.

I said, "Next you have to pick the division problem that will be the answer to your riddle. I'll decide for this one. Let's write a division riddle for thirty divided by fifteen equals two." I chose this equation because a student had suggested it, it wasn't too simple, and the numbers offered students a wide variety of options for clues. I wrote on the board:

$30 \div 15 = 2$

Clue 1:

"Remember, each clue should eliminate some possibilities while pointing to the others as possible solutions," I explained. "For Clue One, we give the quotient. Look at the riddles you solved yesterday for how to do this." While how to write the first clue was obvious to most students, a few looked uncertain. I gave the students a few moments to think, and when all hands were up, I asked them to share their ideas with their neighbors. Then I called the students back to order.

Elise shared her idea. "I think all you have to say is the quotient is equal to two." The others nodded their agreement. I asked Elise to come to the board to write her clue.

$30 \div 15 = 2$

Clue 1: The quotient is 2.

I said, "Think quietly for just a few moments about what the next clue could be." After a few moments, I continued, "Share your idea for Clue Two with your neighbor." The room immediately broke into lively conversations. I listened in as the students shared with one another. From their conversations, it was clear they grasped the idea of each clue reducing the possibilities. I called the students back to order. Hands waved in the air. I called on Yolanda.

Yolanda said, "You could say that the divisor is half the dividend." I recorded Yolanda's suggestion on the board and then called on Katie for another suggestion for Clue 2.

"I think what Yolanda says is true, the divisor is half the dividend, but we already know that because the quotient is two. I think we should say something like the dividend is a multiple of six. I know because the sum of the digits of thirty is three, which means it's divisible by three, *and* thirty is even, so that means it's also divisible by six. Besides, six times five is thirty."

I recorded Katie's suggestion for Clue 2 beneath Yolanda's.

The divisor is half the dividend.

The dividend is a multiple of 6.

I said, "Both of these clues work. Which gives the riddle solver more information without giving too much information?" In a vote, the students indicated the second clue. Beneath the first clue, I wrote Katie's clue:

30 ÷ 15 = 2

Clue 1: The quotient is 2.

Clue 2: The dividend is a multiple of 6.

"I know a clue for Clue Three," Rachel said. "You could say the divisor is a multiple of five, but not of ten."

"Hey, that's a good one," Kaleb responded. "The equation could be thirty divided by fifteen or ninety divided by forty-five, but it can't be sixty divided by thirty." After listening to Kaleb, the students were in agreement that Rachel's idea made an excellent clue. Rachel came to the board and added her clue to the list.

30 ÷ 15 = 2

Clue 1: The quotient is 2.

Clue 2: The dividend is a multiple of 6.

Clue 3: The divisor is a multiple of 5, but not of 10.

"Who has another idea for the next clue?" I asked. Several hands were up, but not as many as had been. I called on Binh.

Binh said, "I have an idea that would take two clues. Is that all right?" I nodded and Binh went on, "Well, you could say for Clue Four that the sum of the digits of the dividend is half the sum of the digits of the divisor." The students sat in absolute silence, faces scrunched in concentration as they considered what Binh said. I waited until faces began to unscrunch and hands started to go up.

"I know what he means," Celena said. "The sum of the digits of the dividend is three and the sum of the digits of the divisor is six. That works because the dividend is thirty and three plus zero equals three, and the divisor is fifteen and one plus five equals six. Three is half as big as six."

"Oh yeah!" "I get it!" "I see now!" "Cool!" were some of the students' responses.

Binh continued, "The last clue that could go with it is the divisor is less than twenty. Then I think no other problems will work except for thirty divided by fifteen." The students agreed that Binh's suggestions made good clues. Binh added them to the list of clues. The completed list of clues looked as follows:

30 ÷ 15 = 2

Clue 1: The quotient is 2.

Clue 2: The dividend is a multiple of 6.

Clue 3: The divisor is a multiple of 5, but not of 10.

Clue 4: The sum of the digits of the dividend is half the sum of the digits of the divisor.

Clue 5: The divisor is less than 20.

To model for the students the importance of checking each clue against the equation used for the riddle, I said, "Let's quickly check that the answer fits all of the clues. Then we'll know that the riddle works." Pointing to Clue 1, I said, "Is the quotient of thirty divided by fifteen two?" The students indicated their agreement with their thumbs. Next I said, pointing to the dividend, "Is the dividend, thirty, a multiple of six?" Again the students should thumbs up. I continued in this way until we'd checked all the clues.

Writing Riddles

"In just a moment, you'll be working with your partner to write your own riddle for a division problem with the quotient of two. You and your partner need to choose a division problem other than the one we used—thirty divided by fifteen. Write the division equation you chose on the back of your paper. For the first clue, write, 'The quotient equals two,' as we did in the riddle we wrote together. Then write three to six additional clues. Each clue should narrow the possible division equations, and your final clue should eliminate all possibilities other than the correct one. If you get stuck or aren't sure, you may refer to the four riddles you solved yesterday or the riddle we wrote together today." I wrote the directions on the board:

1. Choose a division equation that results in a quotient of 2.

2. Write it on the back of your paper.

3. For Clue 1, write The quotient equals 2.

4. Write three to six additional clues. Each clue should narrow the possible division equations. The last clue should eliminate all possibilities other than the correct one.

The students were eager to get started and didn't ask questions. I knew from past experience, however, that while writing a riddle seems easy at first, students sometimes run into difficulties as they get deeper into the activity. Typically, they seem to bump into one of two difficulties: either their clues don't give enough information or give too much information, or their final clue leaves more than one possible solution. Circulating through the class, I read over shoulders, attempting to solve their riddles, and then offered questions or comments to guide their clue writing. This helped eliminate many of these problems.

Observing the Students

Initially, I circulated through the class and answered various questions. As I walked by Yolanda and Kaylee, they announced they had finished their riddle. The girls waited quietly as I read their riddle. I commented, "I think the answer to your riddle could be thirty divided by fifteen." I knew this wasn't the case, as I had asked the students not to use that problem and Kaylee and Yolanda typically followed directions, but it was a possible solution for their clues. The girls looked at each other with confusion and began to talk about my idea.

After a brief discussion, Yolanda said, "I think thirty divided by fifteen equals two works, but that's not our problem. Maybe we need another clue." I nodded and the girls discussed their options. (See Figure 17–1.)

Rachel and Joby ran up to me, very excited to share their riddle. I read their clues and was able to correctly guess that their division equation was $98 \div 46 = 2$. (See Figure 17–2.) "Can we write another one?" they chorused.

I replied, "You may either write another riddle for a different division equation with a quotient of two or write a division riddle for a division equation with a quotient of two remainder one."

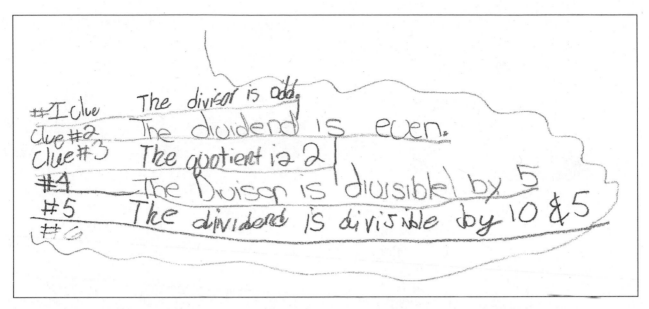

Figure 17–1 *Yolanda and Kaylee made a common error. Their final clue did not eliminate all division problems except the correct one, which was 90 ÷ 45 = 2.*

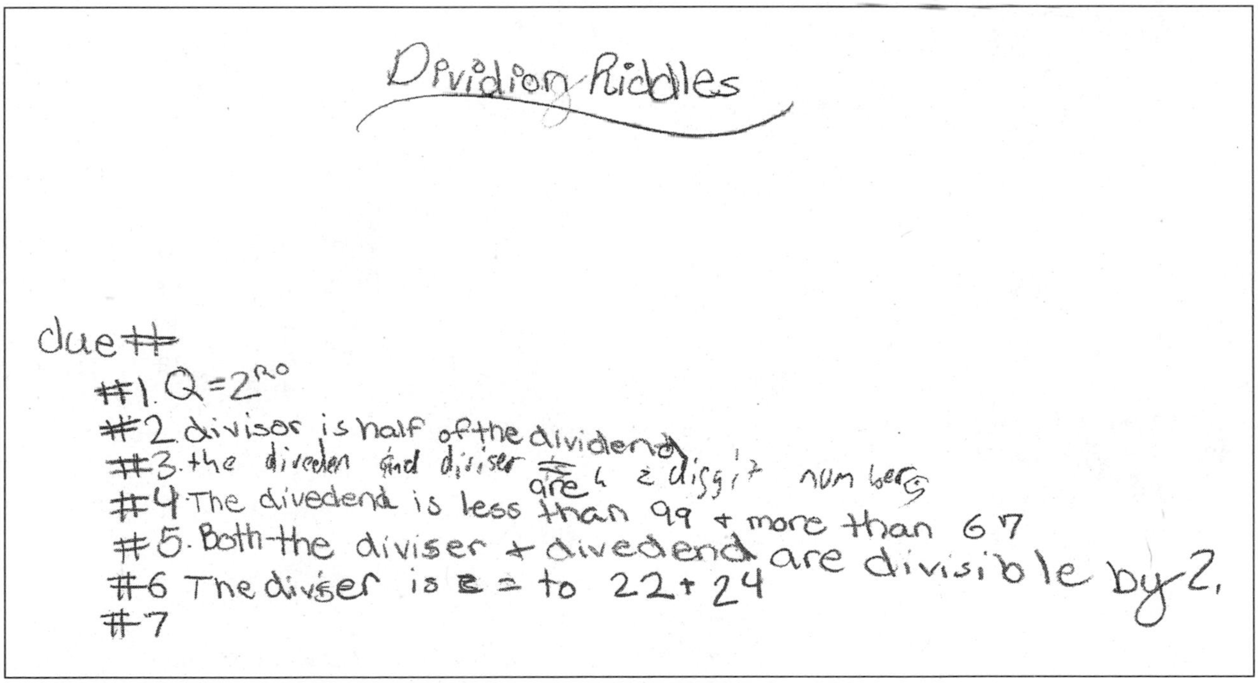

#1 clue   The divisor is odd.
clue #2   The dividend is even.
clue #3   The quotient is 2
#4   The Divisor is divisible by 5
#5   The dividend is divisible by 10 & 5
#6

Division Riddles

clue #
  #1. Q = 2no
  #2 divisor is half of the dividend
  #3. the divedend and divisor are 4 2 diggit numbers
  #4 The divedend is less than 99 + more than 67
  #5. Both the diviser + divedend are divisible by 2.
  #6 The divisor is = to 22 + 24
  #7

Figure 17–2 *Rachel and Joby's division riddle.*

Terrell and Shawn were having difficulty agreeing on their equation. I explained to the boys that if they couldn't agree on a division equation, I'd make the decision for them. They quickly decided on 52 ÷ 26 = 2 and completed the assignment. As other students finished, I read and solved their riddles, giving feedback where needed, and then I gave them the same option I'd given Rachel and Joby: to write a riddle for the quotient of 2 R1. When most students had completed the task, I gave a two-minute warning, and after two minutes, I called the class to order.

Sharing Riddles

I gathered the students on the rug, asking them to sit with their partners and place their papers on the floor. The students enjoyed the activity and were excited to share their riddles. I explained that only one or two pairs of students would get to share their riddles today, but that everyone would have the opportunity to share over the next few days. This seemed to satisfy them.

Nariko and Elise were first to share. Elise read first. "Clue One: The quotient equals two."

Nariko read next. "The divisor is a multiple of nine. What numbers could those be?" Modeling my behavior, Nariko listed on the board multiples of nine as students suggested them.

9

36

18

54

45

27

Elise continued, "The dividend is lower than one hundred and greater than thirty. What does that mean?" She called on Ali, who said the dividend could be ninety-nine down to thirty-one. Elise and Nariko nodded their agreement with Ali.

Nariko read Clue 4. "The divisor is even. Which numbers can I cross off the list we made before?" Nariko crossed off the odd multiples of nine as the students made their suggestions.

~~9~~

36

18

54

~~45~~

~~27~~

Elise read Clue 5. "The divisor is less than ninety." The students realized that this clue didn't give them additional information.

Nariko read Clue 6. "The dividend is a multiple of eight." Again, as students suggested multiples of eight, Nariko listed them on the board. One student suggested that thirty-three was a multiple of eight. Nariko reminded the student to count by eights to check. The student corrected himself, stating thirty-three didn't work, but thirty-two did.

16

0

80

72

88

32

Kaleb raised his hand. "Sixteen and zero don't belong on the list. They're less than thirty, and in Clue Three, you said the dividend was greater than thirty."

"Oh yeah!" Nariko giggled and quickly erased 16 and 0.

Elise read the final clue. "The answer of the divisor is the sum of twenty-five and eleven." Hands shot into the air as the students solved the riddle. I realized that if this clue had been the second clue, then the others could have solved the riddle quickly. However, since the students were engaged, I didn't point this out.

Nariko said to her classmates, "Think it in your heads and I'll write the answer on the board and you can see if you're right." The students watched Nariko carefully as she first wrote on the board the dividend, then the divisor, and finally the quotient.

$$72 \div 36 = 2$$

(See Figure 17–3.)

The students cheered with appreciation of Nariko and Elise and their own

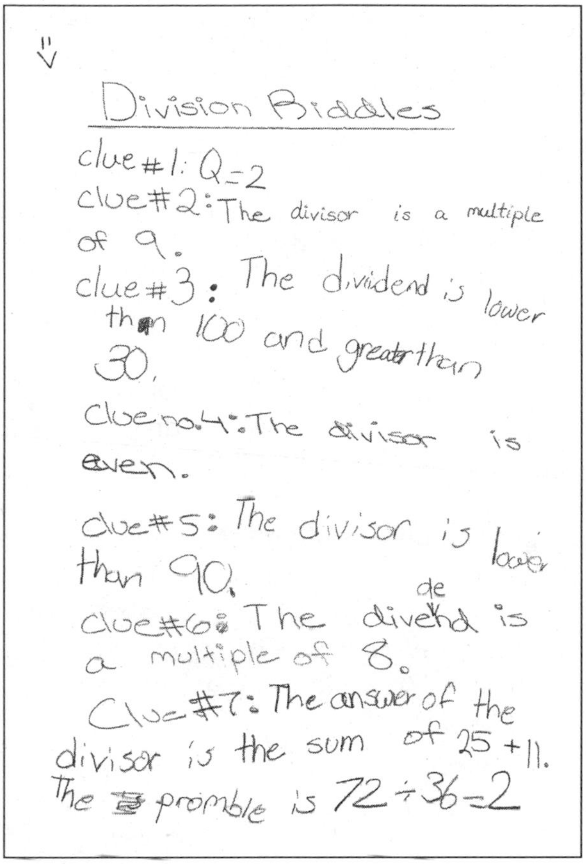

Division Riddles

clue#1: Q=2

clue#2: The divisor is a multiple of 9.

clue#3: The dividend is lower than 100 and greater than 30.

Clue no.4: The divisor is even.

clue#5: The divisor is lower than 90.

clue#6: The divehd is a multiple of 8.

Clue#7: The answer of the divisor is the sum of 25 + 11. The promble is 72 ÷ 36 = 2.

▲▲▲▲▲▲**Figure 17–3** *Nariko and Elise's division riddle.*

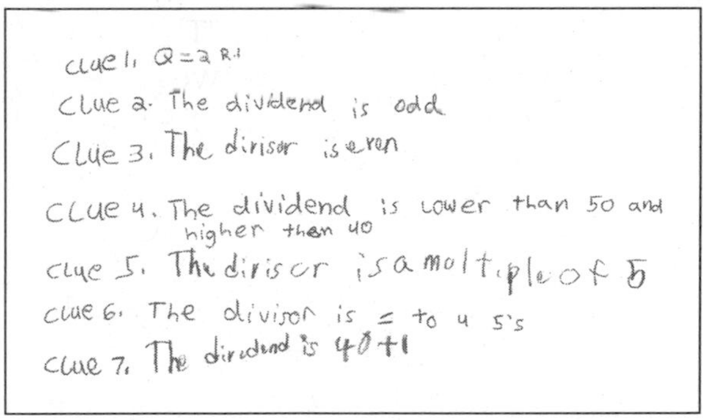

clue 1. Q = 2 R1
Clue 2. The dividend is odd
Clue 3. The divisor is even
Clue 4. The dividend is lower than 50 and higher than 40
clue 5. The divisor is a moltiple of 5
clue 6. The divisor is ≤ to 4 5's
clue 7. The dividend is 40 + 1

▲▲▲▲▲▲**Figure 17–4** *Cody and his partner chose to write a riddle for 2 R1.*

cleverness for having successfully solved the riddle. I had hoped to have at least one more pair share their riddle, but I had not anticipated that Nariko and Elise would take so long. I explained to the class that the others would have a chance to share on other days and then ended class. I collected the students' papers for safekeeping.

EXTENSIONS

Have students write division riddles for other quotients, such as 2 R1, 1 R3, or any other quotient you feel appropriate for your students. Give students the following directions:

1. Write a riddle for a problem with the quotient of _____.
2. Choose a division problem with that quotient that will be the answer to your riddle.
3. For the first clue, write: *Clue 1: The quotient =* _____.
4. Write three to six more clues. Each clue should narrow the possible division equations, and your final clue should eliminate all possibilities other than the correct one.

Or, you may have students choose their own quotients. When they've written their riddles, either have students share their riddles with the class, as was done in the vignette, or collect their riddles and make them into a book. Figure 17–4 shows one pair's riddle for the quotient 2 R1.

Questions and Discussion

▲▲

▲ *How do writing and solving riddles benefit my students?*

As students solve riddles, they are applying ideas they've learned previously. For example, in the vignette, students were applying divisibility rules, practicing division and multiplication, using number theory, and developing their logic skills. Also, as students explain their thinking, you have the opportunity to gain insights into their thinking and understanding. You also have the opportunity to help students revise misconceptions and then correctly apply their new learning as students explain their thinking during class discussions.

▲ *How do I avoid the situation of a student sharing in front of the class a riddle that doesn't work?*

As a pair of students work together to create a riddle, read over their shoulders. Try to solve for yourself the riddle they've created. If you arrive at an answer that is correct but that isn't their solution, or if you can't solve their riddle at all, ask questions or give feedback that will guide the students on how to correct their clues so that they do work. A common problem students have is that their clues leave more than one final possibility. In this case, it's often helpful to redirect their attention to the four riddles solved by the class and point out how each clue eliminates possibilities until only one possibility exists. Another problem students sometimes have when writing riddles is including some clues that don't eliminate additional possibilities, that is, creating clues that don't provide any additional information. For example, stating the quotient is two and then later, in a different clue, stating the divisor is half of the dividend doesn't really provide any additional information. Another problem may be that the last clue, if given earlier, would have eliminated the need for the other clues. However, this didn't seem to bother the students in this class, so I didn't bring it up with them.

ADDITIONAL ACTIVITIES

One goal of fourth- and fifth-grade mathematics instruction is for students to develop proficiency with division computation. The seven activities presented in this section suggest ideas for providing practice with division computation that also enhance and reinforce important concepts presented to students in the earlier chapters of this book.

In the activity *Dividing by Four*, students practice division computation as they divide numbers ending in 5—5, 15, 25, 35, and so on—by 4 and then search the resulting quotients for patterns. This activity is appropriate after students have had experience with the lesson in Chapter 2, "The Divisor Stays the Same," and can be repeated using other divisors throughout students' study of division. Three of the activities, *527 ÷ 3, 400 ÷ 12,* and *Writing Word Problems,* ask students to write division stories. Writing division stories is an activity that helps students connect division to real-world situations. These activities can also be repeated for other problems. *Sharing Pencils* asks students to solve two problems; both have a similar context, but one is a sharing, or partitioning, problem and the other is a grouping problem. This experience further develops students' understanding of the importance of context in interpreting the meaning of answers. *How Many Years Old?* provides division computation practice as students divide by twelve to convert months into years to figure the age in years of a woman reported to have been the longest-living person. The last activity, *A Collection of Division Problems,* provides additional practice with division computation.

Each activity typically takes one class period to complete.

Dividing by Four

OVERVIEW

This activity is appropriate after students have experienced the lesson in Chapter 2, "The Divisor Stays the Same." In this activity, students are provided with division computation practice as they divide numbers that end in 5—5, 15, 25, 35, and so on—by 4. After students solve seven to ten division problems, they search the list of equations for patterns and write about the patterns they find.

MATERIALS

▲ none

TEACHING DIRECTIONS

1. Explain to students that they will be exploring what happens when they divide numbers ending in five by four.

2. Write on the board: $5 \div 4 = ?$ Ask students to solve the problem and share their thinking in a class discussion. Record on the board their answers and strategies for solving the problem.

3. On the board, write $15 \div 4 = ?$ and continue as you did in Step 2.

4. Next write $25 \div 4 = ?$ Continue as you did for Step 2, this time also asking students if they notice any patterns among the three equations. Ask students to predict what the next dividend and quotient will be.

5. Write on the board $35 \div 4 = ?$ Continue as before, focusing students' attention on the patterns emerging in the list of equations.

6. Ask students to record the answers to $45 \div 4$, $55 \div 4$, $65 \div 4$, and $75 \div 4$, then search the list of equations for patterns, and finally, write about the patterns they find.

7. Lead a class discussion for students to share what they found.

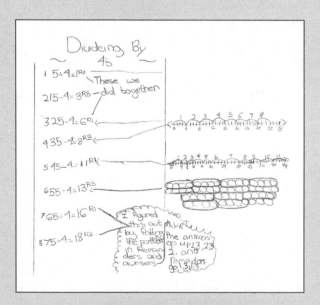

▲▲▲▲▲▲**Figure 1** *Kaylee started the assignment using pictorial representations to help her see patterns and solve the problems. Then she applied the patterns she found and moved to numerical representations.*

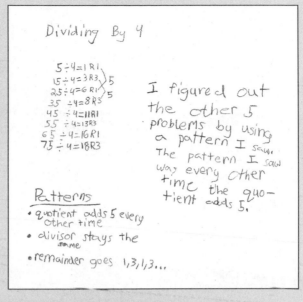

▲▲▲▲▲Figure 2 *Joby noticed that every other quotient increased by 5. When asked why, he explained, "The dividends increase by twenty and that's five groups of four."*

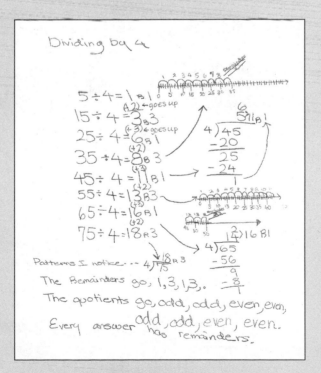

▲▲▲▲▲Figure 3 *Nariko used number lines and long division.*

527 ÷ 3

OVERVIEW

This problem is appropriate for students after they have experienced the lesson in Chapter 4, "An Introduction to Division Computation: If You Hopped Like a Frog." Students first solve the problem 527 ÷ 3 in two ways. They then write a division story that could be represented by 527 ÷ 3. This activity can be repeated throughout the year by changing the numbers. (See the following activity, *400 ÷ 12*, for an example of how to do this.)

MATERIALS

▲ none

TEACHING DIRECTIONS

1. Write on the board *527 ÷ 3 =*.

2. Ask the students to individually solve the problem in two ways.

3. When students have solved the problem in two ways, ask them to each write a division story that could be represented by 527 ÷ 3. If your students have not had previous experience writing division stories, model for the students how to do so, reminding them their division story must include a question that can be answered by 527 ÷ 3.

4. After students have solved the problem and written their division stories, lead a class discussion for students to share their strategies for solving the problem and their division stories.

> there were 527new arivals
> in the zoo there are
> mammals, fishes ,and Reptiles
> there is an equal amount of
> animals in each group
> How many are leftover

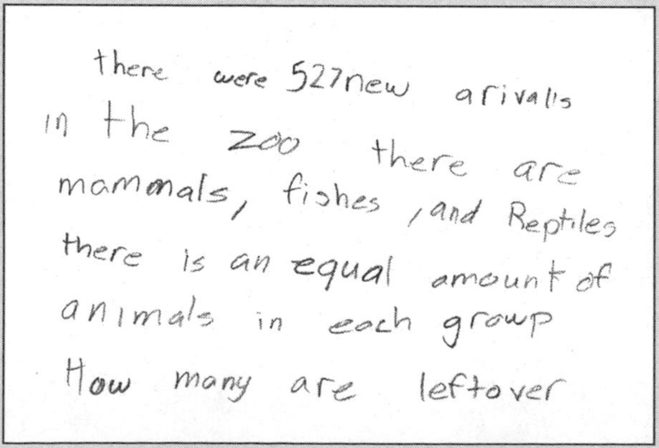

▲▲▲▲▲▲Figure 4 *Juan made a common error in his division story. His question was incomplete.*

175 R2
Marry had 527 marbles and she wanted to divide them between 3 friends. How many will each friend get equally

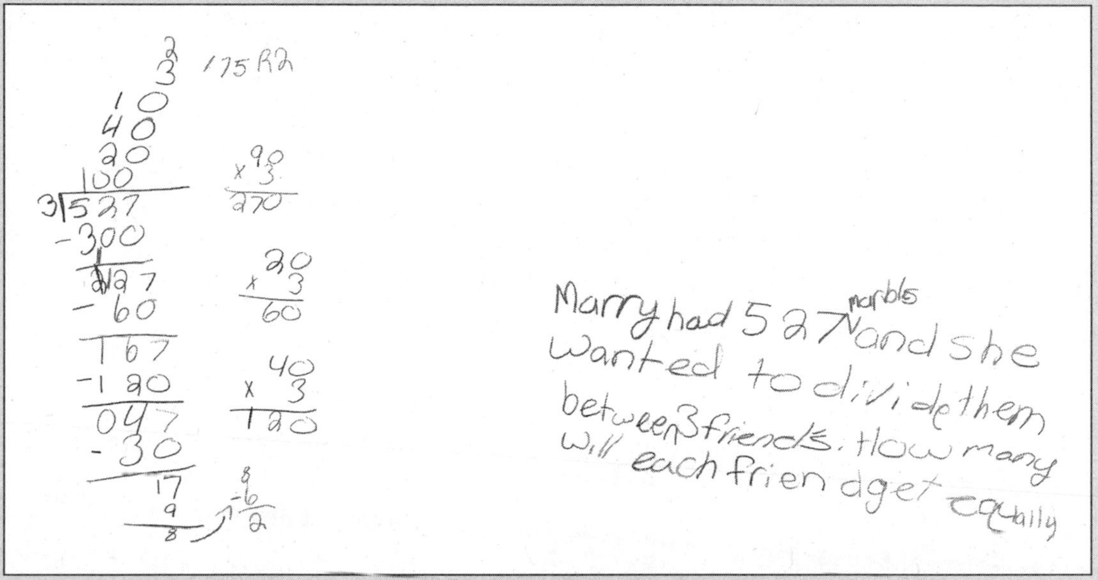

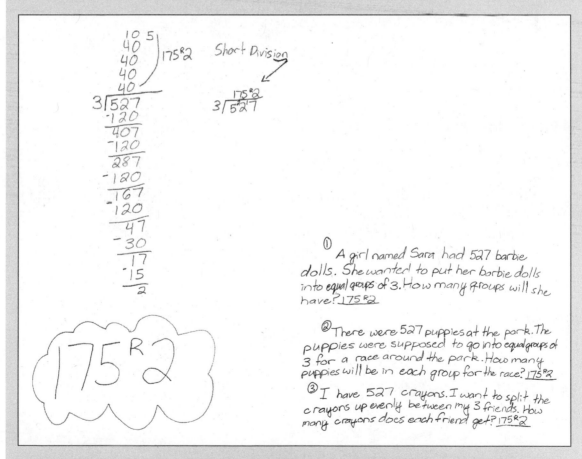

Figure 5 *Wendi used multiplication to help her solve 527 ÷ 3.*

Short Division
175 R2
① A girl named Sara had 527 barbie dolls. She wanted to put her barbie dolls into equal groups of 3. How many groups will she have? 175 R2
② There were 527 puppies at the park. The puppies were supposed to go into equal groups of 3 for a race around the park. How many puppies will be in each group for the race? 175 R2
③ I have 527 crayons. I want to split the crayons up evenly between my 3 friends. How many crayons does each friend get? 175 R2

Figure 6 *Alexa used short division and an alternative algorithm to solve 527 ÷ 3. She wrote three division stories. The first was an example of the grouping model of division and the third was an example of the sharing model. In the second problem, she showed some confusion and inadvertently gave the answer to her problem.*

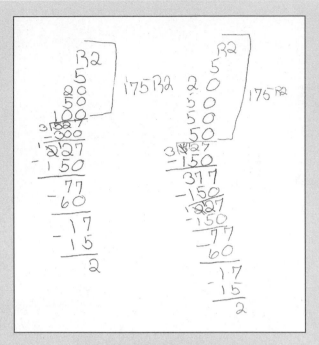

400 ÷ 12

OVERVIEW

This activity is appropriate after students have experienced the lesson in Chapter 4, "An Introduction to Division Computation: If You Hopped Like a Frog." This activity is similar to *527 ÷ 3* but provides students division computation practice using a two-digit divisor. First students solve the problem in two ways, then they write a division story that could be represented by 400 ÷ 12.

MATERIALS

▲ none

TEACHING DIRECTIONS

1. Write on the board 400 ÷ *12 =*.

2. Ask the students to individually solve the problem in two ways.

3. When students have solved the problem in two ways, ask them to each write a division story that could be represented by 400 ÷ 12.

4. After students have solved the problem and written their division stories, lead a class discussion for students to share their strategies for solving the problem and their division stories.

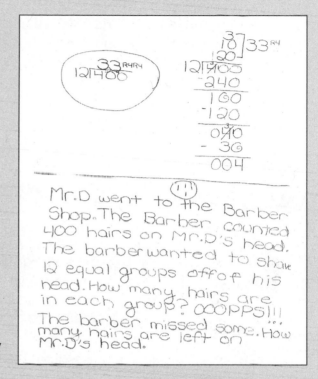

The story reads:

Mr. D went to the Barber Shop. The Barber counted 400 hairs on Mr. D's head. The barber wanted to shave 12 equal groups off of his head. How many hairs are in each group? OOOPPS!!! The barber missed some... How many hairs are left on Mr. D's head.

▲▲▲▲▲▲**Figure 8** *Jewell successfully completed the task.*

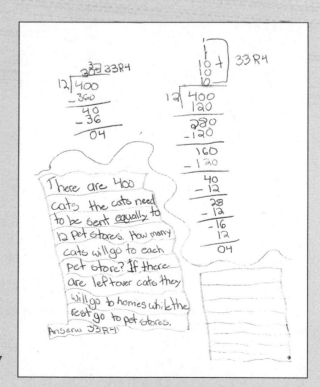

The story reads:

There are 400 cats the cats need to be sent equally to 12 pet stores. How many cats will go to each pet store? If there are leftover cats they will go to homes while the rest go to pet stores. Answer 33R4

▲▲▲▲▲▲**Figure 9** *Nalani solved the problem in two ways. Her division story was an example of the sharing model.*

How Many Years Old?

OVERVIEW

This activity is appropriate after students have experienced the lesson in Chapter 4, "An Introduction to Division Computation: If You Hopped Like a Frog," and provides students with a real-world connection to division. Jeanne Calment was born in France on February 21, 1875, and her death was reported on August 4, 1997, at which time she was about 1,469 months old. She is believed to have been one of the longest-living people. Students figure her age in years by dividing 1,469 by 12.

MATERIALS

▲ none

TEACHING DIRECTIONS

1. Tell students that Jeanne Calment was born in France on February 21, 1875, and is believed to have had one of the longest lives in history. Her death was reported on August 4, 1997, at which time she was about 1,469 months old.

2. Ask the students to figure out how many years old Jeanne Calment was when she died.

3. After the students have solved the problem, lead a class discussion for students to share their strategies.

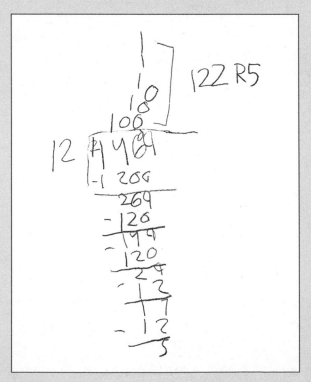

▲▲▲▲▲▲Figure 10 *Michael persisted and successfully solved the problem.*

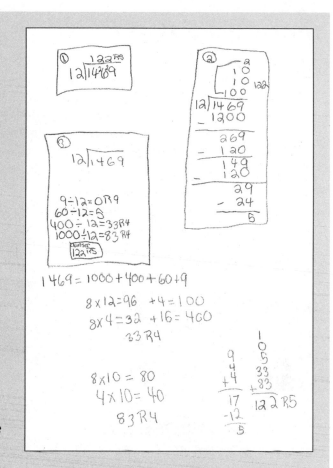

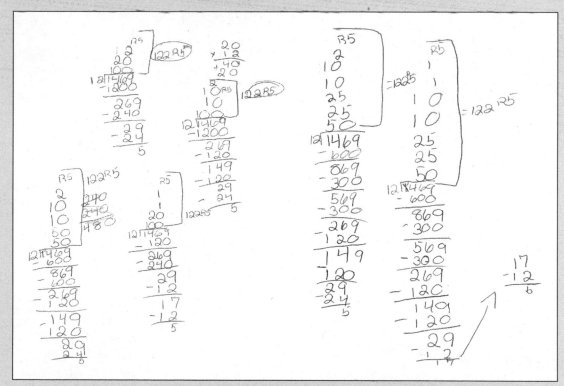

Figure 11 *Natalia's third solution was based on her knowledge of place value and multiplication.*

Figure 12 *Kalani took great pleasure solving 1,469 ÷ 12 in many ways.*

Sharing Pencils

OVERVIEW

This activity is appropriate after students have experienced the lessons in Chapter 12, "The Yarn Lesson," and Chapter 13, "Beans and Scoops." This activity provides students the opportunity to explore both models of division—the sharing, or partitioning, model and the grouping model. First, students figure the number of classes that would get 32 pencils if 1,232 pencils were divided among them so that every student in each class got 1 pencil. This is an example of the grouping model because students must figure the number of groups of 32 that are in 1,232. Next, students share 1,232 pencils among 32 students. This is an example of the sharing model because students share the pencils equally among 32 children. Some children may be surprised that both situations generate the same numerical quotient, though the interpretations of the quotients differ.

MATERIALS

▲ none

TEACHING DIRECTIONS

1. Present the first problem to the students: *The school has 1,232 pencils. The principal wants to know how many classes of 32 students can receive pencils so that every student in each class gets one pencil.* Ask the students to solve the problem.

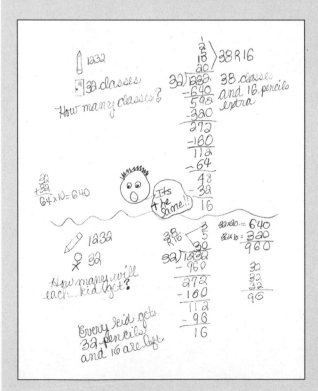

▲▲▲▲▲▲Figure 13 *Jina was surprised that both situations produced the same numerical quotient.*

2. After the students have solved the first problem, lead a class discussion about the strategies they used.

3. Present the second problem to the students: *There are 1,232 pencils to be shared equally among 32 children. How many pencils will each child receive?* Ask the students to solve problem.

4. After students have solved the second problem, lead a class discussion about the strategies they used to solve the problem and what they discovered.

Writing Word Problems

OVERVIEW

This activity provides the opportunity for students to think about situations that could be represented by the following division equations.

$$25 \div 4 = 6 \text{ R1}$$
$$25 \div 4 = 6\frac{1}{4}$$
$$25 \div 4 = 6¢$$
$$25 \div 4 = 7$$
$$25 \div 4 = 6.25$$

Students work in pairs to write a division story for each number sentence.

MATERIALS

▲ none

TEACHING DIRECTIONS

1. Write the following five division sentences on the board:

$$25 \div 4 = 6 \text{ R1}$$
$$25 \div 4 = 6\frac{1}{4}$$
$$25 \div 4 = 6¢$$
$$25 \div 4 = 7$$
$$25 \div 4 = 6.25$$

2. Ask students to work in pairs and write a division story for each number sentence.

3. After students have completed their division stories, lead a class discussion for students to share their work.

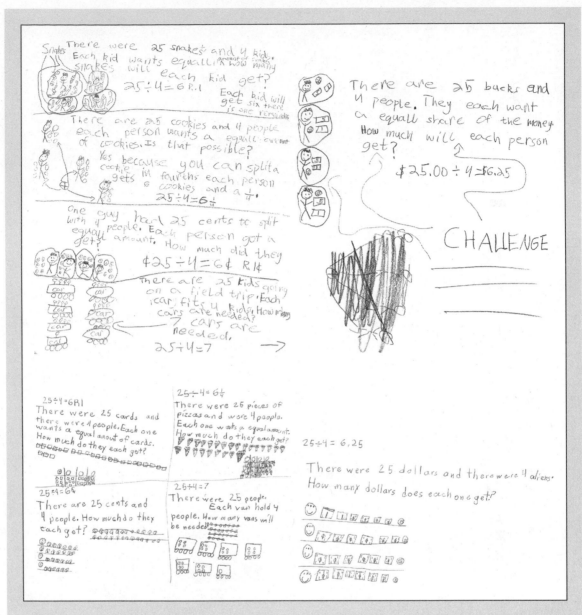

▲▲▲▲▲Figure 14 and Figure 15 *Yolanda and Joby showed strong understanding in their division stories.*

A Collection of Division Problems

OVERVIEW

Seven division problems follow that ask students to apply division to a variety of situations. Each problem can be used as a warm-up followed by a short discussion of the strategies students used to solve the problem.

MATERIALS

▲ none

TEACHING DIRECTIONS

1. Present one of the following problems to students by writing it on the board or on an overhead transparency.

2. Ask students to solve the problem.

3. After students have solved the problem, lead a class discussion for them to share the strategies they used.

The Problems

▲ *Mr. Cortez's weight is 57 kg. He is three times as heavy as Chris. What is Chris's weight?*

▲ *Roger's weight is 70 kg. He is five times as heavy as his son. Find the total weight of Roger and his son.*

▲ *Lily bought fifteen shirts of equal price for $240.00. How much did two shirts cost?*

▲ *A piece of rope measured 3 meters and 66 centimeters long (3 m 66 cm). It was cut into two pieces. The longer piece was twice as long as the shorter piece. What was the length of the longer piece?*

▲ *Twelve people together bought one birthday present for their friend. They paid the cashier $200.00 and received $44.00 change. If they shared the cost equally, how much did each person pay?*

▲ *A blue ribbon is 2,484 centimeters long (2,484 cm). It is eighteen times as long as a red ribbon. How long is the red ribbon?*

▲ *Koji packed 645 oranges into bags of 15 each. If he sold all the oranges at $6.00 a bag, how much money would he receive? If Koji had instead divided all of the 645 oranges equally among 15 bags and sold each bag for $6.00, how much money would he have received?*

ASSESSMENTS

Overview

This section contains nine assessments for evaluating what students are learning as they study division. The first assessment, *What Is Division?* is useful for gaining knowledge about students' prior learning in division. This information provides guidance as you make instructional decisions about what is appropriate for your students. *The Motorcycle Problem* asks students to solve a problem by dividing by ten and is appropriate after students have had experience with the lesson in Chapter 1, "Silent Division." The assessment *4 R3* is appropriate to give to students after they have experienced the lesson in Chapter 6, "The Quotient Stays the Same." *Multiples of Two and Three* and *Divisibility with Candies* are linked to divisibility. *Multiples of Two and Three* elicits information about students' understanding of the divisibility rules for two and three. It should be given after students have completed the activities in Chapter 7, "Exploring Divisibility Rules for Two, Five, and Ten," and Chapter 8, "Exploring Divisibility Rules for Three." *If Shaquille O'Neal Were a Chameleon* assesses what students have learned about division computation and is effective to use after they've experienced the lesson in Chapter 4, "An Introduction to Division Computation: If You Hopped Like a Frog." *Easy, Medium, and Hard* gives students the opportunity to show you what they consider to be easy or hard in terms of division. This assessment can be repeated periodically as students study division. The final two assessments, *593 ÷ 19* and *What Is Division? (Revisited)*, are most appropriate for students later in their study of division. For *593 ÷ 19*, each student must write a story problem that could be solved by 593 ÷ 19 and then solve the problem. *What Is Division? (Revisited)* allows you to examine the students' growth in their understanding of division.

Teaching Notes

Assessment of students needs to be an ongoing, critical part of teaching. Assessments help teachers make appropriate instructional decisions about what concepts to introduce, how and when they should be presented, and how much and what kind of practice is needed for their students to be successful. Assessments also help teachers to know which students need more time, individualized help, or additional challenges.

Often when we think of assessments, we think of paper-and-pencil tests, quizzes, or standardized testing. But assessment of students can take many other forms, including teacher observation of students as they work, a student's contribution during class discussion, or writing assignments.

Class discussions are important to the writing process. Having a discussion before asking students to complete a writing assignment provides students with ideas to consider for writing and the opportunity to clarify their thinking through talk. This can be especially helpful when learning is new and fragile or when students lack confidence. Leading a discussion after students have written provides students with another opportunity to share their thinking while considering the ideas of others. These discussions help students become flexible thinkers.

Often, we ask students to copy the prompt before they begin to write. This helps students focus on the task and what is being asked of them. For students, writing assignments provide opportunities to reflect on their learning, solidify their thinking, raise questions, reinforce new ideas, and review or apply older ideas.

When students are working on writing assignments, I circulate through the class, answering questions and reading over shoulders. Students sometimes need help knowing what to write. When students need help, I begin by asking them to explain what they know about the problem, or I ask them a question to spark their thinking. After I listen to students' explanations, I suggest they begin by writing down the exact words they just spoke. I suggest they send their thoughts from their brains, down their arms, through their hands, out their pencils, and onto their papers. I want students to understand that what they write on their papers should represent the thinking they do in their heads.

Questions that can help spark students' thinking include

▲ How did you get that answer?
▲ What would happen if . . . ?
▲ What pattern do you see?
▲ Does this make sense?
▲ Can you make a simpler problem?

As I observe students at work, some questions I ask myself about the students include

▲ Does the student have a reasonable strategy for solving the problem?
▲ Does the student use good number sense?
▲ Does the student use benchmark or landmark numbers?
▲ Does the student use strategies that are efficient and lead to accurate answers?
▲ Is the student willing to explore new strategies and ideas?
▲ Can the student use new ideas or does the student always use the same approach?
▲ Can the student calculate mentally?
▲ Can the student accurately communicate her or his thinking verbally and in writing?

Typically, division instruction focuses on facts and computation, and assessment is concerned with whether children can "do" division. Teachers test students on their knowledge of division facts, their skills with computing, and their ability to apply their computation skills to solve one-step word problems. The assessments in this section are different.

While it's important for students to gain fluency with computation, enabling them to be accurate and efficient, the purpose of the lessons in this book is to support the development of their conceptual understanding, ultimately leading to accurate and efficient computation. Therefore, these assessments are no different than other activities in this book. Children are asked to work individually to solve problems or relate division to real-world situations. Having to organize their ideas on paper requires thinking and supports their continued learning while giving you valuable information about their learning. Their papers provide valuable information about each child, while a class set provides important insights about the effectiveness of the instruction being provided.

What Is Division?

PROMPT

What is division?

Students in fourth and fifth grade generally have prior experience with division. They may know their basic facts and may be aware that there is a connection between multiplication and division. Perhaps they know that division, like multiplication, involves equal groups. Class discussions and students' written responses to this prompt will inform you about what they bring to their continued study of division. This information will allow you to make appropriate instructional decisions about the learning opportunities you should provide for your students.

To begin, write on the board: *What is division?* Allow students a few moments of quiet time to think about the question. Then, in a class discussion, ask students to share their ideas about division. Record their ideas on the board. After all who want to do so have shared, ask students to write about what they know about division. Encourage students to use words, numbers, and pictures to explain their thinking as clearly as possible.

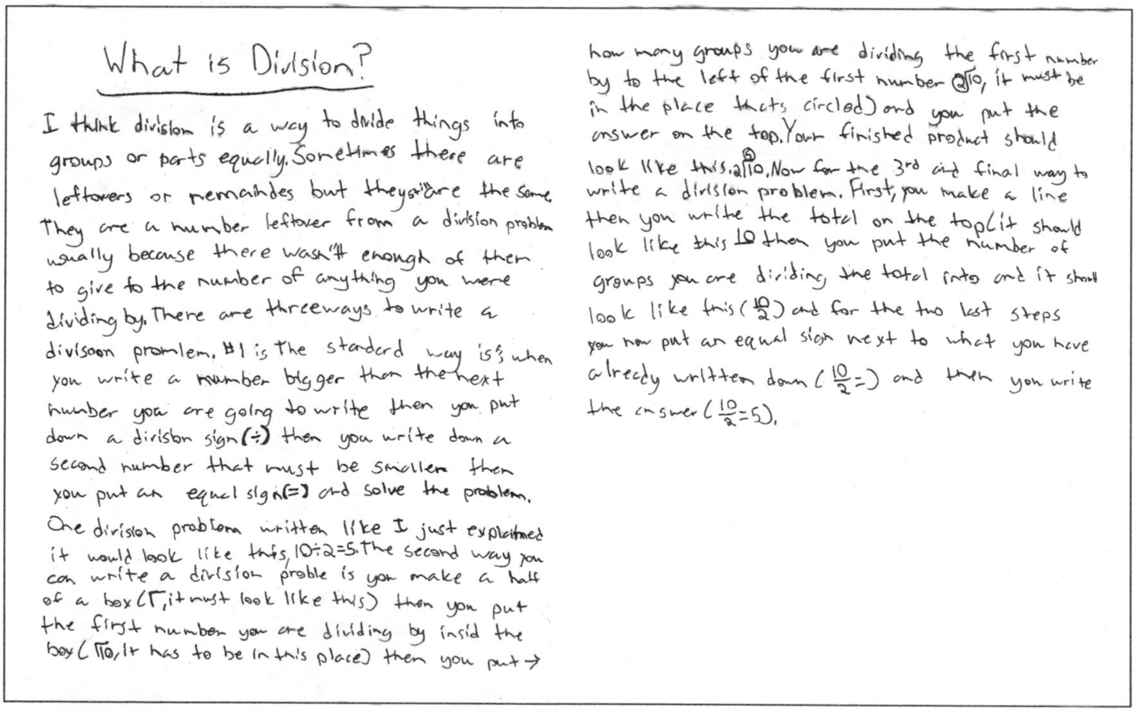
What is Division?

I think division is a way to divide things into groups or parts equally. Sometimes there are leftovers or remaindes but they're the same. They are a number leftover from a division problem usually because there wasn't enough of them to give to the number of anything you were dividing by. There are threeways to write a divisoon promlem. #1 is The standerd way is; when you write a number bigger than the next number you are going to write then you put down a division sign (÷) then you write down a second number that must be smaller then you put an equal sign (=) and solve the problem. One division problem written like I just explained it would look like this, 10÷2=5. The second way you can write a division proble is you make a half of a box (Γ, it must look like this) then you put the first number you are dividing by insid the box (⟌10, it has to be in this place) then you put → how many groups you are dividing the first number by to the left of the first number (2⟌10, it must be in the place thats circled) and you put the answer on the top. Your finished product should look like this. 2⟌10 (5 on top). Now for the 3rd and final way to write a division problem. First, you make a line then you write the total on the top (it should look like this $\overline{10}$) then you put the number of groups you are dividing the total into and it should look like this ($\frac{10}{2}$) and for the two last steps you now put an equal sign next to what you have already written down ($\frac{10}{2}=$) and then you write the answer ($\frac{10}{2}=5$).

Figure 1 ***Robbie's work looked impressive, but he only explained the three ways to represent a division problem. He revealed a common misconception—he believed that the dividend must always be larger than the divisor.***

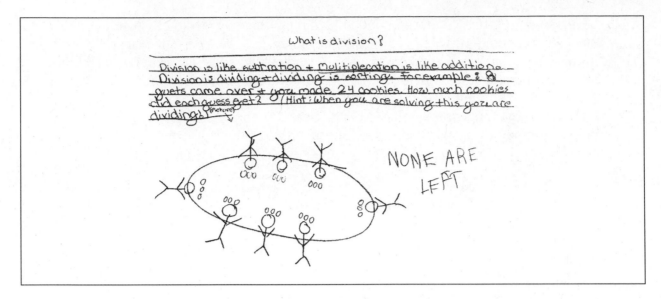

What is division?

Division is like subtration + mulitiplecation is like addition. Division is dividing+dividing is sorting. For example: 8 guets came over + you made 24 cookies. How much cookies did each guess get? (Hint: When you are solving this you are dividing!) (Pictures)

NONE ARE LEFT

▲▲▲▲▲▲Figure 2   *Rachel showed she understood that division involves equal groups.*

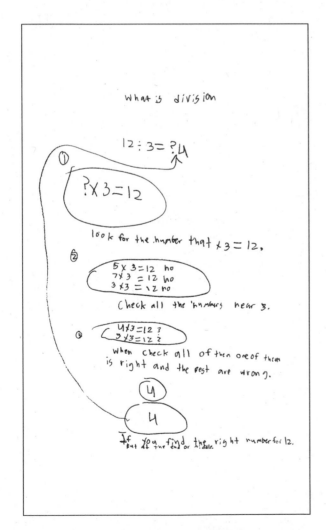

What is division

$12 \div 3 = ? 4$

① $? \times 3 = 12$

look for the number that $\times 3 = 12$.

② $5 \times 3 = 12$ no
$7 \times 3 = 12$ no
$3 \times 3 = 12$ no

Check all the numbers near 3.

③ $4 \times 3 = 12 ?$
$3 \times 3 = 12 ?$

When check all of them one of them is right and the rest are wrong.

4

4

If you find the right number for 12. but it the the end or hidale.

▲▲▲▲▲▲Figure 3   *Shawn indicated a clear understanding of how to use multiplication to solve a division problem.*

What Is Division?

Division is a number divided into equal groups. → Example $25 \div 5 = 5$
Sometimes → Example $8 \div 3 = 2$ R2
there are remainders.

What kinds of things can you divide?

You can divide cookies or numbers.

15 cookies

$$\begin{array}{r} 25 \\ - 5 \\ \hline 20 \\ - 5 \\ \hline 15 \\ - 5 \\ \hline 10 \\ - 5 \\ \hline 5 \end{array}$$

$25 \div 5 = 5$

▲▲▲▲▲▲Figure 4   *Joby showed an understanding that division involves equal groups and that he could solve a division problem by using repeated subtraction.*

The Motorcycle Problem

PROMPT

James rode his motorcycle for a total of 1,530 miles. He rode the same distance each day. He rode for 10 days. How far did he ride daily? Use words, pictures, and/or numbers to show your thinking.

This problem provides students with a real-life context for division by ten. The lesson in Chapter 1, "Silent Division," gives students practice with dividing by ten and multiples of ten. This assessment gives you the opportunity to assess individual student's progress with this skill.

To begin, write the problem on the board and ask students to copy it onto their papers. Ask them to solve the problem and show their thinking using words, numbers, and/or pictures.

Students can use different approaches to solve this problem. Some are comfortable dividing by ten. Others use what they know about multiplication and multiplying by ten and multiples of ten. Some may use repeated subtraction or some combination of ideas to solve the problem.

Asking students to explain why their thinking makes sense or asking them to solve the problem a second way can give you useful insights into their understanding and misconceptions.

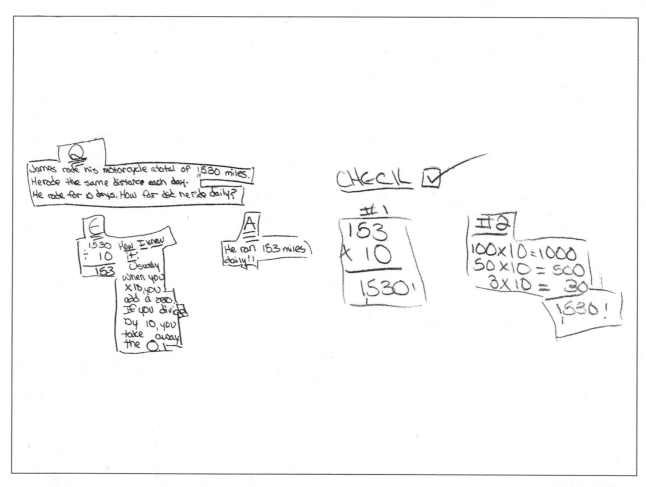

▲▲▲▲▲▲Figure 5   *Celena used her understanding that dividing by 10 results in dropping a 0 from the dividend to find the quotient. She used multiplication to check.*

James rode his motorcycle a total of 1530 miles. He rode the same distance each day. He rode for 10 days. How far did he ride daily?

Answer:
He rode 153 miles daily.

solve
distance
10 × 153 = 1530
amount of days

▲▲▲▲▲▲Figure 6 *Jackson used his knowledge of multiplication by 10 to figure the number of miles James rode each day.*

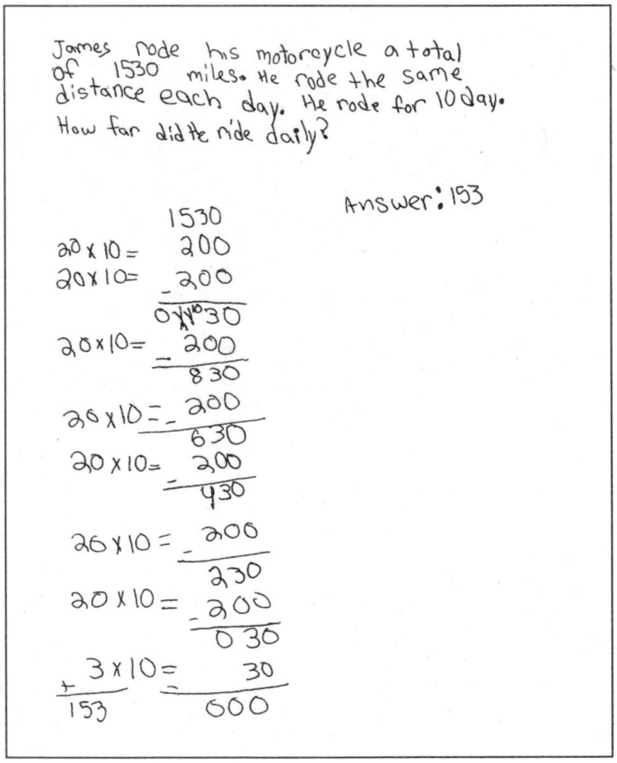

James rode his motorcycle a total of 1530 miles. He rode the same distance each day. He rode for 10 day. How far did he ride daily?

Answer: 153

$$
\begin{array}{r}
1530 \\
20 \times 10 = \underline{200} \\
20 \times 10 = \underline{200} \\
\hline
0\,X^{10}30 \\
20 \times 10 = \underline{200} \\
\hline
830 \\
20 \times 10 = \underline{200} \\
\hline
630 \\
20 \times 10 = \underline{200} \\
\hline
430 \\
20 \times 10 = \underline{200} \\
\hline
230 \\
20 \times 10 = \underline{200} \\
\hline
030 \\
3 \times 10 = \underline{\;30} \\
\hline
153 \quad\quad 600
\end{array}
$$

▲▲▲▲▲▲Figure 7 *Derek solved the problem using a combination of multiplication by multiples of ten and subtraction.*

4 R3

PROMPT

Write three different division problems with a quotient of 4 R3. Choose one of your problems and explain how you know it's correct.

Important understandings students should gain from the lesson in Chapter 6, "The Quotient Stays the Same," are that there are many different division problems that can have the same quotient and that producing the same quotient is the result of a particular relationship between the dividend and the divisor. Asking students to write different problems with the same quotient gives you insight into their grasp of these ideas.

To begin, lead a class discussion for students to share what they learned when they explored *The Quotient Stays the Same*. For many students, this is new, fragile learning, and the class discussion can help students clarify and organize their thoughts before putting them onto paper. After all students who wanted to do so have shared, write the prompt on the board. Ask students to copy the prompt onto their papers.

As students work, circulate through the class. Read over students' shoulders and ask students questions that can help you more clearly understand their thinking. Remind students to choose at least one problem and explain why it makes sense.

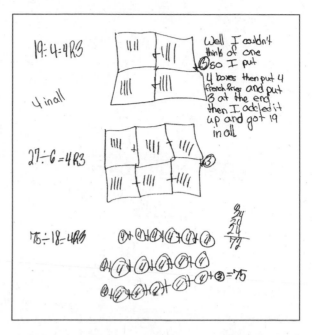

▲▲▲▲▲▲**Figure 8** *Chris used drawings to help him figure the dividend. As he gained confidence, he used larger numbers and substituted numbers for the drawings.*

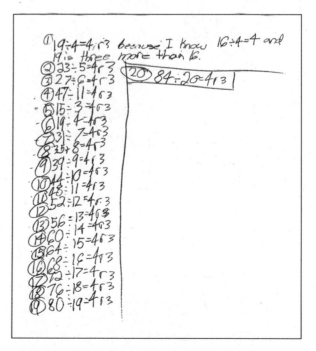

▲▲▲▲▲▲**Figure 9** *Kaleb indicated a clear understanding initially. When he got to the tenth problem, 44 ÷ 10 = 4 R3, he made an error. He multiplied the divisor by 4 and added 4 rather than the remainder of 3. He continued making this error in the rest of the problems.*

$$4\overline{)19} = 4R3$$

$4 \times 4 =$ equals 16 and if you add 3 then it equals 19 so the anser is 4R3

$$4{,}000\overline{)16{,}003} = 4R3$$

4 times 4,000 = 16,000 and if you add 3 then it equals 16,003.

$$6{,}000{,}000\overline{)24{,}000{,}003} = 4R3$$

$4 \times 6{,}000{,}000 = 24{,}000{,}000$ and if you add 3 then it equals 4R3.

$$6\overline{)27} = 4R3$$

6 times 4 = 24 and 24 + 3 = 27 so it is 4R3

$$4{,}000{,}000\overline{)16{,}000{,}003} = 4R3$$

4 times 4,000,000 = 16,000,000 and if you add 3 then it is 16,000,003

4 times the divisor plus 3 equals the dividend

▲▲▲▲▲▲Figure 10 *Toshi enjoyed the challenge of using larger numbers and explained why each of the problems she created made sense. Then she wrote a sentence generalizing what she did in each case.*

$15 \div 3 = 4R3$

because $12 \div 3$ is 4 so $13 \div 3 =$ would be 4R1 and $14 \div 3$ would be 4R2 and then $15 \div 3$ is 4R3. The 4 x divisor, then add 3 and that = the dividend.

$27 \div 6 = 4R3$ $19 \div 4 = 4R3$ $39 \div 9 = 4R3$

$23 \div 5 = 4R3$ $43 \div 10 = 4R3$ $31 \div 7 = 4R3$

$11 \div 2 = 4R3$ $35 \div 8 = 4R3$

▲▲▲▲▲▲Figure 11 *Although Nalani used smaller numbers than Toshi, her understanding was strong.*

Multiples of Two and Three

PROMPT

List at least three numbers that are multiples of BOTH two and three. Explain how you know.

Present this assessment to students after you've taught the lessons in Chapter 7, "Exploring Divisibility Rules for Two, Five, and Ten," and Chapter 8, "Exploring Divisibility Rules for Three," to determine which students understand and can apply the divisibility rules for two and three and to gain insight into the thinking and misconceptions of those who are having difficulty.

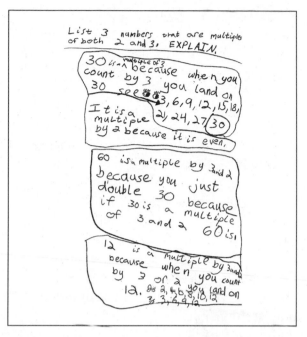

▲▲▲▲▲▲**Figure 12** *Joby used skip-counting to verify 30, 60, and 12 are divisible by both 2 and 3.*

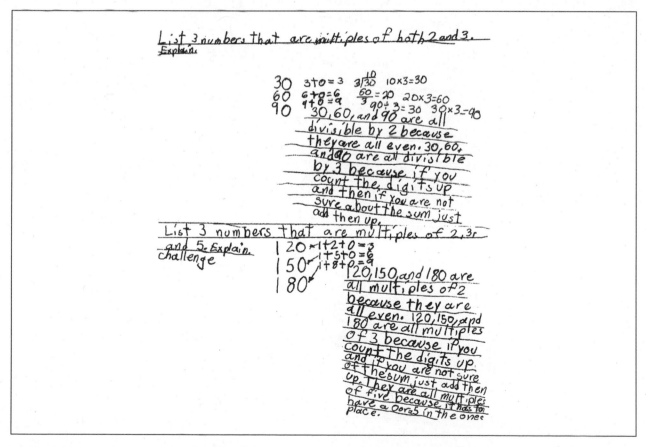

▲▲▲▲▲▲**Figure 13** *Although Yolanda's written explanation was incomplete, she used division to verify that 30, 60, and 90 are indeed divisible by 3. She correctly added the digits to find the sums but went no further.*

To begin, present the prompt to students by writing it on the board. It's important that students understand that the numbers they list must be multiples of, or divisible by, *both* two and three. For example, four is divisible by two but not by three. However, six is a multiple of *both* two and three and is therefore divisible by *both* two and three. Students who have completed the activities Chapters 7 and 8 have had prior experience listing multiples and only a brief discussion of this aspect of the problem should be necessary.

On another day, or for students who finish early and would like an additional challenge, ask students to list numbers that are divisible by 2, 3, and 5 or 2, 3, and 6, and so on.

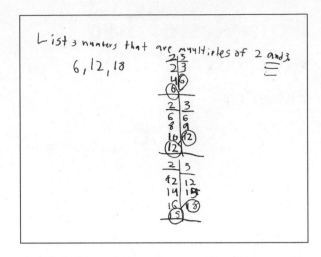

▲▲▲▲▲▲**Figure 14** *Shawn used a chart and skip-counting to show 6, 12, and 18 are divisible by both 2 and 3.*

▲▲▲▲▲▲**Figure 15** *Nariko applied the divisibility rules for 2 and 3 to show that 24, 48, and 36 are divisible by both numbers. She went on to show that 30, 60, 90, and 180 are divisible by 2, 3, and 5.*

Divisibility with Candies

PROMPT

Candies can be packed in boxes of 2, 3, 5, or 6. Zowie Candy Company has 642 candies to box. The same size box must be used for all the candies and no candies can be left over. Which boxes could be used? Explain your thinking.

Divisibility with Candies asks students to apply the divisibility rules for two, three, five, and six and should be used after students have had experience with all three divisibility chapters—7, 8, and 9. Students' explanations about which size boxes can be used to box all 642 candies with none remaining will provide them the opportunity to apply their learning and solidify their thinking. You will gain information about what they understand and what misconceptions students may still have about divisibility by two, three, five, and six.

To begin, explain to students that the Zowie Candy Company has 642 candies ready to be packed into boxes. The candies can be packed in boxes of 2, 3, 5, or 6. The company wants to use only one size box to pack the candy and no candy can be left over. Which size boxes could be used? Write the prompt on the board and ask students to copy it onto their papers.

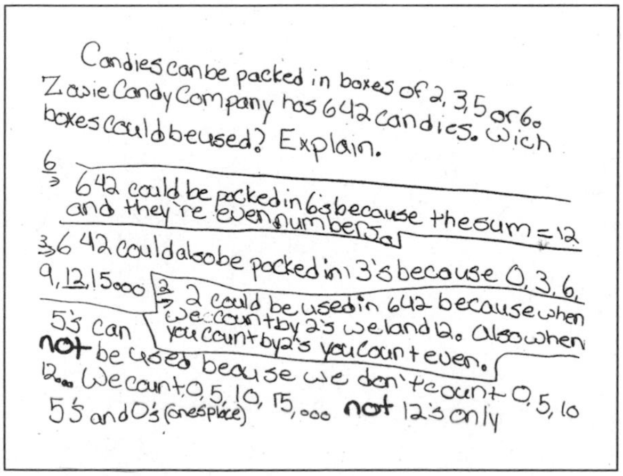

▲▲▲▲▲▲**Figure 17** *Nariko's work showed a clear understanding of how to apply the divisibility rules for 2, 3, 5, and 6. She also used division to verify her application of the divisibility rules.*

▲▲▲▲▲▲**Figure 16** *Celena's paper showed confusion in her application of the divisibility rules for 2, 3, and 5.*

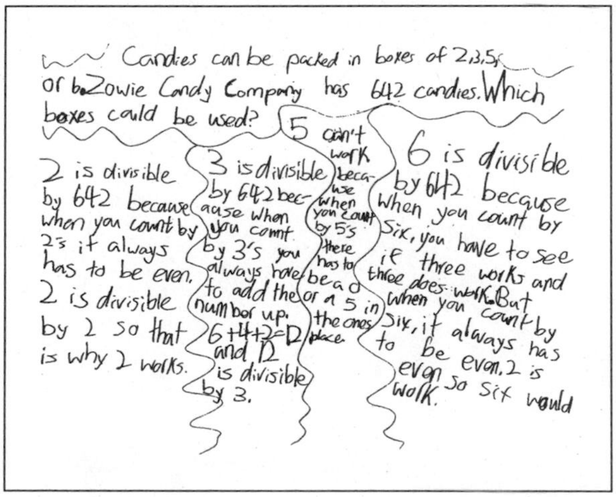

▲▲▲▲▲▲**Figure 18** *Neil showed a good understanding of how to apply the divisibility rules for 2, 3, 5, and 6.*

If Shaquille O'Neal Were a Chameleon

PROMPT

Shaquille O'Neal, a basketball player for the Los Angeles Lakers, is approximately 215 cm tall. If he had a tongue like a chameleon, how long would his tongue be? Show how you figured in at least two ways.
(Reminder: A chameleon's tongue is $\frac{1}{2}$ its body length.)

Use this assessment after teaching the lesson in Chapter 4, "An Introduction to Division Computation: If You Hopped Like a Frog." The methods students use to figure the length of Shaquille's tongue if he were a chameleon will give you information about the development of their division computation skills.

To begin, write the prompt on the board and ask students to copy it onto their papers. Remind students to figure in two ways the length of Shaquille O'Neal's tongue if he were a chameleon. This promotes flexibility in their thinking, and the result of the second method of figuring provides a check of the first answer.

Students may use a variety of methods to compute. Some will use the algorithms introduced in Chapter 4, while others may find the answer by first figuring half of two hundred, then finding half of fifteen. A few may use multiplication, subtraction, or addition. Students' approaches will give you a picture of how they are thinking and show their progress toward becoming accurate, efficient problem solvers. A careful study of their work may reveal misunderstandings or weaknesses, information you can use as guidance in your instructional decisions about how to improve their understanding of division and their division computation skills.

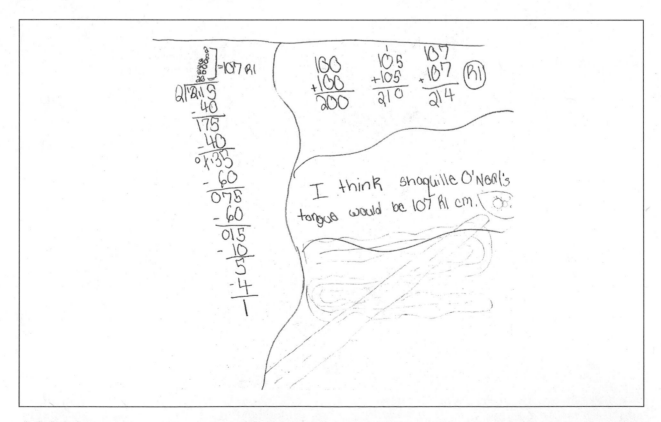

▲▲▲▲▲▲Figure 19 *Alika accurately used the alternative division algorithm introduced in Chapter 4.*

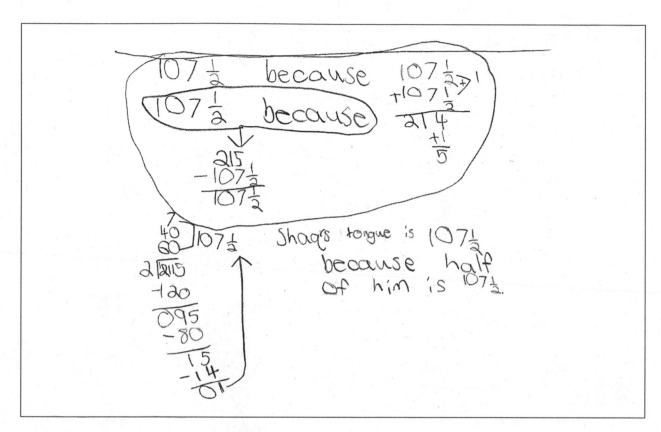

▲▲▲▲▲▲Figure 20   *Mark interpreted the remainder of 1 cm as $\frac{1}{2}$.*

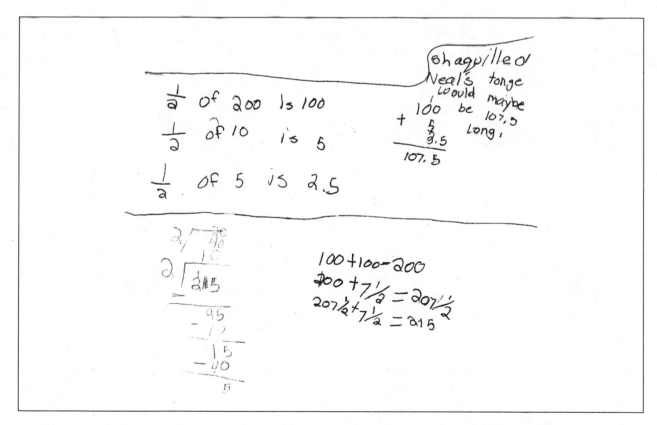

▲▲▲▲▲▲Figure 21   *Belinda thought of 215 as 200 + 10 + 5 and found half of each.*

Easy, Medium, and Hard

PROMPT

Your task is to write three division problems. First, write a problem that you consider to be easy to solve. Next, write a problem you think is of medium difficulty. Finally, write a problem that you feel is hard. Solve all three.

This task can be repeated throughout the students' study of division. Asking students to create problems they consider to be easy, medium, or hard may yield unexpected results. Whether the results are expected or unexpected, you will have information about students' individual perceptions, and when you consider their papers as a whole, you will have insights into what your students think as a group. This information will allow you to choose appropriate levels of difficulty when selecting problems for your students to consider and solve.

To begin, explain to students that they are to write three problems: one that they consider to be easy, one that they think is of medium difficulty, and finally, one that they feel is hard. After students create their three problems, ask them to solve them. After students have completed the task, have students share problems they think are easy, medium, and hard. List their problems on the board and then lead a class discussion about what makes a problem easy, medium, or hard.

As students work, circulate through the class, stopping when appropriate to ask students what makes a particular problem easy, medium, or hard. Their explanations may reveal both strengths and weaknesses in their learning.

By repeating this activity, you will see changes in students' perceptions of easy, medium, and hard with respect to division computation problems.

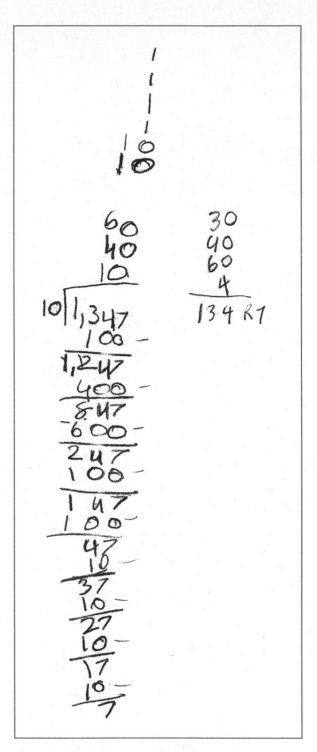

▲▲▲▲▲▲Figure 22 *Jodi thought 1,347 ÷ 10 was of medium difficulty, because of the four-digit dividend.*

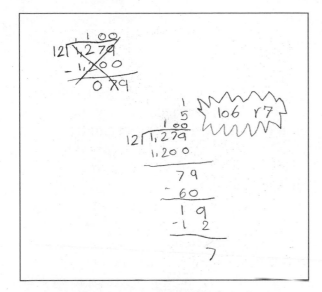

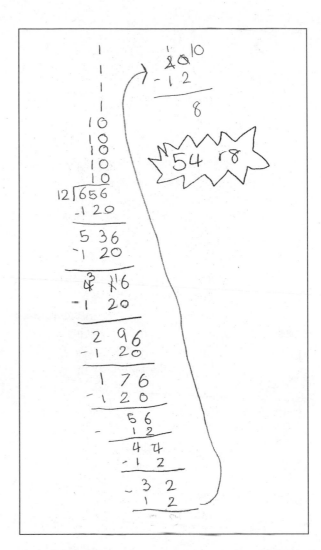

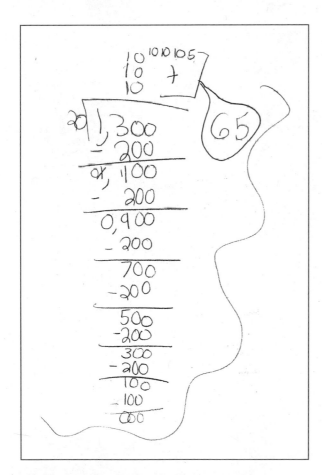

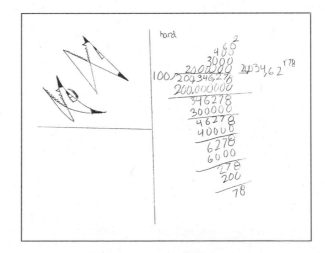

▲▲▲▲▲▲Figure 23 *Pesach considered 1,279 ÷ 12 to be of medium difficulty. He explained it was medium because the dividend had four digits.*

▲▲▲▲▲▲Figure 25 *Pesach thought 656 ÷ 12 was an easy division problem. He accurately solved it.*

▲▲▲▲▲▲Figure 24 *Nalani wrote as a problem of medium difficulty 1,300 ÷ 20, explaining that the 20 and the four-digit dividend made it medium instead of easy.*

▲▲▲▲▲▲Figure 26 *Jay thought 200,346,278 ÷ 100 was hard. He was able to solve the problem correctly.*

593 ÷ 19

PROMPT

Write a division story for 593 ÷ 19. Then solve the problem.

When students write division stories, they must consider what is an appropriate context for a problem. They must also consider what each number in the problems represents. Asking students to write division problems can strengthen their understanding of the numbers and reveal to you areas of strength and weakness in their understanding. If your students have had little or no experience writing division stories, prior to this assessment, have them complete *400 ÷ 12* and *Dividing by Four*.

Both activities can be found in the Additional Activities section of this book and provide students with experience writing division stories.

To begin, write the prompt on the board. Ask the students to copy the prompt onto their papers. As students work, circulate through the class, reading division stories and asking appropriate questions to help you understand how students are thinking. After students have found the answer one way, ask them to solve the problem in a second way. This deepens a student's understanding, helps the student become a more flexible thinker, and provides a check for the first answer. This information also gives you a glimpse into the breadth of a student's understanding.

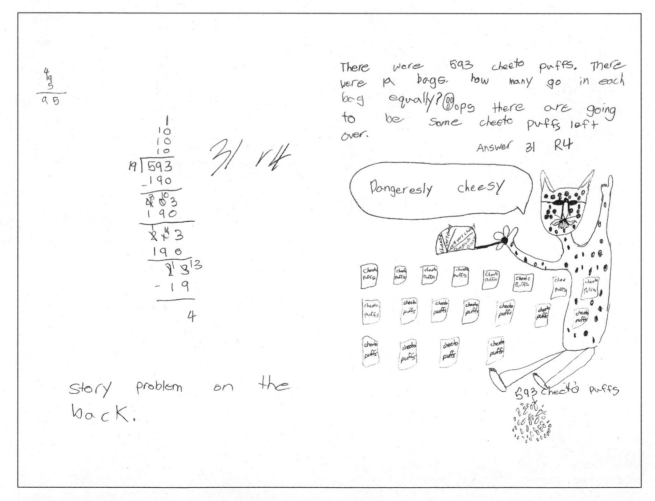

▲▲▲▲▲▲**Figure 27** *Pesach wrote about dividing Chee-tos.*

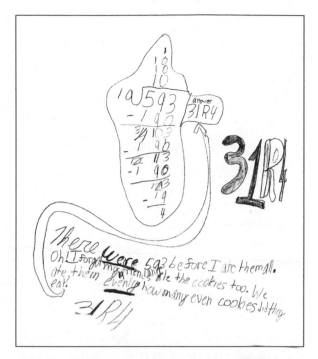

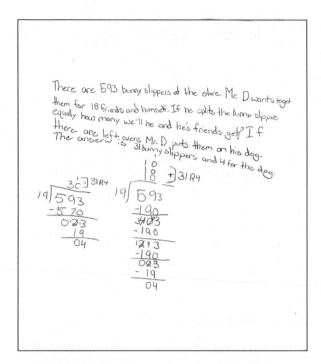

▲▲▲▲▲▲Figure 28 *Ben successfully solved 593 ÷ 19. He made an error in his division story when he stated that he and 19 of his friends, a total of 20 people, split the cookies equally.*

▲▲▲▲▲▲Figure 29 *Nalani successfully wrote a division story and correctly solved it in two ways.*

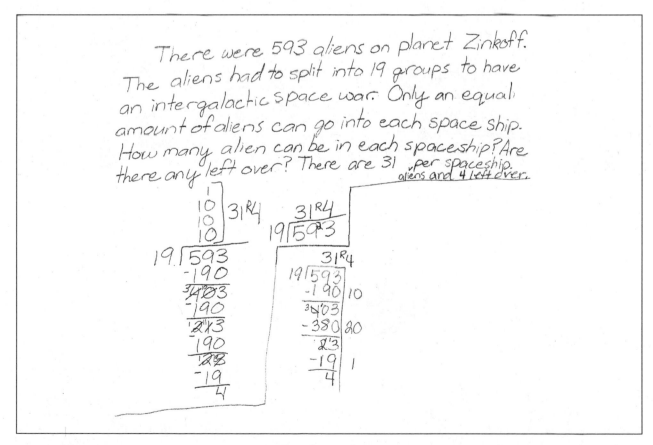

▲▲▲▲▲▲Figure 30 *Alexa correctly wrote a division story and solved the problem in three ways.*

What Is Division? (Revisited)

PROMPT

What is division?

The primary purpose of this prompt is to give students an opportunity to show what they know about division at the end of their study of division. When a student's response from earlier in his or her study of division is compared with this one, you should see increased complexity and clarity in his or her thinking. In their second writing about this question, many students will use examples with larger numbers or make use of divisibility rules. Some will understand more clearly the link between division and multiplication. Many will include their new knowledge about how to compute using larger numbers.

To begin, write the prompt on the board. Ask students to copy the question onto their papers. It's helpful to have a brief class discussion or ask students to talk in pairs before asking them to write, as these are ways for them to gather their thoughts and clarify their ideas. As students write, read over their shoulders, asking and answering questions as necessary.

Individual growth can be seen by comparing the first assessment with this one. The overall growth of the class can be seen by looking at the first assessment papers as a group and then comparing them with the overall results of this assessment. Strengths and weaknesses may be revealed, and with this information, you can continue to support students' division learning as they move on to study other areas of mathematics.

▲▲▲▲▲▲Figure 31 *Jeremy, a struggling student, answered "What is division?" at the beginning of his study of division.*

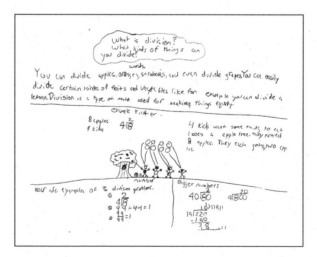

▲▲▲▲▲▲Figure 32 *In Jeremy's second response to "What is division?" he showed growth in how he represented division problems numerically and greater clarity about the meaning of the numbers in division problems, and he accurately solved division problems with larger numbers.*

BLACKLINE MASTERS

Investigating Factors

1. Which numbers from one to fifty have exactly two factors? What do you notice about them?

2. What is the largest prime number from one to fifty? What is the smallest?

3. Which number from one to fifty has the most factors? Which has the fewest?

4. What happens to the number of factors when a number doubles?

5. Which numbers from one to fifty have an odd number of factors? What do you notice about them?

From *Lessons for Extending Division, Grades 4–5* by Maryann Wickett and Marilyn Burns. © 2003 by Math Solutions Publications

1–100 Chart

1	2	3	4	5	6	7	8	9	10
11	12	13	14	15	16	17	18	19	20
21	22	23	24	25	26	27	28	29	30
31	32	33	34	35	36	37	38	39	40
41	42	43	44	45	46	47	48	49	50
51	52	53	54	55	56	57	58	59	60
61	62	63	64	65	66	67	68	69	70
71	72	73	74	75	76	77	78	79	80
81	82	83	84	85	86	87	88	89	90
91	92	93	94	95	96	97	98	99	100

The Division Game

You need:
   a group of five
   1 set of 144 cards with multiples
   1 set of 10 cards with factor pairs
   lists of multiples from 1 to 100 for 2, 3, 4, 5, and 6

Rules

The object of the game is to be the first player to have five cards with multiples of both the numbers on your factor card.

1. Mix and place the ten cards with factor pairs facedown. Then each player takes a factor card and places it faceup in front of him or her.

2. Mix the cards with the multiples. One player deals each player in the group five multiple cards, and players place their multiple cards faceup in front of them. Place the remaining multiple cards facedown in a pile and turn the top multiple card faceup to begin a discard pile.

3. On your turn, you may take the top multiple card from the deck or you may draw the top card from the discard pile. Then you must discard one multiple card, always keeping five cards in your hand. Remember, you want to keep cards that are multiples of both numbers on your factor card. You may refer to the lists of multiples to help you decide if a multiple card is one you want to keep or discard.

4. Players take turns repeating Step 3 until one player has five cards that are multiples of both of the numbers on his or her factor card.

5. The winning player must tell a division sentence to explain how each number on the multiple cards is divisible by both of the factor numbers.

From *Lessons for Extending Division, Grades 4–5* by Maryann Wickett and Marilyn Burns. © 2003 by Math Solutions Publications

The Factor Game Recording Sheet

number list

proof

score

score

proof

_____ had _____ points.

_____ had _____ points.

_____ wins by _____ points.

number list

proof

score

score

proof

_____ had _____ points.

_____ had _____ points.

_____ wins by _____ points.

The Factor Game

You need:
  a partner
  a recording sheet

Rules

The object of the game is to be the player with the higher score.

1. List all numbers to be used in the game at the top of the score sheet.

1 2 3 4 5 6 7 8 9
10 11 12 13 14 15

Player 1		Player 2	
proof	score	score	proof

2. Player 1 selects a number from the list, crosses it off the list, and records the number on the score sheet as the score for that round.

1 2 3 4 5 6 7 8 9
10 11 12 13 14 ~~15~~

Player 1		Player 2	
proof	score	score	proof
	15		

The Factor Game, continued

3. Player 2 identifies all of the proper factors of Player 1's number that haven't yet been crossed out. (Proper factors are smaller than the selected number.) For each factor of Player 1's number, Player 2 writes a division sentence to prove it's a factor and crosses it off the list. Player 2's score for the round is the total of the factors.

<pre>
    ✗   2   ✗   4   ✗   6   7   8   9
   10 11 12 13 14 ✗✗
</pre>

Player 1		Player 2	
proof	score	score	proof
	15		
		5	15 ÷ 3 = 5
		3	15 ÷ 5 = 3
		1	15 ÷ 15 = 1
		9	

4. Player 2 selects a number from the list that isn't crossed out *and* that has at least one factor in the list that isn't crossed out. Player 2 crosses off the selected number and records it on the score sheet and finds his or her new total.

<pre>
    ✗   2   ✗   4   ✗   6   7   8   9   ✗✗
   11 12 13 14 ✗✗
</pre>

Player 1		Player 2	
proof	score	score	proof
	15		
		5	15 ÷ 3 = 5
		3	15 ÷ 5 = 3
		1	15 ÷ 15 = 1
		9	
		10	
		19	

5. Player 1 repeats Steps 3 and 4.

6. Players alternate turns until no more numbers from the list can be used.

7. Players write their scores and who won at the bottom of the score sheet.

   From *Lessons for Extending Division, Grades 4–5* by Maryann Wickett and Marilyn Burns. © 2003 by Math Solutions Publications

Leftovers with 100

You need:
  a partner

Rules

1. Set up a recording sheet as shown.

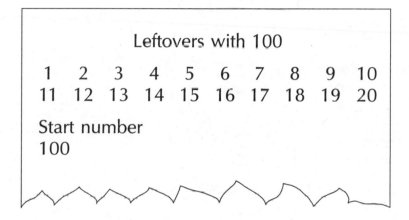

2. Player 1 chooses a divisor from 1 to 20 and divides the start number, 100, by the divisor chosen. Player 2 records the division, crosses out the divisor, and circles and labels the remainder with Player 1's initial.

3. Both players subtract the remainder from the start number to get the next start number.

4. Player 2 uses the new start number, chooses a divisor that hasn't yet been crossed out, and divides. (Divisors can be used only once!) Player 1 records the division, crosses out the divisor, and circles and labels the remainder. Both players subtract the remainder from the start number to get the next start number.

5. Players continue taking turns until the start number reaches 0.

6. Players add their remainders. The player with the larger sum wins.

7. Check that the sum of both players' remainders equals one hundred. If not, you've made an error.

Question: Why should the sum of both players' remainders equal one hundred?

INDEX